Windows Server 2012 R2: Storage, Security, & Networking

Pocket Consultant

William R. Stanek
Author and Series Editor

PUBLISHED BY
Microsoft Press
A Division of Microsoft Corporation
One Microsoft Way
Redmond, Washington 98052-6399

Library of Congress Control Number: 2013956655
ISBN: 978-0-7356-8259-7

Printed and bound in the United States of America.

Second Printing: April 2014

Microsoft Press books are available through booksellers and distributors world-
wide. If you need support related to this book, email Microsoft Press Book
Support at mspinput@microsoft.com. Please tell us what you think of this book
at http://www.microsoft.com/learning/booksurvey.

Microsoft and the trademarks listed at http://www.microsoft.com/en-us/legal/
intellectualproperty/trademarks/en-us.aspx are trademarks of the Microsoft group
of companies. All other marks are property of their respective owners.

The example companies, organizations, products, domain names, email addresses, logos,
people, places, and events depicted herein are fictitious. No association with any real
company, organization, product, domain name, email address, logo, person, place, or
event is intended or should be inferred.

This book expresses the author's views and opinions. The information contained in this
book is provided without any express, statutory, or implied warranties. Neither the authors,
Microsoft Corporation, nor its resellers, or distributors will be held liable for any damages
caused or alleged to be caused either directly or indirectly by this book.

Acquisitions Editor: Anne Hamilton
Developmental Editor: Karen Szall
Editorial Production: Online Training Solutions, Inc. (OTSI)
Project Editor: Karen Szall
Technical Reviewer: Charlie Russell; Technical Review services provided by
Content Master, a member of CM Group, Ltd.
Copyeditor: Denise Bankaitis (OTSI)
Indexer: Krista Wall (OTSI)
Cover: Best & Company Design

Contents

What do you think of this book? We want to hear from you!

Microsoft is interested in hearing your feedback so we can continually improve our
books and learning resources for you. To participate in a brief online survey, please visit:

microsoft.com/learning/booksurvey

Chapter 11 Data backup and recovery 335

What do you think of this book? We want to hear from you!

Microsoft is interested in hearing your feedback so we can continually improve our
books and learning resources for you. To participate in a brief online survey, please visit:

microsoft.com/learning/booksurvey

Acknowledgments

To my readers—thank you for being there with me through many books and many years. It has been an honor and a privilege to be your pocket consultant.

To my wife—for many years, through many books, many millions of words, and many thousands of pages she's been there, providing support and encouragement and making every place we've lived a home.

To my kids—for helping me see the world in new ways, for having exceptional patience and boundless love, and for making every day an adventure.

To Anne, Karen, Martin, Lucinda, Juliana, and many others who've helped out in ways both large and small.

Special thanks to my son Will for not only installing and managing my extensive dev lab for all my books since *Windows 8 Pocket Consultant* but for also performing check reads of all those books as well.

—William R. Stanek

Introduction

Windows Server 2012 R2 Pocket Consultant: Storage, Security, & Networking is designed to be a concise and compulsively usable resource for Windows administrators, developers, and programmers, and for anyone else who wants to use the storage, networking, and security features of Windows Server 2012 R2. This is the readable resource guide that you'll want on your desk or in your pocket at all times. The book discusses everything you need to perform core tasks. Because the focus is directed on providing you with the maximum value in a pocket-sized guide, you don't have to wade through hundreds of pages of extraneous information to find what you're looking for. Instead, you'll find exactly what you need to get the job done.

In short, the book is designed to be the one resource you consult whenever you have questions regarding storage, networking, and security in Windows Server 2012 R2. To this end, the book concentrates on configuration options, frequently used tasks, documented examples, and options that are representative but not necessarily inclusive. One of the goals is to keep the content so concise that the book remains compact and easy to navigate while ensuring that the book is packed with as much information as possible—making it a valuable resource.

Anyone transitioning to Windows Server 2012 R2 from Windows Server 2012 might be surprised at just how much has been updated, as changes both subtle and substantial have been made throughout the operating system. Like Windows Server 2012, Windows Server 2012 R2 supports a touch user interface (UI), in addition to the traditional mouse and keyboard.

Although you might not install Windows Server 2012 R2 on touch UI–capable computers, you can manage Windows Server 2012 R2 from your touch UI–capable computers. If you do end up managing it this way, understanding the touch UI in addition to the revised interface options will be crucial to your success. For this reason, I discuss both the touch UI and the traditional mouse and keyboard techniques throughout this book.

When you are working with touch-enabled computers, you can manipulate on-screen elements in ways that weren't possible previously. You can do any of the following:

- **Tap** Tap an item by touching it with your finger. A tap or double-tap of elements on the screen generally is the equivalent of a mouse click or double-click.

- **Press and hold** Press your finger down and leave it there for a few seconds. Pressing and holding elements on the screen generally is the equivalent of a right-click.

- **Swipe to select** Slide an item a short distance in the opposite direction compared to how the page scrolls. This selects the items and might also bring up related commands. If press and hold doesn't display commands and options for an item, try using swipe to select instead.

- **Swipe from edge (slide in from edge)** Starting from the edge of the screen, swipe or slide in. Sliding in from the right edge opens the Charms panel. Sliding in from the left edge shows open apps and enables you to switch between them easily. Sliding in from the top or bottom edge shows commands for the active element.

- **Pinch** Touch an item with two or more fingers, and then move the fingers toward each other. Pinching zooms out.

- **Stretch** Touch an item with two or more fingers, and then move the fingers away from each other. Stretching zooms in.

You are also able to enter text using the on-screen keyboard. Although the UI changes are substantial, they aren't the most significant changes to the operating system. The most significant changes are below the surface, affecting the underlying architecture and providing many new features. Some of these features are revolutionary in that they forever change the way we use Windows.

As you've probably noticed, a great deal of information about Windows Server 2012 R2 is available on the Web and in other printed books. You can find tutorials, reference sites, discussion groups, and more to make using Windows Server 2012 R2 easier. However, the advantage of reading this book is that much of the information you need to learn about Windows Server 2012 R2 is organized in one place and presented in a straightforward and orderly fashion. This book has everything you need to customize Windows Server 2012 R2 installations, master Windows Server 2012 R2 configurations, and maintain Windows Server 2012 R2 servers.

In this book, I teach you how features work, why they work the way they do, and how to customize them to meet your needs. I also offer specific examples of how certain features can meet your needs, and how you can use other features to troubleshoot and resolve issues you might have. In addition, this book provides tips, best practices, and examples of how to optimize Windows Server 2012 R2. This book won't just teach you how to configure Windows Server 2012 R2, it will teach you how to squeeze every last bit of power out of it and make the most from the features and options it includes.

Unlike many other books about managing Windows Server 2012 R2, this book doesn't focus on a specific user level. This isn't a lightweight beginner book. Regardless of whether you are a beginning administrator or a seasoned professional, many of the concepts in this book will be valuable to you, and you can apply them to your Windows Server 2012 R2 installations.

Who is this book for?

Windows Server 2012 R2 Pocket Consultant: Storage, Security, & Networking covers all editions of Windows Server 2012 R2. The book is designed for the following readers:

- Current Windows system administrators
- Accomplished users who have some administrator responsibilities
- Administrators upgrading to Windows Server 2012 R2 from previous versions
- Administrators transferring from other platforms

To pack in as much information as possible, I had to assume that you have basic networking skills and a basic understanding of Windows Server. With this in mind, I don't devote entire chapters to explaining Windows Server architecture or why you want to use Windows Server. I do, however, cover configuring storage, security, auditing, and much more.

I also assume that you are fairly familiar with Windows commands and procedures in addition to the Windows user interface. If you need help learning Windows basics, you should read other resources (many of which are available from Microsoft Press).

How is this book organized?

Rome wasn't built in a day, nor was this book intended to be read in a day, in a week, or even in a month. Ideally, you'll read this book at your own pace, a little each day as you work your way through all the features Windows Server 2012 R2 has to offer. This book is organized into 11 chapters. The chapters are arranged in a logical order, taking you from planning and deployment tasks to configuration and maintenance tasks.

Ease of reference is an essential part of this hands-on guide. This book has an expanded table of contents and an extensive index for finding answers to problems quickly. Many other quick-reference features have been added to the book as well, including quick step-by-step procedures, lists, tables with fast facts, and extensive cross references.

Conventions used in this book

I've used a variety of elements to help keep the text clear and easy to follow. You'll find code listings in monospace type. When I tell you to actually enter a command, the command appears in **bold** type. When I introduce and define a new term or use a code term in a paragraph of text, I put it in *italics*.

> **NOTE** Group Policy includes both policies and preferences. Under the Computer Configuration and User Configuration nodes, you find two nodes: Policies and Preferences. Settings for general policies are listed under the Policies node. Settings for general preferences are listed under the Preferences node. When referencing settings under the Policies node, I sometimes use shortcut references, such as User Configuration\Administrative Templates\Windows Components, or specify that the policies are found in the Administrative Templates for User Configuration under Windows Components. Both references tell you that the policy setting being discussed is under User Configuration rather than Computer Configuration and can be found under Administrative Templates\Windows Components.

Other conventions include the following:

- **Best Practices**   To examine the best technique to use when working with advanced configuration and maintenance concepts
- **Caution**   To warn you about potential problems

- **Important**   To highlight important concepts and issues
- **More Info**   To provide more information on a subject
- **Note**   To provide additional details on a particular point that needs emphasis
- **Real World**   To provide real-world advice when discussing advanced topics
- **Security Alert**   To point out important security issues
- **Tip**   To offer helpful hints or additional information

I truly hope you find that *Windows Server 2012 R2 Pocket Consultant: Storage, Security, & Networking* provides everything you need to perform the essential administrative tasks on Windows servers as quickly and efficiently as possible. You are welcome to send your thoughts to me at *williamstanek@aol.com*. Follow me on Twitter at WilliamStanek and on Facebook at *www.facebook.com/William.Stanek. Author.*

Other resources

No single magic bullet for learning everything you'll ever need to know about Windows Server 2012 R2 exists. Even though some books are offered as all-in-one guides, there's just no way one book can do it all. With this in mind, I hope you use this book as it is intended to be used—as a concise and easy-to-use resource. It covers everything you need to perform core administration tasks for Windows servers, but it is by no means exhaustive.

Your current knowledge will largely determine your success with this or any other Windows resource or book. As you encounter new topics, take the time to practice what you've learned and read about. Seek out further information as necessary to get the practical hands-on know-how and knowledge you need.

I recommend that you regularly visit the Microsoft website for Windows Server (*microsoft.com/windowsserver*) and *support.microsoft.com* to stay current with the latest changes. To help you get the most out of this book, you can visit my corresponding website at *williamstanek.com/windows*. This site contains information about Windows Server 2012 R2 and updates to the book.

Errata and book support

We've made every effort to ensure the accuracy of this book and its companion content. Any errors that have been reported since this book was published are listed at:

http://aka.ms/WSR2PC2/errata

If you find an error that is not already listed, you can report it to us through the same page.

If you need additional support, email Microsoft Press Book Support at:

mspinput@microsoft.com

Please note that product support for Microsoft software is not offered through the addresses above.

We want to hear from you

At Microsoft Press, your satisfaction is our top priority, and your feedback is our most valuable asset. Please tell us what you think of this book at:

http://aka.ms/tellpress

The survey is short, and we read every one of your comments and ideas. Thanks in advance for your input!

Stay in touch

Let's keep the conversation going! We're on Twitter: *http://twitter.com/MicrosoftPress*.

Managing file systems and drives

A hard drive is the most common storage device used on network workstations and servers. Users depend on hard drives to store their word-processing documents, spreadsheets, and other types of data. Drives are organized into file systems that users can access either locally or remotely.

Local file systems are installed on a user's computer and can be accessed without remote network connections. The C drive, which is available on most workstations and servers, is an example of a local file system. You access the C drive by using the file path C:\.

On the other hand, you access remote file systems through a network connection to a remote resource. You can connect to a remote file system by using the Map Network Drive feature of File Explorer.

Wherever disk resources are located, your job as a system administrator is to manage them. The tools and techniques you use to manage file systems and drives are discussed in this chapter. Chapter 2, "Configuring storage," looks at partition management, volume sets, and fault tolerance.

Managing the File And Storage Services role

A file server provides a central location for storing and sharing files across the network. When many users require access to the same files and application data, you should configure file servers in the domain. Although all servers are configured with basic file services, you must configure the File And Storage Services role and add any additional role services that might be needed.

Table 1-1 provides an overview of the role services associated with the File And Storage Services role. When you add any needed role services to a file server, you might also want to install the following optional features, available through the Add Roles And Features Wizard:

- **Windows Server Backup**   The standard backup utility included with Windows Server 2012 R2.

- **Enhanced Storage**   Supports additional functions made available by devices that support hardware encryption and enhanced storage. Enhanced storage devices support Institute of Electrical and Electronics Engineers (IEEE) standard 1667 to provide enhanced security, which can include authentication at the hardware level of the storage device.

- **Multipath I/O**   Provides support for using multiple data paths between a file server and a storage device. Servers use multiple I/O paths for redundancy in case of the failure of a path and to improve transfer performance.

Binaries needed to install roles and features are referred to as *payloads*. With Windows Server 2012 R2, payloads are stored in subfolders of the %SystemDrive% \Windows\WinSXS folder. If the binaries for the tools have been removed, you might need to install the tools by specifying a source.

TABLE 1-1 Role services for file servers

ROLE SERVICE	DESCRIPTION
BranchCache For Network Files	Enables computers in a branch office to cache commonly used files from shared folders. It takes advantage of data deduplication techniques to optimize data transfers over the wide area networks (WAN) to branch offices.
Data Deduplication	Uses subfile variable-size chunking and compression to achieve greater storage efficiency. This works by segmenting files into 32-KB to 128-KB chunks, identifying duplicate chunks, and replacing the duplicates with references to a single copy. Optimized files are stored as reparse points. After deduplication, files on the volume are no longer stored as data streams and instead are replaced with stubs that point to data blocks within a common chunk store.
DFS Namespaces	Enables you to group shared folders located on different servers into one or more logically structured namespaces. Each namespace appears as a single shared folder with a series of subfolders; however, the underlying structure of a namespace can come from shared folders on multiple servers in different sites.

ROLE SERVICE	DESCRIPTION
DFS Replication	Enables you to synchronize folders on multiple servers across local or WAN connections by using a multimaster replication engine. The replication engine uses the Remote Differential Compression (RDC) protocol to synchronize only the portions of files that have changed since the last replication. You can use DFS Replication with DFS Namespaces or by itself. When a domain is running in a Windows 2008 domain functional level or higher, domain controllers use DFS Replication to provide more robust and granular replication of the SYSVOL directory.
File Server	Enables you to manage file shares that users can access over the network.
File Server Resource Manager (FSRM)	Installs a suite of tools that administrators can use to better manage data stored on servers. By using FSRM, administrators can generate storage reports, configure quotas, and define file-screening policies.
File Server VSS Agent Service	Enables VSS-aware backup utilities to create consistent shadow copies (snapshots) of applications that store data files on the file server.
iSCSI Target Server	Turns any Windows Server into a network-accessible block storage device, which can be used for testing of applications prior to deploying storage area network (SAN) storage. It supports shared storage on both Windows iSCSI initiators and those iSCSI initiators that are not based on Windows as well as network/diskless boot for diskless servers.
iSCSI Target Storage Provider	Supports managing iSCSI virtual disks and shadow copies (snapshots) from an iSCSI initiator.
Server for NFS	Provides a file-sharing solution for enterprises with a mixed Windows and UNIX environment. When you install Server for Network File System (NFS), users can transfer files between Windows Server and UNIX operating systems by using the NFS protocol.
Storage Services	Enables you to manage storage, including storage pools and storage spaces. Storage pools group disks so that you can create virtual disks from the available capacity. Each virtual disk you create is a storage space.
Work Folders	Enables users to synchronize their corporate data to their devices and vice versa. Those devices can be joined to the corporate domain or a workplace.

IMPORTANT If payloads have been removed and you don't specify a source, payloads are restored via Windows Update by default. However, Group Policy can be used to control whether Windows Update is used to restore payloads and to provide alternate source paths for restoring payloads. The policy with which you want to work is Specify Settings For Optional Component Installation And Component Repair, which is under Computer Configuration\Administrative Templates\System. This policy also is used for obtaining payloads needed to repair components.

You can configure the File And Storage Services role on a server by following these steps:

1. In Server Manager, tap or click Manage, and then tap or click Add Roles And Features, or select Add Roles And Features in the Quick Start pane. This starts the Add Roles And Features Wizard. If the wizard displays the Before You Begin page, read the Welcome text, and then tap or click Next.

2. On the Installation Type page, Role-Based Or Feature-Based Installation is selected by default. Tap or click Next.

3. On the Server Selection page, you can choose to install roles and features on running servers or virtual hard disks. Either select a server from the server pool or select a server from the server pool on which to mount a virtual hard disk (VHD). If you are adding roles and features to a VHD, tap or click Browse and then use the Browse For Virtual Hard Disks dialog box to locate the VHD. When you are ready to continue, tap or click Next.

    NOTE Only servers that are running Windows Server 2012 R2 and that have been added for management in Server Manager are listed.

4. On the Server Roles page, select File And Storage Services. Expand the related node, and select the additional role services to install. If additional features are required to install a role, you'll see an additional dialog box. Tap or click Add Features to close the dialog box and add the required features to the server installation. When you are ready to continue, tap or click Next.

5. On the Features page, select the features you want to install. If additional functionality is required to install a feature you selected, you'll see an additional dialog box. Tap or click Add Features to close the dialog box and add the required features to the server installation. When you are ready to continue, tap or click Next. Depending on the added feature, there might be additional steps before you get to the Confirm page.

6. On the Confirm page, tap or click the Export Configuration Settings link to generate an installation report that can be displayed in Internet Explorer.

    REAL WORLD If the server on which you want to install roles or features doesn't have all the required binary source files, the server gets the files via Windows Update by default or from a location specified in Group Policy.

    You can also specify an alternate path for the required source files. To do this, click the Specify An Alternate Source Path link, enter that alternate path in the box provided, and then tap or click OK. For network shares, enter the UNC path to the share, such as \\CorpServer25\WinServer2012R2\. For mounted Windows images, enter the WIM path prefixed with WIM: and including the index of the image to use, such as WIM:\\CorpServer25\WinServer2012R2\install.wim:4.

7. After you review the installation options and save them as necessary, tap or click Install to begin the installation process. The Installation Progress page tracks the progress of the installation. If you close the wizard, tap or click the Notifications icon in Server Manager, and then tap or click the link provided to reopen the wizard.

8. When Setup finishes installing the server with the roles and features you selected, the Installation Progress page will be updated to reflect this. Review the installation details to ensure that all phases of the installation were completed successfully.

   Note any additional actions that might be required to complete the installation, such as restarting the server or performing additional installation tasks.

   If any portion of the installation failed, note the reason for the failure. Review the Server Manager entries for installation problems, and take corrective actions as appropriate.

If the File Services role is already installed on a server and you want to install additional services for a file server, you can add role services to the server by using a similar process.

Adding hard drives

Before you make a hard drive available to users, you need to configure it and consider how it will be used. With Windows Server 2012 R2, you can configure hard drives in a variety of ways. The technique you choose depends primarily on the type of data with which you're working and the needs of your network environment. For general user data stored on workstations, you might want to configure individual drives as stand-alone storage devices. In that case, user data is stored on a workstation's hard drive, where it can be accessed and stored locally.

Although storing data on a single drive is convenient, it isn't the most reliable way to store data. To improve reliability and performance, you might want a set of drives to work together. Windows Server 2012 R2 supports drive sets and arrays by using the redundant array of independent disks (RAID) technology, which is built into the operating system.

Physical drives

Whether you use individual drives or drive sets, you need physical drives. Physical drives are the actual hardware devices that are used to store data. The amount of data a drive can store depends on its size and whether it uses compression. Windows Server 2012 R2 supports both Standard Format and Advanced Format hard drives. Standard Format drives have 512 bytes per physical sector and are also referred to as *512b drives*. Advanced Format drives have 4,096 bytes per physical sector and are also referred to as *512e drives*. 512e represents a significant shift for the hard drive industry, and it allows for large, multiterabyte drives.

Disks perform physical media updates in the granularity of their physical sector size. 512b disks work with data 512 bytes at a time; 512e disks work with data 4,096 bytes at a time. At an elevated, administrator prompt, you can use the command-line utility Fsutil to determine bytes per physical sector by entering the following:

`Fsutil fsinfo ntfsinfo` *DriveDesignator*

DriveDesignator is the designator of the drive to check, such as:

`Fsutil fsinfo sectorinfo c:`

Having a larger physical sector size is what allows drive capacities to jump well beyond previous physical capacity limits. When there is only a 512-byte write, hard drives must perform additional work to complete the sector write. For best perfor-mance, applications must be updated to read and write data properly in this new level of granularity (4096 bytes).

Windows Server 2012 R2 supports many drive interface architectures, including

- Small Computer System Interface (SCSI)
- Parallel ATA (PATA), also known as IDE
- Serial ATA (SATA)

The terms SCSI, IDE, and SATA designate the interface type used by the hard drives. The interface is used to communicate with a drive controller. SCSI drives use SCSI controllers, IDE drives use IDE controllers, and so on.

SCSI is one of the most commonly used interfaces, and there are multiple bus designs for SCSI and multiple interface types. Parallel SCSI (also called SPI) has largely been replaced by Serial Attached SCSI (SAS). Internet SCSI (iSCSI) uses the SCSI architectural model, but it uses TCP/IP as the transport rather than the tradi-tional physical implementation.

SATA was designed to replace IDE. SATA drives are increasingly popular as a low-cost alternative to SCSI. SATA II and SATA III, the most common SATA interfaces, are designed to operate at 3 gigabits per second and 6 per second, respectively. In addition, eSATA (also known as external SATA) is meant for externally connected drives.

NOTE Windows Server 2012 R2 features enhancements to provide improved support for SATA drives. These enhancements reduce metadata inconsistencies and enable drives to cache data more efficiently. Improved disk caching helps to protect cached data in the event of an unexpected power loss.

When setting up a new server, you should give considerable thought to the drive configuration. Start by choosing drives or storage systems that provide the appropriate level of performance. There really is a substantial difference in speed and performance among various drive specifications.

You should consider not only the capacity of the drive but also the following:

- **Rotational speed** A measurement of how fast the disk spins
- **Average seek time** A measurement of how long it takes to seek between disk tracks during sequential I/O operations

Generally speaking, when comparing drives that conform to the same specification, such as Ultra640 SCSI or SATA III, the higher the rotational speed (measured in thousands of rotations per minute) and the lower the average seek time (measured in milliseconds, or msecs), the better. As an example, a drive with a rotational speed of 15,000 RPM gives you 45–50 percent more I/O per second than the average 10,000 RPM drive, all other things being equal. A drive with a seek time of 3.5 msecs gives you a 25–30 percent response time improvement over a drive with a seek time of 4.7 msecs.

Other factors to consider include the following:

- **Maximum sustained data transfer rate**   A measurement of how much data the drive can continuously transfer

- **Mean time to failure (MTTF)**   A measurement of how many hours of operation you can expect to get from the drive before it fails

- **Nonoperational temperatures**   Measurements of the temperatures at which the drive fails

Most drives of comparable quality have similar transfer rates and MTTF. For example, if you compare enterprise SAS drives with 15,000 RPM rotational speed from different vendors, you will probably find similar transfer rates and MTTF. Transfer rates can be expressed in megabytes per second (MBps) or gigabits per second (Gbps). A rate of 1.5 Gbps is equivalent to a data rate of 187.5 MBps, and 3.0 Gbps is equivalent to 375 MBps. Sometimes you'll get a maximum external transfer rate (per the specification to which the drive complies) and an average sustained transfer rate. The average sustained transfer rate is the most important factor.

NOTE   Don't confuse MBps and Mbps. MBps is megabytes per second. Mbps is megabits per second. Because there are 8 bits in a byte, a 100 MBps transfer rate is equivalent to an 800 Mbps transfer rate.

Temperature is another important factor to consider when you're selecting a drive, but it's a factor few administrators take into account. Typically, the faster a drive rotates, the hotter it runs. This is not always the case, but it is certainly something you should consider when making your choice. For example, 15K drives tend to run hot, and you must be sure to carefully regulate temperature. Typical 15K drives can become nonoperational at temperatures of 70 degrees Centigrade or higher (as would most other drives).

Windows Server 2012 R2 adds support for disk drives with hardware encryption (referred to as encrypted hard drives). Encrypted hard drives have built-in processors that shift the encryption-decryption activities from the operating system to hardware, freeing up operating system resources. Windows Server 2012 R2 will use hardware encryption with BitLocker when available. Other security features available in Windows Server 2012 R2 include Secured Boot and Network Unlock. Secured Boot provides boot integrity by validating Boot Configuration Data (BCD) settings according to the Trusted Platform Module (TPM) validation profile settings. Network Unlock can be used to automatically unlock the operating system drive on domain-joined computers. For more information on TPM, BitLocker, Secured Boot, Network Unlock, and encrypted hard drives, see "Using TPM and BitLocker Drive Encryption" in Chapter 2 of *Windows 8.1 Administration Pocket Consultant: Storage, Networking, & Security* (Microsoft Press, 2013).

Preparing a physical drive for use

After you install a drive, you need to configure it for use. You configure the drive by partitioning it and creating file systems in the partitions as needed. A *partition* is a section of a physical drive that functions as if it were a separate unit. After you create a partition, you can create a file system in the partition.

The MBR and GPT partition styles

Two partition styles are used for disks: master boot record (MBR) and GUID partition table (GPT). The MBR contains a partition table that describes where the partitions are located on the disk. With this partition style, the first sector on a hard drive contains the master boot record and a binary code file called the *master boot code* that's used to boot the system. This sector is unpartitioned and hidden from view to protect the system.

With the MBR partitioning style, disks traditionally support volumes of up to 4 terabytes (TB) and use one of two types of partitions: primary or extended. Each MBR drive can have up to four primary partitions or three primary partitions and one extended partition. Primary partitions are drive sections you can access directly for file storage. You make a primary partition accessible to users by creating a file system on it. Although you can access primary partitions directly, you can't access extended partitions directly. Instead, you can configure extended partitions with one or more logical drives that are used to store files. Being able to divide extended partitions into logical drives allows you to divide a physical drive into more than four sections.

GPT was originally developed for high-performance, Itanium-based computers. The key difference between the GPT partition style and the MBR partition style has to do with how partition data is stored. With GPT, critical partition data is stored in the individual partitions, and redundant primary and backup partition tables are used for improved structural integrity. Additionally, GPT disks support volumes of up to 18 exabytes (1 exabyte equals 1,024 x 1,024 terabytes) and as many as 128 partitions. Although the GPT and MBR partitioning styles have underlying differences, most disk-related tasks are performed in the same way.

Legacy and protective MBRs

Most computers ship with Unified Extensible Firmware Interface (UEFI). Although UEFI is replacing BIOS and EFI as the top-level firmware interface, UEFI doesn't replace all the functionality in either BIOS or EFI and typically is wrapped around BIOS or EFI. With respect to UEFI, GPT is the preferred partitioning scheme and a protective MBR may be located on any disk that uses the GPT disk layout. A legacy MBR and a protective MBR differ in many important ways.

A legacy MBR is located at the first logical block on a disk that is not using the GPT disk layout. The first 512 bytes on an MBR disk have the following layout:

- The MBR begins with a 424-byte boot code, which is used to select an MBR partition record and load the first logical block of that partition. The boot code on the MBR is not executed by UEFI.

- The boot code is followed by a 4-byte unique MBR disk signature, which can be used by the operating system to identify the disk and distinguish the disk from other disks on the system. The unique signature is written by the operating system and not used by UEFI.

- A 2-byte separator follows the disk signature. At byte offset 446, there is an array of four MBR partition records, with each record being 16 bytes in length. Block 510 contains 0x55 and block 511 contains 0xAA. Block 512 is reserved.

The four partition records each define the first and last logical blocks that a particular partition uses on a disk:

- Each 16-byte MBR partition record begins with a 1-byte boot indicator. For example, a value of 0x80 identifies a bootable legacy partition. Any other value indicates that this is not a bootable legacy partition. This value is not used by UEFI.

- The boot indicator is followed by a 3-byte address identifying the start of the partition. At byte offset 4, there's a 1-byte value that indicates the operating system type, which is followed by a 3-byte value that identifies the end of the partition. These values are not used by UEFI.

- At byte offset 8, there is a 4-byte value indicating the first logical block of the partition, and this is followed by a 4-byte value indicating size of the partition in units of logical blocks. Both of these values are used by UEFI.

NOTE If an MBR partition has an operating system type value of 0xEF, firmware must add the UEFI system partition GUID to the handle for the MBR partition. This allows boot applications, operating system loaders, drivers, and other lower-level tools to locate the UEFI system partition, which must physically reside on the disk.

A protective MBR may be located at the first logical block on a disk that is using the GPT disk layout. The protective MBR precedes the GUID Partition Table Header and is used to maintain compatibility with tools that do not understand GPT partition structures. The purpose of the protective MBR is to protect the GPT partitions from boot applications, operating system loaders, drivers, and other lower-level tools that don't understand the GPT partitioning scheme. The protective MBR does this by defining a fake partition covering the entire disk. When a disk has a protective MBR, the first 512 bytes on the disk have the following layout:

- The protective MBR begins with a 424-byte boot code, which is not executed by UEFI.

- The boot code is followed by a 4-byte disk signature, which is set to zero and not used by UEFI.

- A 2-byte separator follows the disk signature. This separator is set to zero and not used by UEFI.

- At byte offset 446, there is an array of four MBR partition records, with each record being 16-bytes in length. Only the first partition record—the protective partition record—is used. The other partition records are set to zero.

- Block 510 contains 0x55 and block 511 contains 0xAA. Block 512 is reserved.

The protective partition record reserves the entire space on the disk after the first 512 bytes for the GPT disk layout. The protective partition record begins with a 1-byte boot indicator that is set to 0x00, which indicates a non-bootable partition. The boot indicator is followed by a 3-byte address identifying the start of the partition at 0x000200, which is the first usable block on the disk.

At byte offset 4, there's a 1-byte value set to 0xEE to indicate the operating system type as GPT Protective. This is followed by a 3-byte value that identifies the last usable block on the disk, which is the end of the partition (or 0xFFFFFF if it is not possible to represent this value).

At byte offset 8, there is a 4-byte value set to 0x00000001, which identifies the logical block address of the GPT partition header. This is followed by a 4-byte value indicating size of the disk minus one block (or 0xFFFFFFFF if the size of the disk is too large to be represented).

Disk types and file systems

In addition to a partition style, physical drives have a disk type, which is either basic or dynamic, as discussed later in the chapter in the section "Working with basic, dynamic, and virtual disks." After you set the partition style and disk type for a physical drive, you can format free areas of the drive to establish logical partitions. Formatting creates a file system on a partition. Windows Server 2012 R2 supports the following file systems:

- FAT
- FAT32
- exFAT
- NTFS
- ReFS

With FAT, the number of bits used with the file allocation table determines the variant with which you are working and the maximum volume size. FAT16, also known simply as FAT, defines its file allocation tables using 16 bits. Volumes that are 4 gigabytes (GB) or less in size are formatted with FAT16.

FAT32 defines its file allocation tables using 32 bits, and you can create FAT32 volumes that are 32 GB or less by using the Windows format tools. Although Windows can mount larger FAT32 volumes created with third-party tools, you should use NTFS for volumes larger than 32 GB.

Extended FAT is an enhanced version of FAT. Technically, exFAT could have been called FAT64 (and is called that by some). Because exFAT defines its file allocation tables by using 64 bits, it can overcome the 4-GB file-size limit and the 32-GB volume-size limit of FAT32 file systems. The exFAT format supports allocation unit sizes of up to 128 KB for volumes up to 256 TB.

NTFS volumes have a very different structure and feature set than FAT volumes. The first area of the volume is the boot sector, which stores information about the disk layout, and a bootstrap program executes at startup and boots the operating system. Instead of a file allocation table, NTFS uses a relational database called the master file table (MFT) to store information about files.

The MFT stores a file record of each file and folder on the volume, pertinent volume information, and details about the MFT itself. NTFS gives you many advanced options, including support for the Encrypting File System, compression, and the option to configure file screening and storage reporting. File screening and storage reporting are available when you add the File Server Resource Manager role service to a server as part of the File Services role.

Resilient File System (ReFS) can be thought of as the next generation of NTFS. As such, ReFS remains compatible with core NTFS features while cutting noncore features to focus relentlessly on reliability. This means disk quotas, Encrypting File System (EFS), compression, file screening, and storage reporting are not available but built-in reliability features have been added.

One of the biggest reliability features in ReFS is a data integrity scanner, also called a *data scrubber*. The scrubber provides proactive error identification, isolation, and correction. If the scrubber detects data corruption, a repair process is used to localize the area of corruption and perform automatic online correction. Through an automatic online salvage process, corrupted areas that cannot be repaired, such as those caused by bad blocks on the physical disk, are removed from the live volume so that they cannot adversely affect good data. Because of the automated scrubber and salvage processes, a Check Disk feature is not needed when you use ReFS (and there's no Check Disk utility for ReFS).

NOTE When you are working with File And Storage Services, you can group available physical disks into storage pools so that you can create virtual disks from available capacity. Each virtual disk you create is a storage space. Because only NTFS and ReFS support storage spaces, you'll want to keep that in mind when you are formatting volumes on file servers. For more information about storage spaces, see "Standards-based storage management" in Chapter 2.

Using Disk Management

You use the Disk Management snap-in for the Microsoft Management Console (MMC) to configure drives. Disk Management makes it easy to work with the internal and external drives on a local or remote system. Disk Management is included as part of the Computer Management console. You can also add it to custom MMCs. In Computer Management, you can access Disk Management by expanding the Storage node, and then selecting Disk Management. Alternatively, you can enter **diskmgmt.msc** at the Everywhere prompt, and then press Enter.

Disk Management has three views: Disk List, Graphical View, and Volume List. With remote systems, you're limited in the tasks you can perform with Disk Management. Remote management tasks you can perform include viewing drive details, changing drive letters and paths, and converting disk types. With removable media drives, you can also eject media remotely. To perform more advanced manipulation of remote drives, you can use the DiskPart command-line utility.

NOTE You should be aware that if you create a partition but don't format it, the partition is labeled as Free Space. In addition, if you haven't assigned a portion of the disk to a partition, this section of the disk is labeled Unallocated.

In Figure 1-1, the Volume List view is in the upper-right corner, and the Graphical View is in the lower-right corner. This is the default configuration. You can change the view for the top or bottom pane as follows:

- To change the top view, select View, choose Top, and then select the view you want to use.
- To change the bottom view, select View, choose Bottom, and then select the view you want to use.
- To hide the bottom view, select View, choose Bottom, and then select Hidden.

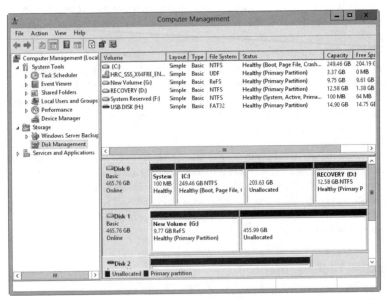

FIGURE 1-1 In Disk Management, the upper view provides a detailed summary of all the drives on the computer, and the lower view provides an overview of the same drives by default.

Windows Server 2012 R2 supports four types of disk configurations:

- **Basic** The standard fixed disk type. Basic disks are divided into partitions and are the original disk type for early Windows operating systems.

- **Dynamic** An enhanced fixed disk type that you can update without having to restart the operating system (in most cases). Dynamic disks are divided into volumes.

- **Removable** The standard disk type associated with removable storage devices.

- **Virtual** The virtual hard disk (VHD) disk type associated with virtualization. Computers can use VHDs just like they use regular fixed disks and can even be configured to boot from a VHD.

These disk configurations can be used with legacy storage approaches as well as standards-based storage. From the Disk Management window, you can get more detailed information on a drive section by pressing and holding or right-clicking it, and then selecting Properties. When you do this, you get a dialog box. Figure 1-2 shows the dialog boxes for two fixed disks. The one on the left uses NTFS, and the one on the right uses ReFS. Both disks have additional tabs based on the server configuration.

FIGURE 1-2 The General tab of the Properties dialog box provides detailed information about a drive.

If you've configured remote management through Server Manager and MMCs, as discussed in Chapter 2, you can use Disk Management to configure and work with disks on remote computers. Keep in mind, however, that your options are slightly different from when you are working with the disks on a local computer.

Tasks you can perform include the following:

- Viewing limited disk properties, but not volume properties. When you are viewing disk properties, you'll see only the General and Volumes tabs. You won't be able to see volume properties.
- Changing drive letters and mount paths.
- Formatting, shrinking, and extending volumes. With mirrored, spanned, and striped volumes, you are able to add and configure related options.
- Deleting volumes (except for system and boot volumes).
- Creating, attaching, and detaching VHDs. When you create and attach VHDs, you need to enter the full file path and won't be able to browse for the .vhd file.

Some tasks you perform with disks and volumes depend on the Plug and Play and Remote Registry services.

Using removable storage devices

Removable storage devices can be formatted with ReFS, NTFS, FAT, FAT32, or exFAT. You connect external storage devices to a computer rather than installing them inside the computer. This makes external storage devices easier and faster to install than most fixed disk drives. Most external storage devices have either a USB or a FireWire interface. When working with USB and FireWire, the transfer speed and overall performance of the device from a user's perspective depends primarily on the version supported. Currently, several versions of USB and FireWire are used.

USB 2.0 is the current industry standard until the world transitions to USB 3.0. USB 2.0 devices can be rated as either full speed (up to 12 Mbps) or high speed (up to 480 Mbps). Although high-speed USB 2.0 supports data transfers at a maximum rate of 480 Mbps, sustained data-transfer rates are usually 10–30 Mbps. The actual sustainable transfer rate depends on many factors, including the type of device, the data you are transferring, and the speed of a computer. Each USB controller on a computer has a fixed amount of bandwidth, which all devices attached to the controller must share. The data transfer rates are significantly slower if a computer's USB port is an earlier version than the device you are using. For example, if you connect a USB 3.0 device to a USB 2.0 port or vice versa, the device operates at the significantly reduced USB 2.0 transfer speed.

USB 1.0, 1.1, and 2.0 ports all look alike; however, most USB 3.0 ports I've seen have a special color to differentiate them. Still, the best way to determine which type of USB ports a computer has is to refer to the documentation that comes with the computer. Newer monitors have USB 2.0 ports to which you can connect devices as well. When you have USB devices connected to a monitor, the monitor acts like a USB hub device. As with any USB hub device, all devices attached to the hub share the same bandwidth, and the total available bandwidth is determined by the speed of the USB input to which the hub is connected on a computer.

FireWire (IEEE 1394) is a high-performance connection standard that uses a peer-to-peer architecture in which peripherals negotiate bus conflicts to determine which device can best control a data transfer. Like USB, several versions of FireWire are currently used. FireWire 400 (IEEE 1394a) has maximum sustained transfer rates of up to 400 Mbps. IEEE 1394b allows 400 Mbps (S400), 800 Mbps (S800), and 1600 Mbps (S1600). As with USB devices, if you connect an IEEE 1394b device to an IEEE 1394a port or vice versa, the device operates at the significantly reduced FireWire 400 transfer speed.

As with USB ports, the sustained transfer rate for IEEE 1394a and IEEE 1394b ports will be considerably less than the maximum rate possible. IEEE 1394a and IEEE 1394b ports and cables have different shapes, making it easier to tell the difference between them—if you know what you're looking for. FireWire 400 cables without bus power have four pins and four connectors. FireWire 400 cables with bus power have six pins and six connectors. FireWire 800 and FireWire 1600 cables always have bus power and have nine pins and nine connectors.

Another option is external SATA (eSATA), which is available on newer computers and is an ultra-high-performance connection for data transfer to and from external mass storage devices. eSATA operates at speeds up to 6 Gbps. If your computer doesn't come with eSATA ports, you can add support for eSATA devices by installing an eSATA controller card.

When you are purchasing an external device for a computer, you'll also want to consider what interfaces it supports. In some cases, you might be able to get a device with more than one interface, such as one that supports USB 3.0 and eSATA. A device with multiple interfaces gives you more options.

Working with removable disks is similar to working with fixed disks. You can do the following:

- Press and hold or right-click a removable disk, and then select Open or Explore to examine the disk's contents in File Explorer.

- Press and hold or right-click a removable disk, and then select Format to format a removable disk as discussed in "Formatting partitions" later in this chapter. Removable disks generally are formatted with a single partition.

- Press and hold or right-click a removable disk, and then select Properties to view or set properties. On the General tab of the Properties dialog box, you can set the volume label as discussed in "Changing or deleting the volume label" in Chapter 2.

When you work with removable disks, you can customize disk and folder views. To do this, press and hold or right-click the disk or folder, select Properties, and then tap or click the Customize tab. You can then specify the default folder type to control the default details displayed. For example, you can set the default folder type as Documents or Pictures And Videos. You can also set folder pictures and folder icons.

Removable disks support network file and folder sharing. You configure sharing on removable disks in the same way you configure standard file sharing. You can assign share permissions, configure caching options for offline file use, and limit the number of simultaneous users. You can share an entire removable disk as well as individual folders stored on the removable disk. You can also create multiple share instances.

Removable disks differ from standard NTFS sharing in that they don't necessarily have an underlying security architecture. With exFAT, FAT, or FAT32, folders and files stored on a removable disk do not have any security permissions or features other than the basic read-only or hidden attribute flags that you can set.

Installing and checking for a new drive

Hot swapping is a feature that allows you to remove internal devices without shutting off the computer. Typically, hot-swappable internal drives are installed and removed from the front of the computer. If your computer supports hot swapping of internal drives, you can install drives without having to shut down. After you have installed a new drive, open Disk Management, and then choose Rescan Disks from the Action menu. New disks that are found are added with the appropriate disk type. If a disk that you've added isn't found, restart the computer.

If the computer doesn't support hot swapping of internal drives, you must turn the computer off and then install the new drives. Then you can scan for new disks as described previously. If you are working with new disks that have not been initialized —meaning they don't have disk signatures—Disk Management will start the Initialize Disk dialog box as soon it starts up and detects the new disks.

You can initialize the disks by following these steps:

1. Each disk you install needs to be initialized. Select the disk or disks you installed.

2. Disks can use either the MBR or GPT partition style. Select the partition style you want to use for the disk or disks you are initializing.

3. Tap or click OK. If you elected to initialize disks, Windows writes a disk signature to the disks and initializes the disks with the basic disk type.

If you don't want to use the Initialize Disk dialog box, you can close it and use Disk Management instead to view and work with the disk. In the Disk List view, the disk is marked with a red downward-pointing arrow icon, the disk's type is listed as Unknown, and the disk's status is listed as Not Initialized. Press and hold or right-click the disk's icon and select Online. Press and hold or right-click the disk's icon again, and select Initialize Disk. You can then initialize the disk as discussed previously.

> **NOTE** At an elevated, administrator Windows PowerShell prompt, you can use Get-Disk to list available disks and Initialize-Disk to initialize new disks.

Understanding drive status

Knowing the status of a drive is useful when you install new drives or troubleshoot drive problems. Disk Management shows the drive status in Graphical View and Volume List view. Table 1-2 summarizes the most common status values.

TABLE 1-2 Common drive status values

STATUS	DESCRIPTION	RESOLUTION
Online	The normal disk status. It means the disk is accessible and doesn't have problems. Both dynamic disks and basic disks display this status.	The drive doesn't have any known problems. You don't need to take any corrective action.
Online (Errors)	I/O errors have been detected on a dynamic disk.	You can try to correct temporary errors by pressing and holding or right-clicking the disk and selecting Reactivate Disk. If this doesn't work, the disk might have physical damage or you might need to run a thorough check of the disk.
Offline	The disk isn't accessible and might be corrupted or temporarily unavailable. If the disk name changes to Missing, the disk can no longer be located or identified on the system.	Check for problems with the drive, its controller, and cables. Make sure that the drive has power and is connected properly. Use the Reactivate Disk command to bring the disk back online (if possible).
Foreign	The disk has been moved to your computer but hasn't been imported for use. A failed drive brought back online might sometimes be listed as Foreign.	Press and hold or right-click the disk, and then tap or click Import Foreign Disks to add the disk to the system.
Unreadable	The disk isn't accessible currently, which can occur when disks are being rescanned. Both dynamic and basic disks display this status.	With FireWire and USB card readers, you might get this status if the card is unformatted or improperly formatted. You might also get this status after the card is removed from the reader. Otherwise, if the drives aren't being scanned, the drive might be corrupted or have I/O errors. Press and hold or right-click the disk, and then tap or click Rescan Disk (on the Action menu) to try to correct the problem. You might also want to restart the system.

STATUS	DESCRIPTION	RESOLUTION
Unrecognized	The disk is of an unknown type and can't be used on the system. A drive from a system that is not based on Windows might display this status.	If the disk is from another operating system, don't do anything. Normally, you can't use the drive on the computer without initializing and formatting it, so try a different drive.
Not Initialized	The disk doesn't have a valid signature. A drive from a system not based on Windows might display this status.	If the disk is from another operating system, don't do anything. You can't use the drive on the computer, so try a different drive. To prepare the disk for use on Windows Server 2012 R2, press and hold or right-click the disk, and then tap or click Initialize Disk.
No Media	No media has been inserted into the DVD or removable drive, or the media has been removed. Only DVD and removable disk types display this status.	Insert a DVD or a removable disk to bring the disk online. With FireWire and USB card readers, this status is usually (but not always) displayed when the card is removed.

Working with basic, dynamic, and virtual disks

Windows Server 2012 R2 supports basic, dynamic, and virtual disk configurations. This section discusses techniques for working with each disk configuration type.

Using basic and dynamic disks

Basic, dynamic, and virtual disk configurations can be used with both legacy storage approaches and standards-based storage. Normally, Windows Server 2012 R2 disk partitions are initialized as basic disks. The exception is when you want to use software-based RAID instead of standards-based storage.

With software-based RAID, you can't create new fault-tolerant drive sets by using the basic disk type. You need to convert to dynamic disks and then create volumes that use striping, mirroring, or striping with parity (referred to as RAID 0, 1, and 5, respectively). The fault-tolerant features and the ability to modify disks without having to restart the computer are the key capabilities that distinguish dynamic disks from basic disks. Other features available on a disk depend on the disk formatting.

You can use both basic and dynamic disks on the same computer; however, volume sets must use the same disk type and partitioning style. For example, if you want to mirror drives C and D, both drives must have the dynamic disk type and use the same partitioning style, which can be either MBR or GPT. Note that Disk Management allows you to start many disk configuration tasks regardless of whether the disks with which you are working use the dynamic disk type. The catch is that during the configuration process, Disk Management will convert the disks to the dynamic disk type. To learn how to convert a disk from basic to dynamic, see "Changing drive types" on the next page.

You can perform different disk configuration tasks with basic and dynamic disks. With basic disks, you can do the following:

- Format partitions, and mark them as active
- Create and delete primary and extended partitions
- Create and delete logical drives within extended partitions
- Convert from a basic disk to a dynamic disk

With dynamic disks, you can do the following:

- Create and delete simple, striped, spanned, mirrored, and RAID-5 volumes
- Remove a mirror from a mirrored volume
- Extend simple or spanned volumes
- Split a volume into two volumes
- Repair mirrored or RAID-5 volumes
- Reactivate a missing or offline disk
- Revert to a basic disk from a dynamic disk (requires deleting volumes and restoring from backup)

With either disk type, you can do the following:

- View properties of disks, partitions, and volumes
- Make drive-letter assignments
- Configure security and drive sharing
- Use Storage Spaces to implement standards-based storage

Special considerations for basic and dynamic disks

Whether you're working with basic or dynamic disks, you need to keep in mind five special types of drive sections:

- **Active**   The active partition or volume is the drive section for system caching and startup. Some devices with removable storage might be listed as having an active partition.
- **Boot**   The boot partition or volume contains the operating system and its support files. The system and boot partition or volume can be the same.
- **Crash dump**   The partition to which the computer attempts to write dump files in the event of a system crash. By default, dump files are written to the %SystemRoot% folder, but they can be located on any partition or volume.

- **Page file** A partition containing a paging file used by the operating system. Because a computer can page memory to multiple disks, according to the way virtual memory is configured, a computer can have multiple page file partitions or volumes.

- **System** The system partition or volume contains the hardware-specific files needed to load the operating system. The system partition or volume can't be part of a striped or spanned volume.

REAL WORLD GPT is becoming the primary disk type for Windows Server. With Windows Server 2012 R2, a typical new disk has the GPT partition style with a recovery partition and an EFI system partition.

NOTE You can mark a partition as active by using Disk Management. In Disk Management, press and hold or right-click the primary partition you want to mark as active, and then tap or click Mark Partition As Active. You can't mark dynamic disk volumes as active. When you convert a basic disk containing the active partition to a dynamic disk, this partition becomes a simple volume that's active automatically.

Changing drive types

You can use dynamic disks with any current version of Windows and many other operating systems, including most UNIX variants. However, keep in mind that you need to create a separate volume for any operating system not based on Windows.

You can't use dynamic disks on portable computers. When you are working with non-portable computers and servers, you only can use dynamic disks with drives connected to internal controllers (as well as some eSATA controllers). Although you can't use dynamic disks with portable or removable drives on these computers, you can connect such a drive to an internal controller or a recognized eSATA controller, and then use Disk Management to import the drive.

Windows Server 2012 R2 provides the tools you need to convert a basic disk to a dynamic disk and to change a dynamic disk back to a basic disk. When you convert to a dynamic disk, partitions are changed to volumes of the appropriate type automatically. You can't change these volumes back to partitions. Instead, you must delete the volumes on the dynamic disk, and then change the disk back to a basic disk. Deleting the volumes destroys all the information on the disk.

Converting a basic disk to a dynamic disk

Before you convert a basic disk to a dynamic disk, you should make sure that you don't need to boot the computer to an operating system that doesn't support dynamic disks. With MBR disks, you should also make sure that the disk has 1 MB of free space at the end of the disk. Although Disk Management reserves this free space when creating partitions and volumes, disk management tools on other operating systems might not. Without the free space at the end of the disk, the conversion will fail.

With GPT disks, you must have contiguous, recognized data partitions. If the GPT disk contains partitions that Windows doesn't recognize, such as those created by another operating system, you can't convert to a dynamic disk.

With either type of disk, the following holds true:

- There must be at least 1 MB of free space at the end of the disk. Disk Management reserves this free space automatically, but other disk management tools might not.

- You can't use dynamic disks on portable computers or with removable media. You can configure these drives only as basic drives with primary partitions.

- You shouldn't convert a disk if it contains multiple installations of the Windows operating system. If you do, you might be able to start the computer only by using the installation which did the conversion.

To convert a basic disk to a dynamic disk, follow these steps:

1. In Disk Management, press and hold or right-click a basic disk that you want to convert, either in the Disk List view or in the left pane of the Graphical View. Then tap or click Convert To Dynamic Disk.

2. In the Convert To Dynamic Disk dialog box, select the check boxes for the disks you want to convert. Tap or click OK to continue. This displays the Disks To Convert dialog box, which shows the disks you're converting.

   The buttons and columns in this dialog box contain the following information:

   - **Name**   Shows the disk number.
   - **Disk Contents**   Shows the type and status of partitions, such as boot, active, or in use.
   - **Will Convert**   Specifies whether the drive will be converted. If the drive doesn't meet the criteria, it won't be converted, and you might need to take corrective action, as described previously.
   - **Details**   Shows the volumes on the selected drive.
   - **Convert**   Starts the conversion.

3. To begin the conversion, tap or click Convert. Disk Management warns you that after the conversion is complete, you won't be able to start previous versions of Windows from volumes on the selected disks. Tap or click Yes to continue.

4. Disk Management restarts the computer if a selected drive contains the boot partition, system partition, or a partition in use.

Changing a dynamic disk back to a basic disk

Before you can change a dynamic disk back to a basic disk, you must delete all dynamic volumes on the disk. After you do this, press and hold or right-click the disk and select Convert To Basic Disk to change the dynamic disk to a basic disk. You can then create new partitions and logical drives on the disk.

Reactivating dynamic disks

If the status of a dynamic disk is Online (Errors) or Offline, you can often reactivate the disk to correct the problem. You reactivate a disk by following these steps:

1. In Disk Management, press and hold or right-click the dynamic disk you want to reactivate, and then tap or click Reactivate Disk. Confirm the action when prompted.

2. If the drive status doesn't change, you might need to reboot the computer. If this still doesn't resolve the problem, check for problems with the drive, its controller, and the cables. Also make sure that the drive has power and is connected properly.

Rescanning disks

Rescanning all drives on a system updates the drive configuration information on the computer. Rescanning can sometimes resolve a problem with drives that show a status of Unreadable. You rescan disks on a computer by choosing Rescan Disks from the Action menu in Disk Management.

Moving a dynamic disk to a new system

An important advantage of dynamic disks over basic disks is that you can easily move dynamic disks from one computer to another. For example, if after setting up a computer you decide that you don't really need an additional hard drive, you can move it to another computer where it can be better used.

Windows Server 2012 R2 greatly simplifies the task of moving disks to a new system. Before moving disks, you should follow these steps:

1. Open Disk Management on the system where the dynamic disks are currently installed. Check the status of the disks, and ensure that they're marked as Healthy. If the status isn't Healthy, you should repair partitions and volumes before you move the disks.

   NOTE Drives with BitLocker Drive Encryption cannot be moved by using this technique. BitLocker Drive Encryption wraps drives in a protected seal so that any offline tampering is detected and results in the disk being unavailable until an administrator unlocks it.

2. Check the hard drive subsystems on the original computer and the computer to which you want to transfer the disk. Both computers should have identical hard drive subsystems. If they don't, the Plug and Play ID on the system drive from the original computer won't match what the destination computer is expecting. As a result, the destination computer won't be able to load the right drivers, and the boot attempt might fail.

3. Check whether any dynamic disks you want to move are part of a spanned, extended, or striped set. If they are, you should make a note of which disks are part of which set and plan on moving all disks in a set together. If you are moving only part of a disk set, you should be aware of the consequences. For

spanned, extended, or striped volumes, moving only part of the set will make the related volumes unusable on the current computer and on the computer to which you are planning to move the disks.

When you are ready to move the disks, follow these steps:

1. On the original computer, start Computer Management. Then, in the left pane, select Device Manager. In the Device list, expand Disk Drives. This shows a list of the physical disk drives on the computer. Press and hold or right-click each disk you want to move, and then tap or click Uninstall. If you are unsure which disks to uninstall, press and hold or right-click each disk and tap or click Properties. In the Properties dialog box, tap or click the Volumes tab and then select Populate to show the volumes on the selected disk.

2. Next, on the original computer, select the Disk Management node in Computer Management. If the disk or disks you want to move are still listed, press and hold or right-click each disk, and then tap or click Remove Disk.

3. After you perform these procedures, you can move the dynamic disks. If the disks are hot-swappable disks and this feature is supported on both computers, remove the disks from the original computer, and then install them on the destination computer. Otherwise, turn off both computers, remove the drives from the original computer, and then install them on the destination computer. When you have finished, restart the computers.

4. On the destination computer, access Disk Management, and then choose Rescan Disks from the Action menu. When Disk Management finishes scanning the disks, press and hold or right-click any disk marked Foreign, and then tap or click Import. You should now be able to access the disks and their volumes on the destination computer.

NOTE In most cases, the volumes on the dynamic disks should retain the drive letters they had on the original computer. However, if a drive letter is already used on the destination computer, a volume receives the next available drive letter. If a dynamic volume previously did not have a drive letter, it does not receive a drive letter when moved to the destination computer. Additionally, if automounting is disabled, the volumes aren't automatically mounted, and you must manually mount volumes and assign drive letters.

Managing virtual hard disks

By using Disk Management, you can create, attach, and detach VHDs. You can create a VHD by choosing Create VHD from the Action menu. In the Create And Attach Virtual Hard Disk dialog box, tap or click Browse. Use the Browse Virtual Disk Files dialog box to select the location where you want to create the .vhd file for the VHD, and then tap or click Save.

In the Virtual Hard Disk Size list, enter the size of the disk in megabytes, gigabytes, or terabytes. Specify whether the size of the VHD dynamically expands to its fixed maximum size as data is saved to it or instead uses a fixed amount of space regardless of the amount of data stored on it. When you tap or click OK, Disk Management creates the VHD.

The VHD is attached automatically and added as a new disk. To initialize the disk for use, press and hold or right-click the disk entry in Graphical View, and then tap or click Initialize Disk. In the Initialize Disk dialog box, the disk is selected for initialization. Specify the disk type as MBR or GPT, and then tap or click OK.

After initializing the disk, press and hold or right-click the unpartitioned space on the disk and create a volume of the appropriate type. After you create the volume, the VHD is available for use.

After you've created, attached, initialized, and formatted a VHD, you can work with a virtual disk in much the same way as you work with other disks. You can write data to and read data from a VHD. You can boot the computer from a VHD. You are able to take a VHD offline or put a VHD online by pressing and holding or right-clicking the disk entry in Graphical View and selecting Offline or Online, respectively. If you no longer want to use a VHD, you can detach it by pressing and holding or right-clicking the disk entry in Graphical View, selecting Detach VHD, and then tapping or clicking OK in the Detach Virtual Hard Disk dialog box.

You can use VHDs created with other programs as well. If you created a VHD using another program or have a detached VHD you want to attach, you can work with the VHD by completing the following steps:

1. In Disk Management, tap or click the Attach VHD option on the Action menu.

2. In the Attach Virtual Hard Disk dialog box, tap or click Browse. Use the Browse Virtual Disk Files dialog box to select the .vhd file for the VHD, and then tap or click Open.

3. If you want to attach the VHD in read-only mode, select Read-Only. Tap or click OK to attach the VHD.

Using basic disks and partitions

When you install a new computer or update an existing computer, you often need to partition the drives on the computer. You partition drives by using Disk Management.

Partitioning basics

In Windows Server 2012 R2, a physical drive using the MBR partition style can have up to four primary partitions and one extended partition. This allows you to configure MBR drives in one of two ways: by using one to four primary partitions, or by using one to three primary partitions and one extended partition. A primary partition can fill an entire disk, or you can size it as appropriate for the workstation or server you're configuring. Within an extended partition, you can create one or more logical drives. A logical drive is simply a section of a partition with its own file system. Generally, you use logical drives to divide a large drive into manageable sections. With this in mind, you might want to divide a 600-GB extended partition into three logical drives of 200 GB each. Physical disks with the GPT partition style can have up to 128 partitions.

After you partition a drive, you format the partitions. This is high-level formatting that creates the file system structure rather than low-level formatting that sets up the drive for initial use. You're probably very familiar with the C drive used by Windows Server 2012 R2. Well, the C drive is simply the designator for a disk partition. If you partition a disk into multiple sections, each section can have its own drive letter. You use the drive letters to access file systems in various partitions on a physical drive. Unlike MS-DOS, which assigns drive letters automatically starting with the letter C, Windows Server 2012 R2 lets you specify drive letters. Generally, the drive letters C through Z are available for your use.

NOTE The drive letter A used to be assigned to a system's floppy disk drive. If the system had a second floppy disk drive, the letter B was assigned to it, so you could use only the letters C through Z. Don't forget that DVD drives and other types of media drives need drive letters as well. The total number of drive letters you can use at one time is 24. If you need additional volumes, you can create them by using drive paths.

By using drive letters, you can have only 24 active volumes. To get around this limitation, you can mount disks to drive paths. A drive path is set as a folder location on another drive. For example, you might mount additional drives as E:\Data1, E:\Data2, and E:\Data3. You can use drive paths with basic and dynamic disks. The only restriction for drive paths is that you mount them on empty folders that are on NTFS drives.

To help you differentiate between primary partitions and extended partitions with logical drives, Disk Management color codes the partitions. For example, primary partitions might be color coded with a dark-blue band and logical drives in extended partitions might be color coded with a light-blue band. The key for the color scheme is shown at the bottom of the Disk Management window. You can change the colors in the Settings dialog box by choosing Settings from the View menu.

Creating partitions and simple volumes

Windows Server 2012 R2 simplifies the Disk Management user interface by using one set of dialog boxes and wizards for both partitions and volumes. The first three volumes on a basic drive are created automatically as primary partitions. If you try to create a fourth volume on a basic drive, the remaining free space on the drive is converted automatically to an extended partition with a logical drive of the size you designate by using the new volume feature in the extended partition. Any subsequent volumes are created in the extended partitions as logical drives automatically.

In Disk Management, you create partitions, logical drives, and simple volumes by following these steps:

1. In Disk Management's Graphical View, press and hold or right-click an unallocated or free area, and then tap or click New Simple Volume. This starts the New Simple Volume Wizard. Read the Welcome page, and then tap or click Next.

2. The Specify Volume Size page in the New Simple Volume Wizard, shown in Figure 1-3, specifies the minimum and maximum size for the volume in megabytes and lets you size the volume within these limits. Size the partition in megabytes in the Simple Volume Size In MB box, and then tap or click Next.

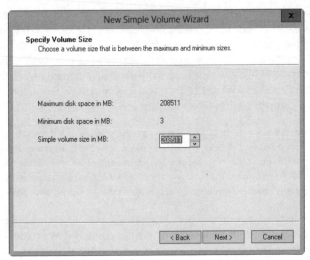

FIGURE 1-3 Set the size of the volume on the Specify Volume Size page in the New Simple Volume Wizard.

3. On the Assign Drive Letter Or Path page, shown in Figure 1-4, specify whether you want to assign a drive letter or path, and then tap or click Next. The following options are available:

- **Assign The Following Drive Letter** Choose this option to assign a drive letter. Then select an available drive letter in the list provided. By default, Windows Server 2012 R2 selects the lowest available drive letter and excludes reserved drive letters as well as those assigned to local disks or network drives.

- **Mount In The Following Empty NTFS Folder** Choose this option to mount the partition in an empty NTFS folder. You must then type the path to an existing folder or tap or click Browse to search for or create a folder to use.

- **Do Not Assign A Drive Letter Or Drive Path** Choose this option if you want to create the partition without assigning a drive letter or path. If you later want the partition to be available for storage, you can assign a drive letter or path at that time.

NOTE You don't have to assign volumes a drive letter or a path. A volume with no designators is considered to be unmounted and is for the most part unusable. An unmounted volume can be mounted by assigning a drive letter or a path at a later date. See "Assigning drive letters and paths" in Chapter 2.

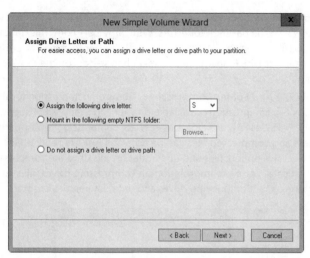

FIGURE 1-4 On the Assign Drive Letter Or Path page, assign the drive designator or choose to wait until later.

4. On the Format Partition page, shown in Figure 1-5, determine whether and how the volume should be formatted. If you want to format the volume, select Format This Volume With The Following Settings, and then configure the following options:

- **File System** Sets the file system type as FAT, FAT32, exFAT, NTFS, or ReFS. The file system types available depend on the size of the volume you are formatting. If you use FAT32, you can later convert to NTFS with the Convert utility. You can't, however, convert NTFS partitions to FAT32.

- **Allocation Unit Size** Sets the cluster size for the file system. This is the basic unit in which disk space is allocated. The default allocation unit size is based on the size of the volume and is set dynamically prior to formatting by default. To override this feature, you can set the allocation unit size to a specific value. If you use many small files, you might want to use a smaller cluster size, such as 512 or 1,024 bytes. With these settings, small files use less disk space. Note that ReFS volumes have a fixed allocation unit size.

- **Volume Label** Sets a text label for the partition. This label is the partition's volume name and is set to New Volume by default. You can change the volume label at any time by pressing and holding or right-clicking the volume in File Explorer, tapping or clicking Properties, and typing a new value in the Label box provided on the General tab.

- **Perform A Quick Format** Tells Windows Server 2012 R2 to format without checking the partition for errors. With large partitions, this option can save you a few minutes. However, it's usually better to check for errors, which enables Disk Management to mark bad sectors on the disk and lock them out.

- **Enable File And Folder Compression** Turns on compression for the disk. Built-in compression is available only for NTFS (and is not supported for FAT, FAT32, exFAT, or ReFS). Under NTFS, compression is transparent to users and compressed files can be accessed just like regular files. If you select this option, files and directories on this drive are compressed automatically. For more information on compressing drives, files, and directories, see "Compressing drives and data" later in this chapter.

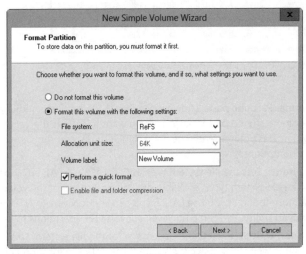

FIGURE 1-5 Set the formatting options for the partition on the Format Partition page.

Formatting partitions

Formatting creates a file system on a partition and permanently deletes any existing data. This is high-level formatting that creates the file system structure rather than low-level formatting that initializes a drive for use. To format a partition, press and hold or right-click the partition, and then tap or click Format. This opens the Format dialog box, shown in Figure 1-6.

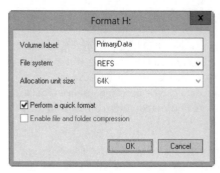

FIGURE 1-6 Format a partition in the Format dialog box by specifying its file system type and volume label.

You use the formatting options as follows:

- **Volume Label** Specifies a text label for the partition. This label is the partition's volume name.

- **File System** Specifies the file system type as FAT, FAT32, exFAT, NTFS, or ReFS. The file system types available depend on the size of the volume you are formatting.

- **Allocation Unit Size** Specifies the cluster size for the file system. This is the basic unit in which disk space is allocated. The default allocation unit size is based on the size of the volume and is set dynamically prior to formatting. To override this feature, you can set the allocation unit size to a specific value. If you use lots of small files, you might want to use a smaller cluster size, such as 512 or 1,024 bytes. With these settings, small files use less disk space.

- **Perform A Quick Format** Tells Windows Server 2012 R2 to format without checking the partition for errors. With large partitions, this option can save you a few minutes. However, it's more prudent to check for errors, which allows Disk Management to mark bad sectors on the disk and lock them out.

When you're ready to proceed, tap or click OK. Because formatting a partition destroys any existing data, Disk Management gives you one last chance to cancel the procedure. Tap or click OK to start formatting the partition. Disk Management changes the drive's status to reflect the formatting and the percentage of completion. When formatting is complete, the drive status changes to reflect this.

Compressing drives and data

When you format a drive for NTFS, Windows Server 2012 R2 allows you to turn on the built-in compression feature. With compression, all files and directories stored on a drive are automatically compressed when they're created. Because this compression is transparent to users, compressed data can be accessed just like regular data. The difference is that you can store more information on a compressed drive than you can on an uncompressed drive.

> **IMPORTANT** File Explorer shows the names of compressed resources in blue. It's also important to point out that ReFS does not support NTFS compression.

> **REAL WORLD** Although compression is certainly a useful feature when you want to save disk space, you can't encrypt compressed data. Compression and encryption are mutually exclusive alternatives for NTFS volumes, which means you have the choice of using compression or using encryption. You can't use both techniques. For more information on encryption, see "Encrypting drives and data" later in this chapter. If you try to compress encrypted data, Windows Server 2012 R2 automatically decrypts the data, and then compresses it. Likewise, if you try to encrypt compressed data, Windows Server 2012 R2 uncompresses the data, and then encrypts it.

Compressing drives

To compress a drive and all its contents, follow these steps:

1. In File Explorer or Disk Management, press and hold or right-click the drive you want to compress, and then tap or click Properties.

2. On the General tab, select Compress Drive To Save Disk Space, and then tap or click OK.

3. In the Confirm Attribute Changes dialog box, select whether to apply the changes to subfolders and files, and then tap or click OK.

Compressing directories and files

If you decide not to compress a drive, Windows Server 2012 R2 lets you selectively compress directories and files. To compress a file or directory, follow these steps:

1. In File Explorer, press and hold or right-click the file or directory you want to compress, and then tap or click Properties.

2. On the General tab of the Properties dialog box, tap or click Advanced. In the Advanced Attributes dialog box, select the Compress Contents To Save Disk Space check box. Tap or click OK twice.

For an individual file, Windows Server marks the file as compressed, and then compresses it. For a directory, Windows Server marks the directory as compressed and then compresses all the files in it. If the directory contains subfolders, Windows Server displays a dialog box that allows you to compress all the subfolders associated with the directory. Simply select Apply Changes To This Folder, Subfolders, And Files, and then tap or click OK. After you compress a directory, any new files added or copied to the directory are compressed automatically.

NOTE If you move an uncompressed file from a different drive, the file is compressed. However, if you move an uncompressed file to a compressed folder on the same NTFS drive, the file isn't compressed. Note also that you can't encrypt compressed files.

Expanding compressed drives

File Explorer shows the names of compressed files and folders in blue. You can remove compression from a drive by following these steps:

1. In File Explorer or Disk Management, press and hold or right-click the drive that contains the data you want to expand, and then tap or click Properties.

2. Clear the Compress Drive To Save Disk Space check box, and then tap or click OK.

3. In the Confirm Attribute Changes dialog box, select whether to apply the change to subfolders and files, and then tap or click OK.

TIP Windows always checks the available disk space before expanding compressed data. You should, too. If less free space is available than used space, you might not be able to complete the expansion. For example, if a compressed drive uses 150 GB of space and has 70 GB of free space available, you won't have enough free space to expand the data. Generally, you need about 1.5 to 2 times as much free space as you have compressed data.

Expanding compressed directories and files

If you decide that you want to expand a compressed file or directory, follow these steps:

1. Press and hold or right-click the file or directory in File Explorer, and then tap or click Properties.

2. On the General tab of the Properties dialog box, tap or click Advanced. Clear the Compress Contents To Save Disk Space check box. Tap or click OK twice.

With files, Windows Server removes compression and expands the file. With directories, Windows Server expands all the files within the directory. If the directory contains subfolders, you also have the opportunity to remove compression from the subfolders. To do this, select Apply Changes To This Folder, Subfolders, And Files when prompted, and then tap or click OK.

TIP Windows Server also provides command-line utilities for compressing and uncompressing data. The compression utility is called Compact (Compact.exe). The uncompression utility is called Expand (Expand.exe).

Encrypting drives and data

NTFS has many advantages over other file systems you can use with Windows Server. One advantage is the capability to automatically encrypt and decrypt data by using the Encrypting File System (EFS). When you encrypt data, you add an extra layer of protection to sensitive data, and this extra layer acts as a security blanket blocking all other users from reading the contents of the encrypted files. Indeed, one of the great benefits of encryption is that only the designated user can access the data. This benefit is also a disadvantage in that the user must remove encryption before authorized users can access the data.

NOTE As discussed previously, you can't compress encrypted files. The encryption and compression features of NTFS are mutually exclusive. You can use one feature or the other, but not both. Note also that ReFS doesn't support this type of encryption.

Understanding encryption and the encrypting file system

File encryption is supported on a per-folder or per-file basis. Any file placed in a folder marked for encryption is automatically encrypted. Files in encrypted format can be read only by the person who encrypted the file. Before other users can read an encrypted file, the user must decrypt the file or grant special access to the file by adding a user's encryption key to the file.

Every encrypted file has the unique encryption key of the user who created the file or currently has ownership of the file. An encrypted file can be copied, moved, backed up, restored, or renamed just like any other file, and in most cases these actions don't affect the encryption of the data. (For details, see "Working with encrypted files and folders" later in this chapter.) The user who encrypts a file always has access to the file, provided that the user's public-key certificate is available on the computer that she is using. For this user, the encryption and decryption process is handled automatically and is transparent.

EFS is the process that handles encryption and decryption. The default setup for EFS allows users to encrypt files without needing special permission. Files are encrypted by using a public/private key that EFS automatically generates on a per-user basis.

Encryption certificates are stored as part of the data in user profiles. If a user works with multiple computers and wants to use encryption, an administrator needs to configure a roaming profile for that user. A roaming profile ensures that the user's profile data and public-key certificates are accessible from other computers. Without this, users won't be able to access their encrypted files on another computer.

SECURITY ALERT An alternative to a roaming profile is to copy the user's encryption certificate to the computers that the user uses. You can do this by using the certificate backup and restore process discussed in "Backing up and restoring the system state" in Chapter 11, "Data backup and recovery." Simply back up the certificate on the user's original computer, and then restore the certificate on each of the other computers the user logs on to.

EFS has a built-in data recovery system to guard against data loss. This recovery system ensures that encrypted data can be recovered if a user's public-key certificate is lost or deleted. The most common scenario for this is when a user leaves the company and the associated user account is deleted. A manager might have been able to log on to the user's account, check files, and save important files to other folders, but if the user account has been deleted, encrypted files will be accessible only if the encryption is removed or if the files are moved to an exFAT, FAT, or FAT32 volume (where encryption isn't supported).

To access encrypted files after the user account has been deleted, you need to use a recovery agent. Recovery agents have access to the file encryption key necessary to unlock data in encrypted files. To protect sensitive data, however, recovery agents don't have access to a user's private key or any private key information.

Windows Server won't encrypt files without designated EFS recovery agents. Therefore, recovery agents are designated automatically, and the necessary recovery certificates are generated automatically as well. This ensures that encrypted files can always be recovered.

EFS recovery agents are configured at two levels:

- **Domain**   The recovery agent for a domain is configured automatically when the first Windows Server domain controller is installed. By default, the recovery agent is the domain administrator. Through Group Policy, domain administrators can designate additional recovery agents. Domain administrators can also delegate recovery agent privileges to designated security administrators.

- **Local computer**   When a computer is part of a workgroup or in a standalone configuration, the recovery agent is the administrator of the local computer by default. Additional recovery agents can be designated. Further, if you want local recovery agents in a domain environment rather than domain-level recovery agents, you must delete the recovery policy from Group Policy for the domain.

You can delete recovery agents if you don't want them to be used. However, if you delete all recovery agents, EFS will no longer encrypt files. One or more recovery agents must be configured for EFS to function.

Encrypting directories and files

With NTFS volumes, Windows Server lets you select files and folders for encryption. When a file is encrypted, the file data is converted to an encrypted format that can be read only by the person who encrypted the file. Users can encrypt files only if they have the proper access permissions. When you encrypt folders, the folder is marked as encrypted, but only the files within it are actually encrypted. All files that are created in or added to a folder marked as encrypted are encrypted automatically. Note that File Explorer shows names of encrypted resources in green.

To encrypt a file or directory, follow these steps:

1. In File Explorer, press and hold or right-click the file or directory you want to encrypt, and then tap or click Properties.

2. On the General tab of the Properties dialog box, tap or click Advanced, and then select the Encrypt Contents To Secure Data check box. Tap or click OK twice.

NOTE You can't encrypt compressed files, system files, or read-only files. If you try to encrypt compressed files, the files are automatically uncompressed and then encrypted. If you try to encrypt system files, you get an error.

For an individual file, Windows Server marks the file as encrypted, and then encrypts it. For a directory, Windows Server marks the directory as encrypted, and then encrypts all the files in it. If the directory contains subfolders, Windows Server displays a dialog box that allows you to encrypt all the subfolders associated with the directory. Simply select Apply Changes To This Folder, Subfolders, And Files, and then tap or click OK.

NOTE On NTFS volumes, files remain encrypted even when they're moved, copied, or renamed. If you copy or move an encrypted file to an exFAT, FAT, or FAT32 volume, the file is automatically decrypted before being copied or moved. Thus, you must have proper permissions to copy or move the file.

You can grant special access to an encrypted file or folder by pressing and holding or right-clicking the file or folder in File Explorer, and then selecting Properties. On the General tab of the Properties dialog box, tap or click Advanced. In the Advanced Attributes dialog box, tap or click Details. In the Encryption Details For dialog box, users who have access to the encrypted file are listed by name. To allow another user access to the file, tap or click Add. If a user certificate is available for the user, select the user's name in the list provided, and then tap or click OK. Otherwise, tap or click Find User to locate the certificate for the user.

Working with encrypted files and folders

Previously, I said you can copy, move, and rename encrypted files and folders just like any other files. This is true, but I qualified this by saying "in most cases." When you work with encrypted files, you'll have few problems as long as you work with NTFS volumes on the same computer. When you work with other file systems or other computers, you might run into problems. Two of the most common scenarios are the following:

- **Copying between volumes on the same computer** When you copy or move an encrypted file or folder from one NTFS volume to another NTFS volume on the same computer, the files remain encrypted. However, if you copy or move encrypted files to a FAT volume, the files are decrypted before transfer and then transferred as standard files, and therefore end up in their destination as unencrypted files. FAT doesn't support encryption.

- **Copying between volumes on a different computer** When you copy or move an encrypted file or folder from one NTFS volume to another NTFS volume on a different computer, the files remain encrypted as long as the destination computer allows you to encrypt files and the remote computer is trusted for delegation. Otherwise, the files are decrypted and then transferred as standard files. The same is true when you copy or move encrypted files to a FAT volume on another computer. FAT doesn't support encryption.

After you transfer a sensitive file that has been encrypted, you might want to confirm that the encryption is still applied. Press and hold or right-click the file, and then select Properties. On the General tab of the Properties dialog box, tap or click Advanced. The Encrypt Contents To Secure Data option should be selected.

Configuring recovery policies

Recovery policies are configured automatically for domain controllers and workstations. By default, domain administrators are the designated recovery agents for domains, and the local administrator is the designated recovery agent for a standalone workstation.

Group Policy Management Console (GPMC) is a feature you can add to any installation of Windows Server 2008 or later by using the Add Roles And Features Wizard. The GPMC is also available on Windows desktops when you install the Remote Server Administration Tools (RSAT). After you add the GPMC to a computer, it is available on the Tools menu in Server Manager. Through the Group Policy console, you can view, assign, and delete recovery agents by following these steps:

1. With the GPMC, you can edit a Group Policy Object (GPO) by pressing and holding or right-clicking the GPO, and then selecting Edit on the shortcut menu. The GPMC then opens the Group Policy Management Editor, which you use to manage policy settings.

2. Open the Encrypted Data Recovery Agents node in Group Policy. To do this, expand Computer Configuration, Windows Settings, Security Settings, and Public Key Policies, and then select Encrypting File System.

3. The pane at the right lists the recovery certificates currently assigned. Recovery certificates are listed according to who issued them, who they are issued to, expiration date, purpose, and more.

4. To designate an additional recovery agent, press and hold or right-click Encrypting File System, and then tap or click Add Data Recovery Agent. This starts the Add Recovery Agent Wizard, which you can use to select a previously generated certificate that has been assigned to a user and mark it as a designated recovery certificate. Tap or click Next.

5. On the Select Recovery Agents page, you can select certificates published in Active Directory or use certificate files. If you want to use a published certificate, tap or click Browse Directory and then—in the Find Users, Contacts, And Groups dialog box—select the user with which you want to work. You'll then be able to use the published certificate of that user. If you want to use a certificate file, tap or click Browse Folders. In the Open dialog box, use the options provided to select and open the certificate file you want to use.

SECURITY ALERT   Before you designate additional recovery agents, you should consider setting up a root certificate authority (CA) in the domain. Then you can use the Certificates snap-in to generate a personal certificate that uses the EFS Recovery Agent template. The root CA must then approve the certificate request so that the certificate can be used.

6. To delete a recovery agent, select the recovery agent's certificate in the right pane, and then press Delete. When prompted to confirm the action, tap or click Yes to permanently and irrevocably delete the certificate. If the recovery policy is empty (meaning that it has no other designated recovery agents), EFS will be turned off so that files can no longer be encrypted; existing EFS-encrypted resources won't have a recovery agent.

Decrypting files and directories

File Explorer shows names of encrypted resources in green. If you want to decrypt a file or directory, follow these steps:

1. In File Explorer, press and hold or right-click the file or directory, and then tap or click Properties.

2. On the General tab of the Properties dialog box, tap or click Advanced. Clear the Encrypt Contents To Secure Data check box. Tap or click OK twice.

With files, Windows Server decrypts the file and restores it to its original format. With directories, Windows Server decrypts all the files within the directory. If the directory contains subfolders, you also have the option to remove encryption from the subfolders. To do this, select Apply Changes To This Folder, Subfolders, And Files when prompted, and then tap or click OK.

> **TIP** Windows Server also provides a command-line utility called Cipher (Cipher. exe) for encrypting and decrypting your data. Entering **cipher** at a command prompt without additional parameters shows you the encryption status of all folders in the current directory.

Configuring storage

S torage management and the ways in which Windows Server works with disks have changed substantially over the past few years. Although traditional storage management techniques relate to physical drives located inside the server, many servers today use attached storage and virtual disks.

Generally, when you work with internal fixed drives, you often need to perform advanced disk setup procedures, such as creating a volume set or setting up a redundant array of independent disks (RAID) array. Here, you create volumes or arrays that can span multiple drives and you know the exact physical layout of those drives.

However, when you work with attached storage, you might not know which actual physical disk or disks the volume you are working with resides on. Instead, you are presented with a virtual disk, also referred to as a *logical unit number* (LUN), which is a logical reference to a portion of the storage subsystem. Although the virtual disk can reside on one or more physical disks (spindles), the layout of the physical disks is controlled separately from the operating system (by the storage subsystem).

When I need to differentiate between the two storage management approaches, I refer to the former technique as *traditional* and the latter technique as *standards-based*. In this chapter, I look at traditional techniques for creating volume sets and arrays first, and then I look at standards-based techniques for creating volumes. Whether a volume is created by using the traditional approach or the standards-based approach, you manage it by using similar techniques. For this reason, in the final section of this chapter, I discuss techniques for working with existing volumes and drives.

REAL WORLD Standards-based approaches to storage management can also be used with a server's internal disks. When internal disks are used in this way, however, the internal disks—such as virtual disks on attached storage—are resources to be allocated by using standards-based approaches. This means you can create virtual disk volumes on the physical disks, add the physical disks to storage pools, and create Internet SCSI (iSCSI) virtual disks that can be targeted. You can also enable data deduplication on your virtual disks. You can't, however, use the operating system's volume set or RAID array features, because standards-based, storage management approaches rely on the storage subsystem to manage the physical disk architecture.

Using volumes and volume sets

You create volume sets and RAID arrays on dynamic drives. With a volume set, you can create a single volume that spans multiple drives. Users can access this volume as if it were a single drive, regardless of how many drives the volume is spread over. A volume that's on a single drive is referred to as a *simple volume*. A volume that spans multiple drives is referred to as a *spanned volume*.

With a RAID array, you can protect important business data and sometimes improve the performance of drives. RAID can be implemented by using the built-in features of the operating system (a software approach) or by using hardware. Windows Server 2012 R2 supports three levels of software RAID: 0, 1, and 5. RAID arrays are implemented as mirrored, striped, and striped with parity volumes.

You create and manage volumes in much the same way in which you create and manage partitions. A *volume* is a drive section you can use to store data directly.

NOTE With spanned and striped volumes on basic disks, you can delete a volume but you can't create or extend volumes. With mirrored volumes on basic disks, you can delete, repair, and resync the mirror. You can also break the mirror. For striped with parity volumes (RAID-5) on basic disks, you can delete or repair the volume, but you can't create new volumes.

Understanding volume basics

Disk Management color codes volumes by type, much like it does partitions. As Figure 2-1 shows, volumes also have the following properties:

- **Layout**   Volume layouts include simple, spanned, mirrored, striped, and striped with parity.
- **Type**   Volumes always have the type *dynamic*. Partitions always have the type *basic*.
- **File System**   Like partitions, each volume can have a different file system type, such as FAT or NTFS file system. Note that FAT16 is available only when the partition or volume is 2 GB or less in size.
- **Status**   The state of the drive. In Graphical View, the state is shown as Healthy, Failed Redundancy, and so on. The next section, "Understanding volume sets," discusses volume sets and the various states you might encounter.

- **Capacity**   The total storage size of the drive.
- **Free Space**   The total amount of available space on the volume.
- **% Free**   The percentage of free space out of the total storage size of the volume.

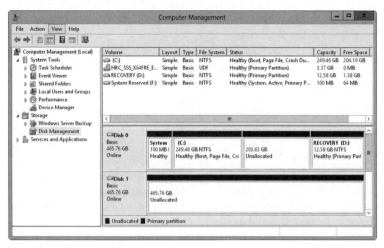

FIGURE 2-1 Disk Management displays volumes much like it does partitions.

An important advantage of dynamic volumes over basic volumes is that dynamic volumes enable you to make changes to volumes and drives without having to restart the system (in most cases). Volumes also let you take advantage of the fault-tolerance enhancements of Windows Server 2012 R2. You can install other operating systems and dual boot a Windows Server 2012 R2 system by creating a separate volume for the other operating system. For example, you could install Windows Server 2012 R2 on volume C and Windows 8.1 on volume D.

With volumes, you can do the following:

- Assign drive letters and drive paths as discussed in "Assigning drive letters and paths" later in this chapter
- Create any number of volumes on a disk as long as you have free space
- Create volumes that span two or more disks and, if necessary, configure fault tolerance
- Extend volumes to increase the volumes' capacity
- Designate active, system, and boot volumes as described in "Special considerations for basic and dynamic disks" in Chapter 1, "Managing file systems and drives"

Understanding volume sets

With volume sets, you can create volumes that span several drives by using free space on different drives to create what users perceive as a single volume. Files are stored on the volume set segment by segment, with the first segment of free space being used to store files before other segments. When the first segment fills up, the second segment is used, and so on.

You can create a volume set using free space on up to 32 hard disk drives. The key advantage to volume sets is that they let you tap into unused free space and create a usable file system. The key disadvantage is that if any hard disk drive in the volume set fails, the volume set can no longer be used, which means that essentially all the data on the volume set is lost.

Understanding the volume status is useful when you install new volumes or are trying to troubleshoot problems. Disk Management shows the drive status in Graphical View and Volume List view. Table 2-1 summarizes status values for dynamic volumes.

TABLE 2-1 Understanding and resolving volume status issues

STATUS	DESCRIPTION	RESOLUTION
Data Incomplete	Spanned volumes on a foreign disk are incomplete. You must have forgotten to add the other disks from the spanned volume set.	Add the disks that contain the rest of the spanned volumes, and then import all the disks at one time.
Data Not Redundant	Fault-tolerant volumes on a foreign disk are incomplete. You must have forgotten to add the other disks from a mirror or RAID-5 set.	Add the remaining disks, and then import all the disks at one time.
Failed	An error disk status. The disk is inaccessible or damaged.	Ensure that the related dynamic disk is online. As necessary, press and hold or right-click the volume, and then tap or click Reactivate Volume. For a basic disk, you might need to check the disk for a faulty connection.
Failed Redundancy	An error disk status. One of the disks in a mirror or RAID-5 set is offline.	Ensure that the related dynamic disk is online. If necessary, reactivate the volume. Next, you might need to replace a failed mirror or repair a failed RAID-5 volume.
Formatting	A temporary status that indicates the volume is being formatted.	The progress of the formatting is indicated as the percent complete unless you choose the Perform A Quick Format option.

STATUS	DESCRIPTION	RESOLUTION
Healthy	The normal volume status.	The volume doesn't have any known problems. You don't need to take any corrective action.
Healthy (At Risk)	Windows had problems reading from or writing to the physical disk on which the dynamic volume is located. This status appears when Windows encounters errors.	Press and hold or right-click the volume, and then tap or click Reactivate Volume. If the disk continues to have this status or has this status periodically, the disk might be failing, and you should back up all data on the disk.
Healthy (Unknown Partition)	Windows does not recognize the partition. This can occur because the partition is from a different operating system or is a manufacturer-created partition used to store system files.	No corrective action is necessary.
Initializing	A temporary status that indicates the disk is being initialized.	The drive status should change after a few seconds.
Regenerating	A temporary status that indicates that data and parity for a RAID-5 volume are being regenerated.	Progress is indicated as the percent complete. The volume should return to Healthy status.
Resynching	A temporary status that indicates that a mirror set is being resynchronized.	Progress is indicated as the percent complete. The volume should return to Healthy status.
Stale Data	Data on foreign disks that are fault tolerant are out of sync.	Rescan the disks or restart the computer, and then check the status. A new status should be displayed, such as Failed Redundancy.
Unknown	The volume cannot be accessed. It might have a corrupted boot sector.	The volume might have a boot sector virus. Check it with an up-to-date antivirus program. Rescan the disks or restart the computer, and then check the status.

Creating volumes and volume sets

You can format simple volumes as exFAT, FAT, FAT32, or NTFS. To make management easier, you should format volumes that span multiple disks as NTFS, which enables you to expand the volume set if necessary. If you find you need more space on a volume, you can extend simple and spanned volumes by selecting an area of free space and adding it to the volume. You can extend a simple volume within the same disk, and you can also extend a simple volume onto other disks. When you do this, you create a spanned volume, which you must format as NTFS.

You create volumes and volume sets by following these steps:

1. In Disk Management's Graphical View, press and hold or right-click an unallocated area, and then tap or click New Spanned Volume or New Striped Volume as appropriate. Read the Welcome page, and then tap or click Next.

2. You should get the Select Disks page, shown in Figure 2-2. Select the disks that you want to be part of the volume, and then size the volume segments on those disks.

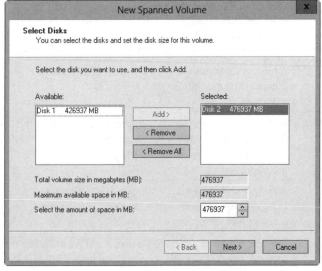

FIGURE 2-2 On the Select Disks page, select disks to be a part of the volume, and then size the volume on each disk.

3. Available disks are shown in the Available list. If necessary, select a disk in this list, and then tap or click Add to add the disk to the Selected list. If you make a mistake, you can remove disks from the Selected list by selecting the disk, and then tapping or clicking Remove.

> **CAUTION** The disk wizards in Windows Server 2012 R2 show both basic and dynamic disks with available disk space. If you add space from a basic disk, the wizard converts the disk to a dynamic disk before creating the volume set. Before tapping or clicking Yes to continue, be sure you really want to do this because it can affect how the disk is used by the operating system.

4. Select a disk in the Selected list, and then specify the size of the volume on the disk in the Select The Amount Of Space In MB box. The Maximum Available Space In MB box shows you the largest area of free space available on the disk. The Total Volume Size In Megabytes box shows you the total disk space selected for use with the volume. Tap or click Next.

> **TIP** Although you can size a volume set any way you want, consider how you'll use volume sets on the system. Simple and spanned volumes aren't fault tolerant; rather than creating one monstrous volume with all the available free space, you might want to create several smaller volumes to help ensure that losing one volume doesn't mean losing all your data.

5. Specify whether you want to assign a drive letter or path to the volume, and then tap or click Next. You use the available options as follows:
   - **Assign The Following Drive Letter**   To assign a drive letter, choose this option, and then select an available drive letter in the list provided.
   - **Mount In The Following Empty NTFS Folder**   To assign a drive path, choose this option, and then type the path to an existing folder on an NTFS drive, or tap or click Browse to search for or create a folder.
   - **Do Not Assign A Drive Letter Or Drive Path**   To create the volume without assigning a drive letter or path, choose this option. You can assign a drive letter or path later if necessary.

6. Specify whether the volume should be formatted. If you elect to format the volume, set the following formatting options:
   - **File System**   Specifies the file system type, such as NTFS or ReFS.
   - **Allocation Unit Size**   Specifies the cluster size for the file system. This is the basic unit in which disk space is allocated. The default allocation unit size is based on the volume's size and is set dynamically prior to formatting. Although you can't change the default size if you select ReFS, you can set the allocation unit size to a specific value with other formats. If you use a lot of small files, you might want to use a smaller cluster size, such as 512 or 1,024 bytes. With these settings, small files use less disk space.
   - **Volume Label**   Specifies a text label for the partition. This label is the partition's volume name.
   - **Perform A Quick Format**   Tells Windows to format without checking the partition for errors. With large partitions, this option can save you a few minutes. However, it's more prudent to check for errors, which allows Disk Management to mark bad sectors on the disk and lock them out.
   - **Enable File And Folder Compression**   Turns on compression for the disk. Compression is transparent to users, and compressed files can be accessed just like regular files. If you select this option, files and directories on this drive are compressed automatically. For more information about compressing drives, files, and directories, see "Compressing drives and data" in Chapter 1. (For NTFS only)

7. Tap or click Next, and then tap or click Finish.

Deleting volumes and volume sets

You use the same technique to delete all volumes, whether they're simple, spanned, mirrored, striped, or RAID-5 (striped with parity). Deleting a volume set removes the associated file system, and all associated data is lost. Before you delete a volume set, you should back up any files and directories the volume set contains.

You can't delete a volume that contains the system, boot, or active paging files for Windows Server 2012 R2.

To delete volumes, follow these steps:

1. In Disk Management, press and hold or right-click any volume in the set, and then tap or click Delete Volume. You can't delete a portion of a spanned volume without deleting the entire volume.

2. Tap or click Yes to confirm that you want to delete the volume.

Managing volumes

You manage volumes much like you manage partitions. Follow the techniques outlined in "Managing existing partitions and drives" later in this chapter.

Improving performance and fault tolerance with RAID

You'll often want to give important data increased protection from drive failures. To do this, you can use RAID technology to add fault tolerance to your file systems. With RAID, you increase data integrity and availability by creating redundant copies of the data. You can also use RAID to improve your disks' performance.

Different implementations of RAID technology are available, and these implementations are described in terms of levels. Each RAID level offers different features. Windows Server 2012 R2 supports RAID levels 0, 1, and 5. You can use RAID-0 to improve the performance of your drives, and you use RAID-1 and RAID-5 to provide fault tolerance for data.

Table 2-2 provides a brief overview of the supported RAID levels. This support is completely software-based.

The most common RAID levels in use on servers running Windows Server 2012 R2 are level 1 (disk mirroring), and level 5 (disk striping with parity). With respect to upfront costs, disk mirroring is the least expensive way to increase data protection with redundancy. Here, you use two identically sized volumes on two different drives to create a redundant data set. If one of the drives fails, you can still obtain the data from the other drive.

However, disk striping with parity requires more disks—a minimum of three—but offers fault tolerance with less overhead than disk mirroring. If any of the drives fail, you can recover the data by combining blocks of data on the remaining disks with a parity record. Parity is a method of error checking that uses an exclusive OR operation to create a checksum for each block of data written to the disk. This checksum is used to recover data in case of failure.

TABLE 2-2 Windows Server 2012 R2 support for RAID

RAID LEVEL	RAID TYPE	DESCRIPTION	MAJOR ADVANTAGES
0	Disk striping	Two or more volumes, each on a separate drive, are configured as a striped set. Data is broken into blocks, called stripes, and then written sequentially to all drives in the striped set.	Speed and performance.
1	Disk mirroring	Two volumes on two drives are configured identically. Data is written to both drives. If one drive fails, no data loss occurs because the other drive contains the data. (This level doesn't include disk striping.)	Redundancy. Better write performance than disk striping with parity.
5	Disk striping with parity	Uses three or more volumes, each on a separate drive, to create a striped set with parity error checking. In the case of failure, data can be recovered.	Fault tolerance with less overhead than mirroring. Better read performance than disk mirroring.

REAL WORLD Although it's true that the upfront costs for mirroring should be less than the upfront costs for disk striping with parity, the actual cost per gigabyte might be higher with disk mirroring. With disk mirroring, you have an overhead of 50 percent. For example, if you mirror two 750-gigabyte (GB) drives (a total storage space of 1500 GB), the usable space is only 750 GB. With disk striping with parity, on though, you have an overhead of around 33 percent. For example, if you create a RAID-5 set by using three 500-GB drives (a total storage space of 1500 GB), the usable space (with one-third lost for overhead) is 1,000 GB.

Implementing RAID on Windows Server 2012 R2

Windows Server 2012 R2 supports disk mirroring, disk striping, and disk striping with parity. Implementing these RAID techniques is discussed in the sections that follow.

CAUTION Some operating systems, such as MS-DOS, don't support RAID. If you dual boot your system to one of these noncompliant operating systems, your RAID-configured drives will be unavailable.

Implementing RAID-0: disk striping

RAID level 0 is disk striping. With disk striping, two or more volumes—each on a separate drive—are configured as a striped set. Data written to the striped set is broken into blocks called *stripes*. These stripes are written sequentially to all drives in the striped set. You can place volumes for a striped set on up to 32 drives, but in most circumstances sets with 2 to 5 volumes offer the best performance improvements. Beyond this, the performance improvement decreases significantly.

The major advantage of disk striping is speed. Data can be accessed on multiple disks by using multiple drive heads, which improves performance considerably. However, this performance boost comes with a price tag. As with volume sets, if any hard disk drive in the striped set fails, the striped set can no longer be used, which essentially means that all data in the striped set is lost. You need to re-create the striped set and restore the data from backups. Data backup and recovery is discussed in Chapter 11, "Data backup and recovery."

> **CAUTION**   The boot and system volumes shouldn't be part of a striped set. Don't use disk striping with these volumes.

When you create striped sets, you should use volumes that are approximately the same size. Disk Management bases the overall size of the striped set on the smallest volume size. Specifically, the maximum size of the striped set is a multiple of the smallest volume size. For example, if you want to create a three-volume striped set but the smallest volume is 20 GB, the maximum size for the striped set is 60 GB, even if the other two values are 2 terabytes (TB) each.

You can maximize performance of the striped set in a couple of ways:

- Use disks that are on separate disk controllers. This allows the system to simultaneously access the drives.
- Don't use the disks containing the striped set for other purposes. This allows the disk to dedicate its time to the striped set.

You can create a striped set by following these steps:

1. In Disk Management's Graphical View, press and hold or right-click an area marked Unallocated on a dynamic disk, and then tap or click New Striped Volume. This starts the New Striped Volume Wizard. Read the Welcome page, and then tap or click Next.

2. Create the volume as described in "Creating volumes and volume sets" earlier in this chapter. The key difference is that you need at least two dynamic disks to create a striped volume.

After you create a striped volume, you can use the volume as you would any other volume. You can't extend a striped set after it's created; therefore, you should carefully consider the setup before you implement it.

Implementing RAID-1: disk mirroring

RAID level 1 is disk mirroring. With disk mirroring, you use identically sized volumes on two different drives to create a redundant data set. The drives are written with identical sets of information, and if one of the drives fails, you can still obtain the data from the other drive.

Disk mirroring offers about the same fault tolerance as disk striping with parity. Because mirrored disks don't need to write parity information, they can offer better write performance in most circumstances. However, disk striping with parity usually offers better read performance because read operations are spread over multiple drives.

The major drawback to disk mirroring is that it effectively cuts the amount of storage space in half. For example, to mirror a 500-GB drive, you need another 500-GB drive. That means you use 1000 GB of space to store 500 GB of information.

TIP If possible, you should mirror boot and system volumes. Mirroring these volumes ensures that you are able to boot the server in case of a single drive failure.

As with disk striping, you'll often want the mirrored disks to be on separate disk controllers to provide increased protection against failure of the disk controller. If one of the disk controllers fails, the disk on the other controller is still available. Technically, when you use two separate disk controllers to duplicate data, you're using a technique known as *disk duplexing*. Figure 2-3 shows the difference between the two techniques. Where disk mirroring typically uses a single drive controller, disk duplexing uses two drive controllers; otherwise, the two techniques are essentially the same.

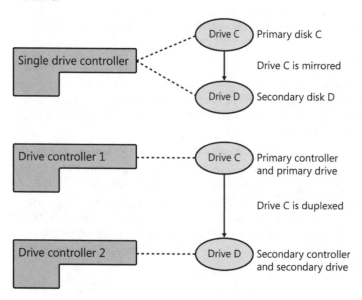

FIGURE 2-3 Although disk mirroring typically uses a single drive controller to create a redundant data set, disk duplexing uses two drive controllers.

If one of the mirrored drives in a set fails, disk operations can continue. Here, when users read and write data, the data is written to the remaining disk. You need to break the mirror before you can fix it. To learn how, see "Managing RAID and recovering from failures" later in this chapter.

Creating a mirror set in Disk Management

You create a mirror set by following these steps:

1. In the Disk Management Graphical View, press and hold or right-click an area marked Unallocated on a dynamic disk, and then tap or click New Mirrored Volume. This starts the New Mirrored Volume Wizard. Read the Welcome page, and then tap or click Next.

2. Create the volume as described in "Creating volumes and volume sets" earlier in this chapter. The key difference when creating the mirror set is that you must create two identically sized volumes, and these volumes must be on separate dynamic drives. You won't be able to continue past the Select Disks window until you select the two disks with which you want to work.

Like other RAID techniques, mirroring is transparent to users. Users experience the mirrored set as a single drive they can access and use like any other drive.

NOTE The status of a normal mirror is Healthy. During the creation of a mirror, you'll get a status of Resynching, which tells you that Disk Management is creating the mirror.

Mirroring an existing volume

Rather than create a new mirrored volume, you can use an existing volume to create a mirrored set. To do this, the volume you want to mirror must be a simple volume, and you must have an area of unallocated space on a second drive of equal or larger size than the existing volume.

In Disk Management, you mirror an existing volume by following these steps:

1. Press and hold or right-click the simple volume you want to mirror, and then tap or click Add Mirror. This displays the Add Mirror dialog box.

2. In the Disks list, shown in Figure 2-4, select a location for the mirror, and then tap or click Add Mirror. Windows Server 2012 R2 begins the mirror creation process. In Disk Management, you'll get a status of Resynching on both volumes. The disk on which the mirrored volume is being created has a warning icon.

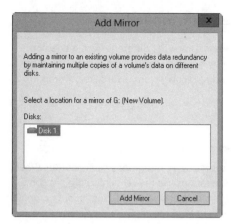

FIGURE 2-4 Select the location for the mirror.

Implementing RAID-5: disk striping with parity

RAID level 5 is disk striping with parity. With this technique, you need a minimum of three hard disk drives to set up fault tolerance. Disk Management sizes the volumes on these drives identically.

RAID-5 distributes data and parity data sequentially across the disks in the array. Fault tolerance ensures that the failure of a single drive won't bring down the entire drive set. Instead, the set continues to function with disk operations directed at the remaining volumes in the set.

To allow for fault tolerance, RAID-5 writes parity checksums with the blocks of data. If any of the drives in the striped set fails, you can use the parity information to recover the data. (This process, called *regenerating the striped set*, is covered in "Managing RAID and recovering from failures" later in the chapter.) If two disks fail, however, the parity information isn't sufficient to recover the data, and you need to rebuild the striped set from backup.

Creating a striped set with parity in Disk Management

In Disk Management, you can create a striped set with parity by following these steps:

1. In Disk Management's Graphical View, press and hold or right-click an area marked Unallocated on a dynamic disk, and then tap or click New RAID-5 Volume. This starts the New RAID-5 Volume Wizard. Read the Welcome page, and then tap or click Next.

2. Create the volume as described previously in "Creating volumes and volume sets." The key difference when creating a striped set with parity is that you must select free space on three separate dynamic drives.

After you create a striped set with parity (RAID-5), users can use the set just like they would a normal drive. Keep in mind that you can't extend a striped set with parity after you create it; therefore, you should carefully consider the setup before you implement it.

Managing RAID and recovering from failures

Managing mirrored drives and striped sets is somewhat different from managing other drive volumes, especially when it comes to recovering from failure. The techniques you use to manage RAID arrays and to recover from failure are covered in this section.

Breaking a mirrored set

You might want to break a mirror for two reasons:

- If one of the mirrored drives in a set fails, disk operations can continue. When users read and write data, these operations use the remaining disk. At some point, however, you need to fix the mirror, and to do this you must first break the mirror, replace the failed drive, and then reestablish the mirror.
- If you no longer want to mirror your drives, you might also want to break a mirror. This allows you to use the disk space for other purposes.

BEST PRACTICES   Although breaking a mirror doesn't delete the data in the set, you should always back up the data before you perform this procedure to ensure that if you have problems, you can recover your data.

In Disk Management, you can break a mirrored set by following these steps:

1. Press and hold or right-click one of the volumes in the mirrored set, and then tap or click Break Mirrored Volume.
2. Confirm that you want to break the mirror by tapping or clicking Yes. If the volume is in use, you'll get another warning dialog box. Confirm that it's okay to continue by tapping or clicking Yes.

   Windows Server 2012 R2 breaks the mirror, creating two independent volumes.

Resynchronizing and repairing a mirrored set

Windows Server 2012 R2 automatically synchronizes mirrored volumes on dynamic drives; however, data on mirrored drives can become out of sync. For example, if one of the drives goes offline, data is written only to the drive that's online.

You can resynchronize and repair mirrored sets, but you must rebuild the set by using disks with the same partition style—either master boot record (MBR) or GUID partition table (GPT). You need to get both drives in the mirrored set online. The mirrored set's status should read Failed Redundancy. The corrective action you take depends on the failed volume's status:

- If the status is Missing or Offline, be sure that the drive has power and is connected properly. Then start Disk Management, press and hold or right-click the failed volume, and tap or click Reactivate Volume. The drive status should change to Regenerating and then to Healthy. If the volume doesn't return to the Healthy status, press and hold or right-click the volume, and then tap or click Resynchronize Mirror.

- If the status is Online (Errors), press and hold or right-click the failed volume, and then tap or click Reactivate Volume. The drive status should change to Regenerating and then to Healthy. If the volume doesn't return to the Healthy status, press and hold or right-click the volume, and then tap or click Resynchronize Mirror.

- If one of the drives shows a status of Unreadable, you might need to rescan the drives on the system by choosing Rescan Disks from Disk Management's Action menu. If the drive status doesn't change, you might need to reboot the computer.

- If one of the drives still won't come back online, press and hold or right-click the failed volume, and then tap or click Remove Mirror. Next, press and hold or right-click the remaining volume in the original mirror, and then tap or click Add Mirror. You now need to mirror the volume on an unallocated area of free space. If you don't have free space, you need to create space by deleting other volumes or replacing the failed drive.

Repairing a mirrored system volume to enable boot

The failure of a mirrored drive might prevent your system from booting. Typically, this happens when you're mirroring the system or boot volume, or both, and the primary mirror drive has failed. In previous versions of the Windows operating system, you often had to go through several procedures to get the system back up and running. With Windows Server 2012 R2, the failure of a primary mirror is usually much easier to resolve.

When you mirror a system volume, the operating system should add an entry to the system's boot manager that allows you to boot to the secondary mirror. Resolving a primary mirror failure is much easier with this entry in the boot manager file than without it because all you need to do is select the entry to boot to the secondary mirror. If you mirror the boot volume and a secondary mirror entry is not created for you, you can modify the boot entries in the boot manager to create one by using the BCD Editor (Bcdedit.exe).

If a system fails to boot to the primary system volume, restart the system and select the Windows Server 2012 R2—Secondary Plex option for the operating system you want to start. The system should start up normally. After you successfully boot the system to the secondary drive, you can schedule the maintenance necessary to rebuild the mirror as described in the following steps:

1. Shut down the system, and replace the failed volume or add a hard disk drive. Then restart the system.

2. Break the mirror set, and then re-create the mirror on the drive you replaced, which is usually drive 0. Press and hold or right-click the remaining volume that was part of the original mirror, and then tap or click Add Mirror. Next, follow the technique in "Mirroring an existing volume" earlier in the chapter.

3. If you want the primary mirror to be on the drive you added or replaced, use Disk Management to break the mirror again. Be sure that the primary drive in the original mirror set has the drive letter that was previously assigned to the complete mirror. If it doesn't, assign the appropriate drive letter.

4. Press and hold or right-click the original system volume, and then tap or click Add Mirror. Now re-create the mirror.

5. Check the boot entries in the boot manager and use the BCD Editor to ensure that the original system volume is used during startup.

Removing a mirrored set

Using Disk Management, you can remove one of the volumes from a mirrored set. When you do this, all data on the removed mirror is deleted and the space it used is marked as Unallocated.

To remove a mirror, follow these steps:

1. In Disk Management, press and hold or right-click one of the volumes in the mirrored set, and then tap or click Remove Mirror to display the Remove Mirror dialog box.

2. In the Remove Mirror dialog box, select the disk from which to remove the mirror.

3. Confirm the action when prompted. All data on the removed mirror is deleted.

Repairing a striped set without parity

A striped set without parity doesn't have fault tolerance. If a drive that's part of a striped set fails, the entire striped set is unusable. Before you try to restore the striped set, you should repair or replace the failed drive. Then you need to re-create the striped set and recover the data contained on the striped set from backup.

Regenerating a striped set with parity

With RAID-5, you can recover the striped set with parity if a single drive fails. You'll know that a striped set with parity drive has failed because the set's status changes to Failed Redundancy and the individual volume's status changes to Missing, Offline, or Online (Errors).

You can repair RAID-5 disks, but you must rebuild the set by using disks with the same partition style—either MBR or GPT. You need to get all drives in the RAID-5 set online. The set's status should read Failed Redundancy. The corrective action you take depends on the failed volume's status:

- If the status is Missing or Offline, make sure the drive has power and is connected properly. Then start Disk Management, press and hold or right-click the failed volume, and select Reactivate Volume. The drive's status should change to Regenerating and then to Healthy. If the drive's status doesn't return to Healthy, press and hold or right-click the volume and select Regenerate Parity.

- If the status is Online (Errors), press and hold or right-click the failed volume, and select Reactivate Volume. The drive's status should change to Regenerating and then to Healthy. If the drive's status doesn't return to Healthy, press and hold or right-click the volume and select Regenerate Parity.

- If one of the drives shows as Unreadable, you might need to rescan the drives on the system by choosing Rescan Disks from Disk Management's Action menu. If the drive status doesn't change, you might need to reboot the computer.

- If one of the drives still won't come back online, you need to repair the failed region of the RAID-5 set. Press and hold or right-click the failed volume, and then select Remove Volume. You now need to select an unallocated space on a separate dynamic disk for the RAID-5 set. This space must be at least as large as the region to repair, and it can't be on a drive that the RAID-5 set is already using. If you don't have enough space, the Repair Volume command is unavailable, and you need to free space by deleting other volumes or by replacing the failed drive.

BEST PRACTICES   If possible, you should back up the data before you perform this procedure to ensure that if you have problems, you can recover your data.

Standards-based storage management

Standards-based storage management focuses on the storage volumes themselves rather than the underlying physical layout, relying on hardware to handle the architecture particulars for data redundancy and the portions of disks that are presented as usable disks. This means the layout of the physical disks is controlled by the storage subsystem instead of by the operating system.

Getting started with standards-based storage

With standards-based management, the physical layout of disks (spindles) is abstracted, so a "disk" can be a logical reference to a portion of a storage subsystem (a virtual disk) or an actual physical disk. This means a disk simply becomes a unit of storage and volumes can be created to allocate space within disks for file systems.

Taking this concept a few steps further, you can pool available space on disks so that units of storage (virtual disks) can be allocated from this pool on an as-needed basis. These units of storage, in turn, are apportioned with volumes to allocate space and create usable file systems.

Technically, the pooled storage is referred to as a *storage pool* and the virtual disks created within the pool are referred to as *storages spaces*. Given a set of "disks," you can create a single storage pool by allocating all the disks to the pool or create multiple storage pools by allocating disks separately to each pool.

REAL WORLD Trust me when I say this all sounds more complicated than it is. When you throw storage subsystems into the mix, it's really a three-layered architecture. In Layer 1, the layout of the physical disks is controlled by the storage subsystem. The storage system likely will use some form of RAID to ensure that data is redundant and recoverable in case of failure. In Layer 2, the virtual disks created by the arrays are made available to servers. The servers simply see the disks as storage that can be allocated. Windows Server can apply software-level RAID or other redundancy approaches to help protect against failure. In Layer 3, the server creates volumes on the virtual disks, and these volumes provide the usable file systems for file and data storage.

Working with standards-based storage

When you are working with File And Storage Services, you can group available physical disks into storage pools so that you can create virtual disks from available capacity. Each virtual disk you create is a storage space. Storage Spaces are made available through the Storage Services role service, which is automatically installed on every server running Windows Server 2012 R2.

To integrate Storage Spaces with standards-based storage management frameworks, you'll want to add the Windows Standards-Based Storage Management feature to your file servers. When a server is configured with the File Services And Storage role, the Windows Standards-Based Storage Management feature adds components and updates Server Manager with the options for working with standards-based volumes. You might also want to do the following:

- Add the Data Deduplication role service if you want to enable data deduplication.
- Add the iSCSI Target Server and iSCSI Target Storage Provider role services if you want the server to host iSCSI virtual disks.

After you configure your servers as appropriate for your environment, you can select the File And Storage Services node in Server Manager to work with your storage volumes, and additional options will be available as well. The Servers subnode lists file servers that have been configured for standards-based management.

As Figure 2-5 shows, the Volumes subnode lists allocated storage on each server according to how volumes are provisioned and how much free space is available. Volumes are listed regardless of whether the underlying disks are physical or virtual. Press and hold or right-click a volume to display management options, including the following:

- **Configure Data Deduplication** Allows you to enable and configure data deduplication for NTFS volumes. If the feature is enabled, you can then also use this option to disable data deduplication.
- **Delete Volume** Allows you to delete the volume. The space that was used is then marked as unallocated on the related disk.
- **Extend Volume** Allows you to extend the volume to unallocated space of the related disk.
- **Format** Allows you to create a new file system on the volume that overwrites the existing volume.

- **Manage Drive Letter And Access Paths**   Allows you to change the drive letter or access path associated with the volume.

- **New iSCSI Virtual Disk**   Allows you to create a new iSCSI virtual disk that is stored on the volume.

- **New Share**   Allows you to create new Server Message Block (SMB) or Network File System (NFS) shares on the volume.

- **Properties**   Displays information about the volume type, file system, health, capacity, used space, and free space. You can also use this option to set the volume label.

- **Repair File System Errors**   Allows you to repair errors detected during an online scan of the file system.

- **Scan File System For Errors**   Allows you to perform an online scan of the file system. Although Windows attempts to repair any errors that are found, some errors can be corrected only by using a repair procedure.

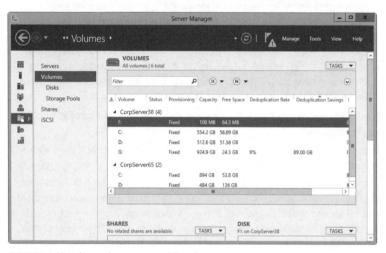

FIGURE 2-5 Note how volumes are provisioned.

As Figure 2-6 shows, the Disks subnode lists the disks available to each server according to total capacity, unallocated space, partition style, subsystem, and bus type. Server Manager attempts to differentiate between physical disks and virtual disks by showing the virtual disk label (if one was provided) and the originating storage subsystem. Press and hold or right-click a disk to display management options, including the following:

- **Bring Online**   Enables you to take an offline disk and make it available for use.

- **Take Offline**   Enables you to take a disk offline so that it can no longer be used.

- **Reset Disk**   Enables you to completely reset the disk, which deletes all volumes on the disk and removes all available data on the disk.

- **New Volume**   Enables you to create a new volume on the disk.

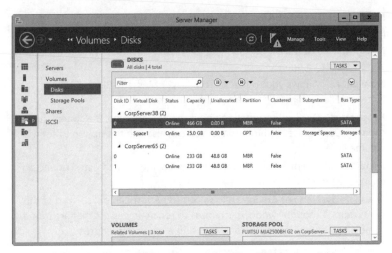

FIGURE 2-6 Note the disks available and how much unallocated space is available.

The version of Storage Spaces that ships with Windows Server 2012 R2 is different from the version that ships with Windows Server 2012. If you have any questions about which version of Storage Spaces is being used, complete the following steps to check the version:

1. Press and hold or right-click the storage pool you want to examine, and then select Properties.

2. In the Properties dialog box, select Details in the left pane, and then choose Version on the Property selection list.

   You also can use this technique to check capacity, status, logical sector size, physical sector size, provisioned space size, thin provisioning alert threshold, and total used space. By default, Storage Space alerts you when storage is approaching capacity and when a storage space reaches 70 percent of the total provisioned size. When you get such an alert, you should consider allocating additional storage.

You can upgrade the version of Storage Spaces being used by a storage pool by pressing and holding or right-clicking a storage pool, and then selecting Upgrade Storage Pool Version. In addition to correcting issues that can result in error and warning states when creating and managing Storage Spaces, the Windows Server 2012 R2 version of Storage Spaces does the following:

- Supports storage spaces that have dual parity, and parity and dual parity spaces on failover clusters. With dual parity, storage spaces are protected against two simultaneous drive failures.

- Supports automatic rebuild of storage spaces from storage pool free space instead of having to use hot spares to recover from drive failures. Here, instead of writing a copy of data that was on a failed disk to a hot spare, the parity or mirrored data is copied to multiple drives in the pool to achieve the previous level of resiliency automatically. As a result, you don't need to specifically allocate hot spares in storage pools, provided that a sufficient number of drives is assigned to the pool to allow for automatic resiliency recovery.

■ Supports storage tiers to automatically move frequently used files from slower physical disks to faster Solid State Drive (SSD) storage. This feature is applicable only when a storage space has a combination of SSD storage and hard disk drive (HDD) storage. Additionally, the storage type must be set as fixed, the volumes created on virtual disks must be the same size as the virtual disk, and enough free space must be available to accommodate the preference. For fine-grained management, use the Set-FileStorageTier cmdlet to assign files to standard physical drive storage or faster SSD storage.

■ Supports write-back caching when a storage pool uses SSD storage. Write-back cache buffers small random writes to SSD storage before later writing the data to HDD storage. Buffering writes in this way helps to protect against data loss in the event of power failures. For write-back cache to work properly, storage spaces with simple volumes must have at least one SSD, storage spaces with two-way mirroring or single-parity must have at least two SSDs, and storage spaces with three-way mirroring or dual parity must have at least three SSDs. When these requirements are met, the volumes automatically will use a 1-GB write-back cache by default. You can designate SSDs that should be used for write-back caching by setting the usage as Journal (the default in this configuration). If enough SSDs are not configured for journaling, the write-back cache size is set to 0 (meaning write-back caching will not be used). The only exception is for parity spaces, which will then have the write-back cache size set to 32 MB.

If you have any question about the size of the write-back cache, complete the following steps to check the cache size:

1. Press and hold or right-click the virtual disk you want to examine, and then select Properties.

2. In the Properties dialog box, select Details in the left pane, and then choose WriteCacheSize on the Property selection list.

You also can use this technique to check allocated size, status, provisioned size, provision type, redundancy type, and more.

Using storage pools and allocating space

In Server Manager, you can work with storage pools and allocate space by selecting the File And Storage Services node, and then selecting the related Storage Pools subnode. As Figure 2-7 shows, the Storage Pools subnode lists the available storage pools, the virtual disks created within storage pools, and the available physical disks. Keep in mind that what's presented as physical disks might actually be LUNs (virtual disks) from a storage subsystem.

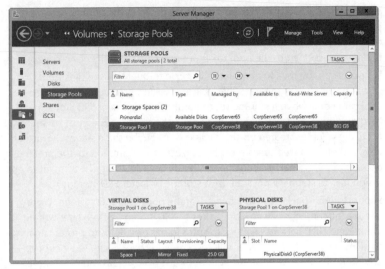

FIGURE 2-7 Create and manage storage pools.

Working with storage pools is a multistep process:

1. You create storage pools to pool available space on one or more disks.
2. You allocate space from this pool to create one or more virtual disks.
3. You create one or more volumes on each virtual disk to allocate storage for file systems.

The sections that follow examine procedures related to each of these steps.

Creating a storage pool

Storage pools allow you to pool available space on disks so that units of storage (virtual disks) can be allocated from this pool. To create a storage pool, you must have at least one unused disk and a storage subsystem to manage it. This storage subsystem can be the one included with the Storage Spaces feature or a subsystem associated with attached storage.

When a computer has extra hard drives in addition to the hard drive on which Windows is installed, you can allocate one or more of the additional drives to a storage pool. However, keep in mind that if you use a formatted drive with a storage pool, Windows permanently deletes all the files on that drive. Additionally, it's important to point out that physical disks with the MBR partition style are converted automatically to the GPT partition style when you add them to a storage pool and create volumes on them.

Each physical disk allocated to the pool can be handled in one of three ways:

- As a data store that is available for use
- As a data store that can be manually allocated for use
- As a hot spare in case a disk in the pool fails or is removed from the subsystem

Types of volumes you can create are as follows:

- **Simple Volumes** Creates a simple volume by writing one copy of your data to one or more drives. With simple volumes, there is no redundancy and no associated overhead. As an example, you can create a single volume that spans two 2-TB drives, making 4 TB of storage available. However, because there is no resiliency, a failure of any drive in a simple volume causes the entire volume to fail.

- **Two-way mirrors** Creates a mirrored set by writing two copies of a computer's data, helping to protect against a single drive failure. Two-way mirrors require at least two drives. With two-way mirrors, there is a 1/2 (50 percent) overhead for redundancy with two drives. As an example, you could allocate two 2-TB drives as a two-way mirror, giving you 2 TB of mirrored storage.

- **Parity volumes** Creates a volume that uses disk striping with parity, helping to provide fault tolerance with less overhead than mirroring. Parity volumes require at least three drives. With parity volumes there is a 1/3 (33.33 percent) overhead for redundancy with three drives. As an example, you could allocate three 2-TB drives as a parity volume, giving you 4 TB of protected storage.

- **Dual parity volumes** Creates a volume that uses disk striping with two sets of parity data, helping to protect against two simultaneous drive failures while requiring less overhead than three-way mirroring. Dual parity volumes require at least seven drives.

- **Three-way mirrors** Creates a mirrored set by writing three copies of a computer's data and by using disk striping with mirroring, helping to protect against two simultaneous drive failures. Although three-way mirrors do not have a penalty for read operations, they do have a performance penalty for write operations because of the overhead associated with having to write data to three separate disks. This overhead can be mitigated by using multiple drive controllers. Ideally, you'll want to ensure that at least three drive controllers are used. Three-way mirrors require at least five drives.

If you are familiar with RAID 6, you are familiar with dual parity volumes. Although dual parity does not have a penalty for read operations, it does have a performance penalty for write operations because of the overhead associated with calculating and writing dual parity values. With standard dual parity volumes, the usable capacity of dual parity volumes is calculated as the sum of the number of volumes minus two times the size of the smallest volume in the array or (N -2) X MinimumVolume-Size. For example, with 7 volumes and the smallest volume size of 1 TB, the usable capacity typically is 5 TB [calculated as (7 - 2) * 1 TB = 5 TB].

Although logically it would seem that you need at least six drives to have three mirrored copies of data, mathematically you need only five. Why? If you want three copies of your data, you need at least 15 logical units of storage to create those three copies. Divide 15 by 3 to come up with the number of disks required, and the answer is that you need 5 disks. Thus, Storage Spaces uses 1/3 of each disk to store original data and 2/3 of each disk to store copies of data. Following this, a three-way mirror with five volumes has a 2/3 (66.66 percent) overhead for redundancy. Or put another way, you could allocate five 3-TB drives as a three-way mirror, giving you 5 TB of mirrored storage (and 10 TB of overhead).

With single parity volumes, data is written out horizontally with parity calculated for each row of data. Dual parity differs from single parity in that row data is not only stored horizontally, it is also stored diagonally. If a single disk fails or a read error from a bad bit or block error occurs, the data is re-created by using only the horizontal row parity data (just as in single parity volumes). In the case of a multiple drive issue, the horizontal and diagonal row data are used for recovery.

To understand how dual parity typically works, consider the following simplified example. Each horizontal row of data has a parity value, the sum of which is stored on the parity disk for that row (and calculated by using an exclusive OR). Each horizontal parity stripe misses one and only one disk. If the parity value is 2, 3, 1, and 4 on disks 0, 1, 2, and 3 respectively, the parity sum stored on the disk 4 (the parity disk for this row) is 10 (2 + 3 + 1 + 4 = 10). If disk 0 were to have a problem, the parity value for the row on this disk could be restored by subtracting the remaining horizontal values from the horizontal parity sum (10 – 3 – 1 – 4 = 2).

The second set of parity data is written diagonally (meaning in different data rows on different disks). Each diagonal row of data has a diagonal parity value, the sum of which is stored on the diagonal parity disk for that row (and calculated by using an exclusive OR). Each diagonal parity stripe misses two disks: one disk in which the diagonal parity sum is stored and one disk that is omitted from the diagonal parity striping. Additionally, the diagonal parity sum includes a data row from the horizontal row parity as part of its diagonal parity sum.

If the diagonal parity value is 1, 4, 3, and 7 on disks 1, 2, 3, and 4 respectively (with four associated horizontal rows), the diagonal parity sum stored on disk 5 (the diagonal parity disk for this row) is 15 (4 + 1 + 3 + 7 = 15) and the omitted disk is disk 0. If disk 2 and disk 4 were to have a problem, the diagonal parity value for the row can be used to restore both of the lost values. The missing diagonal value is restored first by subtracting the remaining diagonal values from the diagonal parity sum. The missing horizontal value is restored next by subtracting the remaining horizontal values for the subject row from the horizontal parity sum for that row.

NOTE Keep in mind that dual parity, as implemented in Storage Spaces, uses seven disks, and the previous example was simplified. Although parity striping with seven disks works differently than as discussed in this example, the basic approach uses horizontal and vertical stripes.

You can create a storage pool by completing the following steps:

1. In Server Manager, select the File And Storage Services node, and then select the related Storage Pools subnode.

2. Select Tasks in the Storage Pools panel, and then select New Storage Pool. This starts the New Storage Pool Wizard. If the wizard displays the Before You Begin page, read the Welcome text, and then click Next.

3. On the Specify A Storage Pool Name And Subsystem page, enter a name and description of the storage pool, and then select the primordial pool with which

you want to work. (A *primordial pool* is simply a group of disks managed by and available to a specific server via a storage subsystem.) Click Next.

TIP Select the primordial pool for the server you want to associate the pool with and allocate storage for. For example, if you are configuring storage for CorpServer38, select the primordial pool that is available to CorpServer38.

4. On the Select Physical Disks For The Storage Pool page, select the unused physical disks that should be part of the storage pool, and then specify the type of allocation for each disk. A storage pool must have more than one disk to use the mirroring and parity features available to protect data in case of error or failure. When setting the Allocation value, keep the following in mind:

   - Choose Automatic to allocate the disk to the pool and make it available for use as needed.

   - Choose Manual to allocate the disk to the pool but not allow it to be used until it is manually allocated.

   - Choose Hot Spare to allocate the disk to the pool as a spare disk that is made available for use if another disk in the pool fails or is removed from the subsystem.

5. When you are ready to continue, click Next. After you confirm your selections, click Create. The wizard tracks the progress of the pool creation. When the wizard finishes creating the pool, the View Results page will be updated to reflect this. Review the details to ensure that all phases were completed successfully, and then click Close.

If any portion of the configuration failed, note the reason for the failure and take corrective actions as appropriate before repeating this procedure.

- If one of the physical disks is currently formatted with a volume, you'll get the following error:

   Could not create storage pool. One of the physical disks specified is not supported by this operation.

   This error occurs because physical disks that you want to add to a storage pool cannot contain existing volumes. To resolve the problem, you'll need to repeat the procedure and select a different physical disk, or remove any existing volumes on the physical disk, repeat the procedure, and then select the disk again. Keep in mind that deleting a volume permanently erases all data it contains.

- If one of the physical disks is unavailable after being select, you'll get the error:

   Could not create storage pool. One or more parameter values passed to the method were invalid.

   This error occurs because a physical disk that was available when you started the New Storage Pool Wizard has become unavailable or is offline. To resolve the problem, you'll need to a) repeat the procedure and select a different physical disk, or b) bring the physical disk online or otherwise make it available for use, repeat the procedure, and then select the disk again.

NOTE External storage can become unavailable for a variety of reasons. For example, an external connected cable might have been disconnected or a LUN previously allocated to the server might have been reallocated by a storage administrator.

Creating a virtual disk in a storage space

After you create a storage pool, you can allocate space from the pool to virtual disks that are available to your servers. Each physical disk allocated to the pool can be handled in one of three ways:

- As a data store that is available for use
- As a data store that can be manually allocated for use
- As a hot spare in case a disk in the pool fails or is removed from the subsystem

When a storage pool has a single disk, your only option for allocating space on that disk is to create virtual disks with a simple layout. A simple layout does not protect against disk failure. If a storage pool has multiple disks, you have these additional layout options:

- **Mirror** With a mirror layout, data is duplicated on disks by using a mirroring technique similar to what I discussed previously in this chapter. However, the mirroring technique is more sophisticated in that data is mirrored onto two or three disks at a time. Like standard mirroring, this approach has its advantages and disadvantages. If a storage space has two or three disks, you are fully protected against a single disk failure, and if a storage space has five or more disks, you are fully protected against two simultaneous disk failures. The disadvantage is that mirroring reduces capacity by up to 50 percent. For example, if you mirror two 1-TB disks, the usable space is 1 TB.

- **Parity** With a parity layout, data and parity information are striped across physical disks by using a striping-with-parity technique similar to what I discussed previously in this chapter. Like standard striping with parity, this approach has its advantages and disadvantages. You need at least three disks to fully protect yourself against a single disk failure. You lose some capacity to the striping, but not as much as with mirroring.

You can create a virtual disk in a storage pool by completing the following steps:

1. In Server Manager, select the File And Storage Services node, and then select the related Storage Pools subnode.

2. Select Tasks in the Virtual Disks panel, and then select New Virtual Disk. This starts the New Virtual Disk Wizard.

3. On the Storage Pool page, select the storage pool in which you want to create the virtual disk, and then click Next. Each available storage pool is listed according to the server it is managed by and available to. Make sure the pool has enough free space to create the virtual disk.

   TIP Select the storage pool for the server you want to associate the virtual disk with and allocate storage from. For example, if you are configuring storage for CorpServer38, select a storage pool that is available to CorpServer38.

4. On the Specify The Virtual Disk Name page, enter a name and description for the virtual disk. If you are using a combination of SSD storage and HDD storage, use the check box provided to specify whether you want to create storage tiers. With storage tiers, the most frequently accessed files are automatically moved from slower HDD to faster SSD storage. This option is not applicable when the server has only HDD or SSD storage. To continue, click Next.

5. On the Select The Storage Layout page, select the storage layout as appropriate for your reliability and redundancy requirements. The simple layout is the only option for storage pools that contain a single disk. If the underlying storage pool has multiple disks, you can choose a simple layout, a mirror layout, or a parity layout. Click Next.

REAL WORLD   If there aren't enough available disks to implement the storage layout, you'll get the error: The storage pool does not contain enough physical disks to support the selected storage layout. Select a different layout or repeat this procedure and select a different storage pool to work with initially.

Keep in mind the storage pool might have one or more disks allocated as hot spares. Hot spares are made available automatically to recover from disk failure when you use mirroring or parity volumes—and cannot otherwise be used. To force Windows to use a hot spare, you can remove the hot spare from the storage pool by pressing and holding or right-clicking it and selecting Remove, and then adding the drive back to the storage pool as an automatically allocated disk by pressing and holding or right-clicking the storage pool and selecting Add Physical Drive. Unfortunately, doing so might cause a storage pool created with a hot spare to report that it is in an Unhealthy state. If you subsequently try to add the drive again in any capacity, you'll get an error stating "Error adding task: The storage pool could not complete the operation because its configuration is read-only." The storage pool is not, in fact, in a read-only state. If the storage pool were in a read-only state you could enter the following command at an elevated Windows PowerShell prompt to clear this state:

```
Get-Storagepool "PoolName" | Set-Storagepool -IsReadonly $false
```

However, entering this command likely will not resolve the problem. To clear this error, I needed to reset Storage Spaces and the related subsystem. You might find it easier to simply restart the server. After you reset or restart the server, the storage pool will transition from an error state (where a red circle with an 'x' is showing) to a warning state (where a yellow triangle with an '!' is showing). You can then remove the physical disk from the storage pool by pressing and holding or right-clicking it and selecting Remove. Afterward, you will be able to add the physical disk as an automatically-allocated disk by pressing and holding or right-clicking the storage pool and selecting Add Physical Drive.

6. On the Specify The Provisioning Type page, select the provisioning type. Storage can be provisioned in a thin disk or a fixed disk. With thin-disk provisioning, the volume uses space from the storage pool as needed, up to the volume size. With fixed provisioning, the volume has a fixed size and uses space from the storage pool equal to the volume size. Click Next.

7. On the Specify The Size Of The Virtual Disk page, use the options provided to set the size of the virtual disk. With fixed provisioning, selecting Maximum Size ensures that the disk is created and sized with the maximum space possible given the available space. For example, if you use a 2-TB disk and a 1.5-TB disk with a mirrored layout, a 1.5-TB fixed disk will be created because this is the maximum mirrored size possible.

8. When you are ready to continue, click Next. After you confirm your selections, click Create. The wizard tracks the progress of the disk creation. When the wizard finishes creating the disk, the View Results page will be updated to reflect this. Review the details to ensure that all phases were completed successfully. If any portion of the configuration failed, note the reason for the failure and take corrective actions as appropriate before repeating this procedure.

9. When you click Close, the New Volume Wizard should start automatically. Use the wizard to create a volume on the disk as discussed in the following section.

Creating a standard volume

Standard volumes can be created on any physical or virtual disk available. You use the same technique regardless of how the disk is presented to the server. This allows you to create standard volumes on a server's internal disks, on virtual disks in a storage subsystem available to a server, and on virtual iSCSI disks available to a server. If you add the data deduplication feature to a server, you can enable data deduplication for standard volumes created for that server.

You can create a standard volume by completing the following steps:

1. Start the New Volume Wizard. If you just created a storage space, the New Volume Wizard might start automatically. If it did not, do one of the following:

   ■ On the Disks subnode, all available disks are listed in the Disks panel. Select the disk with which you want to work, and then under Tasks, select New Volume.

   ■ On the Storage Pools subnode, all available virtual disks are listed in the Virtual Disks panel. Select the disk with which you want to work, and then under Tasks, select New Volume.

2. On the Select The Server And Disk page, select the server for which you are provisioning storage, select the disk where the volume should be created, and then click Next. If you just created a storage space and then New Volume Wizard started automatically, the related server and disk are selected automatically and you simply need to click Next.

3. On the Specify The Size Of The Volume page, use the options provided to set the volume size. By default, the volume size is set to the maximum available on the related disk. Click Next.

4. On the Assign To A Drive Letter Or Folder page, specify whether you want to assign a drive letter or path to the volume, and then click Next. You use these options as follows:

- **Drive Letter** To assign a drive letter, choose this option, and then select an available drive letter in the list provided.

- **The Following Folder** To assign a drive path, choose this option, and then enter the path to an existing folder on an NTFS drive, or select Browse to search for or create a folder.

- **Don't Assign To A Drive Letter Or Drive Path** To create the volume without assigning a drive letter or path, choose this option. You can assign a drive letter or path later if necessary.

5. On the Select File System Settings page, specify how the volume should be formatted by using the following options:

- **File System** Sets the file system type, such as NTFS or ReFS.

- **Allocation Unit Size** Sets the cluster size for the file system. This is the basic unit in which disk space is allocated. The default allocation unit size is based on the volume's size and is set dynamically prior to formatting. To override this feature, you can set the allocation unit size to a specific value.

- **Volume Label** Sets a text label for the partition. This label is the partition's volume name.

6. If you elected to create an NTFS volume and added data deduplication to the server, you can enable and configure data deduplication. When you are ready to continue, click Next.

7. After you confirm your selections, click Create. The wizard tracks the progress of the volume creation. When the wizard finishes creating the volume, the View Results page will be updated to reflect this. Review the details to ensure that all phases were completed successfully. If any portion of the configuration failed, note the reason for the failure and take corrective actions as appropriate before repeating this procedure.

8. Click Close.

REAL WORLD In the Registry under HKLM\SYSTEM\CurrentControlSet\Control \FileSystem, the NtfsDisableLastAccessUpdate and RefsDisableLastAccessUpdate values control whether NTFS and ReFS update the last-access time stamp on each directory when it lists directories on a volume. If you notice that a busy server with a large number of directories isn't very responsive when you list directories, this could be because the filesystem log buffer in physical memory is getting filled with time stamp update records. To prevent this, you can set the value to 1. When the value is set to 1, the filesystem does not update the last-access time stamp, and it does not record time stamp updates in the file system log. Otherwise, when the value is set to 0 (the default), the filesystem updates the last-access time stamp on each directory it detects, and it records each time change in the filesystem log.

Troubleshooting storage spaces

Typical problems creating storage spaces and allocating storage were discussed previously. You also might find that a physical disk that should be available for use isn't available. With the Storage Pools node selected in Server Manager, you can add a physical disk that has been detected but isn't listed as available by selecting Tasks on the Physical Disks panel, and then selecting Add Physical Disk. Next, in the Add Physical Disk dialog box, select the physical disk, and then click OK. Alternatively, if the physical disk has not been detected by the storage system, select Tasks on the Storage Pools panel, and then select Rescan Storage.

Other problems you might experience with storage spaces relate to drive failures and a loss of resiliency. When a storage space uses two-way mirroring, three-way mirroring, parity, or dual parity, you can recover resiliency by reconnecting a disconnected drive or replacing a failed drive. When a storage space uses a simple volume and drives were disconnected, you can recover the volume by reconnecting the drives.

Selecting the notification icon for Action Center displays the related notifications. If there is a problem with storage spaces, Action Center updates the related notification panel in the desktop notification area with a message stating "Check Storage Spaces for issues." To open Server Manager, select the notification icon, and then select the link provided. In Server Manager, you'll need to select the File And Storage Services node, and then select Storage Pools to get the relevant error and warning icons.

To view errors and warnings for storage pools, press and hold or right-click the storage pool with the error or warning icon, and then select Properties. In the Properties dialog box, select Health in the left pane to display the health status and operational status in the main pane. For example, you might find that the health status is listed as Warning and the operation status is listed as Degraded. Degraded is a status you'll get when there is a loss of redundancy.

To view errors and warnings for virtual disks and their associated physical disks, press and hold or right-click the virtual disk with the error or warning icon, and then select Properties. In the Properties dialog box, select Health in the left pane to display the health status and operational status in the main pane. Note the storage layout and the physical disks in use as well. If there is a problem with a physical disk, such as a loss of communication, this status will be displayed. You'll get a Loss of Communication status when a physical disk is missing, failed, or disconnected.

When storage spaces use external drives, a missing drive might be a common problem you encounter. In this case, users can continue to work, and redundancy will be restored when you reconnect the drive. However, if a drive failed, you'd need to complete the following steps to restore redundancy:

1. Physically remove the failed drive. If the drive is connected internally, you'll need to shut down and unplug the computer before you can remove the drive; otherwise, simply disconnect an externally connected drive.

2. Physically add or connect a replacement drive. Next, add the drive to the storage space by doing the following:

   a. On the Storage Spaces panel, press and hold or right-click the storage space you want to configure, and then select Add Physical Drive.

   b. In the Add Physical Disk dialog box, select the drive that should be allocated to the storage pool.

   c. When you click OK, Windows Server will prepare the drive and allocate it to the storage pool.

3. At this point, the failed drive should be listed as "Retired." Remove the failed drive from the storage space by selecting the related Remove Disk option, and then confirm that you want to remove the drive by selecting Yes when prompted.

Windows Server restores redundancy by copying data as necessary to the new disk. During this process, the status of the storage space ordinarily is listed as "Repairing." A value depicting how much of the repair task is completed is also shown. When this value reaches 100 percent, the repair is complete.

Managing existing partitions and drives

Disk Management provides many features to manage existing partitions and drives. Use these features to assign drive letters, delete partitions, set the active partition, and more. In addition, Windows Server 2012 R2 provides other utilities to carry out common tasks such as converting a volume to NTFS, checking a drive for errors, and cleaning up unused disk space.

> **NOTE** Windows Vista and all later releases of Windows support hot-pluggable media that use NTFS volumes. This new feature enables you to format USB flash devices and other similar media with NTFS. There are also enhancements to prevent data loss when ejecting NTFS-formatted removable media.

Assigning drive letters and paths

You can assign drives one drive letter and one or more drive paths, provided that the drive paths are mounted on NTFS drives. Drives don't have to be assigned a drive letter or path. A drive with no designators is considered to be unmounted, and you can mount it by assigning a drive letter or path at a later date. You need to unmount a drive before moving it to another computer.

Windows cannot modify the drive letter of system, boot, or page-file volumes. To change the drive letter of a system or boot volume, you need to edit the registry as described in Microsoft Knowledge Base article 223188 (*support.microsoft.com /kb/223188/*). Before you can change the drive letter of a page-file volume, you might need to move the page file to a different volume.

To manage drive letters and paths, press and hold or right-click the drive you want to configure in Disk Management, and then tap or click Change Drive Letter And Paths to open the dialog box (shown in Figure 2-8). You can now do the following:

- **Add a drive path**   Tap or click Add, select Mount In The Following Empty NTFS Folder, and then type the path to an existing folder, or tap or click Browse to search for or create a folder.
- **Remove a drive path**   Select the drive path to remove, tap or click Remove, and then tap or click Yes.
- **Assign a drive letter**   Tap or click Add, select Assign The Following Drive Letter, and then choose an available letter to assign to the drive.
- **Change the drive letter**   Select the current drive letter, and then tap or click Change. Select Assign The Following Drive Letter, and then choose a different letter to assign to the drive.
- **Remove a drive letter**   Select the current drive letter, tap or click Remove, and then tap or click Yes.

NOTE   If you try to change the letter of a drive that's in use, Windows Server 2012 R2 displays a warning. You need to exit programs that are using the drive and try again, or allow Disk Management to force the change by tapping or clicking Yes when prompted.

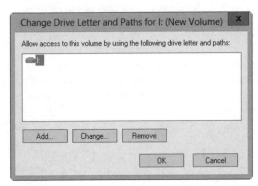

FIGURE 2-8 You can change the drive letter and path assignment in the Change Drive Letter And Paths dialog box.

Changing or deleting the volume label

The volume label is a text descriptor for a drive. With FAT, the volume label can be up to 11 characters and can include spaces. With NTFS, the volume label can be up to 32 characters. Additionally, although FAT doesn't allow you to use some special characters—including * / \ [ ] : ; | = , . + " ? < >—NTFS does allow you to use these special characters.

Because the volume label is displayed when the drive is accessed in various Windows Server 2012 R2 utilities, including File Explorer, it can provide information about a drive's contents. You can change or delete a volume label by using Disk Management or File Explorer.

Using Disk Management, you can change or delete a label by following these steps:

1. Press and hold or right-click the partition, and then tap or click Properties.

2. On the General tab of the Properties dialog box, enter a new label for the volume in the Label text box or delete the existing label. Tap or click OK.

Using File Explorer, you can change or delete a label by following these steps:

1. Press and hold or right-click the drive icon, and then tap or click Properties.

2. On the General tab of the Properties dialog box, enter a new label for the volume in the Label text box or delete the existing label. Tap or click OK.

Deleting partitions and drives

To change the configuration of a drive that's fully allocated, you might need to delete existing partitions and logical drives. Deleting a partition or a drive removes the associated file system, and all data in the file system is lost. Before you delete a partition or a drive, you should back up any files and directories that the partition or drive contains.

NOTE To protect the integrity of the system, you can't delete the system or boot partition. However, Windows Server 2012 R2 does let you delete the active partition or volume if it is not designated as boot or system. Always check to be sure that the partition or volume you are deleting doesn't contain important data or files.

You can delete a primary partition, volume, or logical drive by following these steps:

1. In Disk Management, press and hold or right-click the partition, volume, or drive you want to delete, and then tap or click Explore. Using File Explorer, move all the data to another volume or verify an existing backup to ensure that the data was properly saved.

2. In Disk Management, press and hold or right-click the partition, volume, or drive again, and then tap or click Delete Partition, Delete Volume, or Delete Logical Drive as appropriate.

3. Confirm that you want to delete the selected item by tapping or clicking Yes.

The steps for deleting an extended partition differ slightly from those for deleting a primary partition or a logical drive. To delete an extended partition, follow these steps:

1. Delete all the logical drives on the partition following the steps listed in the previous procedure.

2. Select the extended partition area itself and delete it.

Converting a volume to NTFS

Windows Server 2012 R2 provides a utility for converting FAT volumes to NTFS. This utility, Convert (Convert.exe), is located in the %SystemRoot% folder. When you convert a volume by using this tool, the file and directory structure is preserved and no data is lost. Keep in mind, however, that Windows Server 2012 R2 doesn't provide a utility for converting NTFS to FAT. The only way to go from NTFS to FAT is to delete the partition by following the steps listed in the previous section, and then re-create the partition as a FAT volume.

Understanding the Convert utility syntax

Convert is run at the command prompt. If you want to convert a drive, use the following syntax:

```
convert volume /FS:NTFS
```

Here *volume* is the drive letter followed by a colon, drive path, or volume name. For example, if you want to convert the D drive to NTFS, use the following command:

```
convert D: /FS:NTFS
```

If the volume has a label, you are prompted to enter the volume label for the drive, but you are not prompted if the disk doesn't have a label.

The complete syntax for Convert is shown here:

```
convert volume /FS:NTFS [/V] [/X] [/CvtArea:filename] [/NoSecurity]
```

The options and switches for Convert are used as follows:

volume	Sets the volume with which to work
/FS:NTFS	Converts to NTFS
/V	Sets verbose mode
/X	Forces the volume to dismount before the conversion (if necessary)
/CvtArea: *filename*	Sets the name of a contiguous file in the root directory to be a placeholder for NTFS system files
/NoSecurity	Removes all security attributes, and makes all files and directories accessible to the group Everyone

The following sample statement uses Convert:

```
convert C: /FS:NTFS /V
```

Using the Convert utility

Before you use the Convert utility, determine whether the partition is being used as the active boot partition or a system partition containing the operating system. You can convert the active boot partition to NTFS. Doing so requires that the system gain exclusive access to this partition, which can be obtained only during startup. Thus, if you try to convert the active boot partition to NTFS, Windows Server 2012 R2 displays a prompt asking if you want to schedule the drive to be converted the next time the system starts. If you tap or click Yes, you can restart the system to begin the conversion process.

TIP Often, you will need to restart a system several times to completely convert the active boot partition. Don't panic. Let the system proceed with the conversion.

Before the Convert utility actually converts a drive to NTFS, the utility checks whether the drive has enough free space to perform the conversion. Generally, Convert needs a block of free space that's roughly equal to 25 percent of the total space used on the drive. For example, if the drive stores 200 GB of data, Convert needs about 50 GB of free space. If the drive doesn't have enough free space, Convert aborts and tells you that you need to free up some space. On the other hand, if the drive has enough free space, Convert initiates the conversion. Be patient. The conversion process takes several minutes (longer for large drives). Don't access files or applications on the drive while the conversion is in progress.

You can use the /CvtArea option to improve performance on the volume so that space for the master file table (MFT) is reserved. This option helps to prevent fragmentation of the MFT. How? Over time, the MFT might grow larger than the space allocated to it. The operating system must then expand the MFT into other areas of the disk. Although the Optimize Drives utility can defragment the MFT, it cannot move the first section of the MFT, and it is very unlikely that there will be space after the MFT because this will be filled by file data.

To help prevent fragmentation in some cases, you might want to reserve more space than the default (12.5 percent of the partition or volume size). For example, you might want to increase the MFT size if the volume will have many small or average-size files rather than a few large files. To specify the amount of space to reserve, you can use FSUtil to create a placeholder file equal in size to that of the MFT you want to create. You can then convert the volume to NTFS and specify the name of the placeholder file to use with the /CvtArea option.

In the following example, you use FSUtil to create a 1.5-GB (1,500,000,000 bytes) placeholder file named Temp.txt:

```
fsutil file createnew c:\temp.txt 1500000000
```

To use this placeholder file for the MFT when converting drive C to NTFS, you would then type the following command:

```
convert c: /fs:ntfs /cvtarea:temp.txt
```

Notice that the placeholder file is created on the partition or volume that is being converted. During the conversion process, the file is overwritten with NTFS metadata and any unused space in the file is reserved for future use by the MFT.

Resizing partitions and volumes

Windows Server 2012 R2 doesn't use Ntldr and Boot.ini to load the operating system. Instead, Windows Server 2012 R2 has a preboot environment in which Windows Boot Manager is used to control startup and load the boot application you selected. Windows Boot Manager also finally frees the Windows operating system from its reliance on MS-DOS so that you can use drives in new ways. With Windows Server 2012 R2, you can extend and shrink both basic and dynamic disks. You can use Disk Management, DiskPart, or Windows PowerShell to extend and shrink volumes. You cannot shrink or extend striped, mirrored, or striped-with-parity volumes.

In extending a volume, you convert areas of unallocated space and add them to the existing volume. For spanned volumes on dynamic disks, the space can come from any available dynamic disk, not only from those on which the volume was originally created. Thus, you can combine areas of free space on multiple dynamic disks and use those areas to increase the size of an existing volume.

CAUTION Before you try to extend a volume, be aware of several limitations. First, you can extend simple and spanned volumes only if they are formatted and the file system is NTFS. You can't extend striped volumes, volumes that aren't formatted, or volumes that are formatted with FAT. Additionally, you can't extend a system or boot volume, regardless of its configuration.

You can shrink a simple volume or a spanned volume by following these steps:

1. In Disk Management, press and hold or right-click the volume you want to shrink, and then tap or click Shrink Volume. This option is available only if the volume meets the previously discussed criteria.

2. In the box provided in the Shrink dialog box, shown in Figure 2-9, enter the amount of space to shrink.

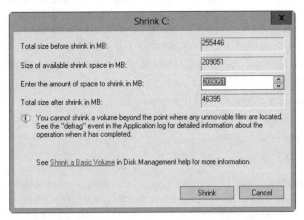

FIGURE 2-9 Specify the amount of space to shrink from the volume.

The Shrink dialog box provides the following information:

- **Total Size Before Shrink In MB**   Lists the total capacity of the volume in megabytes. This is the formatted size of the volume.

- **Size Of Available Shrink Space In MB**   Lists the maximum amount by which the volume can be shrunk. This doesn't represent the total amount of free space on the volume; rather, it represents the amount of space that can be removed, not including any data reserved for the master file table, volume snapshots, page files, and temporary files.

- **Enter The Amount Of Space To Shrink In MB**   Lists the total amount of space that will be removed from the volume. The initial value defaults to the maximum amount of space that can be removed from the volume. For optimal drive performance, you'll want to ensure that the drive has at least 10 percent of free space after the shrink operation.

- **Total Size After Shrink In MB**   Lists what the total capacity of the volume will be (in megabytes) after the shrink. This is the new formatted size of the volume.

3. Tap or click Shrink to shrink the volume.

You can extend a simple volume or a spanned volume by following these steps:

1. In Disk Management, press and hold or right-click the volume you want to extend, and then tap or click Extend Volume. This option is available only if the volume meets the previously discussed criteria and free space is available on one or more of the system's dynamic disks.

2. In the Extend Volume Wizard, read the introductory message, and then tap or click Next.

3. On the Select Disks page, select the disk or disks from which you want to allocate free space. Any disks currently being used by the volume are automatically selected. By default, all remaining free space on those disks is selected for use.

4. With dynamic disks, you can specify the additional space you want to use on other disks by performing the following tasks:

   - Tap or click the disk, and then tap or click Add to add the disk to the Selected list.

   - Select each disk in the Selected list, and then, in the Select The Amount Of Space In MB list, specify the amount of unallocated space to use on the selected disk.

5. Tap or click Next, confirm your options, and then tap or click Finish.

Repairing disk errors and inconsistencies automatically

Windows Server 2012 R2 includes feature enhancements that reduce the amount of manual maintenance you must perform on disk drives. The following enhancements have the most impact on the way you work with disks:

- Transactional NTFS
- Self-healing NTFS

Transactional NTFS allows file operations on an NTFS volume to be performed transactionally, which means programs can use a transaction to group sets of file and registry operations so that all of them succeed or none of them succeed. While a transaction is active, changes are not visible outside the transaction. Changes are committed and written fully to disk only when a transaction is completed successfully. If a transaction fails or is incomplete, the program rolls back the transactional work to restore the file system to the state it was in prior to the transaction.

REAL WORLD Resilient File System (ReFS) takes the transactional and self-healing features of NTFS a few steps further. With ReFS, several background processes are used to maintain disk integrity automatically. The scrubber process checks the disk for inconsistencies and errors. If any are found, a repair process localizes the problems and performs automatic online correction. In the rare case that a physical drive has bad sectors that are causing the problem, ReFS uses a salvage process to mark the bad sectors and remove them from the file system—and all while the volume is online.

Transactions that span multiple volumes are coordinated by the Kernel Transaction Manager (KTM). The KTM supports independent recovery of volumes if a transaction fails. The local resource manager for a volume maintains a separate transaction log and is responsible for maintaining threads for transactions separate from threads that perform the file work.

Traditionally, you had to use the Check Disk tool to fix errors and inconsistencies in NTFS volumes on a disk. Because this process can disrupt the availability of Windows systems, Windows Server 2012 R2 uses self-healing NTFS to protect file systems without requiring you to use separate maintenance tools to fix problems. Because much of the self-healing process is enabled and performed automatically, you might need to perform volume maintenance manually only when you are notified by the operating system that a problem cannot be corrected automatically. If such an error occurs, Windows Server 2012 R2 notifies you about the problem and provides possible solutions.

Self-healing NTFS has many advantages over Check Disk, including the following:

- Check Disk must have exclusive access to volumes, which means system and boot volumes can be checked only when the operating system starts up. On the other hand, with self-healing NTFS, the file system is always available and does not need to be corrected offline (in most cases).

- Self-healing NTFS attempts to preserve as much data as possible if corruption occurs and reduces failed file system mounting that previously could occur if a volume was known to have errors or inconsistencies. During restart, self-healing NTFS repairs the volume immediately so that it can be mounted.

- Self-healing NTFS reports changes made to the volume during repair through existing Chkdsk.exe mechanisms, directory notifications, and update sequence number (USN) journal entries. This feature also allows authorized users and administrators to monitor repair operations through Verification, Waiting For Repair Completion, and Progress Status messages.

- Self-healing NTFS can recover a volume if the boot sector is readable but does not identify an NTFS volume. In this case, you must run an offline tool that repairs the boot sector, and then allow self-healing NTFS to initiate recovery.

Although self-healing NTFS is a terrific enhancement, at times you might want to (or might have to) manually check the integrity of a disk. In these cases, you can use Check Disk (Chkdsk.exe) to check for and (optionally) repair problems found on FAT, FAT32, exFAT, and NTFS volumes.

IMPORTANT Because ReFS is self-correcting, you do not need to use Check Disk to check ReFS volumes for errors. However, it's important to point out that ReFS as originally released did not efficiently correct corruption on parity spaces. With Windows Server 2012 R2, this deficiency has been corrected. ReFS automatically corrects corruption on parity spaces when integrity streams are enabled to detect corrupt data. When corruption is detected, ReFS examines the data copies that the parity spaces contain and then uses the correct version of the data to correct the problem. As ReFS now supports concurrent I/O requests to the same file, the performance of integrity streams also has been improved.

Although Check Disk can check for and correct many types of errors, the utility primarily looks for inconsistencies in the file system and its related metadata. One of the ways Check Disk locates errors is by comparing the volume bitmap to the disk sectors assigned to files in the file system. Beyond this, the usefulness of Check Disk is rather limited. For example, Check Disk can't repair corrupted data within files that appear to be structurally intact.

As part of automated maintenance, Windows Server 2012 R2 performs a proactive scan of NTFS volumes. As with other automated maintenance, Windows scans disks using Check Disk at 2:00 A.M. if the computer is running on AC power and the operating system is idle. Otherwise, Windows scans disks the next time the computer is running on AC power and the operating system is idle. Although automated maintenance triggers the disk scan, the process of calling and managing Check Disk is handled by a separate task. In Task Scheduler, you'll find the ProactiveScan task in the scheduler library under Microsoft\Windows\Chkdsk, and you can get detailed run details by reviewing the information provided on the task's History tab.

REAL WORLD Automatic Maintenance is built on the Windows Diagnostics framework. By default, Windows periodically performs routine maintenance at 2:00 A.M. if the computer is running on AC power and the operating system is idle. Otherwise, maintenance will start the next time the computer is running on AC power and the operating system is idle. Because maintenance runs only when the operating system is idle, maintenance is allowed to run in the background for up to three days. This allows Windows to complete complex maintenance tasks automatically. Maintenance tasks include software updates, security scanning, system diagnostics, checking disks, and disk optimization. You can change the run time for automated maintenance by opening Action Center, expanding the Maintenance panel, selecting Change Maintenance Settings, and then selecting a new run schedule.

Checking disks manually

With Windows Server 2012 R2, Check Disk performs enhanced scan and repair automatically, instead of using the legacy scan and repair available with earlier releases of Windows. Here, when you use Check Disk with NTFS volumes, Check Disk performs an online scan and analysis of the disk for errors. Check Disk writes information about any detected corruptions in the $corrupt system file. If the volume is in use, detected corruptions can be repaired by taking the volume offline temporarily; however, unmounting the volume for the repair invalidates all open file handles. With the boot/system volume, the repairs are performed the next time you start the computer.

Storing the corruption information and then repairing the volume while it is dismounted enables Windows to rapidly repair volumes. You can also keep using the disk while a scan is being performed. Typically, offline repair takes only a few seconds, compared to what otherwise would have been hours for very large volumes using the legacy scan and repair technique.

> **NOTE** FAT, FAT32, and exFAT do not support the enhanced features. When you use Check Disk with FAT, FAT32, or exFAT, Windows Server 2012 R2 uses the legacy scan and repair process. This means the scan and repair process typically requires taking the volume offline and preventing it from being used. You can't use Check Disk with ReFS.

You can run Check Disk from the command prompt or within other utilities. At a command prompt, you can test the integrity of the E drive by entering the following command:

```
chkdsk /scan E:
```

Check Disk then performs an analysis of the disk and returns a status message regarding any problems it encounters. Check Disk won't repair problems, however, unless you specify further options. To repair errors on drive E, use this command:

```
chkdsk /spotfix E:
```

Fixing the volume requires exclusive access to the volume. The way this works depends on the type of volume:

- For nonsystem volumes, you'll get a prompt asking whether you would like to force a dismount of the volume for the repair. In this case, you can enter **Y** to proceed or **N** to cancel the dismount. If you cancel the dismount, you'll get the prompt asking whether you would like to schedule the volume for the repair the next time the computer is started. In this case, you can enter **Y** to schedule the repair or **N** to cancel the repair.

- For system volumes, you'll get a prompt asking whether you would like to schedule the volume for the repair the next time the computer is started. In this case, you can enter **Y** to schedule the repair or **N** to cancel the repair.

You can't run Check Disk with both the *scan* and *spotfix* options because the scan and repair tasks are now independent of each other.

The complete syntax for Check Disk is as follows:

```
CHKDSK [volume[[path]filename]] [/F] [/V] [/R] [/X] [/I] [/C] [/B]
   [/L[:size]] [/scan] [/forceofflinefix] [/perf] [/spotfix]
   [/sdcleanup] [/offlinescanandfix]
```

The options and switches for Check Disk are used as follows:

volume	Sets the volume with which to work.
[path]filename	FAT only. It specifies files to check for fragmentation.
/B	Reevaluates bad clusters on the volume (NTFS only; implies /R).
/C	NTFS only. It skips the checking of cycles within the folder structure.
/F	Fixes errors on the disk by using the offline (legacy) scan and fix behavior.
/I	NTFS only. It performs a minimum check of index entries.
/L:*size*	NTFS only. It changes the log file size.
/R	Locates bad sectors, and recovers readable information (implies /F).
/V	On FAT, it displays the full path and name of every file on the disk. On NTFS, it displays cleanup messages, if there are any.
/X	Forces the volume to dismount first if necessary (implies /F). For NTFS volumes, Check Disk supports these enhanced options:
/forceofflinefix	Must be used with /scan. It bypasses all online repair and queues errors for offline repair.
/offlinescanandfix	Performs an offline scan and fix of the volume.
/perf	Performs the scan as fast as possible by using more system resources.
/scan	Performs an online scan of the volume (the default). Errors detected during the scan are added to the $corrupt system file.
/sdcleanup	Cleans up unneeded security descriptor data. It implies /F (with legacy scan and repair).
/spotfix	Allows certain types of errors to be repaired online (the default).

Running Check Disk interactively

You can run Check Disk interactively through File Explorer or Disk Management by following these steps:

1. Press and hold or right-click the drive, and then tap or click Properties.

2. On the Tools tab of the Properties dialog box, tap or click Check. This displays the Error Checking dialog box, shown in Figure 2-10.

FIGURE 2-10 Use Check Disk to check a disk for errors and repair any that are found.

3. Click Scan Drive to start the scan. If no errors are found, Windows confirms this; otherwise, if errors are found, you'll be prompted with additional options. As with checking disks at a prompt, the way this works depends on whether you are working with a system or nonsystem volume.

NOTE For FAT, FAT32, and exFAT volumes, Windows uses the legacy Check Disk. You tap or click Scan And Repair Drive to start the scan. If the scan finds errors, you might need to restart the computer to repair them.

Analyzing and optimizing disks

Any time you add files to or remove files from a drive, the data on the drive can become fragmented. When a drive is fragmented, large files can't be written to a single continuous area on the disk. As a result, the operating system must write the file to several smaller areas on the disk, which means more time is spent reading the file from the disk. To reduce fragmentation, Windows Server 2012 R2 can manually or automatically analyze and optimize disks by using the Optimize Drives utility.

With manual optimization, Optimize Drives performs an online analysis of volumes, and then reports the percentage of fragmentation. If defragmentation is needed, you can then elect to perform online defragmentation. System and boot volumes can be defragmented online as well, and Optimize Drives can be used with FAT, FAT32, exFAT, NTFS, and ReFS volumes.

You can manually analyze and optimize a disk by following these steps:

1. In Computer Management, select the Storage node and then the Disk Management node. Press and hold or right-click a drive, and then tap or click Properties.

2. On the Tools tab, tap or click Optimize. In the Optimize Drives dialog box, select a disk, and then tap or click Analyze. Optimize Drives then analyzes the disk, as shown in Figure 2-11, to determine whether it needs to be defragmented. If so, it recommends that you defragment at this point.

3. If a disk needs to be defragmented, select the disk, and then tap or click Optimize.

NOTE Depending on the size of the disk, defragmentation can take several hours. You can tap or click Stop Operation at any time to stop defragmentation.

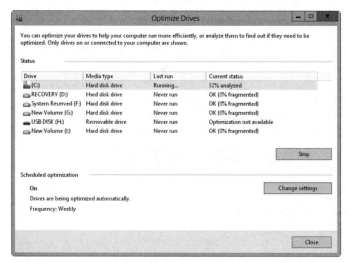

FIGURE 2-11 Optimize Drives analyzes and defragments disks efficiently.

Automatic analysis and optimization of disks can occur while the disks are online, so long as the computer is on AC power and the operating system is running but otherwise idle. By default, disk optimization is a weekly task rather than a daily task—and there's a good reason for this. Normally, you need only to periodically optimize a server's disks, and optimization once a week is sufficient in most cases. Note, however, that although nonsystem disks can be rapidly analyzed and optimized, it can take significantly longer to optimize system disks online.

You can control the approximate start time for the analysis and optimization of disks by changing the automated maintenance start time. Windows Server also notifies you if three consecutive runs are missed. All internal drives and certain external drives are optimized automatically as part of the regular schedule, as are new drives you connect to the server.

NOTE Windows Server 2012 R2 automatically performs cyclic pickup defragmentation. With this feature, when a scheduled defragmentation pass is stopped and rerun, the computer automatically picks up where it left off or starts with the next unfinished volume in line to be defragmented.

You can configure and manage automated defragmentation by following these steps:

1. In Computer Management, select the Storage node and then the Disk Management node. Press and hold or right-click a drive, and then tap or click Properties.

2. On the Tools tab, tap or click Optimize. This displays the Optimize Drives dialog box.

3. If you want to change how optimization works, tap or click Change Settings. This displays the dialog box shown in Figure 2-12. To cancel automated defragmentation, clear the Run On A Schedule check box. To enable automated defragmentation, select Run On A Schedule.

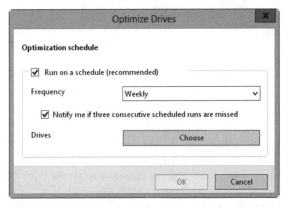

FIGURE 2-12 Set the run schedule for automated defragmentation.

4. The default run frequency is set as shown. In the Frequency list, you can choose Daily, Weekly, or Monthly as the run schedule. If you don't want to be notified about missed runs, clear the Notify Me check box.

5. If you want to manage which disks are defragmented, tap or click Choose, and then select the volumes to defragment. By default, all disks installed within or connected to the computer are defragmented, and any new disks are defragmented automatically as well. Select the check boxes for disks that should be defragmented automatically, and clear the check boxes for disks that should not be defragmented automatically. Tap or click OK to save your settings.

6. Tap or click OK, and then tap or click Close.

CHAPTER 3

Data sharing and redundancy

The Server Message Block (SMB) protocol is the primary file sharing protocol used by computers running Windows. When folders are shared over a network, an SMB client reads and writes to files and requests services from computers hosting SMB-shared folders. With SMB, Windows Server 2012 R2 supports standard file sharing and public folder sharing. Standard file sharing makes it possible for remote users to access network resources such as files, folders, and drives. When you share a folder or a drive, you make all its files and subfolders available to a specified set of users. Because you don't need to move files from their current location, standard file sharing is also referred to as *in-place file sharing*.

You can enable standard file sharing on disks formatted with FAT, FAT32, exFAT, NTFS, or Resilient File System (ReFS). One set of permissions apply to disks formatted with exFAT, FAT, or FAT32. These permissions are called *share permissions*. Two sets of permissions apply to disks formatted with NTFS or ReFS: *NTFS permissions* (also referred to as *access permissions*) and *share permissions*. Having two sets of permissions allows you to determine precisely who has access to shared files and the level of access assigned. With either NTFS permissions or share permissions, you do not need to move the files you are sharing.

With public folder sharing, you share files by just copying or moving files to the computer's Public folder. Public files are available to anyone who logs on to a computer locally regardless of whether that person has a standard user account or an administrator user account on the computer. You can also grant network access to the Public folder; however, if you do this, there are no access restrictions. The Public folder and its contents are open to everyone who can access the computer over the local network.

Using and enabling file sharing

The sharing settings on a computer determine the way files can be shared. The two file sharing models that Windows Server 2012 R2 supports have the following differences:

- **Standard (in-place) file sharing**   Allows remote users to access files, folders, and drives over the network. When you share a folder or a drive, you make all its files and subfolders available to a specified set of users. Share permissions and access permissions together enable you to control who has access to shared files and the level of access assigned. You do not need to move the files you are sharing.

- **Public folder sharing**   Allows local users and (optionally) remote users to access any files placed in the computer's %SystemDrive%\Users\Public folder. Access permissions on the Public folder determine which users and groups have access to publicly shared files in addition to the level of access those users and groups have. When you copy or move files to the Public folder, access permissions are changed to match those of the Public folder. Some additional permissions are added as well. When a computer is part of a workgroup, you can add password protection to the Public folder. Separate password protection isn't needed in a domain because only domain users can access Public folder data.

With standard file sharing, local users don't have automatic access to any data stored on a computer. You control local access to files and folders by using the security settings on the local disk. With public folder sharing, on the other hand, files copied or moved to the Public folder are available to anyone who logs on locally. You can grant network access to the Public folder as well; however, doing so makes the Public folder and its contents open to everyone who can access the computer over the network.

Windows Server 2012 R2 adds new layers of security through compound identities, claims-based access controls, and central access policies. With both Windows 8.1 and Windows Server 2012 R2, you can assign claims-based access controls to file and folder resources on NTFS and ReFS volumes. With Windows Server 2012 R2, users are granted access to file and folder resources, either directly with access permissions and share permissions or indirectly with claims-based access controls and central access policies.

SMB 3.0 makes it possible to encrypt data being transferred over the network. You can enable SMB encryption for shares configured on NTFS and ReFS volumes. SMB encryption works only when the computer requesting data from an SMB-based share (either a standard file share or a DFS share) and the server supplying the data support SMB 3.0. Both Windows 8.1 and Windows Server 2012 R2 support SMB 3.0. (They have an SMB 3.0 client.)

Public folder sharing is designed to enable users to share files and folders from a single location. With public folder sharing, you copy or move files you want to share to a computer's %SystemDrive%\Users\Public folder. You can access public folders in

File Explorer by double-tapping or double-clicking the system drive, and then accessing the Users\Public folder.

The Public folder has several subfolders you can use to help organize public files:

- **Public Desktop** Used for shared desktop items. Any files and program shortcuts placed in the Public Desktop folder appear on the desktop of all users who log on to the computer (and to all network users if network access has been granted to the Public folder).

- **Public Documents, Public Music, Public Pictures, Public Videos** Used for shared document and media files. All files placed in one of these subfolders are available to all users who log on to the computer (and to all network users if network access has been granted to the Public folder).

- **Public Downloads** Used for shared downloads. Any downloads placed in the Public Downloads subfolder are available to all users who log on to the computer (and to all network users if network access has been granted to the Public folder).

NOTE By default, the Public Desktop folder is hidden from view. If hidden items aren't being displayed in File Explorer, tap or click View, and then select Hidden Items.

By default, anyone with a user account and password on a computer can access that computer's Public folder. When you copy or move files to the Public folder, access permissions are changed to match that of the Public folder, and some additional permissions are added as well.

You can change the default Public folder sharing configuration in two key ways:

- Allow users logged on to the computer to view and manage public files but restrict network users from accessing public files. When you configure this option, the implicit groups Interactive, Batch, and Service are granted special permissions on public files and public folders.

- Allow users with network access to view and manage public files. This allows network users to open, change, create, and delete public files. When you configure this option, the implicit group Everyone is granted Full Control permission to public files and public folders.

Windows Server 2012 R2 can use either or both sharing models at any time. However, standard file sharing offers more security and better protection than public folder sharing, and increasing security is essential to protecting your organization's data. With standard file sharing, share permissions are used only when a user attempts to access a file or folder from a different computer on the network. Access permissions are always used, whether the user is logged on to the console or is using a remote system to access a file or folder over the network. When data is accessed remotely, first the share permissions are applied, and then the access permissions are applied.

As shown in Figure 3-1, you can configure the basic file sharing settings for a server by using Advanced Sharing Settings in Network And Sharing Center. Separate options are provided for network discovery, file and printer sharing, and public folder sharing.

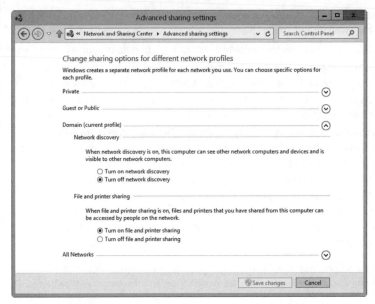

FIGURE 3-1 Network And Sharing Center shows the current sharing configuration.

You can manage a computer's sharing configuration by following these steps:

1. In Control Panel, tap or click View Network Status And Tasks under the Network And Internet heading to open Network And Sharing Center.

2. In Network And Sharing Center, tap or click Change Advanced Sharing Settings in the left pane. Select the network profile for the network on which you want to enable file and printer sharing. Typically, this will be the Domain profile.

3. Standard file and printer sharing controls network access to shared resources. To configure standard file sharing, do one of the following:

   ■ Select Turn On File And Printer Sharing to enable file sharing.

   ■ Select Turn Off File And Printer Sharing to disable file sharing.

4. Public folder sharing controls access to a computer's Public folder. To configure public folder sharing, expand the All Networks panel by tapping or clicking the related expand button. On the Public Folder Sharing panel, choose one of the following options:

   ■ **Turn On Sharing So Anyone With Network Access Can Read And Write Files In The Public Folders** Enables public folder sharing by granting access to the Public folder and all public data to anyone who can access the computer over the network. Windows Firewall settings might prevent external access.

- **Turn Off Public Folder Sharing**   Disables public folder sharing, preventing local network access to the Public folder. Anyone who logs on
  locally to your computer can still access the Public folder and its files.

5. Tap or click Save Changes.

Configuring standard file sharing

You use shares to control access for remote users. Permissions on shared folders
have no effect on users who log on locally to a server or to a workstation that has
shared folders.

Understanding SMB changes

SMB is the primary file sharing protocol used by Windows operating systems. As
Windows itself has changed over the years, so has SMB. To allow for version and
feature changes, SMB was designed to enable clients and servers to negotiate and
then use the highest version supported by both the client attempting to connect an
SMB share and the server hosting the share.

The current version of SMB is version 3.02, which is supported by Windows 8.1
and Windows Server 2012 R2. Thus, when a Windows 8.1 computer connects to an
SMB share hosted on a server running Windows Server 2012 R2, SMB 3.02 is the
version used for the SMB session.

The earliest implementation of SMB was called CIFS, which was introduced with
Windows NT 4.0, followed by SMB 1.0, which was used by all versions of Windows
from Windows 2000 to Windows Server 2003 R2. Beginning with Windows 8.1 and
Windows Server 2012 R2, support for CIFS and SMB 1.0 is an optional feature that
must be enabled. Because CIFS and SMB 1.0 are outdated, perform poorly, and are
less secure than their predecessors, SMB 1.0/CIFS File Sharing Support should not
be enabled unless required. That said, if a computer running Windows 8.1 needs to
connect to a server running a legacy Windows operating system, the computer
must have the SMB 1.0/CIFS File Sharing Support feature enabled. In addition, if a
computer running a legacy Windows operating system needs to connect to a server
running Windows Server 2012 R2, the server must have the SMB 1.0/CIFS File Sharing
Support feature enabled.

Table 3-1 provides a summary of the current versions of SMB, the associated
versions of Windows, and the major features introduced. You can enter **Get-Smb-
Connection** at an elevated, administrator Windows PowerShell prompt to determine
the version of SMB a client has negotiated with a file server. In the command output,
the version is listed in the Dialect column, as shown in the following sample output:

```
ServerName  ShareName   UserName        Credential       Dialect   NumOpens
----------  ---------   --------        ----------       -------   --------
Server36    IPC$        CPANDL\williams CPANDL\williams  3.02      0
Server36    PrimaryData CPANDL\williams CPANDL\williams  3.02      14
```

TABLE 3.1 Overview of current SMB versions

SMB VERSION	WINDOWS VERSION	FEATURES
SMB 2.0	Windows Vista SP1, Windows Server 2008	Increasing scalability and security, asynchronous operations, larger reads/writes, request compounding
SMB 2.1	Windows 7, Windows Server 2008 R2	Large MTU support, BranchCache support
SMB 3.0	Windows 8, Windows Server 2012	Enhancements for server clusters, BranchCache v2 support, SMB over RDMA, improved security
SMB 3.02	Windows 8.1, Windows Server 2012 R2	Improved performance for SMB over RDMA, additional scale-out options, Hyper-V live migration support

IMPORTANT SMB 3.0 and SMB 3.02 brought many enhancements for performance, especially when you use clustered file servers. A key enhancement that doesn't rely on a special configuration is end-to-end encryption of SMB data, which eliminates the need to use Internet Protocol security (IPsec), specialized hardware, or wide area network (WAN) accelerators to protect data from eavesdropping. SMB encryption can be enabled on a per-share basis.

Viewing existing shares

You can use both Computer Management and Server Manager to work with shares. You also can view current shares on a computer by entering **net share** at a command prompt or by entering **get-smbshare** at a Windows PowerShell prompt.

TIP The get-smbshare cmdlet is only one of many cmdlets associated with the smbshare module. To get a list of other cmdlets available for working with SMB shares, enter **get-command –module smbshare** at a Windows PowerShell prompt.

NOTE Computer Management, net share, and get-smbshare display information about SMB-based shares, including standard SMB folder shares, hidden SMB folder shares (those ending with the $ suffix), and SMB folders shared by using Distributed File System (DFS). Server Manager displays information about standard SMB folder shares, SMB folders shared by using DFS, and folders shared by using Network File System (NFS). Server Manager does not display information about hidden SMB folder shares.

In Computer Management, you can view the shared folders on a local or remote computer by following these steps:

1. You're connected to the local computer by default. If you want to connect to a remote computer, press and hold or right-click the Computer Management node and then tap or click Connect To Another Computer. Choose Another Computer, type the name or IP address of the computer you want to connect to, and then tap or click OK.

2. In the console tree, expand System Tools, expand Shared Folders, and then select Shares. The current shares on the system are displayed, as shown in Figure 3-2.

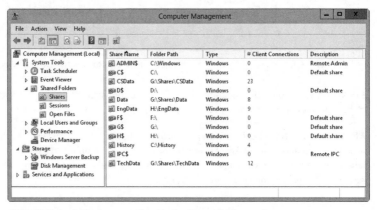

FIGURE 3-2 Available shares are listed in the Shared Folders node.

3. The columns for the Shares node provide the following information:

   - **Share Name** Name of the shared folder.
   - **Folder Path** Complete path to the folder on the local system.
   - **Type** What kind of computers can use the share. This typically shows as Windows because SMB shares are for Windows-based computers.
   - **# Client Connections** Number of clients currently accessing the share.
   - **Description** Description of the share.

In Server Manager, you can view the shared folders on a local or remote computer by following these steps:

1. Select the File And Storage Services node, and then select the related Shares subnode.

2. As Figure 3-3 shows, the Shares subnode provides information about shares on each file server that has been added for management. The columns for the Shares subnode provide the following information:

   - **Share** Name of the shared folder.
   - **Local Path** Complete path to the folder on the local system.
   - **Protocol** What protocol the share uses, either SMB or NFS.
   - **Cluster Role** If the server sharing the folder is part of a cluster, the cluster role is shown here. Otherwise, the cluster role is listed as None.

FIGURE 3-3 Tap or click Shares in the main pane (on the left) to view the available shares.

3. When you tap or click a share in the Shares pane, information about the related volume is displayed in the Volume pane.

REAL WORLD NFS is the file sharing protocol used by UNIX-based systems, which includes computers running Apple OS X. As discussed in "Configuring NFS sharing" later in this chapter, you can enable support for NFS by installing the Server For NFS role service as part of the file server configuration.

Creating shared folders in Computer Management

Windows Server 2012 R2 provides several ways to share folders. You can share local folders by using File Explorer, and you can share local and remote folders by using Computer Management or Server Manager.

When you create a share with Computer Management, you can configure its share permissions and offline settings. When you create a share with Server Manager, you can provision all aspects of sharing, including NTFS permissions, encrypted data access, offline settings for caching, and share permissions. Typically, you create shares on NTFS volumes because NTFS offers the most robust solution.

In Computer Management, you share a folder by following these steps:

1. If necessary, connect to a remote computer. In the console tree, expand System Tools, expand Shared Folders, and then select Shares. The current shares on the system are displayed.

2. Press and hold or right-click Shares, and then tap or click New Share. This starts the Create A Shared Folder Wizard. Tap or click Next.

3. In the Folder Path text box, enter the local file path to the folder you want to share. The file path must be exact, such as **C:\EntData\Documents**. If you don't know the full path, tap or click Browse, use the Browse For Folder dialog box to find the folder you want to share, and then tap or click OK. Tap or click Next.

TIP If the file path you specified doesn't exist, the wizard can create it for you. Tap or click Yes when prompted to create the necessary folder or folders.

4. In the Share Name text box, enter a name for the share, as shown in Figure 3-4. This is the name of the folder to which users will connect. Share names must be unique for each system.

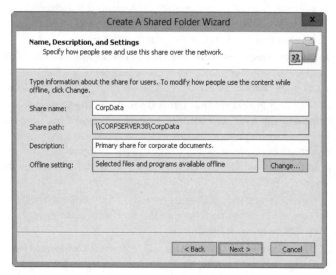

FIGURE 3-4 Use the Create A Shared Folder Wizard to configure the essential share properties, including name, description, and offline resource usage.

TIP If you want to hide a share from users (which means that they won't be able to view the shared resource when they try to browse to it in File Explorer or at the command line), enter a dollar sign ($) as the last character of the shared resource name. For example, you could create a share called PrivEngData$, which would be hidden from File Explorer, NET VIEW, and other similar utilities. Users can still connect to the share and access its data if they've been granted access permission and they know the share's name. Note that the $ must be typed as part of the share name when mapping to the shared resource.

5. If you want to, enter a description of the share in the Description text box. When you view shares on a particular computer, the description is displayed in Computer Management.

6. By default, the share is configured so that only files and programs that users specify are available for offline use. Typically, this is the option you want to use because this option also enables users to take advantage of the new Always Offline feature. If you want to use different offline file settings, tap or click Change, select the appropriate options in the Offline Settings dialog

box, and then tap or click OK. The offline availability settings available include the following:

- **Only The Files And Programs That Users Specify Are Available Offline**   Select this option if you want client computers to cache only the files and programs that users specify for offline use. Optionally, if the BranchCache For Network Files role service is installed on the file server, select Enable BranchCache to enable computers in a branch office to cache files that are downloaded from the shared folder, and then securely share the files to other computers in the branch office.

- **No Files Or Programs From The Shared Folder Are Available Offline**   Select this option if you don't want cached copies of the files and programs in the share to be available on client computers for offline use.

- **All Files And Programs That Users Open From The Shared Folder Are Automatically Available Offline**   Select this option if you want client computers to automatically cache all files and programs that users open from the share. Optionally, select Optimize For Performance to run cached program files from the local cache instead of the shared folder on the server.

7. Tap or click Next, and then set basic permissions for the share. You'll find helpful pointers in "Managing share permissions" later in the chapter. The available options are as follows:

- **All Users Have Read-Only Access**   Gives users access to view files and read data. They can't create, modify, or delete files and folders.

- **Administrators Have Full Access; Other Users Have Read-Only Access** Gives administrators complete control over the share. Full access allows administrators to create, modify, and delete files and folders. On an NTFS volume or partition, it also gives administrators the right to change permissions and to take ownership of files and folders. Other users can view files and read data; however, they can't create, modify, or delete files and folders.

- **Administrators Have Full Access; Other Users Have No Access**   Gives administrators complete control over the share, but prevents other users from accessing the share.

- **Customize Permissions**   Allows you to configure access for specific users and groups, which is usually the best technique to use. Setting share permissions is discussed fully in "Managing share permissions."

8. When you tap or click Finish, the wizard creates the share and displays a status report, which should state "Sharing Was Successful." If an error is displayed instead, note the error and take corrective action as appropriate before repeating this procedure to create the share. Tap or click Finish.

Individual folders can have multiple shares. Each share can have a different name and a different set of access permissions. To create additional shares on an existing share, just follow the preceding steps for creating a share with these changes:

- In step 4, when you name the share, make sure that you use a different name.

- In step 5, when you add a description for the share, use a description that explains what the share is used for and how it's different from the other shares for the same folder.

Creating shared folders in Server Manager

In Server Manager, you share a folder by following these steps:

1. The Shares subnode of the File And Storage Services node shows existing shares for file servers that have been added for management. In the Shares pane, tap or click Tasks, and then tap or click New Share to start the New Share Wizard.

2. Choose one of the available file share profiles, and then tap or click Next. The New Share Wizard has the following file share profiles:

   - **SMB Share—Quick**   A basic profile for creating SMB file shares that allows you to configure the settings and permissions of the shares.

   - **SMB Share—Advanced**   An advanced profile for creating SMB file shares that allows you to configure the settings, permissions, management properties, and NTFS quota profile (if applicable) of the shares.

   - **SMB Share—Applications**   A custom profile for creating SMB file shares with settings appropriate for Hyper-V, certain databases, and other server applications. It's essentially the same as the quick profile, but it doesn't allow you to enable access-based enumeration or offline caching.

   NOTE   If you are using the Server For NFS role service, options are available for creating NFS shares as well.

   REAL WORLD   SMB 3.0 includes enhancements for server-based applications. These enhancements improve performance for small random reads and writes, which are common with server-based applications, such as Microsoft SQL Server OLTP. With SMB 3.0, packets use large Maximum Transmission Units (MTUs) as well, which enhance performance for large, sequential data transfers, such as those used for deploying and copying virtual hard disks (VHDs) over the network, database backup and restore over the network, and SQL Server data warehouse transactions over the network.

3. On the Select The Server And Path For This Share page, select the server and volume on which you want the share to be created. Only file servers you've added for management are available. When you are ready to continue, tap or click Next.

   By default, Server Manager creates the file share as a new folder in the \Shares directory on the selected volume. To override this, choose the Type A Custom Path option, and then either enter the share path, such as C:\Data, or click Browse to use the Select Folder dialog box to select the share path.

4. On the Specify Share Name page, enter a name for the share, as shown in Figure 3-5. This is the name of the folder to which users will connect. Share names must be unique for each system.

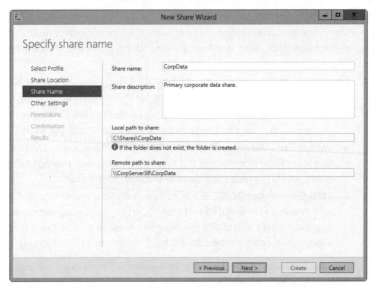

FIGURE 3-5 Set the name and description for the share.

5. If you want to, enter a description of the share in the Description text box. When you view shares on a particular computer, the description is displayed in Computer Management.

6. Note the local and remote paths to the share. These paths are set based on the share location and share name you specified. When you are ready to continue, tap or click Next.

7. On the Configure Share Settings page, use the following options to configure the way the share is used:

   - **Enable Access-Based Enumeration** Configures permissions so that when users browse the folder, only files and folders a user has been granted at least Read access to are displayed. If a user doesn't have at least Read (or equivalent) permission for a file or folder within the shared folder, that file or folder is hidden from view. (This option is dimmed if you are creating an SMB share optimized for applications.)

- **Allow Caching Of Share** Configures the share to cache only the files and programs that users specify for offline use. Although you can later edit the share properties and change the offline files' availability settings, you typically want to select this option because it allows users to take advantage of the new Always Offline feature. Optionally, if the Branch-Cache For Network Files role service is installed on the file server, select Enable BranchCache to enable computers in a branch office to cache files that are downloaded from the shared folder and then securely share the files to other computers in the branch office. (This option is dimmed if you are creating an SMB share optimized for applications.)

- **Encrypt Data Access** Configures the share to use SMB encryption, which protects file data from eavesdropping while being transferred over the network. This option is useful on untrusted networks.

8. On the Specify Permissions To Control Access page, the default permissions assigned to the share are listed. By default, the special group Everyone is granted the Full Control share permission and the underlying folder permissions are as listed. To change share, folder, or both permissions, tap or click Customize Permissions, and then use the Advanced Security Settings dialog box to configure the required permissions. Setting share permissions is discussed fully in "Managing share permissions" later in this chapter. Setting folder permissions is discussed fully in "Understanding file and folder permissions" in Chapter 4 "Data security and auditing."

NOTE If the share will be used for Hyper-V, you might need to enable constrained delegation for remote management of the Hyper-V host.

9. If you are using the advanced profile, optionally set the folder management properties, and then tap or click Next. These properties specify the purpose of the folder and the type of data stored in it so that data management policies, such as classification rules, can then use these properties.

10. If you are using the advanced profile, optionally apply a quota based on a template to the folder, and then tap or click Next. You can select only quota templates that have already been created. For more information, see "Managing disk quota templates" in Chapter 4.

11. On the Confirm Selections page, review your selections. When you tap or click Create, the wizard creates the share, configures it, and sets permissions. The status should state, "The share was successfully created." If an error is displayed instead, note the error and take corrective action as appropriate before repeating this procedure to create the share. Tap or click Close.

Changing shared folder settings

When you create a share, you can configure many basic and advanced settings, including those for access-based enumeration, encrypted data access, offline settings for caching, and management properties. In Server Manager, you can modify these settings by following these steps:

1. The Shares subnode of the File And Storage Services node shows existing shares for file servers that have been added for management. Press and hold or right-click the share with which you want to work, and then tap or click Properties.

2. In the Properties dialog box, shown in Figure 3-6, you have several options panels that can be accessed by using controls in the left pane. You can expand the panels one by one or tap or click Show All to expand all the panels at the same time.

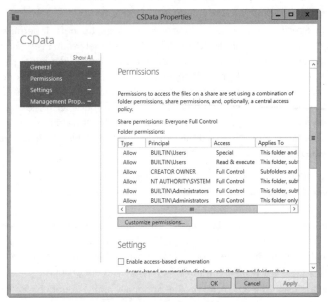

FIGURE 3-6 Modify share settings by using the options provided.

3. Use the options provided to modify the settings as necessary, and then tap or click OK. The options available are the same whether you use the basic, advanced, or applications profile to create the shared folder.

TIP If you're creating a share for general use and general access, you can publish the shared resource in Active Directory. Publishing the resource in Active Directory makes finding the share easier for users; however, this option is not available in Server Manager. To publish a share in Active Directory, press and hold or right-click the share in Computer Management, and then tap or click Properties. On the Publish tab, select the Publish This Share In Active Directory check box, add an optional description and owner information, and then tap or click OK.

Managing share permissions

Share permissions set the maximum allowable actions available within a shared folder. By default, when you create a share, everyone with access to the network has Read access to the share's contents. This is an important security change—in previous editions of Windows Server, the default permission was Full Control.

With NTFS and ReFS volumes, you can use file and folder permissions and ownership, in addition to share permissions, to further constrain actions within the share. With FAT volumes, share permissions control only access.

Understanding the various share permissions

From the most restrictive to the least restrictive, the share permissions available are as follows:

- **No Access**   No permissions are granted for the share.
- **Read**   Users can do the following:
  - View file and subfolder names
  - Access the subfolders in the share
  - Read file data and attributes
  - Run program files
- **Change**   Users have Read permission and the ability to do the following:
  - Create files and subfolders
  - Modify files
  - Change attributes on files and subfolders
  - Delete files and subfolders
- **Full Control**   Users have Read and Change permissions, in addition to the following capabilities on NTFS volumes:
  - Change file and folder permissions
  - Take ownership of files and folders

You can assign share permissions to users and groups. You can even assign permissions to implicit groups. For details on implicit groups, see Chapter 9, "Creating user and group accounts" In Windows Server 2012 R2 Pocket Consultant: Essentials & Configuration.

Viewing and configuring share permissions

You can view and configure share permissions in Computer Management or Server Manager. To view and configure share permissions in Computer Management, follow these steps:

1. In Computer Management, connect to the computer on which the share is created. In the console tree, expand System Tools, expand Shared Folders, and then select Shares.

2. Press and hold or right-click the share with which you want to work, and then tap or click Properties.

3. In the Properties dialog box, tap or click the Share Permissions tab, shown in Figure 3-7. You can now view the users and groups that have access to the share and the type of access they have.

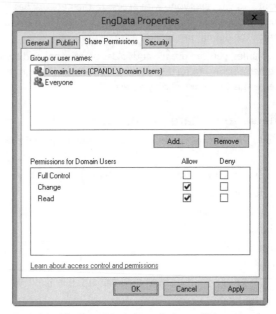

FIGURE 3-7 The Share Permissions tab shows which users and groups have access to the share and what type of access they have.

4. Users or groups that already have access to the share are listed in the Group Or User Names list. You can remove permissions for these users and groups by selecting the user or group you want to remove, and then tapping or clicking Remove. You can change permissions for these users and groups by doing the following:

a. Select the user or group you want to change.

b. Allow or deny access permissions in the Permissions list box.

5. To add permissions for another user or group, tap or click Add. This opens the Select Users, Computers, Service Accounts, Or Groups dialog box, shown in Figure 3-8.

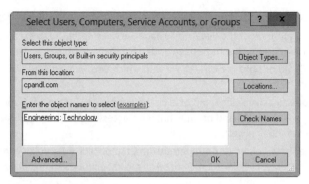

FIGURE 3-8 Add users and groups to the share.

6. Enter the name of a user, computer, or group in the current domain, and then tap or click Check Names. This produces one of the following results:

   ■ If a single match is found, the dialog box is automatically updated and the entry is underlined.

   ■ If no matches are found, you either entered an incorrect name part or you're working with an incorrect location. Modify the name and try again, or tap or click Locations to select a new location.

   ■ If multiple matches are found, select the name or names you want to use, and then tap or click OK. To assign permissions to other users, computers, or groups, enter a semicolon (;) and then repeat this step.

   NOTE The Locations button enables you to access account names in other domains. Tap or click Locations to find a list of the current domains, trusted domains, and other resources you can access. Because of the transitive trusts in Windows Server, you can usually access all the domains in the domain tree or forest.

7. Tap or click OK. The users and groups are added to the Group Or User Names list for the share.

8. Configure access permissions for each user, computer, and group by selecting an account name and then allowing or denying access permissions. Keep in mind that you're setting the maximum allowable permissions for a particular account.

9. Tap or click OK. To assign additional security permissions for NTFS, see "File and folder permissions" in Chapter 4.

IMPORTANT Keep in mind that you can select the opposite permission to override an inherited permission. Note also that Deny typically overrides Allow, so if you explicitly deny permission to a user or group for a child folder or file, this permission should be denied to that user or group of users.

To view and configure share permissions in Server Manager, follow these steps:

1. The Shares subnode of the File And Storage Services node shows existing shares for file servers that have been added for management.

2. Press and hold or right-click the share with which you want to work, and then tap or click Properties.

3. In the Properties dialog box, tap or click the Permissions in the left pane. You can now view the users and groups that have access to the share and the type of access they have.

4. To change share, folder, or both permissions, tap or click Customize Permissions. Next, select the Share tab in the Advanced Security Settings dialog box, as shown in Figure 3-9.

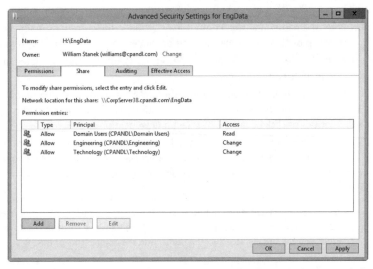

FIGURE 3-9 The Share tab shows which users and groups have access to the share and what type of access they have.

5. Users or groups that already have access to the share are listed in the Permission Entries list. You can remove permissions for these users and groups by selecting the user or group you want to remove, and then tapping or clicking Remove. You can change permissions for these users and groups by doing the following:

    a. Select the user or group you want to change, and then select Edit.

    b. Allow or deny access permissions in the Permission Entries list, and then tap or click OK.

6. To add permissions for another user or group, tap or click Add. This opens the Permission Entry dialog box, shown in Figure 3-10.

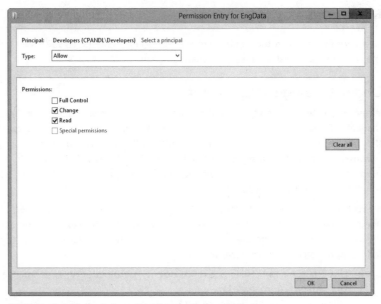

FIGURE 3-10 Add permission entries for a particular user or group.

7. Tap or click Select A Principal to display the Select User, Computer, Service Account Or Group dialog box. Enter the name of a user or a group account. Be sure to reference the user account name rather than the user's full name. Only one name can be entered at a time.

8. Tap or click Check Names. If a single match is found for each entry, the dialog box is automatically updated, and the entry is underlined. Otherwise, you'll get an additional dialog box. If no matches are found, you either entered the name incorrectly or you're working with an incorrect location. Modify the name in the Name Not Found dialog box and try again, or tap or click Locations to select a new location. When multiple matches are found, in the Multiple Names Found dialog box, select the name you want to use, and then tap or click OK.

9. Tap or click OK. The user and group is added as the Principal, and the Permission Entry dialog box is updated to show this.

10. Use the Type list to specify whether you are configuring allowed or denied permissions, and then select the permissions you want to allow or deny.

11. Tap or click OK to return to the Advanced Security Settings dialog box. To assign additional security permissions for NTFS, see "File and folder permissions" in Chapter 4.

Managing existing shares

As an administrator, you often have to manage shared folders. This section covers the common administrative tasks of managing shares.

Understanding special shares

When you install Windows Server, the operating system creates special shares automatically. These shares are known as *administrative shares* and *hidden shares*, and they are designed to help make system administration easier. You can't set access permissions on automatically created special shares; Windows Server assigns access permissions. You can create your own hidden shares by adding the $ symbol as the last character of the share name.

You can delete special shares temporarily if you're certain the shares aren't needed; however, the shares are re-created automatically the next time the operating system starts. To permanently disable the administrative shares, change the following registry values to 0 (zero):

- HKEY_LOCAL_MACHINE\SYSTEM\CurrentControlSet\Services\lanmanserver \parameters\AutoShareServer
- HKEY_LOCAL_MACHINE\SYSTEM\CurrentControlSet\Services\lanmanserver \parameters\AutoShareWks

Which special shares are available depends on your system configuration. Table 3-2 lists special shares you might find and how they're used.

TABLE 3-2 Special shares used by Windows Server 2012 R2

SHARE NAME	DESCRIPTION	USAGE
ADMIN$	A share used during remote administration of a system. It provides access to the operating system %SystemRoot%.	On workstations and servers, administrators and backup operators can access these shares. On domain controllers, server operators also have access.
FAX$	Supports network faxes.	Used by fax clients when sending faxes.
IPC$	Supports named pipes during remote interprocess communications (IPC) access.	Used by programs when performing remote administration and when viewing shared resources.
NETLOGON	Supports the Net Logon service.	Used by the Net Logon service when processing domain logon requests. Everyone has Read access.

SHARE NAME	DESCRIPTION	USAGE
PRINT$	Supports shared printer resources by providing access to printer drivers.	Used by shared printers. Everyone has Read access. Administrators, server operators, and printer operators have Full Control.
SYSVOL	Supports Active Directory.	Used to store data and objects for Active Directory.
Driveletter$	A share that allows administrators to connect to a drive's root folder. These shares are shown as C$, D$, E$, and so on.	On workstations and servers, administrators and backup operators can access these shares. On domain controllers, server operators also have access.

Connecting to special shares

Most special shares end with the $ symbol. Although these shares aren't displayed in File Explorer, administrators and certain operators can connect to them (except for NETLOGON and SYSVOL). If your current logon account has appropriate permissions, you can connect directly to a special share or any standard share by typing the UNC path for the share in File Explorer's address box. The basic syntax is:

*ServerName**ShareName*

ServerName is the DNS name or IP address of the server and *ShareName* is the name of the share. In the following example, you connect to the D$ share on CorpServer25:

\\CorpServer25\D$

If you always want the drive to be listed as a network location in This PC or need to specify credentials, you can connect to a special share by following these steps:

1. When you open File Explorer, the This PC node should be opened by default. If you have an open Explorer window and This PC is not the selected node, select the leftmost option button in the address list, and then select This PC.

2. Next, tap or click the Map Network Drive button on the Computer panel, and then tap or click Map Network Drive. This displays the Map Network Drive dialog box, shown in Figure 3-11.

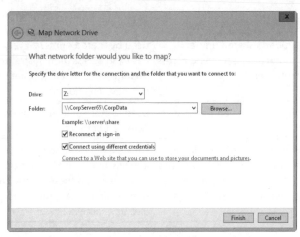

FIGURE 3-11 Connect to special shares by mapping them with the Map Network Drive dialog box.

3. In the Drive list, select a free drive letter. This drive letter is used to access the special share.

4. In the Folder text box, enter the Universal Naming Convention (UNC) path to the share. For example, to access the C$ share on a server called Twiddle, you would use the path \\TWIDDLE\C$.

5. The Reconnect At Sign-In check box is selected automatically to ensure that the network drive is connected each time you log on. If you need to access the share only during the current logon session, clear this check box.

6. If you need to connect to the share using different user credentials, select the Connect Using Different Credentials check box.

7. Tap or click Finish. If you are connecting using different credentials, enter the user name and password when prompted. Enter the user name in Domain \Username format, such as **Cpandl\Williams**. Before tapping or clicking OK, select Remember My Credentials if you want the credentials to be saved. Otherwise, you'll need to provide credentials in the future.

After you connect to a special share, you can access it as you would any other drive. Because special shares are protected, you don't have to worry about ordinary users accessing these shares. The first time you connect to the share, you might be prompted for a user name and password. If you are prompted, provide that information.

Viewing user and computer sessions

You can use Computer Management to track all connections to shared resources on a Windows Server 2012 R2 system. Whenever a user or computer connects to a shared resource, Windows Server 2012 R2 lists a connection in the Sessions node.

To view connections to shared resources, enter **net session** at an elevated command prompt or Get-SMBSession at an elevated Windows PowerShell prompt. You also can follow these steps:

1. In Computer Management, connect to the computer on which you created the shared resource.

2. In the console tree, expand System Tools, expand Shared Folders, and then select Sessions. You can now view connections to shares for users and computers.

The columns for the Sessions node provide the following important information about user and computer connections:

- **User** The names of users or computers connected to shared resources. Computer names are shown with a $ suffix to differentiate them from users.

- **Computer** The name of the computer being used.

- **Type** The type of network connection being used.

- **# Open Files** The number of files with which the user is actively working. For more detailed information, access the Open Files node.

- **Connected Time** The time that has elapsed since the connection was established.

- **Idle Time** The time that has elapsed since the connection was last used.

- **Guest** Whether the user is logged on as a guest.

As shown in the following example, the output of Get-SMBSession provides the session ID, client computer name, client user name and the number of open files for each session:

```
SessionId     ClientComputerName    ClientUserName      NumOpens
---------     ------------------    --------------      --------
601295421497  10.0.0.60             CPANDL\williams     2
```

Managing sessions and shares

Managing sessions and shares is a common administrative task. Before you shut down a server or an application running on a server, you might want to disconnect users from shared resources. You might also need to disconnect users when you plan to change access permissions or delete a share entirely. Another reason to disconnect users is to break locks on files. You disconnect users from shared resources by ending the related user sessions.

ENDING INDIVIDUAL SESSIONS

To disconnect individual users from shared resources, enter **net session** *computername* **/delete** at an elevated command prompt or Close-SMBSession at –Computer Name *computername* an elevated Windows PowerShell prompt. In both instances, *computername* is the DNS name or IP address of computer from which the session originates.

You also can disconnect users by following these steps:

1. In Computer Management, connect to the computer on which you created the share.

2. In the console tree, expand System Tools, expand Shared Folders, and then select Sessions.

3. Press and hold or right-click the user sessions you want to end, and then tap or click Close Session.

4. Tap or click Yes to confirm the action.

ENDING ALL SESSIONS

To disconnect all users from shared resources, follow these steps:

1. In Computer Management, connect to the computer on which you created the share.

2. In the console tree, expand System Tools, expand Shared Folders, and then press and hold or right-click Sessions.

3. Tap or click Disconnect All Sessions, and then tap or click Yes to confirm the action.

NOTE Keep in mind that you're disconnecting users from shared resources, not from the domain. You can use only logon hours and Group Policy to force users to log off after they've logged on to the domain. Thus, disconnecting users doesn't log them off the network. It just disconnects them from the shared resource.

To disconnect individual users from shared resources, enter **net session ** computername **/delete** at an elevated command prompt or Close-SMBSession at –ComputerName computername an elevated Windows PowerShell prompt. In both instances, computername is the DNS name or IP address of computer from which the session originates.

You also can use Windows PowerShell to disconnect all users from a shared resource. The key here is to ensure you only close the sessions you want to close. Consider the following example:

```
ForEach-Object ($Session in (Get-SMBSession)) {
Close-SMBSession -force}
```

This example uses a ForEach loop to get all active SMB sessions and then close each SMB session in turn. Thus, if you enter this example at an elevated Windows PowerShell prompt, you will disconnect all users from all shared resources.

To close all connections only for a specific share, you must create a ForEach loop that only examines the connections for that share, such as:

```
ForEach-Object ($Session in (Get-SMBShare CorpData |
Get-SMBSession)) {Close-SMBSession -force}
```

This example uses a ForEach loop to get all active SMB sessions for the CorpData share and then close each of those sessions in turn. Thus, if you enter this example at an elevated Windows PowerShell prompt, you only disconnect users from the Corp-Data share.

Managing open resources

Any time users connect to shares, the individual file and object resources they are working with are displayed in the Open Files node. The Open Files node might show the files the user has open but isn't currently editing.

You can access the Open Files node by following these steps:

1. In Computer Management, connect to the computer on which you created the share.

2. In the console tree, expand System Tools, expand Shared Folders, and then select Open Files. This displays the Open Files node, which provides the following information about resource usage:

   - **Open File**   The file or folder path to the open file on the local system. The path might also be a named pipe, such as \PIPE\spools, which is used for printer spooling.
   - **Accessed By**   The name of the user accessing the file.
   - **Type**   The type of network connection being used.
   - **# Locks**   The number of locks on the resource.
   - **Open Mode**   The access mode used when the resource was opened, such as read, write, or write+read.

You also can use Get-SMBOpenFile to list open files. As shown in the following example, Get-SMBOpenFile provides the file ID, session ID, path, share relative path, client computer name, and client user name for each open file:

```
FileId       SessionId    Path  ShareRelativePath ClientComputerName ClientUserN
------       ---------    ----  ----------------- ------------------ ------------
601295424973 601295421497 C:\PrimaryData\   10.0.0.60        CPANDL\williams
601295425045 601295421577 C:\Windows\SYSVOL cpan... 10.0.0.60 CPANDL\
CORPPC29$
```

CLOSING AN OPEN FILE

To close an open file on a computer's shares, follow these steps:

1. In Computer Management, connect to the computer with which you want to work.

2. In the console tree, expand System Tools, expand Shared Folders, and then select Open Files.

3. Press and hold or right-click the open file you want to close, and then tap or click Close Open File.

4. Tap or click Yes to confirm the action.

You also can use Close-SMBOpenFile to close open files. When you close a file, you use the –FileID parameter to specify the identifier for the file to close, such as:

```
Close-SMBOpenFile –FileID 601295424973
```

Add the –Force parameter to force close the file if needed. However, if the file has been modified by a user, any changes to the file could be lost.

CLOSING ALL OPEN FILES

To close all open files on a computer's shares, follow these steps:

1. In Computer Management, connect to the computer on which the share is created.

2. In the console tree, expand System Tools, expand Shared Folders, and then press and hold or right-click Open Files.

3. Tap or click Disconnect All Open Files, and then tap or click Yes to confirm the action.

You also can use Windows PowerShell to close all open files on a computer's share. The key here is to ensure that you only close the files you want to close. Consider the following example:

```
ForEach-Object ($Session in (Get-SMBOpenFile)) {
Close-SMBOpenFile –force}
```

This example uses a ForEach loop to get all open SMB files, and then close each SMB file in turn. Thus, if you enter this example at an elevated Windows PowerShell prompt, you will close all open files for all shared resources.

To close open files on a specific share, you must create a ForEach loop that only examines the open files for that share, such as:

```
ForEach-Object ($Session in (Get-SMBShare CorpData |
Get-SMBOpenFile)) {Close-SMBOpenFile –force}
```

This example uses a ForEach loop to get all open SMB files for the CorpData share and then close each of those files in turn. Thus, if you enter this example at an elevated Windows PowerShell prompt, you only close open files for the CorpData share.

Stopping file and folder sharing

To stop sharing a folder, follow these steps:

1. Do one of the following:

   - In Server Manager, select the share you want to manage on the Shares subnode of the File And Storage Services node.

   - In Computer Management, connect to the computer on which you created the share, and then access the Shares node.

2. Press and hold or right-click the share you want to remove, tap or click Stop Sharing, and then tap or click Yes to confirm the action.

CAUTION You should never delete a folder containing shares without first stopping the shares. If you fail to stop the shares, Windows Server 2012 R2 attempts to reestablish the shares the next time the computer is started, and the resulting error is logged in the system event log.

Configuring NFS sharing

As discussed in Chapter 1, "Managing file systems and drives," you can install Server For NFS as a role service on a file server. Server For NFS provides a file sharing solution for enterprises with mixed Windows, OS X, and UNIX environments, allowing users to transfer files between Windows Server 2012 R2, OS X, and UNIX operating systems by using the NFS protocol.

You can configure NFS sharing for local folders on NTFS volumes by using File Explorer. You can also configure NFS sharing of local and remote folders on NTFS volumes by using Server Manager. In File Explorer, follow these steps to enable and configure NFS sharing:

1. Press and hold or right-click the share you want to manage, and then tap or click Properties to display a Properties dialog box for the share.

2. On the NFS Sharing tab, tap or click Manage NFS Sharing.

3. In the NFS Advanced Sharing dialog box, select the Share This Folder check box, as shown in Figure 3-12.

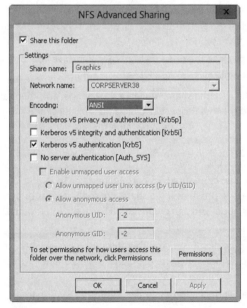

FIGURE 3-12 You can use NFS sharing to share resources between Windows and UNIX computers.

4. In the Share Name text box, enter a name for the share. This is the name of the folder to which UNIX users will connect. NFS share names must be unique for each system and can be the same as those used for standard file sharing.

5. ANSI is the default encoding for text associated with directory listings and file names. If your UNIX computers use a different default encoding, you can choose that encoding in the Encoding list.

6. UNIX computers use Kerberos v5 authentication by default. Typically, you want to allow Kerberos integrity and authentication in addition to standard Kerberos authentication. Select the check boxes for the authentication mechanisms you want to use. Clear the check boxes for those you don't want to use.

7. The share can be configured so that no server authentication is required. If you want to require server authentication, select the No Server Authentication check box, and then choose additional options as appropriate. Unmapped user access can be allowed and enabled. If you want to allow anonymous access to the NFS share, select the Allow Anonymous Access option, and then enter the anonymous user UID and anonymous group GID.

8. For UNIX computers, you configure access primarily based on the computer names (also referred to as *host names*). By default, no UNIX computers have access to the NFS share. If you want to grant read-only or read/write permissions, tap or click Permissions, set the permissions you want to use in the NFS Share Permissions dialog box, and then tap or click OK. You can configure no access, read-only access, or read/write access by client computer name and client computer groups.

9. Tap or click OK twice to close the open dialog boxes and save your settings.

In File Explorer, you can disable NFS sharing by following these steps:

1. Press and hold or right-click the share you want to manage, and then tap or click Properties. This displays a Properties dialog box for the share.

2. On the NFS Sharing tab, tap or click Manage NFS Sharing.

3. In the NFS Advanced Sharing dialog box, clear the Share This Folder check box, and then tap or click OK twice.

With Server Manager, you can configure NFS permissions as part of the initial share configuration when you are provisioning a share. On the Shares subnode of the File And Storage Services node, you can create an NFS share by following these steps:

1. In the Shares pane, tap or click Tasks, and then tap or click New Share to start the New Share Wizard. Choose NFS Share—Quick or NFS Share—Advanced as the share profile, and then tap or click Next.

2. Specify the share name and location as you would for an SMB share.

3. On the Specify Authentication Methods page, configure Kerberos v5 Authentication and No Server Authentication. The options provided are similar to those discussed previously in this section.

4. On the Specify Share Permissions page, configure access for UNIX hosts. Hosts can be set for no access, read-only access, or read/write access to the share.

5. On the Specify Permissions To Control Access, optionally set NTFS permissions for the share.

6. On the Confirm Selections page, review your selections. When you tap or click Create, the wizard creates the share, configures it, and sets permissions. The status should state, "The share was successfully created." If an error is displayed instead, note the error and take corrective action. However, because typical errors relate to configuring host access, you probably won't need to repeat this procedure to create the share. Instead, you might need to modify only the share permissions. Tap or click Close.

Using shadow copies

Any time your organization uses shared folders, you should consider creating shadow copies of these shared folders as well. Shadow copies are point-in-time backups of data files that users can access directly in shared folders. These point-in-time backups can save you and the other administrators in your organization a lot of work, especially if you routinely have to retrieve lost, overwritten, or corrupted data files from backups. The usual procedure for retrieving shadow copies is to use the Previous Versions or Shadow Copy client. Windows Server 2012 R2 includes a feature enhancement that enables you to revert an entire (nonsystem) volume to a previous shadow copy state.

Understanding shadow copies

You can create shadow copies only on NTFS volumes. You use the Shadow Copy feature to create automatic backups of the files in shared folders on a per-volume basis. For example, on a file server that has three NTFS volumes, each containing shared folders, you need to configure this feature for each volume separately.

If you enable this feature in its default configuration, shadow copies are created twice each weekday (Monday–Friday) at 7:00 A.M. and 12:00 P.M. You need at least 100 megabytes (MB) of free space to create the first shadow copy on a volume. The total disk space used beyond this depends on the amount of data in the volume's shared folders. You can restrict the total amount of disk space used by Shadow Copy by setting the allowable maximum size of the point-in-time backups.

You configure and view current Shadow Copy settings on the Shadow Copies tab of the disk's Properties dialog box. In File Explorer or Computer Management, press and hold or right-click the icon for the disk with which you want to work, tap or click Properties, and then tap or click the Shadow Copies tab. The Select A Volume panel shows the following:

- **Volume** The volume label of NTFS volumes on the selected disk drive
- **Next Run Time** The status of Shadow Copy as Disabled, or the next time a shadow copy of the volume will be created
- **Shares** The number of shared folders on the volume
- **Used** The amount of disk space used by Shadow Copy

Individual shadow copies of the currently selected volume are listed in the Shadow Copies Of Selected Volume panel by date and time.

Creating shadow copies

To create a shadow copy on an NTFS volume with shared folders, follow these steps:

1. Open Computer Management. If necessary, connect to a remote computer.

2. In the console tree, expand Storage, and then select Disk Management. The volumes configured on the selected computer are displayed in the details pane.

3. Press and hold or right-click Disk Management, point to All Tasks, and then tap or click Configure Shadow Copies.

4. On the Shadow Copies tab, select the volume with which you want to work in the Select A Volume list.

5. Tap or click Settings to configure the maximum size of all shadow copies for this volume and to change the default schedule. Tap or click OK.

6. After you configure the volume for shadow copying, tap or click Enable if necessary. When prompted to confirm this action, tap or click Yes. Enabling shadow copying creates the first shadow copy and sets the schedule for later shadow copies.

NOTE If you create a run schedule when configuring the Shadow Copy settings, shadow copying is enabled automatically for the volume when you tap or click OK to close the Settings dialog box. However, the first shadow copy won't be created until the next scheduled run time. If you want to create a shadow copy of the volume now, select the volume and then tap or click Create Now.

Restoring a shadow copy

Users working on client computers access shadow copies of individual shared folders by using the Previous Versions or Shadow Copy client. The best way to access shadow copies on a client computer is to follow these steps:

1. In File Explorer, press and hold or right-click the share for which you want to access previous file versions, tap or click Properties, and then tap or click the Previous Versions tab.

2. On the Previous Versions tab, select the folder version with which you want to work. Each folder has a date and time stamp. Tap or click the button corresponding to the action you want to perform:

   - Tap or click Open to open the shadow copy in File Explorer.

   - Tap or click Copy to display the Copy Items dialog box, which lets you copy the snapshot image of the folder to the location you specify.

   - Tap or click Restore to roll back the shared folder to its state at the time of the snapshot image you selected.

Reverting an entire volume to a previous shadow copy

Windows Server 2012 R2 features a shadow copy enhancement that enables you to revert an entire volume to the state it was in when a particular shadow copy was created. Because volumes containing operating system files can't be reverted, the volume you want to revert must not be a system volume. The same goes for volumes on a cluster shared disk.

To revert an entire volume to a previous state, follow these steps:

1. Open Computer Management. If necessary, connect to a remote computer.
2. In the console tree, expand Storage. Press and hold or right-click Disk Management, point to All Tasks, and then tap or click Configure Shadow Copies.
3. On the Shadow Copies tab, select the volume with which you want to work in the Select A Volume list.
4. Individual shadow copies of the currently selected volume are listed by date and time in the Shadow Copies Of Selected Volume panel. Select the shadow copy with the date and time stamp to which you want to revert, and then tap or click Revert.
5. To confirm this action, select the Check Here If You Want To Revert This Volume check box, and then tap or click Revert Now. Tap or click OK to close the Shadow Copies dialog box.

Deleting shadow copies

Each point-in-time backup is maintained separately. You can delete individual shadow copies of a volume as necessary, and this recovers the disk space used by the shadow copies.

To delete a shadow copy, follow these steps:

1. Open Computer Management. If necessary, connect to a remote computer.
2. In the console tree, expand Storage. Press and hold or right-click Disk Management, point to All Tasks, and then tap or click Configure Shadow Copies.
3. On the Shadow Copies tab, select the volume with which you want to work in the Select A Volume list.
4. Individual shadow copies of the currently selected volume are listed by date and time in the Shadow Copies Of Selected Volume panel. Select the shadow copy you want to delete, and then tap or click Delete Now. Tap or click Yes to confirm the action.

Disabling shadow copies

If you no longer want to maintain shadow copies of a volume, you can disable the Shadow Copy feature. Disabling this feature turns off the scheduling of automated point-in-time backups and removes any existing shadow copies.

To disable shadow copies of a volume, follow these steps:

1. Open Computer Management. If necessary, connect to a remote computer.

2. In the console tree, expand Storage. Press and hold or right-click Disk Management, point to All Tasks, and then tap or click Configure Shadow Copies.

3. On the Shadow Copies tab, select the volume with which you want to work in the Select A Volume list, and then tap or click Disable.

4. When prompted, confirm the action by tapping or clicking Yes. Tap or click OK to close the Shadow Copies dialog box.

Connecting to network drives

Users can connect to a network drive and to shared resources available on the network. This connection is shown as a network drive that users can access like any other drive on their systems.

> **NOTE** When users connect to network drives, they're subject not only to the permissions set for the shared resources, but also to Windows Server 2012 R2 file and folder permissions. Differences in these permission sets are usually the reason users might not be able to access a particular file or subfolder within the network drive.

Mapping a network drive

In Windows Server 2012 R2, you connect to a network drive by mapping to it using NET USE and New-PsDrive. The syntax for NET USE is the following:

```
net use DeviceName \\ComputerName\ShareName
```

DeviceName specifies the drive letter or an asterisk (*) to use the next available drive letter, and *ComputerName**ShareName* is the UNC path to the share, such as either of the following:

```
net use g: \\ROMEO\DOCS
```

or

```
net use * \\ROMEO\DOCS
```

> **NOTE** To ensure that the mapped drive is available each time the user logs on, make the mapping persistent by adding the */Persistent:Yes* option.

The syntax for New-PsDrive is:

```
New-PsDrive -Name DriveLetter -Root \\ServerName\ShareName
-PsProvider FileSystem
```

DriveLetter is the drive letter to use and *ServerName* is the DNS name or IP address of the server hosting the share and *ShareName* is the name of the share, such as:

```
New-PsDrive -Name g -Root \\CorpServer21\CorpData
-PsProvider FileSystem
```

NOTE To ensure that the mapped drive is available each time the user logs on, add the –Persist parameter.

If the client computer is running Windows 8.1, you can map network drives by completing the following steps:

1. When you open File Explorer, the This PC node should be opened by default. If you have an open Explorer window and This PC is not the selected node, select the leftmost option button in the address list, and then select This PC.

2. Next, tap or click the Map Network Drive button in the Computer panel, and then tap or click Map Network Drive.

3. Use the Drive list to select a free drive letter to use, and then tap or click the Browse button to the right of the Folder list. In the Browse For Folder dialog box, expand the network folders until you can select the name of the workgroup or the domain with which you want to work.

4. When you expand the name of a computer in a workgroup or a domain, you'll get a list of shared folders. Select the shared folder with which you want to work, and then tap or click OK.

5. Select Reconnect At Logon if you want Windows to connect to the shared folder automatically at the start of each session.

6. Tap or click Finish. If the currently logged-on user doesn't have appropriate access permissions for the share, select Connect Using Different Credentials, and then tap or click Finish. After you tap or click Finish, you can enter the user name and password of the account with which you want to connect to the shared folder. Enter the user name in Domain\UserName format, such as **Cpandl\Williams**. Before tapping or clicking OK, select Remember My Credentials if you want the credentials to be saved. Otherwise, you'll need to provide credentials in the future.

Disconnecting a network drive

In Windows Server 2012 R2, you disconnect a network drive using NET USE and Remove-PsDrive. The syntax for NET USE is:

```
net use DeviceName /delete
```

DeviceName specifies the network drive to remove, such as:

```
net use g: /delete
```

The syntax for Remove-PsDrive is:

```
Remove-PsDrive –Name DriveLetter
```

DriveLetter is the network drive to remove, such as:

```
Remove-PsDrive –Name g
```

NOTE If the network drive has open connections, you can force remove the network drive using –Force parameter.

In File Explorer, you can disconnect a network drive by following these steps:

1. When you open File Explorer, the This PC node should be opened by default. If you have an open Explorer window and This PC is not the selected node, select the leftmost option button in the address list, and then select This PC.

2. Under Network Location, press and hold or right-click the network drive icon, and then tap or click Disconnect.

Configuring synced sharing

Although the standard approach to sharing files requires a computer that is joined and connected to a domain, synced sharing does not. With sync shares, users can use an Internet or corporate network connection to sync data to their devices from folders located on enterprise servers. You implement synced sharing by using Work Folders.

Work Folders is a feature that you can add to servers running Windows Server 2012 R2 or later. Work Folders use a client-server architecture. A Work Folders client is natively integrated into Windows 8.1, and clients for Windows 7, Apple iPad, and other devices are becoming available as well.

Getting started with Work Folders

You deploy Work Folders in the enterprise by performing these procedures:

1. Add the Work Folders role to servers that you want to host sync shares.

2. Use Group Policy to enable discovery of Work Folders.

3. Create sync shares on your sync servers and optionally, enable SMB access to sync shares.

4. Configure clients to access Work Folders.

NOTE Group Policy is discussed in detailed in Chapter 6 "Managing users and computers with Group Policy." For detailed information about configuring Group Policy to enable discovery of Work Folders, see "Automatically configuring Work Folders," in Chapter 6.

Work Folders use a remote web gateway configured as part of the IIS hostable web core. When users access a sync share via a URL provided by an administrator and configured in Group Policy, a user folder is created as a subfolder of the sync share and this subfolder is where the user's data is stored. The folder naming format for the user-specific folder is set when you create a sync share. The folder can be named by using only the user alias portion of the user's logon name or the full logon name in alias@domain format. The format you choose primarily depends on the level of compatibility required. Using the full logon name eliminates potential conflicts when users from different domains have identical user aliases, but this format is not compatible with redirected folders.

To maintain compatibility with redirected folders, you should configure sync folders to use aliases. However, in enterprises with multiple domains, the drawback to this approach is that there could be conflicts between identical user aliases in different domains. Although the automatically configured permissions for a user folder would prevent amyh from the cpandl.com domain from accessing a user folder created for amyh from the pocket-consultant.com domain, the conflict would cause problems. If there was an existing folder for amyh from the cpandl.com domain, the server would not be able to create a user folder for amyh from the pocket-consultant.com.

With Work Folders, you have several important options during initial setup. You can encrypt files in Work Folders on client devices and ensure that the screens on client devices lock automatically and require an access password. Encryption is implemented by using the Encrypting File System (EFS). EFS encrypts files with an enterprise encryption key rather than an encryption key generated by the client device. The enterprise encryption key is specific to the enterprise ID of the user (which by default is the primary SMTP address of the user). Having an enterprise encryption key that is separate from a client's standard encryption key is important to ensure that encrypted personal files and encrypted work files are managed separately.

When files are encrypted, administrators can use a selective wipe to remove enterprise files from a client device. The selective wipe removes the enterprise encryption key and thus renders the work files unreadable. Selective wipe does not affect any encrypted personal files. As the work files remain encrypted, there's no need to actually delete the work files from the client device. That said, you could run Disk Optimizer on the drive where the work files were stored. During optimization, Disk Optimizer should then overwrite the sectors where the work files were stored. Selective wipe only works when you've enabled the encryption option on Work Folders.

Although encryption is one way to protect enterprise data, another way is to con-figure client devices to lock screens and require a password for access. The exact policy enforced requires:

- A minimum password length of 6 characters
- A maximum password retry of 10
- A screen that automatically locks in 15 minutes or less

If you enforce the use of automatic lock screens and passwords, any device that doesn't support these requirements is prevented from connecting to the Work Folder.

By default, sync shares are not available in the same way as standard file shares. Because of this, users can only access sync shares by using the Work Folders client. If you want to make sync shares available to users as standard file shares, you must enable SMB access. After you enable SMB access, users can access files stored in Work Folders by using syncing and by mapping network drives.

When a user makes changes to files in Work Folders, the changes might not be immediately apparent to others using the same Work Folders. For example, if a user deletes a file from a Work Folder by using SMB, other users accessing the Work Folder might still see the file as available. This inconsistency can occur because by default clients only poll the sync server every 10 minutes for SMB changes.

A sync server also uses a Work Folders client to check periodically for changes users have made using SMB; the default polling interval is 5 minutes. When the server identifies changes, the server relays the changes the next time a client syncs. Following this, you can determine that it could take up to 15 minutes for a change made using SMB to fully propagate.

REAL WORLD To minimize support issues related to Work Folders, you'll want to let users know how the technology works. Specifically, you'll want to let users know changes might not be immediately apparent, and they'll need to be patient when waiting for changes to propagate.

You can specify how frequently the server checks for changes made locally on the server or through SMB by using the −MinimumChangeDetectionMins parameter of the Set-SyncServerSetting cmdlet. However, as the server must check the change information for each file stored in the sync share, you need to be careful that you don't configure a server to try to detect changes too frequently. A server that checks for changes too frequently can become overloaded. Remember, change detection uses more resources as the number of files stored in the sync share increases.

If you deploy roles and features that require a full version of the Web (IIS) role, you might find that these roles and features or the Work Folders feature itself don't work together. A conflict can occur because the full version of the Web (IIS) role has a Default Web Site that uses port 80 for HTTP communications and port 443 for secure HTTP communications. For example, running Windows Essentials Experience and Work Folders together on the same server requires a special configuration. Typically, you need to change the ports used by Windows Essentials Experience so that they don't conflict with the ports used by Work Folders.

To enable detailed logging of Work Folders, you can enable and configure the Audit Object Access policy setting for a Group Policy Object (GPO) processed by the server. You'll find this setting in the Administrative Templates for Computer Configuration under Windows Settings\Security Settings\Local Policies Audit Policies. After you enable Audit Object Access, add an audit entry for the specific folders you want to audit. In File Explorer, press and hold or right-click a folder you want to audit, and then select Properties. In the Properties dialog box, on the Security tab, select Advanced. In the Advanced Security Settings dialog box, use the options on the Auditing tab to configure auditing.

Creating sync shares and enabling SMB access

You create a sync share to identify a local folder on a sync server that will be synchronized and accessible to domain users via the Work Folders client. As sync shares are mapped to local paths on sync servers, I recommend that you create any folders that you want to use before creating sync shares. This will make it easier to select the exact folders with which you want to work. For details on adding the Work Folders role and configure Work Folders in Group Policy, see "Automatically configuring Work Folders" in Chapter 6.

To create a sync share, complete the following steps:

1. In Server Manager, select File And Storage Services, and then select Work Folders. On the Work Folders panel, select Tasks, and then select New Sync Share to open the New Sync Share Wizard. If the Before You Begin page is displayed, tap or click Next.

2. On the Select The Server And Path page, shown in Figure 3-13, select the server with which you want to work. Keep in mind that only servers that have the Work Folders role installed are available for selection.

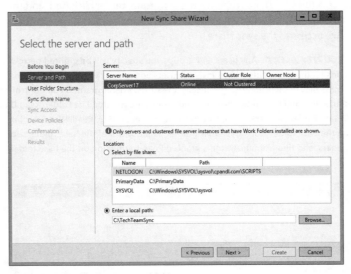

FIGURE 3-13 Specify the server and folder to use.

3. When configuring sync shares, you have several options. You can:

   - Add syncing to an existing file share by choosing the Select By File Share option, and then selecting the file share that should also be synced.

   - Add syncing to an existing local folder by choosing Enter A Local Path, selecting Browse, and then using the Select Folder dialog box to locate and chose the folder to sync.

   - Add syncing to a new local folder by choosing Enter A Local Path, and then entering the path to use.

4. When you are ready to continue, tap or click Next. If you specified a new folder location, you are prompted to confirm whether you want to create this folder. Select OK to create the folder and continue.

5. On the Specify The Structure For User Folders page, choose a folder naming format for the subfolders where user data is stored. To use only the user alias portion of the user's logon name for naming user folders, choose User Alias. To use the full logon name for naming user folders, choose User alias@domain.

6. By default, all folders and files stored under the user folder are synced automatically. If you'd prefer that only a specific folder is synced, select the Sync Only The Following Folder check box, and then enter the name of the folder, such as Documents. Tap or click Next to continue

7. On the Enter The Sync Share Name page, enter a share name and description before tapping or clicking Next to continue.

8. On the Grant Sync Access To Groups page, shown in Figure 3-14, use the options provided to specify the users and groups that should be able to access the sync share. To add a user or group, tap or click Add, and then use the Select User Or Group dialog box to specify the user or group that should have access to the sync share.

SECURITY ALERT Any users and groups you specify will be granted permissions on the base folder that allows the users and groups to create folders and access files in their folders. Specifically, Creator/Owner is granted Full Control on subfolders and files only. The users and groups are granted List Folder/Read Data, Create Folders/Append Data, Traverse Folder/Execute File, Read/Write attributes on the base folder. Local System is granted Full Control of the base folder, subfolders, and files. Administrator is granted Read permission on the base folder.

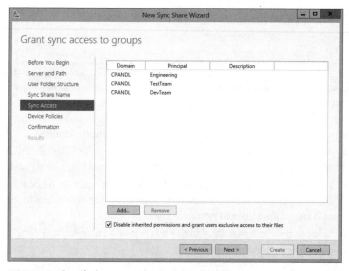

FIGURE 3-14 Specify the users and groups that should have access to the sync share.

9. By default, inherited permissions are disabled and users have exclusive access to their user folders. Because of this, only the user who stores a file has access to this file on the share. If the base folder for the share has permissions that you want to be applied to user folders, such as those that would grant administrators access to user folders, clear the Disable Inherited Permissions check box. When you are ready to continue, tap or click Next.

10. On the Specify Device Policies page, you have two options. You can select Encrypt Work Folders to encrypt files in Work Folders on client devices. You can select Automatically Lock Screen And Require A Password to ensure that the screens on client devices lock automatically and require a password for access.

11. Tap or click Next to continue, and then confirm your selections. Select Create to create the sync share. If the wizard is unable to create the sync share, you'll get an error and will need to note the error and take appropriate corrective action. A common error you might get occurs when the server hosts both Work Folders (which use the hostable web core) and the full Web (IIS) role. Before you can crate sync shares, you'll need to modify the ports used so they do not conflict or install Work Folders on a server that doesn't have the full Web (IIS) role.

12. If you did not select an existing file share during set up and want to enable the sync share for SMB access, open File Explorer. In File Explorer, press and hold or right-click the folder, select Share With, and then select Specific People. Finally, configure file sharing as discussed earlier in this chapter.

Accessing Work Folders on clients

Users with a domain user account can access Work Folders from a client device over the Internet or over the corporate network. You can configure Work Folder Access for a user by completing the following steps:

1. In Control Panel, tap or click System And Security, and then select Work Folders. On the Manage Work Folders page, tap or click Set Up Work Folders.

2. On the Enter Your Work Email Address page, enter the user email address, such as **amyh@cpandl.com**, and then tap or click Next. If the client device is joined to the domain, you will not be prompted for the user's credentials. Otherwise, you are prompted for the user's credentials. After the user enters her credentials, you can select Remember My Credentials to store the user's credentials for future use, and then tap or click OK to continue.

3. On the Introducing Work Folders page, note where the work files for the user will be stored. By default, work files are stored in a user profile subfolder called Work Folders. For example, the work files for Amyh would be stored under %SystemDrive%\Users\Amyh\WorkFolders. To store work files in another location, tap or click Change and then use the options provided to specify a new save location for work files. When you are ready to continue, tap or click Next.

4. On the Security Policies page, review the security policies that will be applied, and then have the user select the I Accept These Policies On My PC check box. You will not be able to continue if you do not select this check box.

5. Select Set Up Work Folders to create Work Folders on the client device.

After you configure Work Folders for initial use on a client device, the user can access Work Folders in File Explorer. When a user opens File Explorer, the This PC node should be opened by default. If so, the user just needs to double-tap or double-click Work Folders to view work files. If a user has an open Explorer window and This PC is not the selected node, she just needs to tap or click the leftmost option button in the address list, and then tap or click This PC.

As the user works with files, the changes the user makes trigger sync actions with the server. If the user doesn't change any files locally for an extended period of time, the client connects to the server every 10 minutes to determine whether there are changes to sync.

Data security and auditing

Data is the heart of any enterprise and few aspects of administration are more important than ensuring that data is protected. Although file and folder permissions protect important resources by restricting access, protecting enterprise data isn't just about file and folder permissions. To secure enterprise data appropriately, you need a firm understanding of object management, ownership, inheritance, and auditing. To help ensure that enterprise data is manageable, you also need to know how to implement quotas that restrict the amount of data that can be stored on servers.

Object management, ownership, and inheritance

Windows Server 2012 R2 takes an object-based approach to describing resources and managing permissions. Objects that describe resources are defined on NTFS volumes and in Active Directory Domain Services (AD DS). With NTFS volumes, you can set permissions for files and folders. With Active Directory, you can set permissions for other types of objects, such as users, computers, and groups. You can use these permissions to control access with precision.

Objects and object managers

Whether defined on an NTFS volume or in Active Directory, each type of object has an object manager and primary management tools. The object manager controls object settings and permissions. The primary management tools are the tools of choice for working with the object. Objects, their managers, and management tools are summarized in Table 4-1.

TABLE 4-1 Windows Server 2012 R2 objects

OBJECT TYPE	OBJECT MANAGER	MANAGEMENT TOOL
Files and folders	NTFS	File Explorer
Printers	Print spooler	Printers in Control Panel
Registry keys	Windows registry	Registry Editor
Services	Service controllers	Security Configuration Tool Set
Shares	Server service	File Explorer, Computer Management, Share And Storage Management

Object ownership and transfer

It's important to understand the concept of object ownership. In Windows Server 2012 R2, the object owner isn't necessarily the object's creator; instead, the object owner is the person who has direct control over the object. Object owners can grant access permissions and give other users permission to take ownership of the object.

As an administrator, you can take ownership of objects on the network to ensure that you can't be locked out of files, folders, printers, and other resources. After you take ownership of files, however, you can't return ownership to the original owner (in most cases). This prevents administrators from accessing files and then trying to hide the fact.

The way ownership is assigned initially depends on the location of the resource being created. In most cases, the Administrators group is listed as the current owner, and the object's actual creator is listed as a person who can take ownership.

Ownership can be transferred in several ways:

- If the Administrators group is initially assigned as the owner, the creator of the object can take ownership, if she does this before someone else takes ownership.

- The current owner can grant the Take Ownership permission to other users, allowing those users to take ownership of the object.

- An administrator can take ownership of an object, if the object is under his administrative control.

To take ownership of an object, follow these steps:

1. Open the management tool for the object. For example, if you want to work with files and folders, start File Explorer.

2. Press and hold or right-click the object you want to take ownership of, and then tap or click Properties. In the Properties dialog box, tap or click the Security tab.

3. On the Security tab, tap or click Advanced to display the Advanced Security Settings dialog box where the current owner is listed under the file or folder name.

4. Tap or click Change. Use the options in the Select User, Computer, Service Account, Or Group dialog box to select the new owner.

5. Tap or click OK twice when you have finished.

TIP If you're taking ownership of a folder, you can take ownership of all subfolders and files within the folder by selecting the Replace Owner On Subcontainers And Objects check box. This option also works with objects that contain other objects, in which case you would take ownership of all child objects.

Object inheritance

Objects are defined by using a parent-child structure. A parent object is a top-level object, and a child object is an object defined below a parent object in the hierarchy. For example, the folder C:\ is the parent of the folders C:\Data and C:\Backups. Any subfolders created in C:\Data or C:\Backups are children of these folders and grandchildren of C:\.

Child objects can inherit permissions from parent objects; in fact, all Windows Server 2012 R2 objects are created with inheritance enabled by default. This means that child objects automatically inherit the permissions of the parent; therefore, the parent object permissions control access to the child object. If you want to change permissions on a child object, you must do one of the following:

- Edit the permissions of the parent object.
- Stop inheriting permissions from the parent object, and then assign permissions to the child object.
- Select the opposite permission to override the inherited permission. For example, if the parent allows the permission, you would deny it on the child object.

To stop inheriting permissions from a parent object, follow these steps:

1. Open the management tool for the object. For example, if you want to work with files and folders, start File Explorer.

2. Press and hold or right-click the object with which you want to work, and then tap or click Properties. In the Properties dialog box, tap or click the Security tab.

3. Tap or click Advanced to display the Advanced Security Settings dialog box.

4. On the Permissions tab, tap or click Change Permissions to display an editable version of the Permissions tab.

5. On the Permissions tab, you'll see a Disable Inheritance button if inheritance currently is enabled. Tap or click Disable Inheritance.

6. You can now either convert the inherited permissions to explicit permissions or remove all inherited permissions and apply only the permissions that you explicitly set on the folder or file.

Keep in mind that if you remove the inherited permissions and no other permissions are assigned, everyone but the owner of the resource is denied access. This effectively locks out everyone except the owner of a folder or file; however, administrators still have the right to take ownership of the resource regardless of the permissions. Thus, if an administrator is locked out of a file or a folder and truly needs access, she can take ownership and then have unrestricted access.

To start inheriting permissions from a parent object, follow these steps:

1. Open the management tool for the object. For example, if you want to work with files and folders, start File Explorer.

2. Press and hold or right-click the object with which you want to work, and then tap or click Properties. In the Properties dialog box, tap or click the Security tab.

3. Tap or click Advanced to display the Advanced Security Settings dialog box.

4. On the Permissions tab, tap or click Enable Inheritance, and then tap or click OK. Note that the Enable Inheritance button is available only if permission inheritance currently is disabled.

File and folder permissions

NTFS permissions are always evaluated when a file is accessed. On NTFS and ReFS volumes, you can set security permissions on files and folders to grant or deny access to the files and folders. Because Windows Server 2012 R2 adds new layers of security, NTFS permissions now encompass the following:

- Basic permissions
- Claims-based permissions
- Special permissions

You can view NTFS permissions for files and folders by following these steps:

1. In File Explorer, press and hold or right-click the file or folder with which you want to work, and then tap or click Properties. In the Properties dialog box, tap or click the Security tab.

2. In the Group Or User Names list, select the user, computer, or group whose permissions you want to view. If the permissions are not available (dimmed), the permissions are inherited from a parent object.

Shared folders have both share permissions and NTFS permissions. You can view the underlying NTFS permissions for shared folders by following these steps:

1. In Server Manager, the Shares subnode of the File And Storage Services node shows existing shares for file servers that have been added for management.

2. Press and hold or right-click the folder with which you want to work, and then tap or click Properties to display a Properties dialog box.

3. When you tap or click Permissions in the left pane, the current share permissions and NTFS permissions are shown in the main pane.

4. To get more information, tap or click Customize Permissions to open the Advanced Security Settings dialog box.

On file servers running Windows Server 2012 R2, you can also use central access policies to precisely define the specific attributes that users and devices must have to access resources.

Understanding file and folder permissions

The basic permissions you can assign to files and folders are summarized in Table 4-2. File permissions include Full Control, Modify, Read & Execute, Read, and Write. Folder permissions include Full Control, Modify, Read & Execute, List Folder Contents, Read, and Write.

TABLE 4-2 File and folder permissions used by Windows Server 2012 R2

PERMISSION	MEANING FOR FOLDERS	MEANING FOR FILES
Read	Permits viewing and listing files and subfolders	Permits viewing or accessing a file's contents
Write	Permits adding files and subfolders	Permits writing to a file
Read & Execute	Does not permit viewing the contents of files. You can list file and folder names, but you can't open files to read, nor can you execute files if that execute requires opening the file (as in a batch or PS1 file). Inherited by files and folders.	Permits viewing and accessing a file's contents in addition to executing a file
List Folder Contents	Permits viewing and listing file names and subfolder names in addition to executing files; inherited by folders only	Not applicable
Modify	Permits reading and writing of files and subfolders; allows deletion of the folder	Permits reading and writing of a file; allows deletion of a file
Full Control	Permits reading, writing, changing, and deleting files and subfolders	Permits reading, writing, changing, and deleting a file

Any time you work with file and folder permissions, you should keep the following in mind:

- Read is the only permission needed to run scripts. Execute permission doesn't matter.
- Read access is required to access a shortcut and its target.
- Giving a user permission to write to a file but not to delete it doesn't prevent the user from deleting the file's contents.
- If a user has full control over a folder, the user can delete files in the folder regardless of the permission on the files.

The basic permissions are created by combining special permissions in logical groups. Table 4-3 shows special permissions used to create the basic permissions for files. By using advanced permission settings, you can assign these special permissions individually, if necessary. As you study the special permissions, keep the following in mind:

- By default, if no access is specifically granted or denied, the user is denied access. Further, if a permission has been explicitly denied, the deny will override any permission grant.

- Actions that users can perform are based on the sum of all the permissions assigned to the user and to all the groups of which the user is a member. For example, if the user GeorgeJ has Read access and is a member of the group Techies, which has Change access, GeorgeJ will have Change access. If Techies is a member of Administrators, which has Full Control, GeorgeJ will have complete control over the file. However, if GeorgeJ has been explicitly denied a permission, the deny will override any grant.

TABLE 4-3 Special permissions for files

| | BASIC PERMISSIONS | | | | |
SPECIAL PERMISSIONS	FULL CONTROL	MODIFY	READ & EXECUTE	READ	WRITE
Traverse Folder/ Execute File	Yes	Yes	Yes		
List Folder/Read Data	Yes	Yes	Yes	Yes	
Read Attributes	Yes	Yes	Yes	Yes	
Read Extended Attributes	Yes	Yes	Yes	Yes	
Create Files/Write Data	Yes	Yes			Yes
Create Folders/Append Data	Yes	Yes			Yes
Write Attributes	Yes	Yes			Yes
Write Extended Attributes	Yes	Yes			Yes
Delete Subfolders And Files	Yes				
Delete	Yes	Yes			
Read Permissions	Yes	Yes	Yes	Yes	Yes
Change Permissions	Yes				
Take Ownership	Yes				

Table 4-4 shows special permissions used to create the basic permissions for folders. As you study the special permissions, keep in mind that when you create files and folders, these files and folders inherit certain permission settings from parent objects. These permission settings are shown as the default permissions.

TABLE 4-4 Special permissions for folders

	BASIC PERMISSIONS					
SPECIAL PERMISSIONS	**FULL CONTROL**	**MODIFY**	**READ & EXECUTE**	**LIST FOLDER CONTENTS**	**READ**	**WRITE**
Traverse Folder/ Execute File	Yes	Yes	Yes	Yes		
List Folder/Read Data	Yes	Yes	Yes	Yes	Yes	
Read Attributes	Yes	Yes	Yes	Yes	Yes	
Read Extended Attributes	Yes	Yes	Yes	Yes	Yes	
Create Files/Write Data	Yes	Yes				Yes
Create Folders/ Append Data	Yes	Yes				Yes
Write Attributes	Yes	Yes				Yes
Write Extended Attributes	Yes	Yes				Yes
Delete Subfolders And Files	Yes					
Delete	Yes	Yes				
Read Permissions	Yes	Yes	Yes		Yes	Yes
Change Permissions	Yes					
Take Ownership	Yes					

Setting basic file and folder permissions

To set basic NTFS permissions for files and folders, follow these steps:

1. In File Explorer, press and hold or right-click the file or folder with which you want to work, and then tap or click Properties. In the Properties dialog box, tap or click the Security tab.

2. Tap or click Edit to display an editable version of the Security tab, as shown in Figure 4-1.

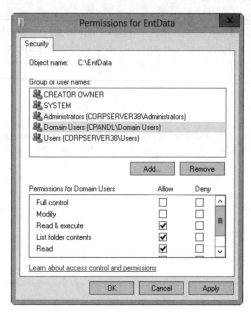

FIGURE 4-1 Configure basic permissions for the file or folder on the Security tab.

3. Users or groups that already have access to the file or folder are listed in the Group Or User Names list. You can change permissions for these users and groups by doing the following:

   a. Select the user or group you want to change.

   b. Grant or deny access permissions in the Permissions box.

   TIP Inherited permissions are shaded (dimmed). If you want to override an inherited permission, select the opposite permission.

4. To set access permissions for additional users, computers, or groups, tap or click Add to display the Select Users, Computers, Service Accounts, Or Groups dialog box.

5. Enter the name of a user, computer, or group in the current domain, and then tap or click Check Names. One of the following actions occurs:

   - If a single match is found, the dialog box is updated and the entry is underlined.

   - If no matches are found, you entered an incorrect name part or are working with an incorrect location. Modify the name and try again, or tap or click Locations to select a new location.

- If multiple matches are found, select the name or names you want to use, and then tap or click OK. To add more users, computers, or groups, enter a semicolon (;), and then repeat this step.

NOTE The Locations button allows you to access account names in other domains. Tap or click Locations to view a list of the current domain, trusted domains, and other resources you can access. Because of the transitive trusts in Windows Server 2012 R2, you can usually access all the domains in the domain tree or forest.

6. In the Group Or User Names list, select the user, computer, or group you want to configure, and in the check boxes in the Permissions list, allow or deny permissions. Repeat for other users, computers, or groups.

7. Tap or click OK.

Because shared folders also have NTFS permissions, you might want to set basic NTFS permissions by using Server Manager. To do this, follow these steps:

1. In Server Manager, select File and Storage Services, select the server with which you want to work, and then Select Shares.

2. Press and hold or right-click the folder with which you want to work, and then tap or click Properties to display a Properties dialog box.

3. When you tap or click Permissions in the left pane, the current share permissions and NTFS permissions are shown in the main pane.

4. Tap or click Customize Permissions to open the Advanced Security Settings dialog box with the Permissions tab selected.

5. Users or groups that already have access to the file or folder are listed under Permission Entries. Use the options provided to view, edit, add, or remove permissions for users and groups.

Setting special permissions on files and folders

To set special NTFS permissions for files and folders, follow these steps:

1. In File Explorer, press and hold or right-click the file or folder with which you want to work, and then tap or click Properties.

2. In the Properties dialog box, select the Security tab, and then tap or click Advanced to display the Advanced Security Settings dialog box. Before you can modify permissions, you must click Change Permissions. As shown in Figure 4-2, the permissions are presented much as they are on the Security tab. The key differences are that you see individual allow or deny permission sets, whether permissions are inherited and where they are from, and the resources to which the permissions apply.

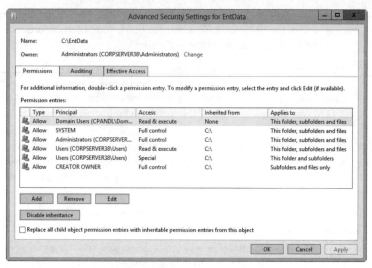

FIGURE 4-2 Configure special permissions on files and folders.

3. If a user or group already has permissions set for the file or folder (and those permissions are not being inherited), you can modify the special permissions by selecting the user or group, and then clicking Edit. Afterward, skip steps 4–7, and then follow the rest of the steps in this procedure.

4. To add special permissions for a user or group, tap or click Add to display the Permission Entry dialog box. Tap or click Select A Principal to display the Select User, Computer, Service Account, Or Group dialog box.

5. Enter the name of a user or a group account. Be sure to reference the user account name rather than the user's full name. Only one name can be entered at a time.

6. Tap or click Check Names. If a single match is found for each entry, the dialog box is automatically updated and the entry is underlined; otherwise, you'll get an additional dialog box. If no matches are found, you either entered the name incorrectly, or you're working with an incorrect location. Modify the name in the Name Not Found dialog box and try again, or tap or click Locations to select a new location. When multiple matches are found, in the Multiple Names Found dialog box, select the name you want to use, and then tap or click OK.

7. Tap or click OK. The user and group are added as the Principal, and the Permission Entry dialog box is updated to show this.

8. When you are editing permissions, only basic permissions are listed by default. Tap or click Show Advanced Permissions to display the special permissions, as shown in Figure 4-3.

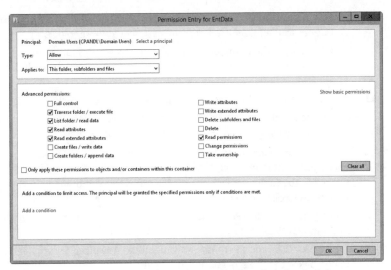

FIGURE 4-3 Configure the special permissions that should be allowed or denied.

9. Use the Type list to specify whether you are configuring allowed or denied special permissions, and then select the special permissions you want to allow or deny. If any permissions are dimmed (unavailable), they are inherited from a parent folder.

> **NOTE** You allow and deny special permissions separately. Therefore, if you want to both allow and deny special permissions, you need to configure the allowed permissions, and then repeat this procedure starting with step 1 to configure the denied permissions.

10. If the options in the Applies To list are available, choose the appropriate option to ensure that the permissions are properly inherited. The options include the following:

- **This Folder Only**   The permissions apply only to the currently selected folder.
- **This Folder, Subfolders And Files**   The permissions apply to this folder, any subfolders of this folder, and any files in any of these folders.
- **This Folder And Subfolders**   The permissions apply to this folder and any subfolders of this folder. They do not apply to any files in any of these folders.
- **This Folder And Files**   The permissions apply to this folder and any files in this folder. They do not apply to any subfolders of this folder.
- **Subfolders And Files Only**   The permissions apply to any subfolders of this folder and any files in any of these folders. They do not apply to this folder itself.

- **Subfolders Only** The permissions apply to any subfolders of this folder but not to the folder itself or any files in any of these folders.

- **Files Only** The permissions apply to any files in this folder and any files in subfolders of this folder. They do not apply to this folder itself or to subfolders.

11. When you have finished configuring permissions, tap or click OK.

Because shared folders also have NTFS permissions, you might want to set special NTFS permissions by using Server Manager. To do this, follow these steps:

1. In Server Manager, select File And Storage Services, select the server with which you want to work, and then select Shares. Next, press and hold or right-click the folder with which you want to work, and then tap or click Properties to display a Properties dialog box.

2. When you tap or click Permissions in the left pane, the current share permissions and NTFS permissions are shown in the main pane.

3. Tap or click Customize Permissions to open the Advanced Security Settings dialog box with the Permissions tab selected.

Users or groups that already have access to the file or folder are listed under Permission Entries. Use the options provided to view, edit, add, or remove permissions for users and groups. When you are editing or adding permissions in the Permission Entry dialog box, follow steps 8–11 of the previous procedure to display and work with special permissions.

Setting claims-based permissions

Claims-based access controls use compound identities that incorporate not only the groups of which a user and the user's computer is a member, but also claim types, which are assertions about objects based on Active Directory attributes, and resource properties, which classify objects and describe their attributes. When resources are remotely accessed, claims-based access controls and central access policies rely on Kerberos with Armoring for authentication of computer device claims. Kerberos with Armoring improves domain security by allowing domain-joined clients and domain controllers to communicate over secure, encrypted channels.

You use claims-based permissions to fine-tune access by defining conditions that limit access as part of a resource's advanced security permissions. Typically, these conditions add device claims or user claims to the access controls. User claims identify users; device claims identify devices. For example, you could define claim types based on business category and country code. The Active Directory attributes are businessCategory and countryCode, respectively. By using these claim types, you could then fine-tune access to ensure that only users, devices, or both that belong to specific business categories and have certain country codes are granted access to a resource. You could also define a resource property called Project to help fine-tune access even more.

MORE INFO With central access policies, you define central access rules in Active Directory and those rules are applied dynamically throughout the enterprise. Central access rules use conditional expressions that require you to determine the resource properties, claim types, and/or security groups required for the policy, in addition to the servers to which the policy should be applied.

Before you can define and apply claim conditions to a computer's files and folders, a claims-based policy must be enabled. For computers that are not joined to the domain, you can do this by enabling and configuring the KDC Support For Claims, Compound Authentication And Kerberos Armoring policy in the Administrative Templates policies for Computer Configuration under System\KDC. The policy must be configured to use one of the following modes:

- **Supported** Domain controllers support claims, compound identities, and Kerberos armoring. Client computers that don't support Kerberos with Armoring can be authenticated.
- **Always Provide Claims** This mode is the same as the Supported mode, but domain controllers always return claims for accounts.
- **Fail Unarmored Authentication Requests** Kerberos with Armoring is mandatory. Client computers that don't support Kerberos with Armoring cannot be authenticated.

The Kerberos Client Support For Claims, Compound Authentication And Kerberos Armoring policy controls whether the Kerberos client running on Windows 8.1 and Windows Server 2012 R2 requests claims and compound authentication. The policy must be enabled for compatible Kerberos clients to request claims and compound authentication for Dynamic Access Control and Kerberos armoring. You'll find this policy in the Administrative Templates policies for Computer Configuration under System\Kerberos.

For application throughout a domain, a claims-based policy should be enabled for all domain controllers in a domain to ensure consistent application. Because of this, you typically enable and configure this policy through the Default Domain Controllers Group Policy Object (GPO), or the highest GPO linked to the domain controllers organizational unit (OU).

After you've enabled and configured the claims-based policy, you can define claim conditions by completing these steps:

1. In File Explorer, press and hold or right-click the file or folder with which you want to work, and then tap or click Properties. In the Properties dialog box, select the Security tab, and then tap or click Advanced to display the Advanced Security Settings dialog box.

   If the user or group already has permissions set for the file or folder, you can edit their existing permissions. Here, tap or click the user with which you want to work, tap or click Edit, and then skip steps 3–6.

2. Tap or click Add to display the Permission Entry dialog box. Tap or click Select A Principal to display the Select User, Computer, Service Account, Or Group dialog box.

3. Enter the name of a user or a group account. Be sure to reference the user account name rather than the user's full name. Only one name can be entered at a time.

4. Tap or click Check Names. If a single match is found for each entry, the dialog box is automatically updated and the entry is underlined. Otherwise, you'll get an additional dialog box. If no matches are found, you either entered the name incorrectly or you're working with an incorrect location. Modify the name in the Name Not Found dialog box and try again, or tap or click Locations to select a new location. When multiple matches are found, in the Multiple Names Found dialog box, select the name you want to use and then tap or click OK.

5. Tap or click OK. The user and group are added as the Principal. Tap or click Add A Condition.

6. Use the options provided to define the condition or conditions that must be met to grant access. With users and groups, set basic claims based on group membership, previously defined claim types, or both. With resource properties, define conditions for property values.

7. When you have finished configuring conditions, tap or click OK.

Because shared folders also have NTFS permissions, you might want to set claims-based permissions by using Server Manager. To do this, follow these steps:

1. In Server Manager, select File and Storage Services, select the server with which you want to work, and then Select Shares.

2. Press and hold or right-click the folder with which you want to work, and then tap or click Properties to display a Properties dialog box.

3. When you tap or click Permissions in the left pane, the current share permissions and NTFS permissions are shown in the main pane.

4. Tap or click Customize Permissions to open the Advanced Security Settings dialog box with the Permissions tab selected.

   Users or groups that already have access to the file or folder are listed under Permission Entries. Use the options provided to view, edit, add, or remove permissions for users and groups. When you are editing or adding permissions in the Permission Entry dialog box, you can add conditions just as I discussed in steps 6–8 of the previous procedure.

Auditing system resources

Auditing is the best way to track what's happening on your Windows Server 2012 R2 systems. You can use auditing to collect information related to resource usage such as file access, system logons, and system configuration changes. Any time an action occurs that you've configured for auditing, the action is written to the system's security log, where it's stored for your review. The security log is accessible from Event Viewer.

NOTE For most auditing changes, you need to be logged on using an account that's a member of the Administrators group or you need to be granted the Manage Auditing And Security Log right in Group Policy.

Setting auditing policies

Auditing policies are essential to help ensure the security and integrity of your systems. Just about every computer system on the network should be configured with some type of security logging. You configure auditing policies for individual computers with local Group Policy and for all computers in domains with Active Directory–based Group Policy. Through Group Policy, you can set auditing policies for an entire site, a domain, or an organizational unit. You can also set policies for an individual workstation or server.

After you access the GPO with which you want to work, you can set auditing policies by following these steps:

1. In the Group Policy Management Editor, shown in Figure 4-4, access the Audit Policy node by working your way down the console tree. Expand Computer Configuration, Policies, Windows Settings, Security Settings, and Local Policies, and then select Audit Policy.

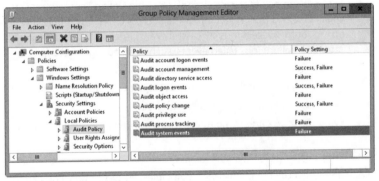

FIGURE 4-4 Set auditing policies by using the Audit Policy node in Group Policy.

2. The auditing options are as follows:
   - **Audit Account Logon Events** Tracks events related to user logon and logoff.
   - **Audit Account Management** Tracks account management by means of Active Directory Users And Computers. Events are generated any time user, computer, or group accounts are created, modified, or deleted.
   - **Audit Directory Service Access** Tracks access to Active Directory. Events are generated any time users or computers access the directory.

- **Audit Logon Events** Tracks events related to user logon, logoff, and remote connections to network systems.
- **Audit Object Access** Tracks system resource usage for files, directories, shares, printers, and Active Directory objects.
- **Audit Policy Change** Tracks changes to user rights, auditing, and trust relationships.
- **Audit Privilege Use** Tracks the use of user rights and privileges, such as the right to back up files and directories.

NOTE The Audit Privilege Use policy doesn't track system access-related events, such as the use of the right to log on interactively or the right to access the computer from the network. You track these events with logon and logoff auditing.

- **Audit Process Tracking** Tracks system processes and the resources they use.
- **Audit System Events** Tracks system startup, shutdown, and restart, in addition to actions that affect system security or the security log.

3. To configure an auditing policy, double-tap or double-click its entry, or press and hold or right-click the entry, and then tap or click Properties.

4. In the dialog box that is displayed, select the Define These Policy Settings check box, and then select either the Success check box, the Failure check box, or both. Success logs successful events, such as successful logon attempts. Failure logs failed events, such as failed logon attempts.

5. Tap or click OK.

When auditing is enabled, the security event log will reflect the following:

- Event IDs of 560 and 562 detailing user audits
- Event IDs of 592 and 593 detailing process audits

Auditing files and folders

If you configure a GPO to enable the Audit Object Access option, you can set the level of auditing for individual folders and files. This enables you to control precisely how folder and file usage is tracked. Auditing of this type is available only on NTFS volumes.

You can configure file and folder auditing by following these steps:

1. In File Explorer, press and hold or right-click the file or folder to be audited, and then tap or click Properties.

2. Tap or click the Security tab, and then tap or click Advanced to display the Advanced Security Settings dialog box.

3. On the Auditing tab, tap or click Continue. You can now view and manage auditing settings by using the options shown in Figure 4-5.

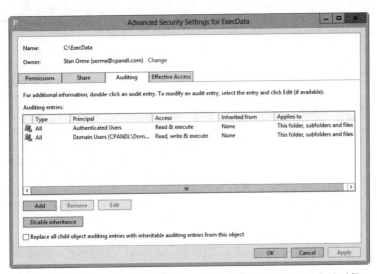

FIGURE 4-5 After you audit object access, you can set auditing policies on individual files and folders on the Auditing tab.

4. The Auditing Entries list shows the users, groups, or computers whose actions you want to audit. To remove an account, select the account in the Auditing Entries list, and then tap or click Remove.

5. To configure auditing for additional users, computers, or groups, tap or click Add. This displays the Select Users, Computers, Service Accounts, Or Groups dialog box.

6. Enter the name of a user, computer, or group in the current domain, and then tap or click Check Names. If a single match is found, the dialog box is automatically updated and the entry is underlined; otherwise, you'll get an additional dialog box. If no matches are found, you either entered the name incorrectly or you're working with an incorrect location. Modify the name in the Name Not Found dialog box and try again, or tap or click Locations to select a new location. When multiple matches are found, in the Multiple Names Found dialog box, select the name you want to use, and then tap or click OK.

7. Tap or click OK. The user and group are added, and the Principal and the Auditing Entry dialog box are updated to show this. Only basic permissions are listed by default. If you want to work with advanced permissions, tap or click Show Advanced Permissions to display the special permissions.

8. As necessary, use the Applies To list to specify where objects are audited. If you are working with a folder and want to replace the auditing entries on all child objects of this folder (and not on the folder itself), select Only Apply These Settings To Objects And/Or Containers Within This Container.

Keep in mind that the Applies To list lets you specify the locations *where* you want the auditing settings to apply. The Only Apply These Settings To Objects And/Or Containers Within This Container check box controls *how* auditing settings are applied. When this check box is selected, auditing settings on the parent object replace settings on child objects. When this check box is cleared, auditing settings on the parent are merged with existing settings on child objects.

9. Use the Type list to specify whether you are configuring auditing for success, failure, or both, and then specify which actions should be audited. Success logs successful events, such as successful file reads. Failure logs failed events, such as failed file deletions. The events you can audit are the same as the special permissions listed in Tables 4-3 and 4-4, except that you can't audit the synchronizing of offline files and folders. For essential files and folders, you'll typically want to track the following:

   ▪ Write Attributes—Successful

   ▪ Write Extended Attributes—Successful

   ▪ Delete Subfolders And Files—Successful

   ▪ Delete—Successful

   ▪ Change Permissions—Successful

   TIP If you want to audit actions for all users, use the special group Everyone; otherwise, select the specific user groups, users, or both that you want to audit.

10. If you're using claims-based policies and want to limit the scope of the auditing entry, you can add claims-based conditions to the auditing entry. For example, if all corporate computers are members of the Domain Computers group, you might want to closely audit access by devices that aren't members of this group.

11. When you have finished configuring auditing, tap or click OK. Repeat this process to audit other users, groups, or computers.

Auditing the registry

If you configure a GPO to enable the Audit Object Access option, you can set the level of auditing for keys within the registry. This enables you to track when key values are set, when subkeys are created, and when keys are deleted.

You can configure registry auditing by following these steps:

1. Open the Registry Editor. At a command prompt, enter **regedit**; or enter **regedit** in the Everywhere search box, and then press Enter.

2. Browse to a key you want to audit. On the Edit menu, select Permissions.

3. In the Permissions dialog box, tap or click Advanced. In the Advanced Security Settings dialog box, tap or click the Auditing tab.

4. Tap or click Add to display the Auditing Entry dialog box. Tap or click Select A Principal to display the Select User, Computer, Service Account, Or Group dialog box.

5. In the Select User, Computer, Service Account, Or Group dialog box, enter **Everyone**, tap or click Check Names, and then tap or click OK.

6. In the Auditing Entry dialog box, only basic permissions are listed by default. Tap or click Show Advanced Permissions to display the special permissions.

7. Use the Applies To list to specify how the auditing entry is to be applied.

8. Use the Type list to specify whether you are configuring auditing for success, failure, or both, and then specify which actions should be audited. Typically, you'll want to track the following advanced permissions:

   - Set Value—Successful and Failed
   - Create Subkey—Successful and Failed
   - Delete—Successful and Failed

9. Tap or click OK three times to close all open dialog boxes and apply the auditing settings.

Auditing Active Directory objects

If you configure a GPO to enable the Audit Directory Service Access option, you can set the level of auditing for Active Directory objects so that you can control precisely how object usage is tracked.

To configure object auditing, follow these steps:

1. In Active Directory Users And Computers, ensure that Advanced Features is selected on the View menu, and then access the container for the object.

2. Double-tap or double-click the object to be audited to open the related Properties dialog box.

3. Tap or click the Security tab, and then tap or click Advanced.

4. In the Advanced Settings dialog box, tap or click the Auditing tab. The Auditing Entries list shows the users, groups, or computers whose actions you are auditing currently (if any). To remove an account, select the account in the Auditing Entries list, and then tap or click Remove.

5. To add specific accounts, tap or click Add to display the Auditing Entry dialog box. Tap or click Select A Principal to display the Select User, Computer, Service Account, Or Group dialog box.

6. Enter the name of a user, computer, or group in the current domain, and then tap or click Check Names. If a single match is found, the dialog box is automatically updated and the entry is underlined; otherwise, you'll get an additional dialog box. If no matches are found, you either entered the name incorrectly or you're working with an incorrect location. Modify the name in the Name Not Found dialog box and try again, or tap or click Locations to select a new location. When multiple matches are found, in the Multiple Names Found dialog box, select the name you want to use, and then tap or click OK.

7. Tap or click OK to return to the Auditing Entry dialog box. Use the Applies To list to specify how the auditing entry is to be applied.

8. Use the Type list to specify whether you are configuring auditing for success, failure, or both, and then specify which actions should be audited. Success logs successful events, such as a successful attempt to modify an object's permissions. Failed logs failed events, such as a failed attempt to modify an object's owner.

9. Tap or click OK. Repeat this process to audit other users, groups, or computers.

Using, configuring, and managing NTFS disk quotas

Windows Server 2012 R2 supports two mutually exclusive types of disk quotas:

- **NTFS disk quotas** NTFS disk quotas are supported on all editions of Windows Server 2012 R2 and enable you to manage disk space usage by users. You configure quotas on a per-volume basis. Although users who exceed limits get warnings, administrators are notified primarily through the event logs.

- **Resource Manager disk quotas** Resource Manager disk quotas are supported on all editions of Windows Server 2012 R2, allowing you to manage disk space usage by folder, by file type, and by volume. Users who are approaching or have exceeded a limit can be automatically notified by email. The notification system also allows for notifying administrators by email, triggering incident reporting, running commands, and logging related events.

The sections that follow discuss NTFS disk quotas.

NOTE Regardless of the quota system being used, you can configure quotas only for NTFS volumes. You can't create quotas for FAT, FAT32, or ReFS volumes.

REAL WORLD When you apply disk quotas, you need to be particularly careful in the way you enforce quotas, especially with respect to system accounts, service accounts, or other special purpose accounts. Improper application of disk quotas to these types of accounts can cause serious problems that are difficult to diagnose and resolve. Enforcing quotas on the System, NetworkService, and LocalService accounts could prevent the computer from completing important operating system tasks. As an example, if these accounts reach their enforced quota limit, you would not be able to apply changes to Group Policy because the Group Policy client runs within a LocalSystem context by default and would not be able to write to the system disk. If the service can't write to the system disk, Group Policy changes cannot be made, and being unable to change Group Policy could have all sorts of unexpected consequences because you would be stuck with the previously configured settings. For example, you would be unable to disable or modify the quota settings through Group Policy.

In this scenario, where service contexts have reached an enforced quota limit, any other configuration settings that use these service contexts and require making changes to files on disk would likely also fail. For example, you would be unable to complete the installation or removal of roles, role services, and features. This would leave the server in a state in which Server Manager always includes a warning that you need to restart the computer to complete configuration tasks, but restarting the computer would not resolve these issues.

To address this problem, you need to edit the disk quota entries for the system disk, raise the enforced limits on the service accounts, and then restart the computer. Restarting the computer triggers the finalization tasks and enables the computer to complete any configuration tasks stuck in a pending status. Because the Group Policy client service could process changes and write them to the system disk, changes to Group Policy would then be applied as well.

Understanding NTFS disk quotas and how NTFS quotas are used

Administrators use NTFS disk quotas to manage disk space usage for critical volumes, such as those that provide corporate data shares or user data shares. When you enable NTFS disk quotas, you can configure two values:

- **Disk quota limit** Sets the upper boundary for space usage, which you can use to prevent users from writing additional information to a volume, to log events regarding the user exceeding the limit, or both.
- **Disk quota warning** Warns users and logs warning events when users are getting close to their disk quota limit.

TIP You can set disk quotas but not enforce them, and you might be wondering why you'd want to do this. Sometimes you want to track disk space usage on a per-user basis and know when users have exceeded some predefined limit, but instead of denying them additional disk space, you log an event in the application log to track the overage. You can then send out warning messages or figure out other ways to reduce the space usage.

NTFS disk quotas apply only to end users and not to administrators. Administrators can't be denied disk space even if they exceed enforced disk quota limits.

In a typical environment, you restrict disk space usage in megabytes (MB) or gigabytes (GB). For example, on a corporate data share used by multiple users in a department, you might want to limit disk space usage from 20 to 100 GB. For a user data share, you might want to set the level much lower, such as from 5 to 20 GB, which restricts the user from creating large amounts of personal data. Often you'll set the disk quota warning as a percentage of the disk quota limit. For example, you might set the warning from 90 to 95 percent of the disk quota limit.

Because NTFS disk quotas are tracked on a per-volume, per-user basis, disk space used by one user doesn't affect the disk quotas for other users. Thus, if one user exceeds his limit, any restrictions applied to this user don't apply to other users. For example, if a user exceeds a 5-GB disk quota limit and the volume is configured to prevent writing over the limit, the user can no longer write data to the volume. Users can, however, remove files and folders from the volume to free up disk space. They can also move files and folders to a compressed area on the volume, which might free up space, or they can elect to compress the files themselves. Moving files to a different location on the volume doesn't affect the quota restriction. The amount of file space is the same unless the user moves uncompressed files and folders to a folder with compression. In any case, the restriction on a single user doesn't affect other users' ability to write to the volume (as long as there's free space on the volume).

You can enable NTFS disk quotas on the following:

- **Local volumes**   To manage disk quotas on local volumes, you work with the local disk itself. When you enable disk quotas on a local volume, the Windows system files are included in the volume usage for the user who installed those files. Sometimes this might cause the user to go over the disk quota limit so to prevent this, you might want to set a higher limit on a local workstation volume.

- **Remote volumes**   To manage disk quotas on remote volumes, you must share the root directory for the volume, and then set the disk quota on the volume. Remember, you set quotas on a per-volume basis, so if a remote file server has separate volumes for different types of data—that is, a corporate data volume and a user data volume—these volumes have different quotas.

Only members of the Domain Admins group or the local system Administrators group can configure disk quotas. The first step in using quotas is to enable quotas in Group Policy, which you can do at two levels:

- **Local**   Through local Group Policy, you can enable disk quotas for an individual computer.

- **Enterprise**   Through Group Policy that applies to a site, a domain, or an organizational unit, you can enable disk quotas for groups of users and computers.

Having to keep track of disk quotas does cause some overhead on computers. This overhead is a function of the number of disk quotas being enforced, the total size of the volumes and their data, and the number of users to which the disk quotas apply.

Although on the surface disk quotas are tracked per user, behind the scenes Windows Server 2012 R2 manages disk quotas according to security identifiers (SIDs). Because SIDs are tracked by disk quotas, you can safely modify user names without affecting the disk quota configuration. Tracking by SIDs does cause some additional overhead when viewing disk quota statistics for users because Windows Server 2012 R2 must correlate SIDs to user account names so that the account names can be displayed in dialog boxes. This means contacting the local user manager and the Active Directory domain controller as necessary.

After Windows Server 2012 R2 looks up names, it caches them to a local file so that they can be available immediately the next time they're needed. The query cache is infrequently updated—if you notice a discrepancy between what's displayed and what's configured, you need to refresh the information. Usually, this means choosing Refresh from the View menu or pressing F5 in the current window.

Setting NTFS disk quota policies

The best way to configure NTFS disk quotas is through Group Policy. When you configure disk quotas through local policy or through unit, domain, and site policy, you define general policies that are set automatically when you enable quota management on individual volumes. Thus, rather than having to configure each volume separately, you can use the same set of rules and apply them in turn to each volume you want to manage.

Policies that control NTFS disk quotas are applied at the system level. You access these policies through Computer Configuration\Administrative Templates\System\Disk Quotas. Table 4-5 summarizes the available policies.

TABLE 4-5 Policies for Setting NTFS disk quotas

POLICY NAME	DESCRIPTION
Apply Policy To Removable Media	Determines whether quota policies apply to NTFS volumes on removable media. If you don't enable this policy, quota limits apply only to fixed media drives.
Enable Disk Quotas	Turns disk quotas on or off for all NTFS volumes of the computer, and prevents users from changing the setting.
Enforce Disk Quota Limit	Specifies whether quota limits are enforced. If quotas are enforced, users will be denied disk space if they exceed the quota. This overrides settings on the Quota tab on the NTFS volume.
Log Event When Quota Limit Exceeded	Determines whether an event is logged when users reach their limit, and prevents users from changing their logging options.
Log Event When Quota Warning Level Exceeded	Determines whether an event is logged when users reach the warning level.
Specify Default Quota Limit And Warning Level	Sets a default quota limit and warning level for all users. This setting overrides other settings and affects only new users.

Whenever you work with quota limits, you should use a standard set of policies on all systems; however, you typically, won't want to enable all the policies. Instead, you'll selectively enable policies and then use the standard NTFS features to control quotas on various volumes. If you want to enable quota limits, follow these steps:

1. Access Group Policy for the system (for example, a file server) with which you want to work. Access the Disk Quotas node by expanding Computer Configuration, Administrative Templates, System, and then selecting Disk Quotas.

2. Double-tap or double-click Enable Disk Quotas. Select Enabled, and then tap or click OK.

3. Double-tap or double-click Enforce Disk Quota Limit. If you want to enforce disk quotas on all NTFS volumes residing on this computer, tap or click Enabled. Otherwise, tap or click Disabled, and then set specific limits on a per-volume basis. Tap or click OK.

4. Double-tap or double-click Specify Default Quota Limit And Warning Level. In the dialog box shown in Figure 4-6, select Enabled.

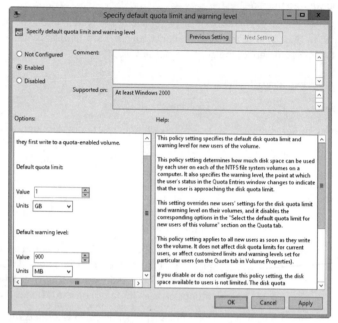

FIGURE 4-6 Enforce disk quotas in the Specify Default Quota Limit And Warning Level dialog box.

5. Under Default Quota Limit, set a default limit that's applied to users when they first write to the quota-enabled volume. The limit doesn't apply to current users or affect current limits in place. On a corporate share, such as a share used by members of a project team, a good limit is between 5 and 10 GB. Of course, this depends on the size of the data files that the users routinely work with, the number of users, and the size of the disk volume. Graphic designers and data engineers might need much more disk space.

6. To set a warning limit, scroll down in the Options window. A good warning limit is about 90 percent of the default quota limit, which means that if you set the default quota limit to 10 GB, you should set the warning limit to 9 GB. Tap or click OK.

7. Double-tap or double-click Log Event When Quota Limit Exceeded. Select Enabled so that limit events are recorded in the application log, and then tap or click OK.

8. Double-tap or double-click Log Event When Quota Warning Level Exceeded. Select Enabled so that warning events are recorded in the application log, and then tap or click OK.

9. Double-tap or double-click Apply Policy To Removable Media. Select Disabled so that the quota limits apply only to fixed media volumes on the computer, and then tap or click OK.

TIP To ensure that the policies are enforced immediately, access the Computer Configuration\Administrative Templates\System\Group Policy node, and then double-tap or double-click Configure Disk Quota Policy Processing. Select Enabled, and then select the Process Even If The Group Policy Objects Have Not Changed check box. Tap or click OK.

Enabling NTFS disk quotas on NTFS volumes

You can set NTFS disk quotas on a per-volume basis. Only NTFS volumes can have disk quotas. After you configure the appropriate group policies, you can use Computer Management to set disk quotas for local and remote volumes.

NOTE If you use the Enforce Disk Quota Limit policy setting to enforce quotas, users are denied disk space if they exceed the quota. This overrides settings on the Quota tab on the NTFS volume.

To enable NTFS disk quotas on an NTFS volume, follow these steps:

1. Open Computer Management. If necessary, connect to a remote computer.

2. In the console tree, expand Storage, and then select Disk Management. The volumes configured on the selected computer are displayed in the details pane.

3. Using Volume List view or Graphical View, press and hold or right-click the volume with which you want to work, and then tap or click Properties.

4. On the Quota tab, select the Enable Quota Management check box, shown in Figure 4-7. If you already set quota management values through Group Policy, the options are unavailable and you can't change them. You must modify options through Group Policy instead.

BEST PRACTICES Whenever you work with the Quota tab, pay particular attention to the Status text and the associated traffic light icon. Both change based on the state of quota management. If quotas aren't configured, the traffic light icon shows a red light and the status is inactive or not configured. If the operating system is working or updating the quotas, the traffic light icon shows a yellow light and the status shows the activity being performed. If quotas are configured, the traffic light icon shows a green light and the status text states that the quota system is active.

5. To set a default disk quota limit for all users, select Limit Disk Space To. In the text boxes provided, set a limit in kilobytes, megabytes, gigabytes, terabytes, petabytes, or exabytes. Then set the default warning limit in the Set Warning Level To text boxes. Again, you'll usually want the disk quota warning limit to be 90–95 percent of the disk quota limit.

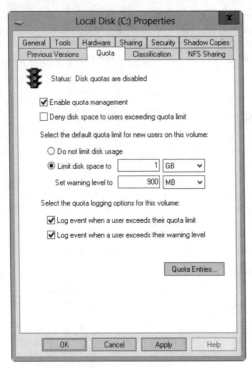

FIGURE 4-7 After you enable quota management, you can configure a quota limit and quota warning for all users.

TIP Although the default quota limit and warning apply to all users, you can configure different levels for individual users. You do this in the Quota Entries dialog box. If you create many unique quota entries and don't want to re-create them on a volume with similar characteristics and usage, you can export the quota entries and import them into a different volume.

6. To enforce the disk quota limit and prevent users from going over the limit, select the Deny Disk Space To Users Exceeding Quota Limit check box. Keep in mind that this creates an actual physical limitation for users (but not for administrators).

7. To configure logging when users exceed a warning limit or the quota limit, select the Log Event check boxes. Tap or click OK to save your changes.

8. If the quota system isn't currently enabled, you'll get a prompt asking you to enable the quota system. Tap or click OK so that Windows Server 2012 R2 can rescan the volume and update disk usage statistics. Actions might be taken against users who exceed the current limit or warning levels. These actions can include preventing additional writing to the volume, notifying them the next time they access the volume, and logging applicable events to the application log.

Viewing disk quota entries

Disk space usage is tracked on a per-user basis. When disk quotas are enabled, each user storing data on a volume has an entry in the disk quota file. This entry is updated periodically to show the current disk space used, the applicable quota limit, the applicable warning level, and the percentage of allowable space being used. As an administrator, you can modify disk quota entries to set different limits and warning levels for particular users. You can also create disk quota entries for users who haven't yet saved data on a volume. The key reason for creating entries is to ensure that when a user does make use of a volume, the user has an appropriate limit and warning level.

To view the current disk quota entries for a volume, follow these steps:

1. Open Computer Management. If necessary, connect to a remote computer.

2. In the console tree, expand Storage, and then select Disk Management. The volumes configured on the selected computer are displayed in the details pane.

3. Using Volume List view or Graphical View, press and hold or right-click the volume with which you want to work, and then tap or click Properties.

4. On the Quota tab, tap or click Quota Entries to display the Quota Entries dialog box. Each quota entry is listed according to a status, which is meant to quickly depict whether a user has gone over a limit. A status of OK means the user is working within the quota boundaries. Any other status usually means the user has reached the warning level or the quota limit.

Creating disk quota entries

You can create disk quota entries for users who haven't yet saved data on a volume. This enables you to set custom limits and warning levels for a particular user. You usually use this feature when a user frequently stores more information than other users and you want to allow the user to go over the normal limit or when you want to set a specific limit for administrators. As you might recall, administrators aren't subject to disk quota limits, so if you want to enforce limits for individual administrators, you must create disk quota entries for each administrator you want to limit.

REAL WORLD You shouldn't create individual disk quota entries haphazardly. You need to track individual entries carefully. Ideally, you should keep a log that details any individual entries so that other administrators understand the policies in place and how those policies are applied. When you modify the base rules for quotas on a volume, you should reexamine individual entries to see whether they're still applicable or need to be updated as well. I've found that certain types of users are exceptions more often than not, and that it's sometimes better to put different classes of users on different volumes and then apply disk quotas to each volume. In this way, each class or category of user has a quota limit that's appropriate for its members' typical usage, and you have fewer (perhaps no) exceptions. For example, you might use separate volumes for executives, managers, and standard users, or you might have separate volumes for management, graphic designers, engineers, and all other users.

To create a quota entry on a volume, follow these steps:

1. Open the Quota Entries dialog box as discussed in "Viewing disk quota entries" earlier in this chapter. Current quota entries for all users are listed. To refresh the listing, press F5 or choose Refresh from the View menu.

2. If the user doesn't have an existing entry on the volume, you can create it by choosing New Quota Entry from the Quota menu. This opens the Select Users dialog box.

3. In the Select Users dialog box, enter the name of a user you want to use in the Enter The Object Names To Select text box, and then tap or click Check Names. If a match is found, select the account you want to use, and then tap or click OK. If no matches are found, update the name you entered and try searching again. Repeat this step as necessary, and then tap or click OK. You also can enter user names separated by semicolons to apply the same quota to multiple users at the same time.

4. After you select a user, the Add New Quota Entry dialog box is displayed, as shown in Figure 4-8. You have two options. You can remove all quota restrictions for this user by selecting Do Not Limit Disk Usage, or you can set a specific limit and warning level by selecting Limit Disk Space To and then entering the appropriate values. Tap or click OK.

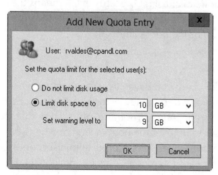

FIGURE 4-8 In the Add New Quota Entry dialog box, you can customize the user's quota limit and warning level or remove quota restrictions altogether.

Deleting disk quota entries

When you've created disk quota entries on a volume and a user no longer needs to use the volume, you can delete the associated disk quota entry. When you delete a disk quota entry, all files owned by the user are collected and displayed in a dialog box so that you can permanently delete the files, take ownership of the files, or move the files to a folder on a different volume.

To delete a disk quota entry for a user and manage the user's remaining files on the volume, follow these steps:

1. Open the Quota Entries dialog box as discussed in "Viewing disk quota entries" earlier in this chapter. Current quota entries for all users are listed. To refresh the listing, press F5 or choose Refresh from the View menu.

2. Select the disk quota entry you want to delete, and then press Delete, or choose Delete Quota Entry from the Quota menu. You can select multiple entries by using the Shift and Ctrl keys.

3. When prompted to confirm the action, tap or click Yes to display the Disk Quota dialog box with a list of current files owned by the selected user or users.

4. In the List Files Owned By list, display files for a user whose quota entry you're deleting. You must now specify how the files for the user are to be handled. You can handle each file separately by selecting individual files and then choosing an appropriate option, or you can select multiple files by using the Shift and Ctrl keys. The following options are available:

   - **Permanently Delete Files** Select the files to delete, and then press Delete. When prompted to confirm the action, tap or click Yes.

   - **Take Ownership Of Files** Select the files you want to take ownership of, and then tap or click Take Ownership Of Files.

   - **Move Files To** Select the files you want to move, and then enter the path to a folder on a different volume. If you don't know the path you want to use, tap or click Browse to display the Browse For Folder dialog box. When you find the folder, tap or click Move.

5. Tap or click Close when you have finished managing the files. If you've appropriately handled all user files, the disk quota entries will be deleted.

Exporting and importing NTFS disk quota settings

Rather than re-creating custom disk quota entries on individual volumes, you can export the settings from a source volume, and then import the settings to another volume. You must format both volumes by using NTFS. To export and then import disk quota entries, follow these steps:

1. Open the Quota Entries dialog box as discussed in "Viewing disk quota entries" earlier in this chapter. Current quota entries for all users are listed. To refresh the listing, press F5 or choose Refresh from the View menu.

2. Select Export from the Quota menu to display the Export Quota Settings dialog box. Choose the save location for the file containing the quota settings, and then enter a name for the file in the File Name text box. Tap or click Save.

   NOTE If you save the settings file to a mapped drive on the target volume, you'll have an easier time importing the settings. Quota files are usually small, so you don't need to worry about disk space usage.

3. On the Quota menu, tap or click Close to exit the Quota Entries dialog box.

4. Press and hold or right-click Computer Management in the console tree, and then tap or click Connect To Another Computer. In the Select Computer dialog box, choose the computer containing the target volume. The target volume is the one on which you want to use the exported settings.

5. As explained previously, open the Properties dialog box for the target volume. Then tap or click Quota Entries on the Quota tab to display the Quota Entries dialog box for the target volume.

6. Tap or click Import on the Quota menu. In the Import Quota Settings dialog box, select the quota settings file you saved previously. Tap or click Open.

7. If the volume had previous quota entries, you are given the choice to replace existing entries or keep existing entries. When prompted about a conflict, tap or click Yes to replace an existing entry, or tap or click No to keep the existing entry. To apply the option to replace or keep existing entries to all entries on the volume, select the Do This For All Quota Entries check box prior to tapping or clicking Yes or No.

Disabling NTFS disk quotas

You can disable quotas for individual users or all users on a volume. When you disable quotas for a particular user, the user is no longer subject to the quota restrictions but disk quotas are still tracked for other users. When you disable quotas on a volume, quota tracking and management are completely removed. To disable quotas for a particular user, follow the technique outlined earlier in the chapter in "Viewing disk quota entries." To disable quota tracking and management on a volume, follow these steps:

1. Open Computer Management. If necessary, connect to a remote computer.

2. Open the Properties dialog box for the volume on which you want to disable NTFS quotas.

3. On the Quota tab, clear the Enable Quota Management check box. Tap or click OK. When prompted to confirm, tap or click OK.

IMPORTANT Disabling quota tracking doesn't delete existing quota entries on a volume. If you later enable quota management, the previously created quota entries will be available and will be enforced.

Using, configuring, and managing Resource Manager disk quotas

Windows Server 2012 R2 supports an enhanced quota management system called *Resource Manager disk quotas*. By using Resource Manager disk quotas, you can manage disk space usage by folder and by volume.

TIP Because you manage Resource Manager disk quotas separately from NTFS disk quotas, you can configure a single volume to use both quota systems; however, it's recommended that you use one quota system or the other. Alternatively, if you've already configured NTFS disk quotas, you might want to continue by using NTFS disk quotas on a per-volume basis and supplement this quota management with Resource Manager disk quotas for important folders.

Understanding Resource Manager disk quotas

When you're working with Windows Server 2012 R2, Resource Manager disk quotas are another tool you can use to manage disk usage. You can configure Resource Manager disk quotas on a per-volume or per-folder basis. You can set disk quotas with a specific hard limit—meaning a limit can't be exceeded—or a soft limit, meaning a limit can be exceeded.

Generally, you should use hard limits when you want to prevent users from exceeding a specific disk-usage limitation. Use soft limits when you want to monitor usage and simply warn users who exceed or are about to exceed usage guidelines. All quotas have a quota path, which designates the base file path on the volume or folder to which the quota is applied. The quota applies to the designated volume or folder and all subfolders of the designated volume or folder. The particulars of how quotas work and how users are limited or warned are derived from a source template that defines the quota properties.

Windows Server 2012 R2 includes the quota templates listed in Table 4-6. By using the File Server Resource Manager, you can easily define additional templates that would then be available whenever you define quotas, or you can set single-use custom quota properties when defining a quota.

Quota templates or custom properties define the following:

- **Limit** The disk space usage limit
- **Quota type** Hard or soft
- **Notification thresholds** The types of notification that occur when usage reaches a specific percentage of the limit

Although each quota has a specific limit and type, you can define multiple notification thresholds as either a warning threshold or a limit threshold. Warning thresholds are considered to be any percentage of the limit that is less than 100 percent. Limit thresholds occur when the limit reached is 100 percent. For example, you could define warning thresholds that are triggered at 85 percent and 95 percent of the limit and a limit threshold that is triggered when 100 percent of the limit is reached.

Users who are approaching or have exceeded a limit can be automatically notified by email. The notification system also allows for notifying administrators by email, triggering incident reporting, running commands, and logging related events.

TABLE 4-6 Disk quota templates

QUOTA TEMPLATE	LIMIT	QUOTA TYPE	DESCRIPTION
100 MB Limit	100 MB	Hard	Sends warnings to users as the limit is approached and exceeded
200 MB Limit Reports To User	200 MB	Hard	Sends storage reports to the users who exceed the threshold
200 MB Limit With 50 MB Extension	200 MB	Hard	Uses the DIRQUOTA command to grant an automatic, one-time, 50-MB extension to users who exceed the quota limit
250 MB Extended Limit	250 MB	Hard	Meant to be used by those whose limit has been extended from 200 MB to 250 MB
Monitor 200 GB Volume Usage	200 GB	Soft	Monitors volume usage, and warns when the limit is approached and exceeded
Monitor 500 MB Share	500 MB	Soft	Monitors share usage, and warns when the limit is approached and exceeded

Managing disk quota templates

You use disk quota templates to define quota properties, including the limit, quota type, and notification thresholds. In File Server Resource Manager, you can view the currently defined disk quota templates by expanding the Quota Management node, and then selecting Quota Templates. Table 4-6, shown earlier, provides a summary of the default disk quota templates. Table 4-7, which follows, shows variables that can be used for automatically generated messages and events.

TABLE 4-7 Key variables available for disk quota messages and event logging

VARIABLE NAME	DESCRIPTION
[Admin Email]	Inserts the email addresses of the administrators defined under the global options
[File Screen Path]	Inserts the local file path, such as C:\Data
[File Screen Remote Path]	Inserts the remote path, such as \\server\share
[File Screen System Path]	Inserts the canonical file path, such as \\?\VolumeGUID
[Server Domain]	Inserts the domain of the server on which the notification occurred
[Server]	Inserts the server on which the notification occurred
[Source File Owner]	Inserts the user name of the owner of the file/folder
[Source File Owner Email]	Inserts the email address of the owner of the file/folder
[Source File Path]	Inserts the source path of the file/folder

You can modify existing disk quota templates by following these steps:

1. In File Server Resource Manager, expand the Quota Management node, and then select Quota Templates.

   Currently defined disk quota templates are listed by name, limit, and quota type.

2. To modify disk quota template properties, double-tap or double-click the disk quota template name. This displays a related Properties dialog box, as shown in Figure 4-9.

3. On the Settings tab, you can set the template name, limit, and quota type. Current notification thresholds are listed. To modify an existing threshold, select it and then tap or click Edit. To define a new threshold, tap or click Add.

4. When you have finished modifying the quota template, tap or click OK to save the changes.

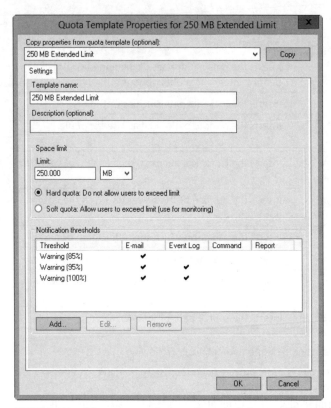

FIGURE 4-9 Use disk quota properties to configure the limit, quota type, and notification thresholds.

You can create a new disk quota template by following these steps:

1. In File Server Resource Manager, expand the Quota Management node, and then select Quota Templates.

2. On the Action menu or in the Actions pane, tap or click Create Quota Template to display the Create Quota Template dialog box.

3. On the Settings tab, set the template name, limit, and quota type. You should create a limit threshold first, and then create additional warning thresholds as necessary. In the Limit list, enter the limit value and specify whether you are setting the limit in kilobytes, megabytes, gigabytes, or terabytes.

4. Tap or click Add to add warning thresholds. In the Add Threshold dialog box, enter a percentage value under Generate Notifications When Usage Reaches (%). Warning thresholds are considered to be any percentage of the limit that is less than 100 percent. Limit thresholds occur when the limit reached is 100 percent.

5. On the E-Mail Message tab, you can configure notification as follows:

   - To notify an administrator when the disk quota is triggered, select the Send E-Mail To The Following Administrators check box, and then enter the email address or addresses to use. Be sure to separate multiple email addresses with a semicolon. Use the value [Admin Email] to specify the default administrator as configured previously under the global options.

   - To notify users, select the Send E-Mail To The User Who Exceeded The Threshold check box.

   - Specify the contents of the notification message in the Subject and Message Body text boxes. Table 4-7 lists available variables and their meanings.

6. On the Event Log tab, you can configure event logging. Select the Send Warning To Event Log check box to enable logging, and then specify the text of the log entry in the Log Entry text box. Table 4-7 lists available variables and their meanings.

7. On the Command tab, you can optionally specify a command or script to run, arguments to pass in to the command or script, and a working directory. The default security context for commands is Local Service, which grants standard user access to local resources but denies access to network resources. If the command requires access to both local and network resources, you can run the command as Network Service.

8. On the Report tab, select the Generate Reports check box to enable incident reporting, and then select the types of reports to generate. Incident reports are stored under %SystemDrive%\StorageReports\Incident by default, and they can also be sent to designated administrators. Use the value [Admin Email] to specify the default administrator as configured previously under the global options.

9. Repeat steps 5–7 to define additional notification thresholds.

10. Tap or click OK when you have finished creating the template.

Creating Resource Manager disk quotas

You use disk quotas to designate file paths that have specific usage limits. In File Server Resource Manager, you can view current disk quotas by expanding the Quota Management node, and then selecting Quotas. Before you define disk quotas, you should specify screening file groups and disk quota templates that you will use, as discussed in "Managing disk quota templates" earlier in this chapter.

After you define the necessary file groups and disk quota templates, you can create a disk quota by following these steps:

1. In File Server Resource Manager, expand the Quota Management node, and then select Quotas.

2. Tap or click Create Quota on the Action menu or in the Actions pane.

3. In the Create Quota dialog box, set the local computer path for the quota by tapping or clicking Browse and then by using the Browse For Folder dialog box to select the path, such as C:\Data. Tap or click OK.

4. In the Derive Properties From This Quota Template list, choose the disk quota template that defines the quota properties you want to use.

5. Tap or click Create.

CHAPTER 5

Enhancing computer security

S̲ound security practices and settings are essential to successful system administration. Two key methods to configure security settings are to use security
templates and security policies. Both of these features manage system settings
that you would otherwise manage through Group Policy.

Using security templates

Security templates provide a centralized way to manage security-related settings
for workstations and servers. You use security templates to apply customized sets
of Group Policy definitions to specific computers. These policy definitions generally affect the following policies:

- **Account policies**   Control security for passwords, account lockout, and
  Kerberos security
- **Local policies**   Control security for auditing, user rights assignment, and
  other security options
- **Event log policies**   Control security for event logging
- **Restricted groups policies**   Control security for local group membership
  administration
- **System services policies**   Control security and startup mode for local
  services
- **File system policies**   Control security for file and folder paths in the local
  file system
- **Registry policies**   Control the permissions on security-related registry keys

NOTE   Security templates are available in all Windows Server installations and can
be imported into any Group Policy object (GPO). Security templates apply only to
the Computer Configuration area of Group Policy. They do not apply to the User
Configuration area. In Group Policy, you'll find applicable settings under Computer
Configuration\Windows Settings\Security Settings. Some security settings are not
included, such as those that apply to wireless networks, public keys, software restrictions, and IP security.

Working with security templates is a multipart process that involves the following steps:

1. Use the Security Templates snap-in to create a new template, or select an existing template that you want to modify.

2. Use the Security Templates snap-in to make necessary changes to the template settings, and then save the changes.

3. Use the Security Configuration And Analysis snap-in to analyze the differences between the template with which you are working and the current computer security settings.

4. Revise the template as necessary after you review the differences between the template settings and the current computer settings.

5. Use the Security Configuration And Analysis snap-in to apply the template and overwrite existing security settings.

When you first start working with security templates, you should determine whether you can use an existing template as a starting point. Other administrators might have created templates, or your organization might have baseline templates that should be used. You can also create a new template to use as your starting point, as shown in Figure 5-1.

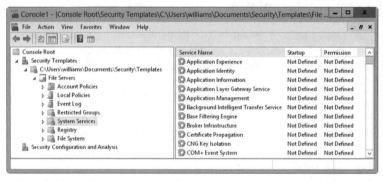

FIGURE 5-1 View and create security templates with the Security Templates snap-in.

> **TIP** If you select a template that you want to use as a starting point, you should go through each setting that the template applies and evaluate how the setting affects your environment. If a setting doesn't make sense, you should modify it appropriately or delete it.

You should use the Security Configuration And Analysis snap-in to apply templates rather than the Security Templates snap-in. You can also use the Security Configuration And Analysis snap-in to compare the settings in a template to the current settings on a computer. The results of the analysis highlight areas in which the current settings don't match those in the template. This is useful to determine whether security settings have changed over time.

Using the Security Templates and Security Configuration And Analysis snap-ins

You can open the security snap-ins by following these steps:

1. Start the Microsoft Management Console (MMC) by pressing the Windows key, entering **mmc.exe**, and then pressing Enter.

2. In the Microsoft Management Console, tap or click File, and then tap or click Add/Remove Snap-In.

3. In the Add Or Remove Snap-Ins dialog box, tap or click Security Templates, and then tap or click Add.

4. Tap or click Security Configuration And Analysis, and then tap or click Add. Tap or click OK.

By default, the Security Templates snap-in looks for security templates in the %SystemDrive%\Users\%UserName%\Documents\Security\Templates folder. You can add other search paths for templates by following these steps:

1. With the Security Templates snap-in selected in the MMC, choose New Template Search Path from the Action menu.

2. In the Browse For Folder dialog box, select the template location to add, such as %SystemRoot%\Security\Templates\Policies. Tap or click OK.

   Now that you've located the template search path with which you want to work, you can select a template and expand the related notes to review its settings.

You can create a template by following these steps:

1. In the Security Templates snap-in, either press and hold or right-click the search path where the template should be created, and then tap or click New Template.

2. Enter a name and description for the template in the text boxes provided.

3. Tap or click OK to create the template. The template will not have settings configured, so you need to modify the settings carefully before the template is ready for use.

4. After you modify the template, save the changes by pressing and holding or right-clicking the template in the Security Templates snap-in and selecting Save. Alternatively, you can select Save As to assign a different name to the modified template.

Reviewing and changing template settings

The sections that follow discuss how to work with template settings. As you'll learn, you manage each type of template setting in a slightly different way.

Changing settings for account, local, and event log policies

Account policy settings control security for passwords, account lockout, and Kerberos security. Local policy settings control security for auditing, user rights assignment, and other security options. Event log policy settings control security for event logging. For detailed information on account policy, local policy settings, and configuring event logging, see Chapter 9, "Creating User and Group Accounts" and Chapter 3, "Monitoring Services, Processes, and Events" in Windows Server 2012 R2 Pocket Consultant: Essentials & Configuration.

With account, local, and event log policies, you can change template settings by following these steps:

1. In the Security Templates snap-in, expand the Account Policies or Local Policies node as necessary, and then select a related subnode, such as Password Policy or Account Lockout Policy.

2. In the right pane, policy settings are listed alphabetically. The value in the Computer Setting column shows the current setting. If the template changes the setting so that it is no longer defined, the value is listed as Not Defined.

3. Double-tap or double-click a setting to display its Properties dialog box, as shown in Figure 5-2. To determine the purpose of the setting, tap or click the Explain tab. To define and apply the policy setting, select the Define This Policy Setting In The Template check box. To clear this policy and not apply it, clear this check box.

FIGURE 5-2 Change template settings for account and local policies in the Security Templates snap-in.

4. If you enable the policy setting, specify how the policy setting is to be used by configuring any additional options.

5. Tap or click OK to save your changes. You might get the Suggested Value Changes dialog box, shown in Figure 5-3. This dialog box informs you of other values that are changed to suggested values based on your setting

change. For example, when you change the Account Lockout Threshold setting, Windows might also change the Account Lockout Duration and Reset
Account Lockout Counter After settings, as shown in the figure.

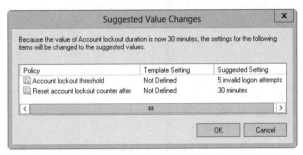

FIGURE 5-3 Review the suggested value changes.

Configuring restricted groups

Restricted groups policy settings control the list of members of groups and the groups
to which the configured group belongs. You can restrict a group by following these
steps:

1. In the Security Templates snap-in, select the Restricted Groups node. In the
   right pane, any currently restricted groups are listed by name. Members of
   the group are listed as well, and so are groups of which the restricted group
   is a member.

2. You can add a restricted group by pressing and holding or right-clicking the
   Restricted Groups node in the left pane, and then tapping or clicking Add
   Group. In the Add Group dialog box, tap or click Browse.

3. In the Select Groups dialog box, enter the name of a group you want to
   restrict, and then tap or click Check Names. If multiple matches are found,
   select the account you want to use, and then tap or click OK. If no matches
   are found, update the name you entered and try searching again. Repeat this
   step as necessary, and then tap or click OK.

4. In the Properties dialog box, shown in Figure 5-4, you can use the Add
   Members option to add members to the group. Tap or click Add Members,
   and then specify the members of the group. If the group should not have
   any members, remove all members by tapping or clicking Remove. Any
   members who are not specified in the policy setting for the restricted
   group are removed when the security template is applied.

5. In the Properties dialog box, tap or click Add Groups to specify the groups to
   which this group belongs. If you specify membership in groups, the groups
   to which this group belongs are listed exactly as you've applied them (if the
   groups are valid in the applicable workgroup or domain). If you do not specify membership in groups, the groups to which this group belongs are not
   modified when the template is applied.

6. Tap or click OK to save your settings.

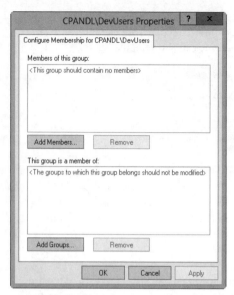

FIGURE 5-4 Configure membership for the selected group.

You can remove a restriction on a group by following these steps:

1. In the Security Templates snap-in, select the Restricted Groups node. In the right pane, any currently restricted groups are listed by name. Members of the group are listed along with the groups of which the restricted group is a member.

2. Press and hold or right-click the group that should not be restricted, and then tap or click Delete. When prompted to confirm the action, tap or click Yes.

Enabling, disabling, and configuring system services

Policy settings for system services control the general security and startup mode for local services. You can enable, disable, and configure system services by following these steps:

1. In the Security Templates snap-in, select the System Services node. In the right pane, all currently installed services on the computer with which you are working are listed by name, startup setting, and permission configuration. Keep the following in mind when working with system services:

   - If the template does not change the startup configuration of the service, the value for the Startup column is listed as Not Defined. Otherwise, the startup configuration is listed as one of the following values: Automatic, Manual, or Disabled.

   - If the template does not change the security configuration of the service, the value for the Permission column is listed as Not Defined. Otherwise, the security configuration is listed as Configured.

2. Double-tap or double-click the entry for a system service to display its Properties dialog box, shown in Figure 5-5. To define and apply the policy setting, select the Define This Policy Setting In The Template check box. To clear this policy and not apply it, clear this check box.

FIGURE 5-5 Change template settings for system services.

3. If you enable the policy setting, specify the service startup mode by selecting Automatic, Manual, or Disabled. Keep the following in mind:

   - Automatic ensures that the service starts automatically when the operating system starts. Choose this setting for essential services that you know are secure and that you want to be sure are run if they are installed on the computer to which the template is being applied.

   - Manual prevents the service from starting automatically and allows the service only to be started manually, either by a user, application, or other service. Choose this setting when you want to restrict unnecessary or unused services or when you want to restrict services that you know are not entirely secure.

   - Disabled prevents the service from starting automatically or manually. Choose this setting only with unnecessary or unused services that you want to prevent from running.

4. If you know the security configuration that the service should use, tap or click Edit Security, and then set the service permissions in the Security For dialog box. You can set permissions to allow specific users and groups to start, stop, and pause the service on the computer.

5. Tap or click OK.

Configuring security settings for registry and file system paths

Policy settings for the file system control security for file and folder paths in the local file system. Policy settings for the registry control the values of security-related registry keys. You can view or change security settings for currently defined registry and file system paths by following these steps:

1. In the Security Templates snap-in, select the Registry node or the File System node, depending on which type of file path with which you want work. In the right pane, all currently secured paths are listed.

2. Double-tap or double-click a registry or file path to view its current settings, as shown in Figure 5-6.

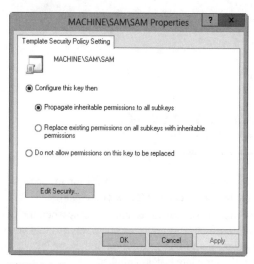

FIGURE 5-6 Change template settings for paths and keys.

3. To ensure that permissions on the path or key are not replaced, select Do Not Allow Permissions On This Key To Be Replaced, and then tap or click OK. Skip the remaining steps in this procedure.

4. To configure the path or key and replace permissions, select Configure This Key Then, and then choose one of the following options:

   - **Propagate Inheritable Permissions To All Subkeys** Choose this option to apply all inheritable permissions to this registry or file path and to all registry and file paths below this path. Existing permissions are replaced only if they conflict with a security permission set for this path.

   - **Replace Existing Permissions On All Subkeys With Inheritable Permissions** Choose this option to replace all existing permissions on this registry or file path and on all registry and file paths below this path. Any existing permissions are removed, and only the current permissions remain.

5. Tap or click Edit Security. In the Security For dialog box, configure security permissions for users and groups. You have the same options for permissions, auditing, and ownership as you do for files and folders used with NTFS. See Chapter 3, "Data sharing and redundancy" for details on permissions, auditing, and ownership.

6. Tap or click OK twice to save the settings.

You can define security settings for registry paths by following these steps:

1. In the Security Templates snap-in, select and then press and hold or right-click the Registry node, and then tap or click Add Key to display the Select Registry Key dialog box, shown in Figure 5-7.

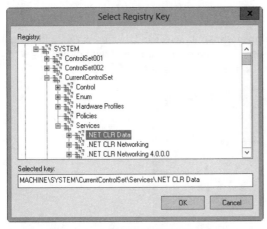

FIGURE 5-7 Select the registry path or value to secure.

2. In the Select Registry Key dialog box, select the registry path or value with which you want to work, and then tap or click OK. Entries under CLASSES_ ROOT are for HKEY_CLASSES_ROOT. Entries under MACHINE are for HKEY_ LOCAL_MACHINE. Entries under USERS are for HKEY_USERS.

3. In the Security For dialog box, configure security permissions for users and groups. You have the same options for permissions, auditing, and ownership as you do for files and folders used with NTFS. See Chapter 3 for details on permissions, auditing, and ownership.

4. Tap or click OK. The Add Object dialog box is displayed. To ensure that per-missions on the path or key are not replaced, select Do Not Allow Permis-sions On This Key To Be Replaced, and then tap or click OK. Skip the remaining steps in this procedure.

5. To configure the path or key and replace permissions, select Configure This Key Then, and then do one of the following:

- Choose Propagate Inheritable Permissions To All Subkeys to apply all inheritable permissions to this registry path and all registry paths below this path. Existing permissions are replaced only if they conflict with a security permission set for this path.

- Choose Replace Existing Permissions On All Subkeys With Inheritable Permissions to replace all existing permissions on this registry path and on all registry paths below this path. Any existing permissions are removed, and only the current permissions remain.

6. Tap or click OK.

You can define security settings for file paths by following these steps:

1. In the Security Templates snap-in, select and then press and hold or right-click the File System node, and then tap or click Add File to display the Add A File Or Folder dialog box, shown in Figure 5-8.

FIGURE 5-8 Select the file or folder path to secure.

2. In the Add A File Or Folder dialog box, select the file or folder path or value with which you want to work, and then tap or click OK.

3. In the Database Security For dialog box, configure security permissions for users and groups. You have the same options for permissions, auditing, and ownership as you do for files and folders used with NTFS. See Chapter 12 for details on permissions, auditing, and ownership.

4. Tap or click OK. The Add Object dialog box is displayed. To ensure that permissions on the path are not replaced, select Do Not Allow Permissions On This File Or Folder To Be Replaced, and then tap or click OK. Skip the remaining steps in this procedure.

5. To configure the path and replace permissions, select Configure This Path Then, and then do one of the following:

- Choose Propagate Inheritable Permissions To All Subfolders to apply all inheritable permissions to this file path and all file paths below this path. Existing permissions are replaced only if they conflict with a security permission set for this path.

- Choose Replace Existing Permissions On All Subfolders With Inheritable Permissions to replace all existing permissions on this file path and on all file paths below this path. Any existing permissions are removed, and only the current permissions remain.

6. Tap or click OK.

Analyzing, reviewing, and applying security templates

As stated previously, you use the Security Configuration And Analysis snap-in to apply templates and to compare the settings in a template to the current settings on a computer. Applying a template ensures that a computer conforms to a specific security configuration. Comparing settings can help you identify any discrepancies between what is implemented currently and what is defined in a security template. This can also be useful to determine whether security settings have changed over time.

REAL WORLD The key drawback to using the Security Configuration And Analysis snap-in is that you cannot configure multiple computers at once. You can configure security only on the computer on which you are running the snap-in. If you want to use this tool to deploy security configurations, you must log on to and run the tool on each computer. Although this technique works for standalone computers, it is not the optimal approach in a domain. In a domain setting, you'll want to import the security template settings into a Group Policy object (GPO), and then deploy the security configuration to multiple computers. For more information, see "Deploying security templates to multiple computers" later in this chapter.

The Security Configuration And Analysis snap-in uses a working database to store template security settings, and then applies the settings from this database. For analysis and comparisons, the template settings are listed as the effective database settings and the current computer settings are listed as the effective computer settings. Keep in mind that if you are actively editing a template in the Security Templates snap-in, you need to save the template so that the changes can be analyzed and used.

After you create a template or determine that you want to use an existing template, you can analyze and then configure the template by following these steps:

1. Open the Security Configuration And Analysis snap-in.

2. Press and hold or right-click the Security Configuration And Analysis node, and then tap or click Open Database to display the Open Database dialog box.

3. By default, the Open Database dialog box's search path is set to %System-Drive%\Users\%UserName%\Documents\Security\Database. As necessary, select options in the Open Database dialog box to navigate to a new location in which to save the database. In the File Name text box, enter a descriptive name for the database, such as **Current Config Comparison**, and then tap or click Open. The security database is created in the Security Database Files format with the .sdb file extension.

4. The Import Template dialog box is displayed with the default search path set to %SystemDrive%\Users\%UserName%\Documents\Security\Templates. As necessary, select options in the Import Template dialog box to navigate to a new template location. Select the security template you want to use, and then tap or click Open. Security template files end with the .inf file extension.

5. Press and hold or right-click the Security Configuration And Analysis node, and then tap or click Analyze Computer Now. When prompted to set the error log path, enter a new path or tap or click OK to use the default path.

6. Wait for the snap-in to complete the analysis of the template. If an error occurs during the analysis, you can view the error log by pressing and holding or right-clicking the Security Configuration And Analysis node and choosing View Log File.

When you are working with the Security Configuration And Analysis snap-in, you can review the differences between the template settings and the current computer settings. As Figure 5-9 shows, the template settings stored in the analysis database are listed in the Database Setting column, and the current computer settings are listed in the Computer Setting column. If a setting has not been analyzed, it is listed as Not Defined.

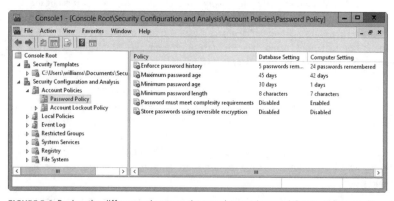

FIGURE 5-9 Review the differences between the template settings and the current computer settings.

You can make changes to a setting stored in the database by following these steps:

1. In the Security Configuration And Analysis snap-in, double-tap or double-click the setting with which you want to work.

2. In the Properties dialog box, shown in Figure 5-10, note the current computer setting. If information about the purpose of the setting is available, you can view this information by tapping or clicking the Explain tab.

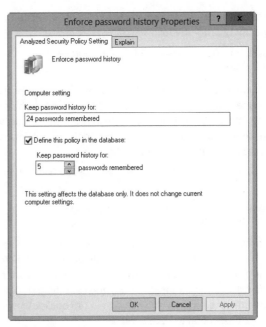

FIGURE 5-10 Change a policy setting in the database before applying the template.

3. To define and apply the policy setting, select the Define This Policy In The Database check box. To clear this policy and not apply it, clear this check box.

4. If you enable the policy setting, specify how the policy setting is to be used by configuring any additional options.

5. Repeat this process as necessary. To save your database changes to the template, press and hold or right-click the Security Configuration And Analysis node, and then tap or click Save.

You can also use the Secedit command-line utility to analyze, review, and apply security templates. The basic technique is as follows:

1. Open an elevated administrator prompt.

2. Use Secedit /Import to import a security template into a working database.

3. Use Secedit /Analyze to compare the template settings to a computer's current settings.

4. Use Secedit /Configure to apply the template settings.

Whether you are working with the graphical wizard or the command-line utility, you might want to create a rollback template before applying any settings. A rollback template is a reverse template that allows you to remove most settings applied with a template. The only settings that cannot be removed are those for access control lists on file system and registry paths.

At an elevated administrator prompt, you can create a rollback template by using the Secedit command-line utility. Enter the following:

```
secedit /generaterollback /db DatabaseName /cfg TemplateName
/rbk RollBackName /log LogName
```

DatabaseName is the name of a new database that will be used to perform the rollback, *TemplateName* is the name of an existing security template for which you are creating a rollback template, *RollBackName* sets the name of a new security template in which the reverse settings should be stored, and *LogName* sets the name of an optional file for tracking the status of the rollback process.

In the following example, you create a rollback template for the "File Servers" template:

```
secedit /generaterollback /db rollback.db /cfg "file servers.inf"
/rbk fs-orig.inf /log rollback.log
```

When you're ready to apply the template, press and hold or right-click the Security Configuration And Analysis node, and then tap or click Configure Computer Now. When prompted to set the error log path, tap or click OK because the default path should be sufficient. To view the configuration error log, press and hold or right-click the Security Configuration And Analysis node, and then tap or click View Log File. Note any problems, and take action as necessary.

If you created a rollback template prior to applying a security template, you can restore the computer's security settings to its previous state. To apply a rollback template, follow these steps:

1. In the Security Configuration And Analysis snap-in, press and hold or right-click the Security Configuration And Analysis node, and then tap or click Import Template.

2. In the Import Template dialog box, select the rollback template.

3. Select the Clear This Database Before Importing check box, and then tap or click Open.

4. Press and hold or right-click the Security Configuration And Analysis node, and then tap or click Configure Computer Now. Tap or click OK.

The only settings that cannot be restored are for access control lists on file system and registry paths. After the permissions on file system and registry paths have been applied, you cannot reverse the process automatically and must instead manually reverse the changes one at a time.

Deploying security templates to multiple computers

Rather than applying security templates to one computer at a time, you can deploy your security configurations to multiple computers through Group Policy. To do this, you need to import the security template into a GPO processed by the computers to which the template settings should apply. Then, when policy is refreshed, all computers within the scope of the GPO receive the security configuration.

Security templates apply only to the Computer Configuration portion of Group Policy. Before you deploy security configurations in this way, you should take a close look at the domain and organizational unit (OU) structure of your organization and make changes as necessary to ensure that the security configuration is applied only to relevant types of computers. Essentially, this means that you need to create OUs for the different types of computers in your organization, and then move the computer accounts for these computers into the appropriate OUs. Afterward, you need to create and link a GPO for each of the computer OUs. For example, you could create the following computer OUs:

- **Domain Controllers** An OU for your organization's domain controllers. This OU is created automatically in a domain.

- **High-Security Member Servers** An OU for servers that require higher than usual security configurations.

- **Member Servers** An OU for servers that require standard server security configurations.

- **Laptop and Mobile Devices** An OU for laptops and mobile devices, which are inherently less secure and might require enhanced security configurations.

- **High-Security User Workstations** An OU for workstations that require higher than usual security configurations.

- **User Workstations** An OU for workstations that require standard workstation security configurations.

- **Remote Access Computers** An OU for computers that remotely access the organization's network.

- **Restricted Computers** An OU for computers that require restrictive security configurations, such as computers that are used in labs or kiosks.

REAL WORLD You need to be extra careful when you deploy security templates through GPOs. If you haven't done this before, practice in a test environment first, and be sure to also practice recovering computers to their original security settings. If you create a GPO and link the GPO to the appropriate level in the Active Directory structure, you can recover the computers to their original state by removing the link to the GPO. This is why it's extremely important to create and link a new GPO rather than use an existing GPO.

To deploy a security template to a computer GPO, follow these steps:

1. After you configure a security template and have tested it to ensure that it is appropriate, open the GPO you previously created and linked to the appropriate level of your Active Directory structure. In the Group Policy Management editor, open Computer Configuration\Windows Settings\Security Settings.

2. Press and hold or right-click Security Settings, and then tap or click Import Policy.

3. In the Import Policy From dialog box, select the security template to import, and then tap or click Open. Security templates end with the .inf file extension.

4. Check the configuration state of the security settings to verify that the settings were imported as expected, and then close the policy editor. Repeat this process for each security template and computer GPO you've configured. In the default configuration of Group Policy, it will take 90 to 120 minutes for the settings to be pushed out to computers in the organization.

Using the Security Configuration Wizard

The Security Configuration Wizard can help you create and apply a comprehensive security policy. A security policy is an XML file you can use to configure services, network security, registry values, and audit policies. Because security policies are role-based and feature-based, you generally need to create a separate policy for each of your standard server configurations. For example, if your organization uses domain controllers, file servers, and print servers, you might want to create a separate policy for each of these server types. If your organization has mail servers, database servers, and combined file/print servers in addition to domain controllers, you should create separate policies tailored to these server types.

You can use the Security Configuration Wizard to do the following:

- Create a security policy
- Edit a security policy
- Apply a security policy
- Roll back the last-applied security policy

Security policies can incorporate one or more security templates. Much like you can with security templates, you can apply a security policy to the currently logged-on computer by using the Security Configuration Wizard. Through Group Policy, you can also apply a security policy to multiple computers. By default, security policies created with the Security Configuration Wizard are saved in the %SystemRoot% \security\msscw\Policies folder.

The command-line counterpart to the graphical wizard is the Scwcmd (Scwcmd.exe) utility. At an elevated administrator prompt, you can use Scwcmd Analyze to determine whether a computer is in compliance with a security policy and Scwcmd Configure to apply a security policy.

Creating security policies

The Security Configuration Wizard allows you to configure policies only for roles and features that are installed on a computer when you run the wizard. The precise step-by-step process for creating security policies depends on the server roles and features available on the computer that is currently logged on. That said, the general configuration sections presented in the wizard are the same regardless of the computer configuration.

The Security Configuration Wizard has the following configuration sections:

- **Role-Based Service Configuration**   Configures the startup mode of system services based on a server's installed roles, installed features, installed options, and required services.

- **Network Security**   Configures inbound and outbound security rules for Windows Firewall With Advanced Security based on installed roles and installed options.

- **Registry Settings**   Configures protocols used to communicate with other computers based on installed roles and installed options.

- **Audit Policy**   Configures auditing on the selected server based on your preferences.

- **Save Security Policy**   Allows you to save and view the security policy. You can also include one or more security templates.

With the fact that the step-by-step process can vary in mind, you can create a security policy by following these steps:

1. Start the Security Configuration Wizard in Server Manager by tapping or clicking Tools, Security Configuration Wizard. On the Welcome page of the wizard, tap or click Next.

2. On the Configuration Action page, review the actions you can perform. (See Figure 5-11.) Create A New Security Policy is selected by default. Tap or click Next.

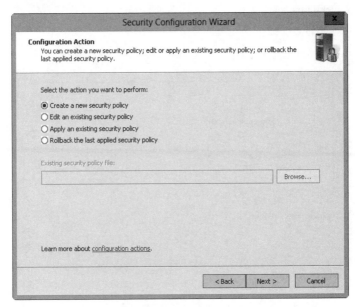

FIGURE 5-11 Review the actions you can perform.

3. On the Select Server page, select the server you want to use as a baseline for this security policy. The baseline server is the server on which the roles, features, and options with which you want to work are installed. The computer that is logged on is selected by default. To choose a different computer, tap or click Browse. In the Select Computer dialog box, enter the name of the computer, and then tap or click Check Names. Select the computer account you want to use, and then tap or click OK.

4. When you tap or click Next, the wizard collects the security configuration and stores it in a security configuration database. On the Processing Security Configuration Database page, tap or click View Configuration Database to view the settings in the database. After you review the settings in the SCW Viewer, return to the wizard and tap or click Next to continue.

5. Each configuration section has an introductory page. The first introductory page is the one for Role-Based Service Configuration. Tap or click Next.

6. The Select Server Roles page, shown in Figure 5-12, lists the installed server roles. Select each role that should be enabled. Clear the check box for each role that should be disabled. Selecting a role enables services, inbound ports, and settings required for that role. Clearing a role disables services, inbound ports, and settings required for that role, provided that they aren't required by an enabled role. Tap or click Next.

FIGURE 5-12 Select the server roles to enable.

7. On the Select Client Features page, you'll find the installed client features used to enable services. Select each feature that should be enabled, and clear each feature that should be disabled. Selecting a feature enables services required for that feature. Clearing a feature disables services required for that feature, if they aren't required by an enabled feature. Tap or click Next.

8. On the Select Administration And Other Options page, you'll see the installed options used to enable services and open ports. Select each option that should be enabled, and clear each option that should be disabled. Selecting an option enables services required for that option. Clearing an option disables services required for that option, if they aren't required by an enabled option. Tap or click Next.

9. On the Select Additional Services page, you'll find a list of additional services found on the selected server while processing the security configuration database. Select each service that should be enabled, and clear each service that should be disabled. Selecting a service enables services required for that service. Clearing a service disables services required for that service, if they aren't required by an enabled service. Tap or click Next.

10. On the Handling Unspecified Services page, indicate how unspecified services should be handled. Unspecified services are services that are not installed on the selected server and are not listed in the security configuration database. By default, the startup mode of unspecified services is not changed. To disable unspecified services instead, select Disable The Service. Tap or click Next.

11. On the Confirm Service Changes page, review the services that will be changed on the selected server if the security policy is applied. Note the current startup mode and the startup mode that will be applied by the policy. Tap or click Next.

12. On the introductory page for Network Security, tap or click Next. On the Network Security Rules page, you'll find a list of firewall rules needed for the roles, features, and options you previously selected. You can add, edit, or remove inbound and outbound rules by using the options provided. Tap or click Next when you are ready to continue.

13. On the introductory page for Registry Settings, tap or click Next. On the Require SMB Security Signatures page, review the server message block (SMB) security signature options. By default, minimum operating system requirements and digital signing are used, and you won't want to change these settings. Tap or click Next.

14. For domain controllers and servers with LDAP, on the Require LDAP Signing page, you can set minimum operating system requirements for all directory-enabled computers that access Active Directory Domain Services.

15. On the Outbound Authentication Methods page, choose the methods that the selected server uses to authenticate with remote computers. Your choices set the outbound LAN Manager authentication level that will be used. If the computer communicates only with domain computers, select Domain Accounts, but do not select the other options. This will ensure that the computer uses the highest level of outbound LAN Manager authentication. If the computer communicates with both domain and workgroup computers, select Domain Accounts and Local Accounts On The Remote Computers. In most cases, you won't want to select the file-sharing option because this will result in a substantially lowered authentication level. Tap or click Next.

16. The outbound authentication methods you choose determine what additional Registry Settings pages are displayed. Keep the following in mind:

    ■ If you don't select any outbound authentication methods, the outbound LAN Manager authentication level is set as Send NTLMv2 Response Only, and an additional page is displayed to enable you to set the inbound authentication method. On the Inbound Authentication Using Domain Accounts page, choose the types of computers from which the selected server will accept connections. Your choices set the inbound LAN Manager authentication level that will be used. If the computer communicates only with Windows XP Professional or later computers, clear both options to ensure that the computer uses the highest level of inbound LAN Manager authentication. If the computer communicates with older PCs, accept the default selections. Tap or click Next.

    ■ If you select domain accounts, local accounts, or both, you'll have additional related pages that enable you to set the LAN Manager authentication level used when making outbound connections. You'll also be able to specify that you want to synchronize clocks with this server's clock. Inbound authentication is set as Accept All.

    ■ If you allow file sharing passwords for early releases of Windows, the outbound LAN Manager authentication level is set as Send LM & NTLM Only and the inbound authentication level is set as Accept All. Because of this, when you tap or click Next, the Registry Settings Summary page is displayed.

17. On the Registry Settings Summary page, review the values that will be changed on the selected server if the security policy is applied. Note the current value and the value that will be applied by the policy. Tap or click Next.

18. On the introductory page for Audit Policy, tap or click Next. On the System Audit Policy page, configure the level of auditing you want. To disable auditing, select Do Not Audit. To enable auditing for successful events, select Audit Successful Activities. To enable auditing for all events, select Audit Successful And Unsuccessful Activities. Tap or click Next.

19. On the Audit Policy Summary page, review the settings that will be changed on the selected server if the security policy is applied. Note the current setting and the setting that will be applied by the policy. Tap or click Next.

20. On the introductory page for Save Security Policy, tap or click Next. On the Security Policy File Name page, you can configure options for saving the security policy and adding one or more security templates to the policy. To view the security policy in the SCW Viewer, tap or click View Security Policy. When you have finished viewing the policy, return to the wizard.

21. To add security templates to the policy, tap or click Include Security Templates. In the Include Security Templates dialog box, tap or click Add. In the Open dialog box, select a security template to include in the security policy. If you add more than one security template, you can prioritize them in case any security configuration conflicts occur between them. Settings from templates higher in the list have priority. Select a template, and then tap or click the Up and Down buttons to prioritize the templates. Tap or click OK.

22. By default, the security policy is saved in the %SystemRoot%\Security\Msscw \Policies folder. Tap or click Browse. In the Save As dialog box, select a different save location for the policy if necessary. After you enter a name for the security policy, tap or click Save. The default or selected folder path and file name are then listed in the Security Policy File Name text box.

23. Tap or click Next. On the Apply Security Policy page, you can choose to apply the policy now or later. Tap or click Next, and then tap or click Finish.

Editing security policies

You can use the Security Configuration Wizard to edit a security policy by following these steps:

1. Start the Security Configuration Wizard in Server Manager by tapping or clicking Tools, Security Configuration Wizard. When the wizard starts, tap or click Next.

2. On the Configuration Action page, select Edit An Existing Security Policy, and then tap or click Browse. In the Open dialog box, select the security policy with which you want to work, and then tap or click Open. Security policies end with the .xml extension. Tap or click Next.

3. Follow steps 3–23 of the procedure in the section "Creating security policies" to edit the configuration of the security policy.

Applying security policies

You can use the Security Configuration Wizard to apply a security policy by following these steps:

1. Start the Security Configuration Wizard in Server Manager by tapping or clicking Tools, Security Configuration Wizard. When the wizard starts, tap or click Next.

2. On the Configuration Action page, select Apply An Existing Security Policy, and then tap or click Browse. In the Open dialog box, select the security policy with which you want to work and then tap or click Open. Security policies end with the .xml extension. Tap or click Next.

3. On the Select Server page, select the server to which you want to apply the security policy. The computer that is logged on is selected by default. To choose a different computer, tap or click Browse. In the Select Computer dialog box, enter the name of the computer, and then tap or click Check Names. Select the computer account you want to use, and then tap or click OK.

4. Tap or click Next. On the Apply Security Policy page, tap or click View Security Policy to view the security policy in the SCW Viewer. When you have finished viewing the policy, return to the wizard.

5. Tap or click Next to apply the policy to the selected server. When the wizard finishes applying the policy, tap or click Next, and then tap or click Finish.

Rolling back the last applied security policy

You can use the Security Configuration Wizard to roll back the last security policy you applied by following these steps:

1. Start the Security Configuration Wizard inn Server Manager by tapping or clicking Tools, Security Configuration Wizard. When the wizard starts, tap or click Next.

2. On the Configuration Action page, select Rollback The Last Applied Security Policy, and then tap or click Next.

3. On the Select Server page, select the server on which you want to roll back the last security policy you applied. The computer that is logged on is selected by default. To choose a different computer, tap or click Browse. In the Select Computer dialog box, enter the name of the computer, and then tap or click Check Names. Select the computer account you want to use, and then tap or click OK.

4. Tap or click Next. On the Rollback Security Configuration page, tap or click View Rollback File to view the details of the last applied security policy in the SCW Viewer. When you finish viewing the policy, return to the wizard.

5. Tap or click Next to roll back the policy to the selected server. When the wizard finishes the rollback process, tap or click Next, and then tap or click Finish.

Deploying a security policy to multiple computers

In an organization with many computers, you probably won't want to apply a security policy to each computer separately. As discussed in "Deploying security templates to multiple computers" earlier in this chapter, you might want to apply a security policy through Group Policy, and you might want to create computer OUs for this purpose.

After you've created the necessary OUs, you can use the Scwcmd utility's transform command to create a GPO that includes the settings in the security policy (and any security templates attached to the policy). You then deploy the settings to computers by linking the new GPO to the appropriate OU or OUs. By default, security policies created with the Security Configuration Wizard are saved in the %SystemRoot%\security\msscw\Policies folder.

Use the following syntax to transform a security policy:

```
scwcmd transform /p:FullFilePathToSecurityPolicy /g:GPOName
```

FullFilePathToSecurityPolicy is the full file path to the security policy's .xml file, and *GPOName* is the display name for the new GPO. Consider the following example:

```
scwcmd transform /p:"c:\users\wrs\documents\fspolicy.xml"
/g: "FileServer GPO"
```

When you create the GPO, you can link the GPO by following these steps:

1. In the Group Policy Management Console (GPMC), select the OU with which you want to work. In the right pane, the Linked Group Policy Objects tab shows the GPOs that are currently linked to the selected OU (if any).

2. Press and hold or right-click the OU to which you want to link the previously created GPO, and then select Link An Existing GPO. In the Select GPO dialog box, select the GPO to which you want to link, and then tap or click OK.

   When Group Policy is refreshed for computers in the applicable OU, the policy settings in the GPO are applied.

Because you created a new GPO and linked the GPO to the appropriate level in the Active Directory structure, you can restore the computers to their original state by removing the link to the GPO. To remove a link to a GPO, follow these steps:

1. In the GPMC, select and then expand the OU with which you want to work. In the right pane, the Linked Group Policy Objects tab shows the GPOs that are currently linked to the selected OU.

2. Press and hold or right-click the GPO. On the shortcut menu, the Link Enabled option should have a check mark to show it is enabled. Clear this option to remove the link.

CHAPTER 6

Managing users and computers with Group Policy

You can use Group Policy to manage users and computers in many different ways. In the sections that follow, I'll describe some specific management areas, including the following:

- Folder redirection
- Computer and user scripts
- Software deployment
- Work Folders options
- Computer and user certificate enrollment
- Automatic update settings

Centrally managing special folders

You can centrally manage special folders used by Windows Server through folder redirection. You do this by redirecting special folders to a central network location instead of using multiple default locations on each computer. For Windows Vista and later releases of Windows, the special folders you can manage are AppData (Roaming), Desktop, Start Menu, Documents, Pictures, Music, Videos, Favorites, Contacts, Downloads, Links, Searches, and Saved Games.

Note that even though current releases of Windows store personal folders in slightly different ways, you manage the folders in the same way within Group Policy.

You have two general options for redirection. You can redirect a special folder to the same network location for all users, or you can designate locations based on user membership in security groups. In either case, you should make sure that the network location you plan to use is available as a network share. See Chapter 4, "Data security and auditing," for details on sharing data on a network.

By default, users can redirect folders no matter which computer they're using within the domain. Windows 8.1 and Windows Server 2012 R2 enable you to modify this behavior by specifying from which computers a user can access roaming profiles and redirected folders. You do this by designating certain computers as primary computers, and then configuring domain policy to restrict the downloading of profiles, redirected folders, or both to primary computers. For more information, see Chapter 10, "Managing existing user and group accounts" in Windows Server 2012 R2: Essentials & Configuration.

Redirecting a special folder to a single location

You can redirect a special folder to a single location by following these steps:

1. In the Group Policy Management Console (GPMC), press and hold or right-click the Group Policy object (GPO) for the site, domain, or organizational unit with which you want to work, and then tap or click Edit to open the policy editor for the GPO.

    NOTE If you'd rather create a new GPO, press and hold or right-click the site, domain or organizational unit and then select Create A GPO... And Link It Here. In the New GPO dialog box, enter a name for the GPO, and then select OK.

2. In the policy editor, expand the following nodes: User Configuration, Policies, Windows Settings, and Folder Redirection.

3. Under Folder Redirection, press and hold or right-click the special folder with which you want to work, such as AppData(Roaming), and then tap or click Properties to open a Properties dialog box similar to the one shown in Figure 6-1.

4. In the Setting list on the Target tab, choose Basic—Redirect Everyone's Folder To The Same Location.

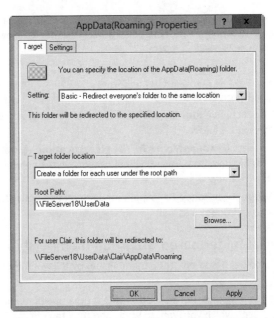

FIGURE 6-1 Set options for redirection by using a special folder's Properties dialog box.

5. Under Target Folder Location, you have several options depending on the folder with which you're working, and those options include the following:

- **Redirect To The User's Home Directory** If you select this option, the folder is redirected to a subdirectory within the user's home directory. You set the location of the user's home directory with the %HomeDrive% and %HomePath% environment variables.

- **Create A Folder For Each User Under The Root Path** If you select this option, a folder is created for each user at the location you enter in the Root Path text box. The folder name is the user account name as specified by %UserName%. Thus, if you enter the root path value \\Zeta\UserDocuments, the folder for Williams will be located at \\Zeta \UserDocuments\Williams.

- **Redirect To The Following Location** If you select this option, the folder is redirected to the location you enter in the Root Path text box. Here, you typically want to use an environment variable to customize the folder location for each user. For example, you could use the root path value \\Zeta\UserData\%UserName%\docs.

- **Redirect To The Local Userprofile Location** If you select this option, the folder is redirected to a subdirectory within the user profile directory. You set the location of the user profile with the %UserProfile% variable.

IMPORTANT When specifying the root path, be sure to specify the UNC path for the server and not a local path. The basic syntax for a UNC path is \\ServerName \ShareName, such as \\CorpServer38\CorpData.

6. Tap or click the Settings tab, configure the following additional options, and then tap or click OK to complete the process:

- **Grant The User Exclusive Rights To** Gives users full rights to access their data in the special folder.

- **Move The Contents Of *FolderName* To The New Location** Moves the data in the special folders from the individual systems on the network to the central folder or folders.

- **Also Apply Redirection Policy To** Applies the redirection policy to previous releases of Windows as well.

Redirecting a special folder based on group membership

You can redirect a special folder based on group membership by following these steps:

1. In the GPMC, press and hold or right-click the GPO for the site, domain, or organizational unit with which you want to work, and then tap or click Edit to open the policy editor for the GPO.

2. In the policy editor, expand the following nodes: User Configuration, Policies, Windows Settings, and Folder Redirection.

3. Under Folder Redirection, press and hold or right-click the special folder with which you want to work, such as AppData(Roaming), and then tap or click Properties.

4. In the Setting list on the Target tab, choose Advanced – Specify Locations For Various User Groups. As shown in Figure 6-2, a Security Group Membership panel is added to the Properties dialog box.

5. Tap or click Add to open the Specify Group And Location dialog box. Or select a group entry, and then tap or click Edit to modify its settings.

6. In the Security Group Membership text box, enter the name of the security group for which you want to configure redirection, or tap or click Browse to find a security group to add.

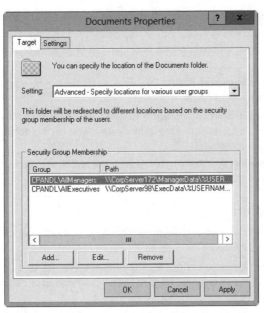

FIGURE 6-2 Configure advanced redirection by using the Security Group Membership panel.

7. As with basic redirection, the options available depend on the folder with which you're working and include the following:

- **Redirect To The User's Home Directory** If you select this option, the folder is redirected to a subdirectory within the user's home directory. You set the location of the user's home directory with the %HomeDrive% and %HomePath% environment variables.

- **Create A Folder For Each User Under The Root Path** If you select this option, a folder is created for each user at the location you enter in the Root Path text box. The folder name is the user account name as specified by %UserName%. Thus, if you enter the root path value \\Zeta\UserDocuments, the folder for Williams will be located at \\Zeta\UserDocuments\Williams.

- **Redirect To The Following Location** If you select this option, the folder is redirected to the location you enter in the Root Path text box. Here, you typically want to use an environment variable to customize the folder location for each user. For example, you could use the root path value \\Zeta\UserData\%UserName%\docs.

- **Redirect To The Local Userprofile Location** If you select this option, the folder is redirected to a subdirectory within the user profile directory. You set the location of the user profile with the %UserProfile% variable.

8. Tap or click OK. Repeat steps 5–7 for other groups you want to configure.

9. When you're done creating group entries, tap or click the Settings tab, configure the following additional options, and then tap or click OK to complete the process:

   - **Grant The User Exclusive Rights To**   Gives users full rights to access their data in the special folder.

   - **Move The Contents Of *FolderName* To The New Location**   Moves the data in the special folders from the individual systems on the network to the central folder or folders.

   - **Also Apply Redirection Policy To**   Applies the redirection policy to early releases of Windows as well.

Removing redirection

Sometimes you might want to remove redirection from a particular special folder. You remove redirection by following these steps:

1. In the GPMC, press and hold or right-click the GPO for the site, domain, or organizational unit with which you want to work, and then tap or click Edit to open the policy editor for the GPO.

2. In the policy editor, expand the following nodes: User Configuration, Policies, Windows Settings, and Folder Redirection.

3. Under Folder Redirection, press and hold or right-click the special folder with which you want to work, and then tap or click Properties.

4. Tap or click the Settings tab, and then make sure that an appropriate Policy Removal option is selected. The following two options are available:

   - **Leave The Folder In The New Location When Policy Is Removed**   When you select this option, the folder and its contents remain at the redirected location and current users are still permitted to access the folder and its contents at this location.

   - **Redirect The Folder Back To The Local Userprofile Location When Policy Is Removed**   When you select this option, the folder and its contents are copied back to the original location; however, the contents aren't deleted from the previous location.

5. If you changed the Policy Removal option, tap or click Apply, and then tap or click the Target tab. Otherwise, just tap or click the Target tab.

6. To remove all redirection definitions for the special folder, choose Not Configured in the Setting list.

7. To remove redirection for a particular security group, select the security group in the Security Group Membership panel, and then tap or click Remove. Tap or click OK.

User and computer script management

You can configure four types of scripts with Windows Server:

- **Computer Startup**   Executed during startup
- **Computer Shutdown**   Executed prior to shutdown
- **User Logon**   Executed when a user logs on
- **User Logoff**   Executed when a user logs off

Windows supports scripts written as command-shell batch scripts ending with the .bat or .cmd extension or scripts that use the Windows Script Host (WSH). WSH is a feature of Windows Server that enables you to use scripts written in a scripting language, such as VBScript, without needing to insert the script into a webpage. To provide a multipurpose scripting environment, WSH relies on scripting engines. A scripting engine is the component that defines the core syntax and structure of a particular scripting language. Windows Server ships with scripting engines for VBScript and JScript. Other scripting engines are also available.

Beginning with Windows 7 and Windows Server 2008 R2, current Windows operating systems also support Windows PowerShell scripts. When Windows PowerShell is installed on computers that process a particular GPO, you can use Windows PowerShell scripts in much the same way as you use other scripts. You have the option of running Windows PowerShell scripts before or after other types of scripts.

Assigning computer startup and shutdown scripts

Computer startup and shutdown scripts are assigned as part of a GPO; as a result, all computers that are members of the site, domain, or organizational unit—or all three—execute scripts automatically when they're started or shut down.

To assign a computer startup or shutdown script, follow these steps:

1. In File Explorer, open the folder containing the script or scripts you want to use.

2. In the GPMC, press and hold or right-click the GPO for the site, domain, or organizational unit with which you want to work, and then tap or click Edit to open the policy editor for the GPO.

3. In the Computer Configuration\Policies node, double-tap or double-click the Windows Settings folder, and then tap or click Scripts.

4. To work with startup scripts, press and hold or right-click Startup, and then tap or click Properties. To work with shutdown scripts, press and hold or right-click Shutdown and select Properties to open a dialog box similar to the one shown in Figure 6-3.

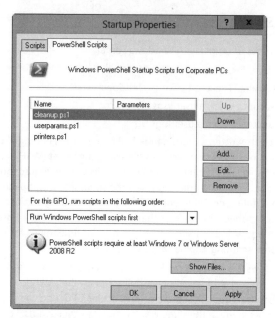

FIGURE 6-3 Add, edit, and remove computer startup scripts by using the Startup Properties dialog box.

5. On the Scripts tab, you can manage command-shell batch scripts ending with the .bat or .cmd extension and scripts that use the Windows Script Host. On the PowerShell Scripts tab, you can manage Windows PowerShell scripts. When working with either tab, tap or click Show Files.

6. Copy the files in the open File Explorer window, and then paste them into the window that opened when you clicked Show Files.

7. Tap or click Add to open the Add A Script dialog box and assign a script. In the Script Name text box, enter the name of the script you copied to the Machine\Scripts\Startup or the Machine\Scripts\Shutdown folder for the related policy. In the Script Parameters text box, enter any parameters to pass to the script. Repeat this step to add other scripts.

8. During startup or shutdown, scripts are executed in the order in which they're listed in the Properties dialog box. On the Scripts tab, use the Up and Down buttons to reorder scripts as necessary. Do the same on the PowerShell Scripts tab. On the PowerShell Scripts tab, you can also use the selection list to specify whether Windows PowerShell scripts should run before or after other types of scripts.

9. If you want to edit the script name or parameters later, select the script in the Script For list, and then tap or click Edit. To delete a script, select the script in the Script For list, and tap or click Remove.

10. To save your changes, tap or click OK.

Assigning user logon and logoff scripts

You can assign user scripts in one of the three following ways:

- You can assign logon and logoff scripts as part of a GPO; and as a result, all users who are members of the site, domain, or organizational unit—or all three—execute scripts automatically when they log on or log off.

- You can also assign logon scripts individually through the Active Directory Users And Computers console, which enables you to assign a separate logon script to each user or group.

- You can also assign individual logon scripts as scheduled tasks by using the Scheduled Task Wizard.

To assign a logon or logoff script in a GPO, follow these steps:

1. In File Explorer, open the folder containing the script or scripts you want to use.

2. In the GPMC, press and hold or right-click the GPO for the site, domain, or organizational unit with which you want to work, and then tap or click Edit to open the policy editor for the GPO.

3. Double-tap or double-click the Windows Settings folder in the User Configuration\Policies node, and then tap or click Scripts.

4. To work with logon scripts, press and hold or right-click Logon, and then tap or click Properties. To work with logoff scripts, press and hold or right-click Logoff, and then tap or click Properties. This opens a dialog box similar to the one shown in Figure 6-4.

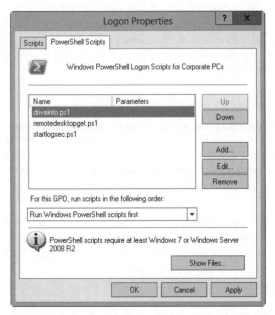

FIGURE 6-4 Add, edit, and remove user logon scripts by using the Logon Properties dialog box.

5. On the Scripts tab, you can manage command-shell batch scripts ending with the .bat or .cmd extension and scripts that use the Windows Script Host. On the PowerShell Scripts tab, you can manage Windows PowerShell scripts. When working with either tab, tap or click Show Files.

6. Copy the files in the open File Explorer window, and then paste them into the window that opened when you clicked Show Files.

7. Tap or click Add to open the Add A Script dialog box and assign a script. In the Script Name text box, enter the name of the script you copied to the User\Scripts\Logon or the User\Scripts\Logoff folder for the related policy. In the Script Parameter text box, enter any parameters to pass to the script. Repeat this step to add other scripts.

8. During logon or logoff, scripts are executed in the order in which they're listed in the Properties dialog box. On the Scripts tab, use the Up and Down buttons to reorder scripts as necessary. Do the same on the PowerShell Scripts tab, on which you can also use the selection list to specify whether Windows PowerShell scripts should run before or after other types of scripts.

9. If you want to edit the script name or parameters later, select the script in the Script For list, and then tap or click Edit. To delete a script, select the script in the Script For list, and then tap or click Remove.

10. To save your changes, tap or click OK.

Deploying software through Group Policy

Group Policy includes basic functionality, called Software Installation policy, for deploying software. Although Software Installation policy is not designed to replace enterprise solutions such as System Center 2012 R2, you can use it to automate the deployment and maintenance of software in just about any size organization if your computers are running the Windows operating system.

Getting to know Software Installation policy

In Group Policy, you can deploy software on a per-computer or per-user basis. Per-computer applications are available to all users of a computer and configured under Computer Configuration\Policies\Software Settings\Software Installation. Per-user applications are available to individual users and configured under User Configuration\Policies\Software Settings\Software Installation.

You deploy software in three key ways:

- **Computer assignment** Assigns the software to client computers so that it is installed when the computer starts. This technique requires no user intervention, but it does require a restart to install the software. Installed software is then available to all users on the computer.

- **User assignment** Assigns the software to users so that it is installed when a user logs on. This technique requires no user intervention, but it does require the user to log on to install or advertise the software. The software is associated with the user only and not the computer.

- **User publishing** Publishes the software so that users can install it manually through Programs And Features. This technique requires the user to explicitly install software or activate installation. The software is associated with the user only.

When you use user assignment or user publishing, you can advertise the software so that a computer can install the software when it is first used. With advertisements, the software can be installed automatically in the following situations:

- When a user accesses a document that requires the software
- When a user opens a shortcut to the application
- When another application requires a component of the software

When you configure Software Installation policy, you should generally not use existing GPOs. Instead, you should create GPOs that configure software installation, and then link those GPOs to the appropriate containers in Group Policy. When you use this approach, it's much easier to redeploy software and apply updates.

After you create a GPO for your software deployment, you should set up a distribution point. A distribution point is a shared folder that is available to the computers and users to which you are deploying software. With basic applications, you prepare the distribution point by copying the installer package file and all required application files to the share and configuring permissions so that these files can be accessed. With other applications, you may need to prepare the distribution point by performing an administrative installation to the share. The advantage of an administrative installation is that the software can be updated and redeployed through Software Installation policy.

You can update applications deployed through Software Installation policy by using an update or service pack or by deploying a new version of the application. Each task is performed in a slightly different way.

Deploying software throughout your organization

Software Installation policy uses either Windows Installer Packages (.msi) or ZAW Down-Level Application Packages (.zap). When you use computer assignment, user assignment, or user publishing, you can deploy software by using Windows Installer Packages. When you use user publishing, you can deploy software by using either Windows Installer Packages or ZAW Down-Level Application Packages. With either technique, you must set file permissions on the installer package so that the appropriate computer and user accounts have read access.

Because Software Installation policy is applied only during foreground processing of policy settings, per-computer application deployments are processed at startup and per-user application deployments are processed at logon. You can customize installation by using transform (.mst) files. Transform files modify the installation process according to the settings you defined for specific computers and users.

You can deploy software by following these steps:

1. In the GPMC, press and hold or right-click the GPO you want to use for the deployment, and then tap or click Edit.

2. In the policy editor, open Computer Configuration\Policies\Software Settings \Software Installation or User Configuration\Policies\Software Settings \Software Installation as appropriate for the type of software deployment.

3. Press and hold or right-click Software Installation. On the shortcut menu, tap or click New, and then tap or click Package.

4. In the Open dialog box, go to the network share where your package is located, tap or click the package to select it, and then tap or click Open.

   NOTE Windows Installer Packages (.msi) is selected by default in the Files Of Type list. If you are performing a user publishing deployment, you can also choose ZAW Down-Level Application Packages (.zap) as the file type.

5. In the Deploy Software dialog box, shown in Figure 6-5, select one of the following deployment methods, and then tap or click OK:

   - **Published**   To publish the application without modifications
   - **Assigned**   To assign the application without modifications
   - **Advanced**   To deploy the application by using advanced configuration options

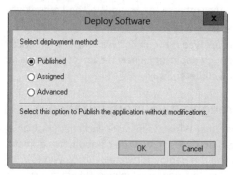

FIGURE 6-5 Select the deployment method.

Configuring software deployment options

You can view and set general options for a software package by following these steps:

1. In the GPMC, press and hold or right-click the GPO you want to use for the deployment, and then tap or click Edit.

2. In the policy editor, access Computer Configuration\Policies\Software Settings \Software Installation or User Configuration\Policies\Software Settings \Software Installation as appropriate for the type of software deployment.

3. Double-tap or double-click the Software Installation package. In the Properties dialog box, review or modify software deployment options.

4. On the Deployment tab, shown in Figure 6-6, you can change the deployment type and configure the following deployment and installation options:

- **Auto-Install This Application By File Extension Activation** Advertises any file extensions associated with this package for install-on-first-use deployment. This option is selected by default.

- **Uninstall This Application When It Falls Out Of The Scope Of Management** Removes the application if it no longer applies to the user.

- **Do Not Display This Package In The Add/Remove Programs Control Panel** Prevents the application from appearing in Add/Remove Programs, which prevents a user from uninstalling an application.

- **Install This Application At Logon** Configures full installation—rather than advertisement—of an application when the user logs on. This option cannot be set when you publish a package for users.

- **Installation User Interface Options** Controls how the installation is performed. With the default setting, Maximum, the user gets all setup screens and messages during installation. With the Basic option, the user gets only error and completion messages during installation.

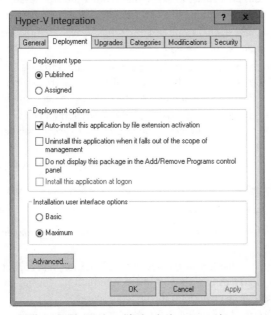

FIGURE 6-6 Review and modify the deployment options as necessary.

5. Tap or click OK.

Updating deployed software

When an application uses a Windows Installer package, you can apply an update or service pack to a deployed application by following these steps:

1. After you obtain an .msi file or .msp (security update) file containing the update or service pack to be applied, copy the .msi or .msp file and any new installation files to the folder containing the original .msi file. Overwrite any duplicate files as necessary.

2. In the GPMC, press and hold or right-click the GPO you want to use for the deployment, and then tap or click Edit.

3. In the policy editor, access Computer Configuration\Policies\Software Settings \Software Installation or User Configuration\Policies\Software Settings \Software Installation as appropriate for the type of software deployment.

4. Press and hold or right-click the package with which you want to work. On the shortcut menu, tap or click All Tasks, and then tap or click Redeploy Application.

5. When prompted to confirm the action, tap or click Yes. The application is then redeployed to all users and computers as appropriate for the GPO with which you are working.

When an application uses an Installer package that is not Windows-based, you can update a deployed application or apply a service pack by following these steps:

1. In the GPMC, press and hold or right-click the GPO you want to use for the deployment, and then tap or click Edit.

2. In the policy editor, access Computer Configuration\Policies\Software Settings \Software Installation or User Configuration\Policies\Software Settings \Software Installation as appropriate for the type of software deployment.

3. Press and hold or right-click the package. On the shortcut menu, tap or click All Tasks, and then tap or click Remove. Tap or click OK to accept the default option of immediate removal.

4. Copy the new .zap file and all related files to a network share, and redeploy the application.

Upgrading deployed software

You can upgrade a previously deployed application to a new version by following these steps:

1. Obtain a Windows Installer file for the new software version, and copy it along with all required files to a network share. Alternatively, you can per-form an administrative installation to the network share.

2. In the GPMC, press and hold or right-click the GPO you want to use for the deployment, and then tap or click Edit.

3. In the policy editor, access Computer Configuration\Policies\Software Settings \Software Installation or User Configuration\Policies\Software Settings \Software Installation as appropriate for the type of software deployment.

4. Press and hold or right-click Software Installation. On the shortcut menu, tap or click New, and then tap or click Package. Create an assigned or published application by using the Windows Installer file for the new software version.

5. Press and hold or right-click the upgrade package, and then tap or click Properties. On the Upgrades tab, tap or click Add. In the Add Upgrade Package dialog box, do one of the following:

   ■ If the original application and the upgrade are in the current GPO, select Current Group Policy Object, and then select the previously deployed application in the Package To Upgrade list.

   ■ If the original application and the upgrade are in different GPOs, select A Specific GPO, tap or click Browse, and then select the GPO from the Browse For A Group Policy Object dialog box. Select the previously deployed application in the Package To Upgrade list.

6. Choose an upgrade option. If you want to replace the application with the new version, select Uninstall The Existing Package, Then Install The Upgrade Package. If you want to perform an in-place upgrade over the existing instal-lation, select Package Can Upgrade Over The Existing Package.

7. Tap or click OK to close the Add Upgrade Package dialog box. If you want to make this a required upgrade, select the Required Upgrade For Existing Packages check box, and then tap or click OK to close the upgrade package's Properties dialog box.

Automatically configuring Work Folders

Computers that are members of a workplace can access internal network resources, such as internal websites and business applications. Work Folders enable users to synchronize their corporate data to their devices and vice versa. Those devices can be joined to the corporate domain or a workplace. Devices access Work Folders via a remote web gateway running on Microsoft Internet Information Services (IIS).

To deploy Work Folders, you add the File And Storage Services \ Work Folders role to a file server, and then configure Work Folders by using Server Manager. Afterward, you can use policy settings to control related options, such as the server to which users can connect remotely and access Work Folders. You control the con-nection server in one of two ways:

■ By specifying the exact URL of a file server hosting the Work Folders for the user, such as *https://server29.cpandl.com*

■ By specifying the URL used within your organization for Work Folders discov-ery, such as *https://workfolders.cpandl.com*

REAL WORLD Clients use secure encrypted communications to connect to work folders as long as the file servers hosting the Work Folders have valid SSL certificates. When a device initiates an SSL connection, the server sends the certificate to the client. The client evaluates the certificate and continues only if the certificate is valid and can be trusted. If you configure a connection to an exact URL, the client can connect directly to the specified sever and synchronize data in Work Folders. The server's certificate must have a Common Name (CN) or a Subject Alternative Name (SAN) that matches the host header in the request. For example, if the client makes a request to https://server18.cpandl.com, the CN or SAN must be server18.cpandl.com.

In Group Policy, you specify the URL used within your organization for Work Folders discovery by using the Specify Work Folders Settings policy found under Administrative Templates policies for User Configuration\Windows Components \Work Folders. Any server configured with Work Folders acts as a discovery server by default. If you configure a discovery URL, a client connects to one of several servers, and the email address of the user is used to discover which specific server hosts the Work Folders for the client. The client is then connected to this server. Each discovery server will need to have a certificate with multiple Subject Alternative Names, which includes the server name and the discovery name. For example, if a client makes a request to *https://workfolders.cpandl.com* and connects to *FileServer11.cpandl.com*, the server's certificate must have a CN or SAN of *fileserver11. cpandl.com* and a SAN of *workfolders.cpandl.com*.

If you want to configure Work Folders in Group Policy, use the following technique:

1. Access Group Policy for the system, site, domain, or OU with which you want to work. Next, access the Work Folders node by using the Administrative Templates policies for User Configuration under Windows Components \Work Folders.

2. Double-tap or double-click Specify Work Folders Settings, and then select Enabled.

3. In the World Folders URL text box, enter the URL of the file server that hosts the Work Folders for the user or the URL used within your organization for Work Folders discovery.

4. If you want to prevent users from changing settings when setting up Work Folders, select Force Automatic Setup.

5. Tap or click OK.

Automatically enrolling computer and user certificates

A server designated as a certificate authority (CA) is responsible for issuing digital certificates and managing certificate revocation lists (CRLs). Servers running Windows Server can be configured as certificate authorities by installing Active Directory Certificate Services. Computers and users can use certificates for authentication and encryption.

In an enterprise configuration, enterprise CAs are used for automatic enrollment. This means authorized users and computers can request a certificate, and the certificate authority can automatically process the certificate request so that the users and computers can immediately install the certificate.

Group Policy controls the way automatic enrollment works. When you install enterprise CAs, automatic enrollment policies for users and computers are enabled automatically. The policy for computer certificate enrollment is Certificate Services Client—Auto-Enrollment Settings under Computer Configuration\Policies\Windows Settings\Security Settings\Public Key Policies. The policy for user certificate enrollment is Certificate Services Client—Auto-Enrollment under User Configuration\Policies \Windows Settings\Security Settings\Public Key Policies.

You can configure automatic enrollment by following these steps:

1. In the GPMC, press and hold or right-click the GPO with which you want to work, and then tap or click Edit.

2. In the policy editor, access User Configuration\Policies\Windows Settings \Security Settings\Public Key Policies or Computer Configuration\Policies \Windows Settings\Security Settings\Public Key Policies as appropriate for the type of policy you want to review.

3. Double-tap or double-click Certificate Services Client—Auto-Enrollment. To disable automatic enrollment, select Disabled from the Configuration Model list, tap or click OK, and then skip the remaining steps in this procedure. To enable automatic enrollment, select Enabled from the Configuration Model list.

4. To automatically renew expired certificates, update pending certificates, and remove revoked certificates, select the related check box.

5. To ensure that the latest version of certificate templates are requested and used, select the Update Certificates That Use Certificate Templates check box.

6. To notify users when a certificate is about to expire, specify when notifications are sent using the box provided. By default, notifications are sent when 10 percent of the certificate lifetime remains.

7. Tap or click OK to save your settings.

Managing Automatic Updates in Group Policy

Automatic Updates help you keep the operating system up to date. Although you can configure Automatic Updates on a per-computer basis, you'll typically want to configure this feature for all users and computers that process a GPO—this is a much more efficient management technique.

Note that by default, Windows 8.1 and Windows Server 2012 R2 use Windows Update to download Windows Components in addition to binaries for roles, role services, and features. If the Windows diagnostics framework detects that a Windows component needs to be repaired, Windows uses Windows Update to download the component. If an administrator is trying to install a role, role service, or feature and the payload is missing, Windows uses Windows Update to download the related binaries.

Configuring Automatic Updates

When you manage Automatic Updates through Group Policy, you can set the update configuration to any of the following options:

- **Auto Download And Schedule The Install**   Updates are automatically downloaded and installed according to a schedule you specify. When updates have been downloaded, the operating system notifies the user so that she can review the updates that are scheduled to be installed. The user can install the updates at that time or wait for the scheduled installation time.

- **Auto Download And Notify For Install**   The operating system retrieves all updates as they become available, and then prompts the user when they're ready to be installed. The user can then accept or reject the updates. Accepted updates are installed. Rejected updates aren't installed but remain on the system, where they can be installed at a later date.

- **Notify For Download And Notify For Install**   The operating system notifies the user before retrieving any updates. If a user elects to download the updates, the user still has the opportunity to accept or reject them. Accepted updates are installed. Rejected updates aren't installed but remain on the system, where they can be installed at a later date.

- **Allow Local Admin To Choose Setting**   Allows the local administrator to configure Automatic Updates on a per-computer basis. Note that if you use any other setting, local users and administrators are unable to change settings for Automatic Updates.

You can configure Automatic Updates in Group Policy by following these steps:

1. In the GPMC, press and hold or right-click the GPO with which you want to work, and then tap or click Edit.

2. In the policy editor, access Computer Configuration\Policies\Administrative Templates\Windows Components\Windows Update.

3. Double-tap or double-click Configure Automatic Updates. In the Properties dialog box, you can now enable or disable Group Policy management of Automatic Updates. To enable management of Automatic Updates, select Enabled. To disable management of Automatic Updates, select Disabled, tap or click OK, and then skip the remaining steps.

4. Choose an update configuration from the options in the Configure Automatic Updating list. On Windows 8 and later as well as Windows Server 2012 and later, updates can be automatically installed during the scheduled maintenance window by selecting the Install During Automatic Maintenance check box.

5. If you select Auto Download And Schedule The Install, you can schedule the installation day and time by using the lists provided. Tap or click OK to save your settings.

By default, Windows Update runs daily at 2:00 A.M. as part of other automatic maintenance. With desktop operating systems running Windows 8 or later, Windows Update uses the computer's power management features to wake the computer from hibernation or sleep at the scheduled update time, and then install updates.

Generally, this wake-up-and-install process will occur whether the computer is on battery or AC power.

If a restart is required to finalize updates applied as part of automatic maintenance and there is an active user session, Windows caches the credentials of the user currently logged on to the console, and then restarts the computer automatically. After the restart, Windows uses the cached credentials to sign in as this user. Next, Windows restarts applications that were running previously, and then locks the session using the Secure Desktop. If BitLocker is enabled, the entire process is protected by BitLocker encryption as well.

The maintenance process does not need a user to be logged on. The maintenance process runs whether a user is logged on or not. If no user is logged on when scheduled maintenance begins and a restart is required, Windows restarts the computer without caching credentials or storing information about running applications. When Windows restarts, Windows does not log on as any user.

Because Windows automatically wakes computers to perform automatic maintenance and updates, you'll also want to carefully consider the power options that are applied. Unless a power plan is configured to turn off the display and put the computer to sleep, the computer may remain powered on for many hours after automatic maintenance and updates.

Optimizing Automatic Updates

Generally, most automatic updates are installed only when a computer is shut down and restarted. Some automatic updates can be installed immediately without interrupting system services or requiring system restart. To ensure that some updates can be installed immediately, follow these steps:

1. In the GPMC, press and hold or right-click the GPO with which you want to work, and then tap or click Edit.

2. In the policy editor, access Computer Configuration\Policies\Administrative Templates\Windows Components\Windows Update.

3. Double-tap or double-click Allow Automatic Updates Immediate Installation. In the Properties dialog box, select Enabled, and then tap or click OK.

By default, only users with local administrator privileges receive notifications about updates. You can enable any user logged on to a computer to receive update notifications by following these steps:

1. In the GPMC, press and hold or right-click the GPO with which you want to work, and then tap or click Edit.

2. In the policy editor, access Computer Configuration\Policies\Administrative Templates\Windows Components\Windows Update.

3. Double-tap or double-click Allow Non-Administrators To Receive Update Notifications. In the Properties dialog box, select Enabled, and then tap or click OK.

Another useful policy is Remove Access To Use All Windows Update Features. This policy prohibits access to all Windows Update features. If enabled, all Automatic Updates features are removed and can't be configured. This includes the Automatic Updates tab in the System utility and driver updates from the Windows Update website in Device Manager. This policy is located in User Configuration \Policies\Administrative Templates\Windows Components\Windows Update.

Using intranet update service locations

On networks with hundreds or thousands of computers, the Automatic Updates process can use a considerable amount of network bandwidth, and having all the computers check for updates and install them over the Internet doesn't make sense. Instead, consider using the Specify Intranet Microsoft Update Service Location policy, which tells individual computers to check a designated internal server for updates.

The designated update server must run Windows Server Update Services (WSUS), be configured as a web server running IIS, and be able to handle the additional workload, which might be considerable on a large network during peak usage times. Additionally, the update server must have access to the external network on port 80. The use of a firewall or proxy server on this port shouldn't present any problems.

The update process also tracks configuration information and statistics for each computer. This information is necessary for the update process to work properly, and it can be stored on a separate statistics server (an internal server running IIS) or on the update server itself.

To specify an internal update server, follow these steps:

1. After you install and configure an update server, open the GPO with which you want to work for editing. In the policy editor, access Computer Configuration\Policies\Administrative Templates\Windows Components\Windows Update.

2. Double-tap or double-click Specify Intranet Microsoft Update Service Location. In the Properties dialog box, select Enabled.

3. In the Set The Intranet Update Service For Detecting Updates text box, enter the URL of the update server. In most cases, this is http://*servername*, such as *http://CorpUpdateServer01*.

4. Enter the URL of the statistics server in the Set The Intranet Statistics Server text box. This doesn't have to be a separate server; you can specify the update server in this text box.

   NOTE If you want a single server to handle both updates and statistics, enter the same URL in both boxes. Otherwise, if you want a different server for updates and statistics, enter the URL for each server in the appropriate box.

5. Tap or click OK. After the applicable GPO is refreshed, systems running appropriate versions of Windows will look to the update server for updates. You'll want to monitor the update and statistics servers closely for several days or weeks to ensure that everything is working properly. Directories and files will be created on the update and statistics servers.

CHAPTER 7

Managing TCP/IP networking

A s an administrator, you enable networked computers to communicate by using the basic networking protocols built into Windows Server 2012 R2. The key protocol you use is TCP/IP, which is a suite of protocols and services used for communicating over a network and is the primary protocol used for internetwork communications. Compared to configuring other networking protocols, configuring TCP/IP communications is fairly complicated, but TCP/IP is the most versatile protocol available.

> **NOTE** Group Policy settings can affect your ability to install and manage TCP/IP networking. The key policies you should examine are in User Configuration \Administrative Templates\Network\Network Connections and Computer Configuration\Administrative Templates\System\Group Policy. Group Policy is discussed in Chapter 6, "Managing users and computers with Group Policy."

Navigating networking in Windows Server 2012 R2

Windows Server 2012 R2 has an extensive set of networking tools:

- **Network Explorer**   Provides a central console for browsing computers and devices on the network
- **Network And Sharing Center**   Provides a central console for viewing and managing a computer's networking and sharing configuration
- **Network Diagnostics**   Provides automated diagnostics to help diagnose and resolve networking problems

Before I describe how these networking tools are used, let's first look at the following Windows Server 2012 R2 features on which these tools rely:

- **Network Discovery** Controls the ability to view other computers and devices
- **Network Awareness** Reports changes in network connectivity and configuration

REAL WORLD Computers running Windows Vista with SP1 or later, in addition to later releases of Windows, support extensions to network awareness. These extensions enable a computer connected to one or more networks via two or more interfaces (regardless of whether they are wired or wireless) to select the route with the best performance for a particular data transfer. As part of selecting the best route, Windows chooses the best interface (either wired or wireless) for the transfer. This mechanism improves the selection of wireless over wired networks when both interfaces are present.

Network discovery settings for the computer with which you are working determine the computers and devices you can browse or view in Windows Server 2012 R2 networking tools. Discovery settings work in conjunction with a computer's Windows Firewall settings to block or allow the following:

- Discovery of network computers and devices
- Discovery of your computer by others

Network discovery settings are meant to provide the appropriate level of security for each of the various categories of networks to which a computer can connect. The three categories of networks are defined as follows:

- **Domain network** Designates a network in which computers are connected to the corporate domain to which they are joined
- **Private network** Designates a network in which computers are configured as members of a homegroup or workgroup and are not connected directly to the public Internet
- **Public network** Designates a network in a public place, such as a coffee shop or an airport, rather than an internal network

Because a computer saves settings separately for each category of network, different block and allow settings can be used for each network category. When you connect a computer's network adapter to a network for the first time, Windows sets the network category based on the configuration of the computer. Based on the network category, Windows Server 2012 R2 automatically configures settings that turn discovery on or off. The On (Enabled) state means

- The computer can discover other computers and devices on the network.
- Other computers on the network can discover the computer.

The Off (Disabled) state means

- The computer cannot discover other computers and devices on the network.
- Other computers on the network cannot discover the computer.

Typically, you will find that a network adapter is set as public before you join a computer to the domain. Network Explorer, shown in Figure 7-1, displays a list of discovered computers and devices on the network. To access Network Explorer, tap or click File Explorer on the Start screen. In File Explorer, tap or click the location path selection button, and then tap or click Network.

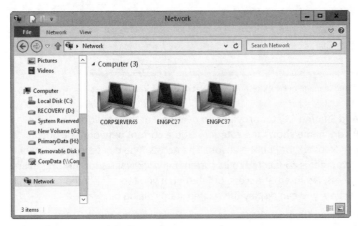

FIGURE 7-1 Use Network Explorer to browse network resources.

The computers and devices listed in Network Explorer depend on the network discovery settings of the computer, the operating system, and whether the computer is a member of a domain. If discovery is blocked and a server running Windows Server 2012 R2 is not a member of a domain, you'll get a warning message about this. When you tap or click the warning message and then select Turn On Network Discovery And File Sharing, you enable network discovery, file sharing, and printer sharing. In addition, related Windows Firewall ports open.

Network And Sharing Center, shown in Figure 7-2, provides the current network status, in addition to an overview of the current network configuration. In Control Panel, you can access Network And Sharing Center by tapping or clicking View Network Status And Tasks under the Network And Internet heading.

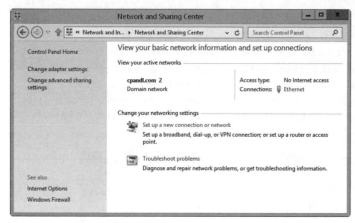

FIGURE 7-2 View and manage network settings with Network And Sharing Center.

Network And Sharing Center provides an overview of the network. The value below the network name shows the category of the current network as Domain Network, Private Network, or Public Network. The Access Type box specifies whether and how the computer is connected to its current network. Values for this option are No Network Access, No Internet Access, or Internet. If you tap or click the name of a network connection, you can display the related status dialog box.

Tapping or clicking Change Adapter Settings displays the Network Connections page, which you can use to manage network connections. Tapping or clicking Change Advanced Sharing Settings provides options for configuring the computer's sharing and discovery settings for each network profile. To manage a profile, expand the profile's view panel by tapping or clicking the Expand button (showing a down arrow), tap or click the setting with which you want to work, and then tap or click Save Changes. To turn on or off network discovery, tap or click Turn On Network Discovery or Turn Off Network Discovery as appropriate, and then tap or click Save Changes.

From Network And Sharing Center, you can attempt to diagnose a networking problem. To do this, tap or click Troubleshoot Problems, and then tap or click a troubleshooter to run, such as Incoming Connections or Network Adapter, and then follow the prompts. Windows Network Diagnostics then attempts to identify the network problem and provide a possible solution.

NOTE To quickly access Network Connections without opening Network And Sharing Center, enter **ncpa.cpl** in the Everywhere search box. Alternatively, enter **ncpa.cpl** at a command prompt or a Windows PowerShell prompt.

Managing networking in Windows 8.1 and Windows Server 2012 R2

In Group Policy, you'll find network management policies for both wired networks (IEEE 802.3) and wireless networks (IEEE 802.11) are located in the Administrative Templates for Computer Configuration under Windows Settings\Security Settings. Only one wired policy and one wireless policy can be created and applied at a time. This means you can establish both a wired policy and a wireless policy for computers running Windows Vista and later releases of Windows. You also can create a wireless policy for computers running Windows XP.

If you press and hold or right-click the Wired Network (IEEE 802.3) node, you can create a policy for Windows Vista and later releases that specifies whether the Wire AutoConfig service is used to configure and connect these clients to 802.3 wired Ethernet networks. For Windows 7 and later releases of Windows, you have options for preventing the sharing of user credentials and for specifying whether to prohibit computers from making autoconnection attempts to the network for a specified amount of time.

If you press and hold or right-click the Wireless Network (IEEE 802.11) node, you can create separate policies for Windows XP computers and computers running later releases that enable WLAN autoconfiguration, define the specific networks that can be used, and set network permissions. For Windows 7 and later releases of Windows, you have options for preventing the sharing of user credentials, for specifying whether to prohibit computers from making autoconnection attempts to the network for a specified amount of time, and for preventing the use of hosted networks.

Windows Vista SP1 or later and later releases of Windows support several wired and wireless enhancements. These enhancements enable users to change their password when connecting to a wired or wireless network (as opposed to using the Winlogon change password feature), to correct a wrong password entered during sign on, and to reset an expired password—all as part of the network logon process.

Network security enhancements include the following:

- Secure Socket Tunneling Protocol (SSTP)
- Secure Remote Access (SRA)
- CryptoAPI Version 2 (CAPI2)
- Online Certificate Status Protocol (OCSP) extensions
- Port preservation for Teredo
- Remote Desktop Protocol (RDP) file signing

Secure Socket Tunneling Protocol allows data transmission at the data link layer over an HTTPS connection. Secure Remote Access enables secure access to remote networks over HTTPS. Together these technologies enable users to securely access a private network by using an Internet connection. Secure Socket Tunneling Protocol and Secure Remote Access represent improvements over the Point-to-Point Tunneling

Protocol (PPTP) and Layer Two Tunneling Protocol/Internet Protocol Security (L2TP/IPsec) protocols because they use the standard TCP/IP ports for secure web traffic, and this allows them to traverse most firewalls in addition to Network Address Translation (NAT) and web proxies.

Secure Socket Tunneling Protocol uses HTTP over Secure Sockets Layer (SSL), which is also known as Transport Layer Security (TLS). HTTP over SSL (which uses TCP port 443) is commonly used for protected communications with websites. Whenever users connect to a web address that begins with *https://*, they are using HTTP over SSL. Using HTTP over SSL solves many of the virtual private network (VPN) protocol connectivity problems. Because SSTP supports both IPv4 and IPv6, users can establish secure tunnels using either IP technology. Essentially, you get VPN technology that works everywhere, which should mean that you receive far fewer support calls.

CAPI2 extends support for public key infrastructure (PKI) and X.509 certificates and implements additional functionality for certificate path validation, certificate stores, and signature verification. One of the steps during certificate path validation is revocation checking, which involves verifying the certificate status to ensure that it has not been revoked by its issuer; this is where Online Certificate Status Protocol comes into the picture.

OCSP is used to check the revocation status of certificates. CAPI2 also supports independent OCSP signer chains and specifying additional OCSP download locations on a per-issuer basis. Independent OCSP signer chains modify the original OCSP implementation so that it can work with OCSP responses that are signed by trusted OCSP signers that are separate from the issuer of the certificate being validated. Additional OCSP download locations make it possible to specify OCSP download locations for issuing CA certificates as URLs that are added as a property to the CA certificate.

To ensure IPv4/IPv6 coexistence, Windows enables applications to use IPv6 on an IPv4 network, and it also supports related technologies such as port preservation for Teredo, which is a User Datagram Protocol (UDP)–based tunneling technology that can traverse NATs. This feature enables Teredo communications between "port preserving" symmetric NATs and other types of NATs. A NAT is port preserving if it chooses to use the same external port number as the internal port number.

Current releases of Windows Server support TCP Chimney offloading. This feature enables the networking subsystem to offload the processing of a TCP/IP connection from a server's processors to its network adapters, as long as the network adapters support TCP/IP offload processing. Both TCP/IPv4 connections and TCP/IPv6 connections can be offloaded. By default, TCP connections are offloaded on 10–gigabits per second (Gbps) network adapters but are not offloaded on 1-Gbps network adapters. To modify the related settings, you can use Netsh.

Network Diagnostic Framework (NDF) simplifies network troubleshooting by automating many common troubleshooting steps and solutions. When you run Windows Network Diagnostics, each diagnostic session generates a report with diagnostics results, and you can view this information in Action Center by tapping or clicking the Troubleshooting link, and then tapping or clicking View History. On the Troubleshooting History page, each diagnostic session is listed by type and date run. To get detailed information, select the session you want to review, and then tap or click View Details.

The diagnostic information shown in Action Center comes from an Event Trace Log (ETL) file created as part of diagnostics. If you press and hold or right-click a diagnostic session and then select Open File Location, you can view the files generated as part of diagnostics for the selected diagnostic session.

You can use the Netsh Trace context to perform comprehensive tracing in addition to network packet capturing and filtering. You perform traces by using predefined or custom scenarios and providers. Tracing scenarios are collections of providers. Providers are the actual components in the network protocol stack that you want to work with, such as TCP/IP, Windows Filtering Platform and Firewall, Wireless LAN Services, Winsock, or NDIS. Typically, you use Network Monitor (Netmon) to analyze trace data. If you collect trace data on a computer where Netmon isn't installed, you can just copy the trace file to a computer where Netmon is installed so that you can analyze the data.

Windows Vista with SP1 or later and later releases of Windows use an RDP 6.1 or later compatible client. Here, RDP files can be digitally signed to prevent users from opening or running potentially dangerous RDP files from unknown sources. Administrators can sign RDP files by using a signing tool provided by Microsoft. Three related settings can be configured through Group Policy or through the registry. These settings include a comma-separated list of certificate hashes that are trusted by the administrator (known as the *trusted publishers list*), an option to enable users to decide to accept untrusted publishers (enabled by default), and an option to enable users to accept unsigned files (enabled by default).

Windows 8.1 and Windows Server 2012 R2 have a number of enhancements in their built-in DNS clients that improve name resolution on IPv4 and IPv6 networks. With adaptive query timeout, the DNS client adapts the timeout interval based on the time required for previous queries. Thus, instead of waiting 1000 milliseconds (ms) before timing out a query, the timeout is adjusted based on past performance for the network, resulting in timeouts between 25 ms and 1000 ms.

The DNS client for Windows 8.1 and Windows Server 2012 R2 also supports query coalescing, parallel queries, and persistent caching. With query coalescing, the DNS client combines multiple DNS queries for the same name. This results in only one query and optimizes performance. With parallel queries, the DNS client issues IPv4 and IPv6 queries for A and AAAA records in parallel when both IP interfaces are enabled, which streamlines the query process and improves performance. Link-local multicast name resolution (LLMNR) and NETBIOS queries are also issued in parallel for IPv4 and IPv6. With a persistent cache, the DNS client maintains the DNS cache across changes that occur on the same network. For example, the DNS client now persists the cache after address change notifications and when the computer is resuming from the sleep or standby state.

Installing TCP/IP networking

To install networking on a computer, you must install TCP/IP networking and a network adapter. Windows Server 2012 R2 uses TCP/IP as the default wide area network (WAN) protocol. Typically, you install networking during Windows Server 2012 R2 setup. You can also install TCP/IP networking through network connection properties.

To install TCP/IP after installing Windows Server 2012 R2, log on to the computer by using an account with administrator privileges, and then follow these steps:

1. In Control Panel, access Network And Sharing Center by tapping or clicking View Network Status And Tasks under the Network And Internet heading.

2. In Network And Sharing Center, tap or click Change Adapter Settings.

3. In Network Connections, press and hold or right-click the connection with which you want to work, and then tap or click Properties. This displays a Properties dialog box for the connection, shown in Figure 7-3.

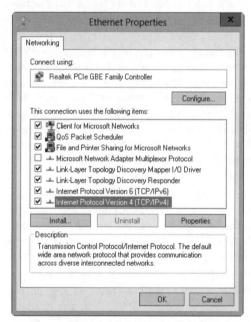

FIGURE 7-3 Install and configure TCP/IP protocols.

4. If Internet Protocol Version 6 (TCP/IPv6), Internet Protocol Version 4 (TCP/IPv4), or both aren't shown in the list of installed components, you need to install them. Tap or click Install. Tap or click Protocol, and then tap or click Add. In the Select Network Protocol dialog box, select the protocol to install, and then tap or click OK. If you are installing both TCP/IPv6 and TCP/IPv4, repeat this procedure for each protocol.

5. In the Properties dialog box for the network connection, be sure that Internet Protocol Version 6 (TCP/IPv6), Internet Protocol Version 4 (TCP/IPv4), or both are selected, and then tap or click OK.

6. As necessary, follow the instructions in the next section for configuring network connections for the computer.

Configuring TCP/IP networking

A network connection is created automatically if a computer has a network adapter and is connected to a network. If a computer has multiple network adapters and is connected to a network, one network connection is created for each adapter. If no network connection is available, you should connect the computer to the network or create a different type of connection.

Computers use IP addresses to communicate over TCP/IP. Windows Server 2012 R2 provides the following ways to configure IP addresses:

- **Manually** IP addresses that are assigned manually are called *static IP addresses*. Static IP addresses are fixed and don't change unless you change them. You usually assign static IP addresses to Windows servers, and when you do this, you need to configure additional information to help the server navigate the network.

- **Dynamically** A DHCP server (if one is installed on the network) assigns dynamic IP addresses at startup, and the addresses might change over time. Dynamic IP addressing is the default configuration.

- **Alternate addresses (IPv4 only)** When a computer is configured to use DHCPv4 and no DHCPv4 server is available, Windows Server 2012 R2 assigns an alternate private IP address automatically. By default, the alternate IPv4 address is in the range 169.254.0.1 to 169.254.255.254 with a subnet mask of 255.255.0.0. You can also specify a user-configured alternate IPv4 address, which is particularly useful for laptop users.

Configuring static IP addresses

When you assign a static IP address, you need to tell the computer the IP address you want to use, the subnet mask for this IP address, and, if necessary, the default gateway to use for internetwork communications. An IP address is a numeric identifier for a computer. IP addressing schemes vary according to how your network is configured, but they're typically assigned based on a particular network segment.

IPv6 addresses and IPv4 addresses are very different. With IPv6, the first 64 bits represent the network ID and the remaining 64 bits represent the network interface. With IPv4, a variable number of the initial bits represent the network ID and the rest of the bits represent the host ID. For example, if you're working with IPv4 and a computer on the network segment 10.0.10.0 with a subnet mask of 255.255.255.0, the first three octets (8-bit groups) represent the network ID, and the address range you have available for computer hosts is 10.0.10.1 to 10.0.10.254. In this range, the address 10.0.10.255 is reserved for network broadcasts.

If you're on a private network that is indirectly connected to the Internet, you should use private IPv4 addresses. Table 7-1 summarizes private network IPv4 addresses.

TABLE 7-1 Private IPv4 network addressing

PRIVATE NETWORK ID	SUBNET MASK	NETWORK ADDRESS RANGE
10.0.0.0	255.0.0.0	10.0.0.0–10.255.255.255
172.16.0.0	255.240.0.0	172.16.0.0–172.31.255.255
192.168.0.0	255.255.0.0	192.168.0.0–192.168.255.255

All other IPv4 network addresses are public and must be leased or purchased. If the network is connected directly to the Internet and you've obtained a range of IPv4 addresses from your Internet service provider, you can use the IPv4 addresses you've been assigned.

Using the *ping* command to check an address

Before you assign a static IP address, you should make sure that the address isn't already in use or reserved for use with DHCP. With the *ping* command, you can check whether an address is in use. Open a command prompt and enter **ping**, followed by the IP address you want to check.

To test the IPv4 address 10.0.10.12, you would use the following command:

```
ping 10.0.10.12
```

To test the IPv6 address FEC0::02BC:FF:BECB:FE4F:961D, you would use the following command:

```
ping FEC0::02BC:FF:BECB:FE4F:961D
```

If you receive a successful reply from the ping test, the IP address is in use and you should try another one. If the request times out for all four ping attempts, the IP address isn't active on the network at this time and probably isn't in use; however, a firewall could be blocking your ping request. Your company's network administrator would also be able to confirm whether an IP address is in use.

Configuring a static IPv4 or IPv6 address

One LAN connection is available for each network adapter installed. These connections are created automatically. To configure static IP addresses for a particular connection, follow these steps:

1. In Network And Sharing Center, tap or click Change Adapter Settings. In Network Connections, press and hold or right-click the connection with which you want to work, and then tap or click Properties.

2. Double-tap or double-click Internet Protocol Version 6 (TCP/IPv6) or Internet Protocol Version 4 (TCP/IPv4) as appropriate for the type of IP address you are configuring.

3. For an IPv6 address, do the following:

■ Tap or click Use The Following IPv6 Address, and then enter the IPv6 address in the IPv6 Address text box. The IPv6 address you assign to the computer must not be in use anywhere else on the network.

■ The Subnet Prefix Length option ensures that the computer communicates over the network properly. Windows Server 2012 R2 should insert a default value for the subnet prefix into the Subnet Prefix Length text box. If the network doesn't use variable-length subnetting, the default value should suffice, but if it does use variable-length subnets, you need to change this value as appropriate for your network.

4. For an IPv4 address, do the following:

■ Tap or click Use The Following IP Address, and then enter the IPv4 address in the IP Address text box. The IPv4 address you assign to the computer must not be in use anywhere else on the network.

■ The Subnet Mask option ensures that the computer communicates over the network properly. Windows Server 2012 R2 should insert a default value for the subnet mask into the Subnet Mask text box. If the network doesn't use variable-length subnetting, the default value should suffice, but if it does use variable-length subnets, you need to change this value as appropriate for your network.

5. If the computer needs to access other TCP/IP networks, the Internet, or other subnets, you must specify a default gateway. Enter the IP address of the network's default router in the Default Gateway text box.

6. Domain Name System (DNS) is needed for domain name resolution. Enter a preferred address and an alternate DNS server address in the text boxes provided.

7. When you have finished, tap or click OK twice. Repeat this process for other network adapters and IP protocols you want to configure.

8. With IPv4 addressing, configure WINS as necessary.

Configuring dynamic IP addresses and alternate IP addressing

Although most servers have static IP addresses, you can configure servers to use dynamic addressing, alternate IP addressing, or both. You configure dynamic and alternate addressing by following these steps:

1. In Network And Sharing Center, tap or click Change Adapter Settings. In Network Connections, one LAN connection is shown for each network adapter installed. These connections are created automatically. If you don't find a LAN connection for an installed adapter, check the driver for the adapter. It might be installed incorrectly. Press and hold or right-click the connection with which you want to work, and then tap or click Properties.

2. Double-tap or double-click Internet Protocol Version 6 (TCP/IPv6) or Internet Protocol Version 4 (TCP/IPv4) as appropriate for the type of IP address you are configuring.

3. Select Obtain An IPv6 Address Automatically or Obtain An IP Address Automatically as appropriate for the type of IP address you are configuring. You can select Obtain DNS Server Address Automatically, or you can select Use The Following DNS Server Addresses, and then enter a preferred and alternate DNS server address in the text boxes provided.

4. When you use dynamic IPv4 addressing, you can configure an automatic alternate address or manually configure the alternate address. To use an automatic configuration, on the Alternate Configuration tab, select Automatic Private IP Address. Tap or click OK, tap or click Close, and then skip the remaining step.

5. To use a manual configuration, on the Alternate Configuration tab, select User Configured, and then enter the IP address you want to use in the IP Address text box. The IP address you assign to the computer should be a private IP address, as shown earlier in Table 7-1, and it must not be in use anywhere else when the settings are applied. Complete the alternate configuration by entering a subnet mask, default gateway, DNS server, and Windows Internet Name Service (WINS) settings. When you have finished, tap or click OK, and then tap or click Close.

Configuring multiple gateways

To provide fault tolerance in case of a router outage, you can choose to configure Windows Server 2012 R2 computers so that they use multiple default gateways. When you assign multiple gateways, Windows Server 2012 R2 uses the gateway metric to determine which gateway is used and at what time. The gateway metric indicates the routing cost of using a gateway. The gateway with the lowest routing cost, or metric, is used first. If the computer can't communicate with this gateway, Windows Server 2012 R2 tries to use the gateway with the next lowest metric.

The best way to configure multiple gateways depends on the configuration of your network. If your organization's computers use DHCP, you probably want to configure the additional gateways through settings on the DHCP server. If computers use static IP addresses or you want to set gateways specifically, assign them by following these steps:

1. In Network And Sharing Center, tap or click Change Adapter Settings. In Network Connections, press and hold or right-click the connection with which you want to work, and then tap or click Properties.

2. Double-tap or double-click Internet Protocol Version 6 (TCP/IPv6) or Internet Protocol Version 4 (TCP/IPv4) as appropriate for the type of IP address you are configuring.

3. Tap or click Advanced to open the Advanced TCP/IP Settings dialog box, shown in Figure 7-4.

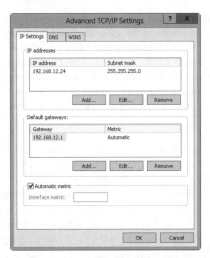

FIGURE 7-4 Configure multiple IP addresses and gateways in the Advanced TCP/IP Settings dialog box.

4. The Default Gateways panel shows the current gateways that have been manually configured (if any). You can enter additional default gateways as necessary.

   a. Tap or click Add, and then enter the gateway address in the Gateway text box.

   b. By default, Windows Server 2012 R2 automatically assigns a metric to the gateway. You can also assign the metric yourself. To do this, clear the Automatic Metric check box, enter a metric in the text box provided, and then tap or click Add.

   c. Repeat steps a through b for each gateway you want to add.

5. Tap or click OK, and then tap or click Close.

Configuring networking for Hyper-V

After you install Hyper-V and create an external virtual network, your server uses a virtual network adapter to connect to the physical network. When you work with the Network Connections page, you will find the original network adapter and a new virtual network adapter. The original network adapter will have nothing bound to it except the Microsoft Virtual Network Switch Protocol, and the virtual network adapter will have all the standard protocols and services bound to it. The virtual network adapter that appears under Network Connections will have the same name as the virtual network switch with which it is associated.

NOTE As part of the Hyper-V configuration, you can create an internal virtual network, which enables communications only between the server and hosted virtual machines. This configuration exposes a virtual network adapter to the parent server without the need to have a physical network adapter associated with it and isolates the virtual machine from the Internet and the rest of the LAN. Hyper-V binds the virtual network service to a physical network adapter only when an external virtual network is created. An external virtual network is required for communications on the LAN and the Internet.

Following this, when you install Hyper-V on a server and enable external virtual networking, you'll find that virtual network switching is being used. As shown in Figure 7-5, the server has a network connection with the Hyper-V Extensible Virtual Switch protocol enabled and all other networking components not enabled in the dialog box on the left and an entry for a virtual connection with the key networking components enabled and the Hyper-V Extensible Virtual Switch Protocol disabled in the dialog box on the right. This is the configuration you want to use to ensure proper communications for the server and any hosted virtual machines that use networking. If this configuration is changed, virtual machines won't be able to connect to the external network.

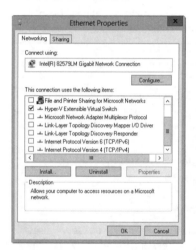 

FIGURE 7-5 Use switched virtual networking to ensure communications with hosted virtual machines.

Managing network connections

Network connections make it possible for computers to access resources on the network and the Internet. One network connection is created automatically for each network adapter installed on a computer. This section examines techniques you can use to manage these connections.

Checking the status, speed, and activity for network connections

To check the status of a network connection, follow these steps:

1. In Network And Sharing Center, tap or click Change Adapter Settings. In Network Connections, press and hold or right-click the connection with which you want to work, and then tap or click Status to display the Status dialog box for the network connection.

2. If the connection is disabled or the media is unplugged, you won't be able to access the Status dialog box. Enable the connection or connect the network cable to resolve the problem, and then try to display the Status dialog box again.

Enabling and disabling network connections

Network connections are created and connected automatically. If you want to disable a connection so that it cannot be used, follow these steps:

1. In Network And Sharing Center, tap or click Change Adapter Settings. In Network Connections, press and hold or right-click the connection, and then tap or click Disable to deactivate the connection and disable it.

2. If you want to enable the connection later, press and hold or right-click the connection in Network Connections, and then tap or click Enable.

If you want to disconnect from a network, follow these steps:

1. In Network And Sharing Center, tap or click Change Adapter Settings. In Network Connections, press and hold or right-click the connection and then tap or click Disconnect. Typically, only remote access connections have a Disconnect option.

2. If you want to activate the connection later, press and hold or right-click the connection in Network Connections, and then tap or click Connect.

Renaming network connections

Windows Server 2012 R2 initially assigns default names to network connections. In Network Connections, you can rename a connection at any time by pressing and holding or right-clicking the connection, tapping or clicking Rename, and then entering a new name. If a computer has multiple network connections, a descriptive name can help you and others better understand the uses of a particular connection.

Running DHCP clients and servers

You can use Dynamic Host Configuration Protocol (DHCP) to simplify administration of Active Directory domains, and in this chapter you'll learn how to do that. You use DHCP to dynamically assign TCP/IP configuration information to network clients. This not only saves time during system configuration, but also provides a centralized mechanism for updating the configuration. To enable DHCP on the network, you need to install and configure a DHCP server. This server is responsible for assigning the necessary network information.

Understanding DHCP

DHCP gives you centralized control over IP addressing and more. After DHCP is installed, you rely on the DHCP server to supply the basic information necessary for TCP/IP networking. This basic information can include the following: IP address, subnet mask, and default gateway; primary and secondary Domain Name System (DNS) servers; primary and secondary Windows Internet Name Service (WINS) servers; and the DNS domain name. DHCP servers can assign a dynamic IP version 4 (IPv4) address, a dynamic IP version 6 (IPv6) address, or both addresses to any of the network interface cards (NICs) on a computer.

Using dynamic IPv4 addressing and configuration

A computer that uses dynamic IPv4 addressing and configuration is called a *DHCPv4 client*. When you start a DHCPv4 client, a 32-bit IPv4 address can be retrieved from a pool of IPv4 addresses defined for the network's DHCP server.

The address is assigned to the client for a specified time period known as a *lease*. When the lease is approximately 50 percent expired, the client tries to renew it. If the client can't renew the lease at that time, it tries again before the lease expires. If this attempt fails, the client tries to contact an alternate DHCP server. IPv4 addresses that aren't renewed are returned to the address pool. If the client is able to contact the DHCP server but the current IP address can't be reassigned, the DHCP server assigns a new IPv4 address to the client.

The availability of a DHCP server doesn't affect startup or logon (in most cases). DHCPv4 clients can start and users can log on to the local computer even if a DHCP server isn't available. During startup, the DHCPv4 client looks for a DHCP server. If a DHCP server is available, the client gets its configuration information from the server. If a DHCP server isn't available and the client's previous lease is still valid, the client pings the default gateway listed in the lease. A successful ping tells the client that it's probably on the same network it was on when it was issued the lease, and the client continues to use the lease as described previously. A failed ping tells the client that it might be on a different network. In this case, the client uses IPv4 autoconfiguration. The client also uses IPv4 autoconfiguration if a DHCP server isn't available and the previous lease has expired.

IPv4 autoconfiguration works like this:

1. The client computer selects an IP address from the Microsoft-reserved class B subnet 169.254.0.0 and uses the subnet mask 255.255.0.0. Before using the IPv4 address, the client performs an Address Resolution Protocol (ARP) test to be sure that no other client is using this IPv4 address.

2. If the IPv4 address is in use, the client repeats step 1, testing up to 10 IPv4 addresses before reporting failure. When a client is disconnected from the network, the ARP test always succeeds. As a result, the client uses the first IPv4 address it selects.

3. If the IPv4 address is available, the client configures the NIC with this address. The client then attempts to contact a DHCP server, sending out a broadcast every five minutes to the network. When the client successfully contacts a server, the client obtains a lease and reconfigures the network interface.

As part of your planning, you need to consider how many DHCP servers should be installed on the network. Typically, you'll want to install at least two DHCP servers on each physical network segment. Windows Server 2012 R2 includes DHCP failover for IPv4. DHCP failover enables high availability of DHCP services by synchronizing IPv4 address leases between two DHCP servers in one of two modes:

- **Load Balance** When you load balance the servers, you specify the percentage of the load each server should handle. Typically, you use a 50/50 approach to make each server equally share the load. You also could use other approaches, such as 60/40 to make one server carry 60 percent of the load and the other 40 percent of the load.

- **Hot Standby** With hot standby, one of the servers acts as the primary server and handles the DHCP services. The other acts as a standby server in case the primary fails or runs out of addresses to lease. A specific percentage of available IP addresses are reserved for the hot standby—5 percent by default.

The configuration of DHCP failover is simple and straightforward, and it does not require clustering or any advanced configuration. To configure DHCP failover, all you need to do is complete the following steps:

1. Install and configure two DHCP servers. The servers should be on the same physical network.

2. Create a DHCPv4 scope on one of the servers. Scopes are pools of IPv4 or IPv6 addresses you can assign to clients through leases.

3. When you establish the other server as a failover partner for the DHCPv4 scope, the scope is replicated to the partner.

Using dynamic IPv6 addressing and configuration

Both IPv4 and IPv6 are enabled by default when networking hardware is detected during installation. As discussed in Chapter 7, "Managing TCP/IP networking," IPv4 is the primary version of IP used on most networks, and IPv6 is the next generation version of IP. IPv6 uses 128-bit addresses. In a standard configuration, the first 64 bits represent the network ID, and the last 64 bits represent the network interface on the client computer.

You can use DHCP to configure IPv6 addressing in two key ways:

- **DHCPv6 stateful mode**   In DHCPv6 stateful mode, a client acquires its IPv6 address in addition to its network configuration parameters through DHCPv6.

- **DHCPv6 stateless mode**   In DHCPv6 stateless mode, a client uses auto-configuration to acquire its IP address and acquires its network configuration parameters through DHCPv6.

A computer that uses dynamic IPv6 addressing, configuration, or both mechanisms is called a *DHCPv6 client*. As with DHCPv4, the components of the DHCPv6 infrastructure consist of DHCPv6 clients that request configuration, DHCPv6 servers that provide configuration, and DHCPv6 relay agents that convey messages between clients and servers when clients are on subnets that do not have a DHCPv6 server.

Unlike in DHCPv4, you must also configure your IPv6 routers to support DHCPv6. A DHCPv6 client performs autoconfiguration based on the following flags in the Router Advertisement message sent by a neighboring router:

- Managed Address Configuration flag, which is also known as the *M flag*. When set to 1, this flag instructs the client to use a configuration protocol to obtain stateful addresses.

- Other Stateful Configuration flag, which is also known as the *O flag*. When set to 1, this flag instructs the client to use a configuration protocol to obtain other configuration settings.

Windows includes a DHCPv6 client. The DHCPv6 client attempts DHCPv6-based configuration depending on the values of the M and O flags in the Router Advertisement messages it receives. If there is more than one advertising router for a given subnet, the additional router or routers should be configured to advertise the same stateless address prefixes and the same values for the M and O flags. All current

Windows desktop and server operating systems include IPv6 clients and, therefore, accept the values of the M and O flags in router advertisements they receive.

You can configure an IPv6 router to set the M flag to 1 in router advertisements by entering the following command at an elevated command prompt, where *InterfaceName* is the actual name of the interface:

```
netsh interface ipv6 set interface InterfaceName managedaddress=enabled
```

Similarly, you can set the O flag to 1 in router advertisements by entering the following command at an elevated command prompt:

```
netsh interface ipv6 set interface InterfaceName otherstateful=enabled
```

If the interface name contains spaces, enclose the related value in quotation marks, as shown in the following example:

```
netsh interface ipv6 set interface "Wired Ethernet Connection 2"
managedaddress=enabled
```

Keep the following in mind when you are working with the M and O flags:

- If the M and O flags are both set to 0, the network is considered not to have DHCPv6 infrastructure. Clients use router advertisements for non-link-local addresses and manual configuration to configure other settings.

- If the M and O flags are both set to 1, DHCPv6 is used for both IP addressing and other configuration settings. This combination is known as *DHCPv6 stateful mode*, in which DHCPv6 assigns stateful addresses to IPv6 clients.

- If the M flag is set to 0 and the O flag is set to 1, DHCPv6 is used only to assign other configuration settings. Neighboring routers are configured to advertise non-link-local address prefixes from which IPv6 clients derive stateless addresses. This combination is known as *DHCPv6 stateless mode*.

- If the M flag is set to 1 and the O flag is set to 0, DHCPv6 is used for IP address configuration but not for other settings. Because IPv6 clients typically need to be configured with other settings, such as the IPv6 addresses of DNS servers, this combination typically is not used.

Windows obtains dynamic IPv6 addresses by using a process similar to dynamic IPv4 addresses. Typically, IPv6 autoconfiguration for DHCPv6 clients in stateful mode works like this:

1. The client computer selects a link-local unicast IPv6 address. Before using the IPv6 address, the client performs an ARP test to make sure that no other client is using this IPv6 address.

2. If the IPv6 address is in use, the client repeats step 1. Keep in mind that when a client is disconnected from the network, the ARP test always succeeds. As a result, the client uses the first IPv6 address it selects.

3. If the IPv6 address is available, the client configures the NIC with this address. The client then attempts to contact a DHCP server, sending out a broadcast every five minutes to the network. When the client successfully contacts a server, the client obtains a lease and reconfigures the network interface.

This is not how IPv6 autoconfiguration works for DHCPv6 clients in stateless mode. In stateless mode, DHCPv6 clients configure both link-local addresses and additional non-link-local addresses by exchanging Router Solicitation and Router Advertisement messages with neighboring routers.

Like DHCPv4, DHCPv6 uses User Datagram Protocol (UDP) messages. DHCPv6 clients listen for DHCP messages on UDP port 546. DHCPv6 servers and relay agents listen for DHCPv6 messages on UDP port 547. The structure for DHCPv6 messages is much simpler than for DHCPv4, which had its origins in Bootstrap Protocol (BOOTP) to support diskless workstations.

DHCPv6 messages start with a 1-byte Msg-Type field that indicates the type of DHCPv6 message. This is followed by a 3-byte Transaction-ID field determined by a client and used to group together the messages of a DHCPv6 message exchange. Following the Transaction-ID field, DHCPv6 options are used to indicate client and server identification, addresses, and other configuration settings.

Three fields are associated with each DHCPv6 option. A 2-byte Option-Code field indicates a specific option. A 2-byte Option-Len field indicates the length of the Option-Data field in bytes. The Option-Data field contains the data for the option.

Messages exchanged between relay agents and servers use a different message structure to transfer additional information. A 1-byte Hop-Count field indicates the number of relay agents that have received the message. A receiving relay agent can discard the message if the message exceeds a configured maximum hop count. A 15-byte Link-Address field contains a non-link-local address that is assigned to an interface connected to the subnet on which the client is located. Based on the Link-Address field, the server can determine the correct address scope from which to assign an address. A 15-byte Peer-Address field contains the IPv6 address of the client that originally sent the message or the previous relay agent that relayed the message. Following the Peer-Address field are DHCPv6 options. A key option is the Relay Message option. This option provides an encapsulation of the messages being exchanged between the client and the server.

IPv6 does not have broadcast addresses. The use of the limited broadcast address for some DHCPv4 messages has been replaced with the use of the All_DHCP_Relay _Agents_and_Servers address of FF02::1:2 for DHCPv6. A DHCPv6 client attempting to discover the location of the DHCPv6 server on the network sends a Solicit message from its link-local address to FF02::1:2. If there is a DHCPv6 server on the client's subnet, it receives the Solicit message and sends an appropriate reply. If the client and server are on different subnets, a DHCPv6 relay agent on the client's subnet that receives the Solicit message forwards it to a DHCPv6 server.

Checking IP address assignment

You can use ipconfig to check the currently assigned IP address and other configuration information. To obtain information for all network adapters on the computer, enter the command **ipconfig /all** at the command prompt. If the IP address has been assigned automatically, you'll notice an entry for Autoconfiguration IP Address.

In the following example, the autoconfiguration IPv4 address is 169.254.98.59:

```
Windows IP Configuration
        Host Name ................: DELTA
        Primary DNS Suffix ........: microsoft.com
        Node Type ................: Hybrid
        IP Routing Enabled.........: No
        WINS Proxy Enabled.........: No
        DNS Suffix Search List.....: microsoft.com
Ethernet adapter Ethernet:
        Connection-specific DNS Suffix...:
        Description ................: Intel Pro/1000 Network Connection
        Physical Address............: 23-15-C6-F8-FD-67
        DHCP Enabled................: Yes
        Autoconfiguration Enabled...: Yes
        Autoconfiguration IP Address: 169.254.98.59
        Subnet Mask ................: 255.255.0.0
        Default Gateway ............:
        DNS Servers ................:
```

Understanding scopes

Scopes are pools of IPv4 or IPv6 addresses you can assign to clients through leases. DHCP also provides a way to permanently assign a lease on an address. To do this, you need to create a reservation by specifying the IPv4 address to reserve and the media access control (MAC) address of the computer that will hold the IPv4 address. The reservation thereafter ensures that the client computer with the specified MAC address always gets the designated IPv4 address. With IPv6, you can specify that a lease is temporary or nontemporary. A nontemporary lease is similar to a reservation.

You create scopes to specify IP address ranges that are available for DHCP clients. For example, you could assign the IP address range 192.168.12.2 to 192.168.12.250 to a scope called Enterprise Primary. Scopes can use public or private IPv4 addresses on the following networks:

- **Class A networks** IP addresses from 1.0.0.0 to 126.255.255.255
- **Class B networks** IP addresses from 128.0.0.0 to 191.255.255.255
- **Class C networks** IP addresses from 192.0.0.0 to 223.255.255.255
- **Class D networks** IP addresses from 224.0.0.0 to 239.255.255.255

NOTE The IP address 127.0.0.1 is used for local loopback (and so are any other IP addresses in the 127.x.y.z address range).

Scopes can also use link-local unicast, global unicast, and multicast IPv6 addresses. Link-local unicast addresses begin with FE80. Multicast IPv6 addresses begin with FF00. Global (site-local) unicast addresses include all other addresses except :: (unspecified) and ::1 (loopback) addresses.

A single DHCP server can manage multiple scopes. With IPv4 addresses, four types of scopes are available:

- **Normal scopes** Used to assign IPv4 address pools for class A, B, and C networks.

- **Multicast scopes** Used to assign IP address pools for IPv4 class D networks. Computers use multicast IP addresses as secondary IP addresses in addition to a standard IP address.

- **Superscopes** Containers for other scopes that are used to simplify management of multiple scopes and also support DHCP clients on a single physical network where multiple logical IP networks are used.

- **Failover scopes** Scopes split between two DHCP servers to increase fault tolerance, provide redundancy, and enable load balancing.

With IPv6, only normal scopes are available. Although you can create scopes on multiple network segments, you'll usually want these segments to be in the same network class, such as all IP addresses that are class C.

TIP Don't forget that you must configure DHCPv4 and DHCPv6 relays to relay DHCPv4 and DHCPv6 broadcast requests between network segments. You can configure relay agents with the Routing and Remote Access Service (RRAS) and the DHCP Relay Agent Service. You can also configure some routers as relay agents. These services can be installed as part of the Remote Access role. On a server with no other policy and access role services configured, you can install the Remote Access role by using the Add Roles And Features Wizard.

Installing a DHCP server

Dynamic IP addressing is available only if a DHCP server is installed on the network. By using the Add Roles And Features Wizard, you install the DHCP server as a role service, configure its initial settings, and authorize the server in Active Directory Domain Services (AD DS). Only authorized DHCP servers can provide dynamic IP addresses to clients.

Installing DHCP components

On a server running Windows Server 2012 R2, follow these steps to enable the server to function as a DHCP server:

1. DHCP servers should be assigned a static IPv4 and IPv6 address on each subnet to which they are connected and will service. Be sure that the server has static IPv4 and IPv6 addresses.

2. In Server Manager, tap or click Manage, and then tap or click Add Roles And Features, or select Add Roles And Features in the Quick Start pane. This starts the Add Roles And Features Wizard. If the wizard displays the Before You Begin page, read the Welcome text, and then tap or click Next.

3. On the Installation Type page, Role-Based Or Feature-Based Installation is selected by default. Tap or click Next.

4. On the Server Selection page, you can choose to install roles and features on running servers or virtual hard disks. Either select a server from the server pool or select a server from the server pool on which to mount a virtual hard disk (VHD). If you are adding roles and features to a VHD, tap or click Browse, and then use the Browse For Virtual Hard Disks dialog box to locate the VHD. When you are ready to continue, tap or click Next.

   NOTE Only servers running Windows Server 2012 R2 and that have been added for management in Server Manager are listed.

5. On the Select Roles page, select DHCP Server. If additional features are required to install a role, you'll get an additional dialog box. Tap or click Add Features to close the dialog box and add the required features to the server installation. When you are ready to continue, tap or click Next three times.

6. If the server on which you want to install the DHCP Server role doesn't have all the required binary source files, the server gets the files via Windows Update by default or from a location specified in Group Policy.

   NOTE You also can specify an alternate path for the required source files. To do this, click the Specify An Alternate Source Path link, enter that alternate path in the box provided, and then tap or click OK. For network shares, enter the UNC path to the share, such as \\CorpServer82\WinServer2012\. For mounted Windows images, enter the Windows Imaging (WIM) path prefixed with *WIM:* and including the index of the image to use, such as WIM:\\CorpServer82 \WinServer2012\install.wim:4.

7. After you review the installation options and save them as necessary, tap or click Install to begin the installation process. The Installation Progress page tracks the progress of the installation. If you close the wizard, tap or click the Notifications icon in Server Manager, and then tap or click the link provided to reopen the wizard.

8. When Setup finishes installing the DHCP Server role, the Installation Progress page will be updated to reflect this. Review the installation details to ensure that all phases of the installation were completed successfully.

9. As stated in the Post-Deployment Configuration task panel, additional configuration is required for the DHCP server. Tap or click the Complete DHCP Configuration link to start the DHCP Post-Install Configuration Wizard.

10. The Description page states that the DHCP Administrators and DHCP Users groups will be created in the domain for delegation of DHCP Server administration. Additionally, if the DHCP server is joined to a domain, the server will be authorized in Active Directory. Tap or click Next.

11. On the Authorization page, do one of the following to specify the credentials to use to authorize the DHCP server in Active Directory:

- Your current user name is shown in the User Name text box. If you have administrator privileges in the domain that the DHCP server is a member of and you want to use your current credentials, tap or click Commit to attempt to authorize the server by using these credentials.

- If you want to use alternate credentials or if you are unable to authorize the server by using your current credentials, select Use Alternate Credentials, and then tap or click Specify. In the Windows Security dialog box, enter the user name and password for the authorized account, and then tap or click OK. Tap or click Commit to attempt to authorize the server by using these credentials.

- If you want to authorize the DHCP server later, select Skip AD Authorization, and then tap or click Commit. Keep in mind that in domains, only authorized DHCP servers can provide dynamic IP addresses to clients.

12. When the wizard finishes the post-install configuration, review the installation details to ensure that tasks were completed successfully, and then tap or click Close.

13. Next, you need to restart the DHCP Server service on the DHCP server so that the DHCP Administrators and DHCP Users groups can be used. To do this, tap or click DHCP in the left pane of Server Manager. Next, in the main pane, on the Servers panel, select the DHCP server. Finally, on the Services panel, press and hold or right-click the entry for the DHCP Server, and then tap or click Restart Service.

14. To complete the installation, you need to do the following:

- If the server has multiple network cards, review the server bindings and specify the connections that the DHCP server supports for servicing clients. See "Configuring server bindings" later in this chapter.

- Configure server options to assign common configuration settings for DHCPv4 and DHCPv6 clients, including 003 Router, 006 DNS Servers, 015 DNS Domain Name, and 044 WINS/NBNS Servers. See "Setting scope options" later in the chapter.

- Create and activate any DHCP scopes that the server will use, as discussed in "Creating and managing scopes" later in the chapter.

Starting and using the DHCP console

After you install a DHCP server, you use the DHCP console to configure and manage dynamic IP addressing. In Server Manager, tap or click Tools, and then tap or click DHCP to open the DHCP console. Alternatively, enter **Dhcpmgmt.msc** in the Everywhere search box or at a prompt.

The main window for the DHCP console is shown in Figure 8-1. You'll notice that the main window is divided into two panes. The left pane lists the DHCP servers in the domain according to their fully qualified domain name (FQDN). You can expand a server listing to show subnodes for IPv4 and IPv6. If you expand the IP nodes, you'll find the scopes and options defined for the related IP version. The right pane shows the expanded view of the current selection.

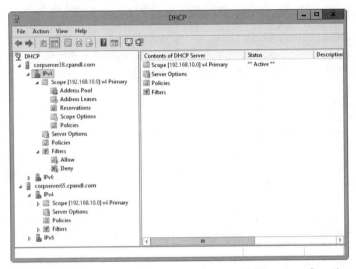

FIGURE 8-1 Use the DHCP console to create and manage DHCP server configurations.

Icons on the various nodes show the current status of the nodes. For server and IP nodes, you might find the following icons:

- A server icon with a green circle with a check mark indicates that the DHCP service is running and the server is active.

- A server icon with red circle with an X through it indicates that the console can't connect to the server. The DHCP service has been stopped or the server is inaccessible.

- A red down arrow indicates that the DHCP server hasn't been authorized.

- A blue warning icon indicates that the server's state has changed or a warning has been issued.

For scopes, you might find the following icons:

- A red down arrow indicates that the scope hasn't been activated.

- A blue warning icon indicates that the scope's state has changed or a warning has been issued.

Connecting to remote DHCP servers

When you start the DHCP console, you are connected directly to a local DHCP server, but you won't find entries for remote DHCP servers. You can connect to remote servers by following these steps:

1. Press and hold or right-click DHCP in the console tree, and then tap or click Add Server to open the dialog box shown in Figure 8-2.

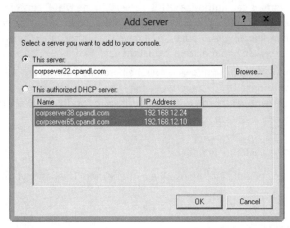

FIGURE 8-2 If your DHCP server isn't listed, you need to add it to the DHCP console by using the Add Server dialog box.

2. Select This Server, and then enter the IP address or computer name of the DHCP server you want to manage.

3. Tap or click OK. An entry for the DHCP server is added to the console tree.

TIP When you work with remote servers, you might find that you can't select certain options. A simple refresh of the server information might resolve this problem. To refresh the server information press and hold or right-click the server node, and then select Refresh.

Starting and stopping a DHCP server

You manage DHCP servers through the DHCP Server service. As with any other service, you can start, stop, pause, and resume the DHCP Server service in the Services node of Computer Management or from the command line. You can also manage the DHCP Server service in the DHCP console. Press and hold or right-click the server you want to manage in the DHCP console, point to All Tasks, and then tap or click Start, Stop, Pause, Resume, or Restart, as appropriate.

NOTE You also can use Server Manager to start and stop a DHCP server. Tap or click DHCP in the left pane of Server Manager. Next, in the main pane, on the Servers panel, select the DHCP server. Finally, on the Services panel, press and hold or right-click the entry for the DHCP Server, and then tap or click Start Service, Stop Service, Pause Service, Resume Service, or Restart Service, as appropriate.

Authorizing a DHCP server in Active Directory

Before you can use a DHCP server in the domain, you must authorize it in Active Directory. By authorizing the server, you specify that the server is authorized to provide dynamic IP addressing in the domain. Windows Server 2012 R2 requires authorization to prevent unauthorized DHCP servers from serving domain clients. This in turn ensures that network operations can run smoothly.

Only Enterprise Admins can authorize DHCP servers. In the DHCP console, you authorize a DHCP server by pressing and holding or right-clicking the server entry in the tree view, and then selecting Authorize. To remove the authorization, press and hold or right-click the server, and then select Unauthorize.

At an elevated, administrator Windows PowerShell prompt, you can use Add-DhcpServerInDC to authorize DHCP servers. Use the –DnsName parameter to specify the name of the server to authorize or the –IpAddress to specify the IP address ofthe server to authorize as shown in the following examples:

```
Add-DhcpServerInDC –DnsName CorpSvr03.cpand1.com
Add-DhcpServerInDC –IpAddress 192.168.1.1
```

Use Remove-DhcpServerInDC to remove the authorization. The basic syntax is the same.

Configuring DHCP servers

After you install a new DHCP server, you need to configure and optimize the server for the network environment. A separate set of options are provided for IPv4 and IPv6.

Configuring server bindings

A server with multiple NICs has multiple local area network connections and can provide DHCP services on any of these network connections. However, you might not want DHCP to be served over all available connections. For example, if the server has both a 100–megabits per second (Mbps) connection and a 1–gigabit per second (Gbps) connection, you might want all DHCP traffic to go over the 1-Gbps connection.

To bind DHCP to a specific network connection, follow these steps:

1. In the DHCP console, press and hold or right-click the server with which you want to work, and then tap or click Add/Remove Bindings.

2. Select the IPv4 or IPv6 tab as appropriate for the type of binding with which you want to work.

3. The Bindings dialog box displays a list of available network connections for the DHCP server. If you want the DHCP Server service to use a connection to service clients, select the check box for the connection. If you don't want the service to use a connection, clear the related check box. If there are no network connections listed for the protocol with which you are working, ensure that the server has a static address for that protocol.

4. Tap or click OK when you have finished.

Updating DHCP statistics

The DHCP console provides statistics concerning IPv4 and IPv6 address availability and usage. In the DHCP console, you can view these statistics by expanding the node for the server with which you want to work, pressing and holding or right-clicking IPv4 or IPv6 as appropriate for the type of address with which you want to work, and then tapping or clicking Display Statistics.

By default, these statistics are updated only when you start the DHCP console or when you select the server and then tap or click the Refresh button on the toolbar. If you monitor DHCP routinely, you might want these statistics to be updated automatically, which you can do by following these steps:

1. In the DHCP console, expand the node for the server with which you want to work, press and hold or right-click IPv4 or IPv6 as appropriate for the type of address with which you want to work, and then tap or click Properties.

2. On the General tab, select Automatically Update Statistics Every and enter an update interval in hours and minutes. Tap or click OK.

Auditing and troubleshooting DHCP

Windows Server 2012 R2 is configured to audit DHCP processes by default. Auditing tracks DHCP processes and requests in log files.

You can use audit logs to help you troubleshoot problems with a DHCP server. Just as you enable and configure logging separately for IPv4 and IPv6, the two protocols use different log files. The default location for DHCP logs is %SystemRoot% \System32\DHCP. In this directory, you'll find a different log file for each day of the week. The IPv4 log file for Monday is named DhcpSrvLog-Mon.log, the log file for Tuesday is named DhcpSrvLog-Tue.log, and so on. The IPv6 log file for Monday is named DhcpV6SrvLog-Mon.log, the log file for Tuesday is named DhcpV6SrvLog-Tue.log, and so on.

When you start the DHCP server or a new day arrives, a header message is written to the log file. This header provides a summary of DHCP events and their meanings. Stopping and starting the DHCP Server service doesn't clear a log file. Log data is kept for a week. For example, the DCHP Server service clears and starts over Monday's log the following Monday. You don't have to monitor space usage by the DHCP Server service. The service is configured to monitor itself and restricts disk space usage by default.

You can enable or disable DHCP auditing by following these steps:

1. In the DHCP console, expand the node for the server with which you want to work, press and hold or right-click IPv4 or IPv6 as appropriate for the type of address with which you want to work, and then tap or click Properties.

2. On the General tab, select or clear the Enable DHCP Audit Logging check box, and then tap or click OK.

By default, DHCP logs are stored in %SystemRoot%\System32\DHCP. You can change the location of DHCP logs by following these steps:

1. In the DHCP console, expand the node for the server with which you want to work, press and hold or right-click IPv4 or IPv6 as appropriate for the type of address with which you want to work, and then tap or click Properties.

2. Tap or click the Advanced tab. Audit Log File Path shows the current folder location for log files. Enter a new folder location, or tap or click Browse to select a new location.

3. Tap or click OK. Windows Server 2012 R2 now needs to restart the DHCP Server service. When prompted to restart the service, tap or click Yes. The service will be stopped and then started again.

The DHCP server has a self-monitoring system that checks disk space usage. By default, the maximum size of all DHCP server logs is 70 megabytes (MB), with each individual log being limited to one-seventh of this space. If the server reaches the 70-MB limit or an individual log grows beyond the allocated space, logging of DHCP activity stops until log files are cleared or space is otherwise made available. Typically, this happens at the beginning of a new day when the server clears the previous week's log file for that day.

Registry keys that control log usage and other DHCP settings are located under HKEY_LOCAL_MACHINE\SYSTEM\CurrentControlSet\Services\DHCPServer \Parameters.

The following keys control the logging:

- **DhcpLogFilesMaxSize** Sets the maximum file size for all logs. The default is 70 MB.

- **DhcpLogDiskSpaceCleanupInterval** Determines how often DHCP checks disk space usage and cleans up as necessary. The default interval is 60 minutes.

- **DhcpLogMinSpaceOnDisk** Sets the free space threshold for writing to the log. If the disk has less free space than the value specified, logging is temporarily disabled. The default value is 20 MB.

DhcpLogMinSpaceOnDisk is considered an optional key and is not created automatically. You need to create this key as necessary and set appropriate values for your network.

Integrating DHCP and DNS

DNS is used to resolve computer names in Active Directory domains and on the Internet. Thanks to the DNS dynamic update protocol, you don't need to manually register DHCP clients in DNS. The protocol allows the client or the DHCP server to register the forward-lookup and reverse-lookup records in DNS as necessary. When configured by using the default setup for DHCP, current DHCP clients automatically update their own DNS records after receiving an IP address lease. You can modify this behavior globally for each DHCP server or on a per-scope basis.

Name protection is an additional feature in Windows Server 2012 R2. With name protection, the DHCP server registers records on behalf of the client only if no other client with this DNS information is already registered. You can configure name protection for IPv4 and IPv6 at the network adapter level or at the scope level. Name protection settings configured at the scope level take precedence over the settings at the IPv4 or IPv6 level.

Name protection is designed to prevent name squatting. Name squatting occurs when a computer not based on the Windows operating system registers a name in DNS that is already registered to a computer running a Windows operating system. By enabling name protection, you can prevent name squatting by computers not based on the Windows operating system. Although name squatting generally does not present a problem when you use Active Directory to reserve a name for a single user or computer, it usually is a good idea to enable name protection on all Windows networks.

Name protection is based on the Dynamic Host Configuration Identifier (DHCID) and support for the DHCID RR (resource record) in DNS. The DHCID is a resource record stored in DNS that maps names to prevent duplicate registration. DHCP uses the DHCID resource record to store an identifier for a computer along with related information for the name, such as the A and AAAA records of the computer. The DHCP server can request a DHCID record match and then refuse the registration of a computer with a different address attempting to register a name with an existing DHCID record.

You can view and change the global DNS integration settings by following these steps:

1. In the DHCP console, expand the node for the server with which you want to work, press and hold or right-click IPv4 or IPv6, and then tap or click Properties.

2. Tap or click the DNS tab. Figure 8-3 shows the default DNS integration settings for DHCP. Because these settings are configured by default, you usually don't need to modify the configuration. However, if you only want host (A) records to be dynamically updated instead of both host (A) and pointer (PTR) records, select the Disable Dynamic Updates For DNS PTR Records check box.

IMPORTANT The default configuration, which registers and maintains both A and PTR records, assumes that you've configured reverse lookup zones for your organization. If you haven't, attempts to register and update PTR records will fail. You can prevent repeated failed attempts to register and update PTR records by disabling dynamic updates for PTR records. If you disable this option in the IPv4 properties, you are disabling the option for all IPv4 scopes. Alternatively, you can use scope properties to disable the option on a per scope basis.

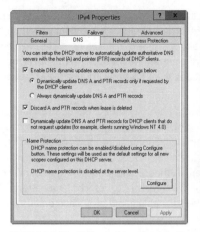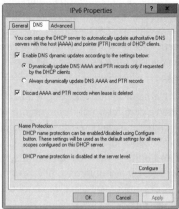

FIGURE 8-3 The DNS tab shows the default settings for DNS integration with DHCP.

3. Optionally, you can enable or disable the name protection feature. With name protection, the DHCP server registers records on behalf of the client only if no other client with this DNS information is already registered. To enable or disable name protection, tap or click Configure. In the Name Protection dialog box, select or clear Enable Name Protection, and then tap or click OK.

You can view and change the per-scope DNS integration settings by following these steps:

1. In the DHCP console, expand the node for the server with which you want to work, and then expand IPv4 or IPv6.

2. Press and hold or right-click the scope with which you want to work, and then tap or click Properties.

3. Tap or click the DNS tab. The options available are the same as those shown in Figure 8-3. Because these settings are configured by default, you usually don't need to modify the configuration.

4. Optionally, you can enable or disable the name-protection feature. Tap or click Configure. In the Name Protection dialog box, select or clear Enable Name Protection, and then tap or click OK.

Integrating DHCP and NAP

Network Access Protection (NAP) is designed to protect the network from clients that do not have the appropriate security measures in place. The easiest way to enable NAP with DHCP is to set up the DHCP server as a Network Policy Server. To do this, you need to install the Network Policy And Access Services role, configure a compliant policy for NAP and DHCP integration on the server, and then enable NAP for DHCP. This process enables NAP for network computers that use DHCP, but it does not fully configure NAP for use.

You can create a NAP and DHCP integration policy by following these steps:

1. On the server that you want to designate as the Network Policy Server, use the Add Roles And Features Wizard to install the Network Policy And Access Services role. You should install the Network Policy Server role service at a minimum.

2. In the Network Policy Server Console (Nps.msc), available from the Tools menu in Server Manager, select the NPS (Local) node in the console tree, and then tap or click Configure NAP in the main pane to start the Configure NAP Wizard.

3. In the Network Connection Method list, choose Dynamic Host Configuration Protocol (DHCP) as the connection method you want to deploy on your network for NAP-capable clients. As shown in Figure 8-4, the policy name is set to NAP DHCP by default. Tap or click Next.

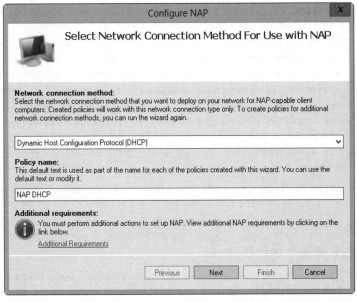

FIGURE 8-4 Configure Network Access Protection policy for the local DHCP server.

4. On the Specify NAP Enforcement Servers Running DHCP Server page, you need to identify all remote DHCP servers on your network by doing the following:

   ■ Tap or click Add. In the New RADIUS Client dialog box, enter a friendly name for the remote server in the Friendly Name text box. Then enter the DNS name of the remote DHCP server in the Address text box. Tap or click Verify to ensure that the DNS name is valid.

- In the Shared Secret panel, select Generate, and then tap or click the Generate button to create a long shared-secret keyphrase. You need to enter this keyphrase in the NAP DHCP policy on all remote DHCP servers. Be sure to write down this keyphrase, or copy it to Notepad and save it in a file stored in a secure location. Tap or click OK.

5. Tap or click Next. On the Specify DHCP Scopes page, you can identify the DHCP scopes to which this policy should apply. If you do not specify any scopes, the policy applies to all NAP-enabled scopes on the selected DHCP servers. Tap or click Next twice to skip the Configure Machine Groups page.

6. On the Specify A NAP Remediation Server Group And URL page, select a Remediation Server, or tap or click New Group to define a remediation group and specify servers to handle remediation. Remediation servers store software updates for NAP clients that need them. In the text box provided, enter a URL for a webpage that provides users with instructions on how to bring their computers into compliance with NAP health policy. Be sure that all DHCP clients can access this URL. Tap or click Next to continue.

7. On the Define NAP Health Policy page, use the options provided to determine how NAP health policy works. In many cases, the default settings work fine, though you may want to use the Allow option while you fine-tune policy. With the default settings, NAP-ineligible clients are denied access to the network, and NAP-capable clients are checked for compliance and automatically remediated, which allows them to get needed software updates that you've made available. Tap or click Next, and then tap or click Finish.

You can modify NAP settings globally for each DHCP server or on a per-scope basis. To view or change the global NAP settings, follow these steps:

1. In the DHCP console, expand the node for the server with which you want to work, press and hold or right-click IPv4, and then tap or click Properties.

2. On the Network Access Protection tab, shown in Figure 8-5, tap or click Enable On All Scopes or Disable On All Scopes to enable or disable NAP for all scopes on the server.

> **NOTE** When the local DHCP server is also a Network Policy Server, the Network Policy Server should always be reachable. If you haven't configured the server as a Network Policy Server or the DHCP server is unable to contact the designated Network Policy Server, you'll get an error stating this on the Network Access Protection tab.

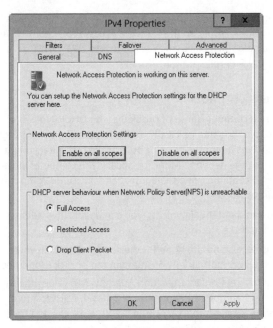

FIGURE 8-5 The Network Access Protection tab controls the protection options for DHCP.

3. Choose one of the following options to specify how the DHCP server behaves if the Network Policy Server is unreachable, and then tap or click OK to save your settings:

- **Full Access**   Gives DHCP clients full (unrestricted) access to the network. This means clients can perform any permitted actions.

- **Restricted Access**   Gives DHCP clients restricted access to the network. This means clients can work only with the server to which they are connected.

- **Drop Client Packet**   Blocks client requests, and prevents the clients from accessing the network. This means clients have no access to resources on the network.

You can view and change the NAP settings for individual scopes by following these steps:

1. In the DHCP console, expand the node for the server with which you want to work, and then expand IPv4.

2. Press and hold or right-click the scope with which you want to work, and then tap or click Properties.

3. On the Network Access Protection tab, tap or click Enable For This Scope or Disable For This Scope to enable or disable NAP for this scope.

4. If you're enabling NAP and want to use a NAP profile other than the default, tap or click Use Custom Profile on the Network Access Protection tab, and then enter the name of the profile, such as **Alternate NAP DHCP**.

5. Tap or click OK to save your settings.

Avoiding IP address conflicts

IPv4 address conflicts are a common cause of problems with DHCP. No two computers on the network can have the same unicast IP address. If a computer is assigned the same unicast IPv4 address as another, one or both of the computers might become disconnected from the network. More specifically, the computer already using the IPv4 address can continue using the address and any other computer that tries to use that IPv4 address is blocked from using it.

To better detect and avoid potential conflicts, you can enable IPv4 address conflict detection by following these steps:

1. In the DHCP console, expand the node for the server with which you want to work, press and hold or right-click IPv4, and then tap or click Properties.

2. On the Advanced tab, set Conflict Detection Attempts to a value other than 0. The value you enter determines the number of times the DHCP server checks an IP address before leasing it to a client. The DHCP server checks IP addresses by sending a ping request over the network.

REAL WORLD A unicast IPv4 address is a standard IP address for class A, B, and C networks. When a DHCP client requests a lease, a DHCP server checks its pool of available addresses and assigns the client a lease on an available IPv4 address. By default, the server checks only the list of current leases to determine whether an address is available. It doesn't actually query the network to determine whether an address is in use. Unfortunately, in a busy network environment, an administrator might have assigned this IPv4 address to another computer or an offline computer might have been brought online with a lease that it believes hasn't expired, even though the DHCP server believes the lease has expired. Either way, you have an address conflict that will cause problems on the network. To reduce these types of conflicts, set the conflict detection to a value greater than 0.

Saving and restoring the DHCP configuration

After you configure all the necessary DHCP settings, you might want to save the DHCP configuration so that you can restore it on the DHCP server. To save the configuration, enter the following command at the command prompt:

```
netsh dump DHCP > dhcpconfig.dmp
```

In this example, *dhcpconfig.dmp* is the name of the configuration script you want to create. By default, the script is created in the current working directory. Alternatively, you can specify the full file path in which to save the script. After you create this script, you can restore the configuration by executing the script. If you saved the script in the current working directory, you can enter the following command at the command prompt:

```
netsh exec dhcpconfig.dmp
```

If you saved the script in another directory, you can specify the full path to the script, such as:

```
netsh exec d:\dhcp\scripts\dhcpconfig.dmp
```

> **TIP** You can also use this technique to set up another DHCP server with the same configuration. Just copy the configuration script to a folder on the destination computer, and then execute it.

You can save or restore the DHCP configuration by using the DHCP console as well. To save the configuration, press and hold or right-click the DHCP server entry, tap or click Backup, use the dialog box provided to select the folder for the backup, and then tap or click OK. To restore the configuration, press and hold or right-click the DHCP server entry, tap or click Restore, use the dialog box provided to select the backup folder, and then tap or click OK. When prompted to confirm, tap or click Yes.

At an elevated Windows PowerShell prompt, you use Export-DhcpServer to save the configuration settings. The basic syntax is:

```
Export-DhcpServer –ComputerName ServerID –File SavePath
```

Here, *ServerID* is the DNS name or IP address of the DHCP server, and *SavePath* is the path and name of the file in which you want to store the configuration settings. If you omit the name of the server to work with, the local server is used. If you don't specify a save path along with the file name, the configuration file is created in the current working directory. In the following example, you store the configuration settings in the d:\dhcp\scripts directory with the name dhcpconfig.dmp:

```
Export-DhcpServer-File d:\dhcp\scripts\dhcpconfig.dmp
```

You can restore the configuration using Import-DhcpServer. The basic syntax is:

```
Import-DhcpServer –ComputerName ServerID –BackupPath CurrentConfigSavePath
–File SavePath
```

Here, *SavePath* is the path and name of the file in which you stored the configuration settings and *CurrentConfigSavePath* specifies the path where the current configuration should be saved prior to importing and overwriting existing settings. In the following example, you back up the settings to d:\dhcp\backup\origconfig.dmp and then apply the saved configuration from d:\dhcp\scripts\dhcpconfig.dmp:

```
Import-DhcpServer-BackupPath d:\dhcp\backup\origconfig.dmp
–File d:\dhcp\scripts\dhcpconfig.dmp
```

Managing DHCP scopes

After you install a DHCP server, you need to configure the scopes that the DHCP server will use. Scopes are pools of IP addresses you can lease to clients. As explained earlier in "Understanding scopes," you can create superscopes, normal scopes, multicast scopes, and failover scopes with IPv4 addresses, but you can create only normal scopes with IPv6 addresses.

Creating and managing superscopes

A superscope is a container for IPv4 scopes in much the same way that an organizational unit is a container for Active Directory objects. Superscopes help you manage scopes available on the network by grouping them into a single point of management. For example, with a superscope, you can activate or deactivate multiple scopes through a single action. You can also view statistics for all scopes in the superscope rather than having to check statistics for each scope. Superscopes also support DHCP clients on a single physical network where multiple logical IP networks are used, or put another way, you can create superscopes to distribute IP addresses from different logical networks to the same physical network segment.

Creating superscopes

After you create at least one normal or multicast IPv4 scope, you can create a superscope by following these steps:

1. In the DHCP console, expand the node for the server with which you want to work, press and hold or right-click IPv4, and then tap or click New Superscope to start the New Superscope Wizard. Tap or click Next.

2. Enter a name for the superscope, and then tap or click Next.

3. Select scopes to add to the superscope. Select individual scopes by tapping or clicking their entry in the Available Scopes list. Select multiple scopes by tapping or clicking entries while holding down Shift or Ctrl.

4. Tap or click Next, and then tap or click Finish.

Adding scopes to a superscope

You can add scopes to a superscope when you create it, or you can add the scopes later. To add a scope to a superscope, follow these steps:

1. Press and hold or right-click the scope you want to add to a superscope, and then tap or click Add To Superscope.

2. In the Add Scope To A Superscope dialog box, select a superscope.

3. Tap or click OK. The scope is then added to the superscope.

Removing scopes from a superscope

To remove a scope from a superscope, follow these steps:

1. Press and hold or right-click the scope you want to remove from a superscope, and then tap or click Remove From Superscope.

2. Confirm the action by tapping or clicking Yes when prompted. If this is the last scope in the superscope, the superscope is deleted automatically.

Activating and deactivating a superscope

When you activate or deactivate a superscope, you make all the scopes within the superscope active or inactive. To activate a superscope, press and hold or right-click the superscope, and then select Activate. To deactivate a superscope, press and hold or right-click the superscope, and then select Deactivate.

Deleting a superscope

Deleting a superscope removes the superscope container but doesn't delete the scopes it contains. If you want to delete the member scopes, you'll need to do that separately. To delete a superscope, press and hold or right-click the superscope, and then select Delete. When prompted, tap or click Yes to confirm the action.

Creating and managing scopes

Scopes provide a pool of IP addresses for DHCP clients. A normal scope is a scope with class A, B, or C network addresses. A multicast scope is a scope with class D network addresses. Although you create normal scopes and multicast scopes differently, you manage them in much the same way. The key differences are that multicast scopes can't use reservations, and you can't set additional options for WINS, DNS, routing, and so forth.

Creating normal scopes for IPv4 addresses

You can create a normal scope for IPv4 addresses by following these steps:

1. In the DHCP console, expand the node for the server with which you want to work, and then press and hold or right-click IPv4. If you want to add the new scope to a superscope automatically, press and hold or right-click the super-scope instead.

2. On the shortcut menu, tap or click New Scope to start the New Scope Wizard. Tap or click Next.

3. Enter a name and description for the scope, and then tap or click Next.

4. The Start IP Address and End IP Address boxes define the valid IP address range for the scope. On the IP Address Range page, enter a start address and an end address in these boxes.

   NOTE Generally, the scope doesn't include the x.x.x.0 and x.x.x.255 addresses, which are usually reserved for network addresses and broadcast messages, respectively. Accordingly, you would use a range such as 192.168.10.1 to 192.168.10.254 rather than 192.168.10.0 to 192.168.10.255.

5. When you enter an IP address range, the bit length and subnet mask are filled in for you automatically (as shown in Figure 8-6). Unless you use subnets, you should use the default values.

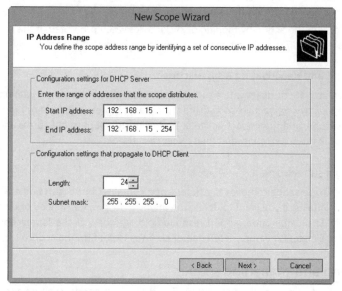

FIGURE 8-6 In the New Scope Wizard, enter the IP address range for the scope.

6. Tap or click Next. If the IP address range you entered is on multiple networks, you're given the opportunity to create a superscope that contains separate scopes for each network and, in this case, select the Yes option button to continue, and then move on to step 8. If you make a mistake, tap or click Back, and then modify the IP address range you entered.

7. Use the Start IP Address and End IP Address boxes on the Add Exclusions And Delay page to define IP address ranges that are to be excluded from the scope. You can exclude multiple address ranges as follows:

   ■ To define an exclusion range, enter a start address and an end address in the Exclusion Range's Start IP Address and End IP Address boxes, and then tap or click Add. To exclude a single IP address, use that address as both the start IP address and the end IP address.

   ■ To track which address ranges are excluded, use the Excluded Address Range list.

   To delete an exclusion range, select the range in the Excluded Address Range list, and then tap or click Remove.

8. Tap or click Next. Specify the duration of leases for the scope by using the Day(s), Hour(s), and Minutes boxes. The default duration is eight days. Tap or click Next.

NOTE A lease duration that's set too long can reduce the effectiveness of DHCP and might eventually cause you to run out of available IP addresses, especially on networks with mobile users or other types of computers that aren't fixed members of the network. A good lease duration for most networks is from one to three days.

9. You have the opportunity to configure common DHCP options for DNS, WINS, gateways, and more. If you want to set these options now, select Yes, I Want To Configure These Options Now; otherwise, select No, I Will Configure These Options Later and skip steps 10–15.

10. Tap or click Next. The first option you can configure is the default gateway. In the IP Address box, enter the IP address of the primary default gateway, and then tap or click Add. Repeat this process for other default gateways.

11. The first gateway listed is the one clients try to use first. If the gateway isn't available, clients try to use the next gateway, and so on. Use the Up and Down buttons to change the order of the gateways, as necessary.

12. Tap or click Next. As shown in Figure 8-7, configure default DNS settings for DHCP clients. Enter the name of the parent domain to use for DNS resolution of computer names that aren't fully qualified.

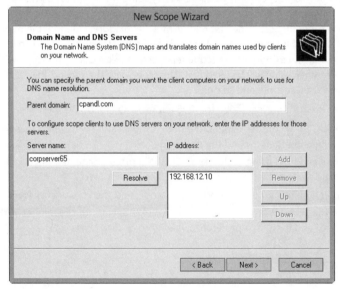

FIGURE 8-7 Use the Domain Name And DNS Servers page to configure default DNS settings for DHCP clients.

13. In the IP Address box, enter the IP address of the primary DNS server, and then tap or click Add. Repeat this process to specify additional DNS servers. Again, the order of the entries determines which IP address is used first. Change the order as necessary by using the Up and Down buttons. Tap or click Next.

   TIP If you know the name of a server instead of its IP address, enter the name in the Server Name box, and then tap or click Resolve. The IP address is then entered in the IP Address box, if possible. Add the server by tapping or clicking Add. Using this approach helps to ensure that you've entered the correct information.

14. Configure default WINS settings for the DHCP clients. The techniques you use are the same as those previously described. Tap or click Next.

15. If you want to activate the scope, select Yes, I Want To Activate This Scope Now, and then tap or click Next. Otherwise, select No, I Will Activate This Scope Later and then tap or click Next.

16. Tap or click Finish to complete the process.

Creating normal scopes for IPv6 addresses

You create normal scopes for IPv6 addresses by using the New Scope Wizard. When you are configuring DHCP for IPv6 addresses, you must enter the network ID and a preference value. Typically, the first 64 bits of an IPv6 address identify the network, and a 64-bit value is what the New Scope Wizard expects you to enter. The preference value sets the priority of the scope relative to other scopes. The scope with the lowest preference value will be used first. The scope with the second-lowest preference will be used second, and so on.

You can create a normal scope for IPv6 addresses by following these steps:

1. In the DHCP console, expand the node for the server with which you want to work and then expand the IPv6 node.

2. Press and hold or right-click IPv6. On the shortcut menu, tap or click New Scope to start the New Scope Wizard. Tap or click Next.

3. Enter a name and description for the scope, and then tap or click Next.

4. On the Scope Prefix page, shown in Figure 8-8, enter the 64-bit network prefix, and then set a preference value. Tap or click Next.

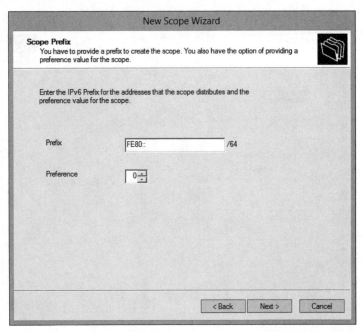

FIGURE 8-8 In the New Scope Wizard, enter the network prefix and preference value.

5. Use the Start IPv6 Address and End IPv6 Address boxes on the Add Exclusions page to define IPv6 address ranges that are to be excluded from the scope. You can exclude multiple address ranges as follows:

   ■ To define an exclusion range, enter a start address and an end address in the Exclusion Range's Start IPv6 Address and End IPv6 Address boxes, and then tap or click Add. To exclude a single IPv6 address, use that address as the start IPv6 address, and then tap or click Add.

   ■ To track which address ranges are excluded, use the Excluded Address Range list.

   To delete an exclusion range, select the range in the Excluded Address Range list, and then tap or click Remove.

6. Tap or click Next. Dynamic IPv6 addresses can be temporary or nontemporary. A nontemporary address is similar to a reservation. On the Scope Lease page, shown in Figure 8-9, specify the duration of leases for nontemporary addresses by using the Days, Hours, and Minutes boxes under Preferred Life Time and Valid Life Time. The preferred lifetime is the preferred amount of time the lease should be valid. The valid lifetime is the maximum amount of time the lease is valid. Tap or click Next.

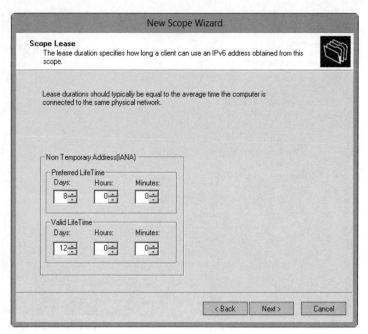

FIGURE 8-9 Specify the duration of nontemporary leases.

NOTE A lease lifetime that's set too long can reduce the effectiveness of DHCP. A good lease duration for nontemporary leases is from 8 to 30 days.

7. If you want to activate the scope, select Yes under Activate Scope Now, and then tap or click Finish. Otherwise, select No under Activate Scope Now, and then tap or click Finish.

Creating multicast scopes

To create a multicast scope, follow these steps:

1. In the DHCP console, expand the node for the server with which you want to work. Select and then press and hold or right-click IPv4. If you want to add the new scope to a superscope, select and then press and hold or right-click the superscope instead.

2. On the shortcut menu, tap or click New Multicast Scope to start the New Multicast Scope Wizard. Tap or click Next.

3. Enter a name and description for the scope, and then tap or click Next.

4. The Start IP Address and End IP Address boxes define the valid IP address range for the scope. Enter a start address and an end address in these boxes. You must define multicast scopes by using Class D IP addresses. This means the valid IP address range is 224.0.0.0 to 239.255.255.255.

5. Messages sent by computers using multicast IP addresses have a specific time-to-live (TTL) value. The TTL value specifies the maximum number of routers the message can go through. The default value is 32, which is sufficient on most networks. If you have a large network, you might need to increase this value to reflect the actual number of routers that might be used.

6. Tap or click Next. If you make a mistake, tap or click Back, and then modify the IP address range you entered.

7. Use the exclusion range to define IP address ranges that are to be excluded from the scope. You can exclude multiple address ranges as follows:

   ■ To define an exclusion range, enter a start address and an end address in the Start IP Address and End IP Address boxes, and then tap or click Add.

   ■ To track which address ranges are excluded, use the Excluded Addresses list.

   ■ To delete an exclusion range, select the range in the Excluded Addresses list, and then tap or click Remove.

8. Tap or click Next. Specify the duration of leases for the scope by using the Day(s), Hour(s), and Minutes boxes. The default duration is 30 days. Tap or click Next.

   TIP If you haven't worked a lot with multicast, you shouldn't change the default value. Multicast leases aren't used in the same way as normal leases. Multiple computers can use a multicast IP address, and all of these computers can have a lease on the IP address. A good multicast lease duration for most networks is from 30 to 60 days.

9. If you want to activate the scope, select Yes, and then tap or click Next. Otherwise, select No, and then tap or click Next.

10. Tap or click Finish to complete the process.

Setting scope options

Scope options enable you to precisely control a scope's functioning and to set default TCP/IP settings for clients that use the scope. For example, you can use scope options to enable clients to automatically find DNS servers on the network. You can also define settings for default gateways, WINS, and more. Scope options apply only to normal scopes, not to multicast scopes.

You can set scope options in any of the following ways:

■ Globally for all scopes by setting default server options

■ On a per-scope basis by setting scope options

■ On a per-client basis by setting reservation options

■ On a client-class basis by configuring user-specific or vendor-specific classes

IPv4 and IPv6 have different scope options. Scope options use a hierarchy to determine when certain options apply. The previous list shows the hierarchy. Basically, this means the following:

- Per-scope options override global options
- Per-client options override per-scope and global options
- Client-class options override all other options

VIEWING AND ASSIGNING SERVER OPTIONS

Server options are applied to all scopes configured on a particular DHCP server. You can view and assign server options by following these steps:

1. In the DHCP console, double-tap or double-click the server with which you want to work, and then expand its IPv4 and IPv6 folders in the tree view.

2. To view current settings, select the Server Options node under IPv4 or IPv6, depending on the type of address with which you want to work. Currently configured options are displayed in the right pane.

3. To assign new settings, press and hold or right-click Server Options, and then tap or click Configure Options to open the Server Options dialog box. Under Available Options, select the check box for the first option you want to configure. Then, with the option selected, enter any required information in the Data Entry panel. Repeat this step to configure other options.

4. Tap or click OK to save your changes.

VIEWING AND ASSIGNING SCOPE OPTIONS

Scope options are specific to an individual scope and override the default server options. You can view and assign scope options by following these steps:

1. In the DHCP console, expand the entry for the scope with which you want to work.

2. To view current settings, select Scope Options. Currently configured options are displayed in the right pane.

3. To assign new settings, press and hold or right-click Scope Options, and then tap or click Configure Options. This opens the Scope Options dialog box. Under Available Options, select the check box for the first option you want to configure. Then, with the option selected, enter any required information in the Data Entry panel, as shown in Figure 8-10. Repeat this step to configure other options.

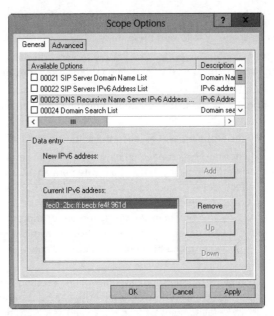

FIGURE 8-10 Select the option you want to configure in the Scope Options dialog box, and then enter the required information on the Data Entry panel.

4. Tap or click OK.

VIEWING AND ASSIGNING RESERVATION OPTIONS

You can assign reservation options to a client that has a reserved IPv4 or IPv6 address. These options are specific to an individual client and override server-specific and scope-specific options. To view and assign reservation options, follow these steps:

1. In the DHCP console, expand the entry for the scope with which you want to work.

2. Double-tap or double-click the Reservations folder for the scope.

3. To view current settings, tap or click the reservation you want to examine. Currently configured options are displayed in the right pane.

4. To assign new settings, press and hold or right-click the reservation, and then tap or click Configure Options to open the Reservation Options dialog box. Under Available Options, select the check box for the first option you want to configure. Then, with the option selected, enter any required information in the Data Entry panel. Repeat this step to configure other options.

Modifying scopes

You can modify an existing scope by following these steps:

1. In the DHCP console, double-tap or double-click the server with which you want to work, and then expand its IPv4 and IPv6 folders in the tree view. This should display the currently configured scopes for the server.

2. Press and hold or right-click the scope you want to modify, and then tap or click Properties.

3. You can now modify the scope properties. Keep the following in mind:

   - When you modify normal IPv4 scopes, you have the option of setting an unlimited lease expiration time. If you do, you create permanent leases that reduce the effectiveness of pooling IP addresses with DHCP. Permanent leases aren't released unless you physically release them or deactivate the scope. As a result, you might eventually run out of addresses, especially as your network grows. A better alternative to unlimited leases is to use address reservations, and then only for specific clients that need fixed IP addresses.

   - When you modify multicast scopes, you have the option of setting a lifetime for the scope. The scope lifetime determines the amount of time the scope is valid. By default, multicast scopes are valid as long as they're activated. To change this setting, tap or click the Lifetime tab, select Multicast Scope Expires On, and then set an expiration date.

Activating and deactivating scopes

In the DHCP console, inactive scopes are displayed with an icon showing a red arrow pointing down. Active scopes display the standard folder icon.

You can activate an inactive scope by pressing and holding or right-clicking it in the DHCP console, and then selecting Activate. You can deactivate an active scope by pressing and holding or right-clicking it in the DHCP console, and then selecting Deactivate.

> **IMPORTANT** Deactivating turns off a scope but doesn't terminate current client leases. If you want to terminate leases, follow the instructions in "Releasing addresses and leases" later in this chapter.

Enabling the Bootstrap Protocol

Bootstrap Protocol (BOOTP) is a dynamic IPv4 addressing protocol that predates DHCP. Normal scopes don't support BOOTP. To enable a scope to support BOOTP, follow these steps:

1. Press and hold or right-click the normal scope for IPv4 addresses that you want to modify, and then tap or click Properties.

2. On the Advanced tab, tap or click Both to support DHCP and BOOTP clients.

3. As necessary, set a lease duration for BOOTP clients, and then tap or click OK.

NOTE The typical lease duration for a BOOTP address is much longer than for a DHCP address. For BOOTP, the default of 30 days is a good compromise, though some scenarios might lend themselves to an unlimited lease duration.

Removing a scope

Removing a scope permanently deletes the scope from the DHCP server. To remove a scope, follow these steps:

1. In the DHCP console, press and hold or right-click the scope you want to remove, and then tap or click Delete.
2. When prompted to confirm that you want to delete the scope, tap or click Yes.

Configuring multiple scopes on a network

You can configure multiple scopes on a single network. A single DHCP server or multiple DHCP servers can serve these scopes. However, any time you work with multiple scopes, it's extremely important that the address ranges used by different scopes not overlap. Each scope must have a unique address range. If it doesn't, the same IP address might be assigned to different DHCP clients, which can cause severe problems on the network.

To understand how you can use multiple scopes, consider the following scenario, in which each server has its respective DHCP scope IP address range on the same subnet:

- **Server A** 192.168.10.1 to 192.168.10.99
- **Server B** 192.168.10.100 to 192.168.10.199
- **Server C** 192.168.10.200 to 192.168.10.254

Each of these servers responds to DHCP discovery messages, and any of them can assign IP addresses to clients. If one of the servers fails, the other servers can continue to provide DHCP services to the network. To introduce fault tolerance and provide redundancy, you can use failover scopes as discussed in the next section.

Creating and managing failover scopes

Failover scopes are split between two DHCP servers to increase fault tolerance, provide redundancy over using a single DHCP server, and enable load balancing. With a failover scope, you identify the two DHCP servers that split the scope. If one of the servers becomes unavailable or overloaded, the other server can take its place by continuing to lease new IP addresses and renew existing leases. A failover scope can also help to balance server loads.

Creating failover scopes

Failover scopes apply only to IPv4 addresses. You can split a single scope or a superscope that contains multiple scopes.

You create a failover scope on the DHCP server that you want to designate as the primary server by splitting an existing scope or superscope. During the failover-scope creation process, you need to specify the partner server with which you want to split the primary server's scope. This additional server acts as the secondary server for the scope. Because failover scopes are a server-side enhancement, no additional configuration is required for DHCP clients.

The way scope splitting works depends on the failover scope configuration settings. You do one of the following:

- **Optimize for load balancing** A failover scope optimized for load balancing has little or no time delay configured in its scope properties. With no time delay, both the primary and the secondary servers can respond to DHCP DISCOVER requests from DHCP clients. This enables the fastest server to respond to and accept a DHCPOFFER first. Fault tolerance continues to be a part of the scope. If one of the servers becomes unavailable or overloaded and is unable to respond to requests, the other server handles requests and continues distributing addresses until the normal process is restored. For load balancing, set Load Balance as the failover mode.

- **Optimize for fault tolerance** A failover scope optimized for fault tolerance has an extended time delay configured in its scope properties. The time delay on the secondary DHCP server causes the server to respond with a delay to DHCP DISCOVER requests from DHCP clients. The delay on the secondary server enables the primary DHCP server to respond to and accept the DHCPOFFER first. However, if the primary server becomes unavailable or overloaded and is unable to respond to requests, the secondary server handles requests and continues distributing addresses until the primary server is available to service clients again. For fault tolerance, set Hot Standby as the failover mode.

You can create a failover scope by completing the following steps:

1. In the DHCP console, connect to the primary DHCP server for the failover scope. Double-tap or double-click the entry for the primary server, and then expand its IPv4 folder in the tree view.

2. The scope with which you want to work must already be defined. Press and hold or right-click the scope or superscope that you want to configure for failover, and then tap or click Configure Failover to start the Configure Failover Wizard. Tap or click Next.

3. Next, you need to specify the partner server to use for failover. Tap or click Add Server. Use the options in the Add Server dialog box to select the secondary DHCP server for the failover scope, and then tap or click OK. Clear the Reuse Existing Failover Relationships check box, and then tap or click Next to continue.

4. On the Create A New Failover Relationship page, shown in Figure 8-11, use the Mode list to set the failover mode as Load Balance or Hot Standby.

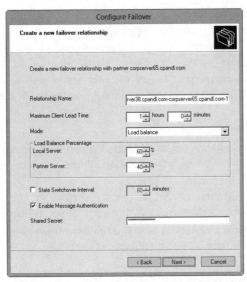

FIGURE 8-11 Specify the load balance percentage for the local server and the partner server.

5. If you set the failover mode for Load Balance, use the Load Balance Percentage combo boxes to specify the relative percentage for how to allocate the IP addresses to each of the servers. Here are configuration examples:

- An 80/20 split works best when you want one server to handle most of the workload and want another server to be available as needed.

- An 60/40 split works best when you want one server to handle a little more of the workload than the other, but you want both servers to have regular workloads.

- A 50/50 split works best when you want to evenly balance the load between two servers.

6. If you set the failover mode to Hot Standby, set the role of the partner as either Active or Standby and then specify the relative percentage of IP addresses to reserve. By default, 5 percent of the IP addresses are reserved for the standby server.

7. Enter a shared secret for the partners. The shared secret is a password that the partners use when synchronizing the DHCP database and performing other tasks related to maintaining the DHCP failover partnership. When you are ready to continue, tap or click Next.

8. Tap or click Finish. Review the summary of the failover scope configuration. If any errors were encountered, you might need to take corrective action. Tap or click Close.

Modifying or removing failover scopes

Failover scopes are not identified as such in the DHCP console. You can identify a failover scope by its network ID and IP address pool. Generally, you'll find a scope with the same network ID on two DHCP servers, and the scope properties will include information about the failover partnership. To view this information, press and hold or right-click the scope, and then select Properties. In the Properties dialog box, select the Failover tab.

You can manage the partnership in several ways:

- If you suspect the configuration details related to the partnership are out of sync, press and hold or right-click the scope, and then select Replicate Partnership.

- If you suspect the DHCP database that the partners share is out of sync, press and hold or right-click the scope, and then select Replicate Scope.

- If you no longer want the scope to fail over, you can deconfigure failover by pressing and holding or right-clicking the scope, and then selecting Deconfigure Failover.

You can't modify the failover settings after the partnership is established; however, you can deconfigure failover and then reconfigure failover.

Managing the address pool, leases, and reservations

Scopes have separate folders for address pools, leases, and reservations. By accessing these folders, you can view current statistics for the related data and manage existing entries.

Viewing scope statistics

Scope statistics provide summary information about the address pool for the current scope or superscope. To view statistics, press and hold or right-click the scope or superscope, and then select Display Statistics.

The primary columns in the Scope Statistics dialog box are used as follows:

- **Total Scopes** Shows the number of scopes in a superscope.
- **Total Addresses** Shows the total number of IP addresses assigned to the scope.
- **In Use** Shows the total number (as a numerical value and as a percentage of the total available addresses) of addresses being used. If the total reaches 85 percent or more, you might want to consider assigning additional addresses or freeing up addresses for use.
- **Available** Shows the total number (as a numerical value and as a percentage of the total available addresses) of addresses available for use.

Enabling and configuring MAC address filtering

MAC address filtering (aka *link-layer filtering*) is a feature for IPv4 addresses that enables you to include or exclude computers and devices based on their MAC address. When you configure MAC address filtering, you can specify the hardware types that are exempted from filtering. By default, all hardware types defined in RFC 1700 are exempted from filtering. To modify hardware type exemptions, follow these steps:

1. In the DHCP console, press and hold or right-click the IPv4 node, and then tap or click Properties.

2. On the Filters tab, tap or click Advanced. In the Advanced Filter Properties dialog box, select the check box for hardware types to exempt from filtering. Clear the check box for hardware types to filter.

3. Tap or click OK to save your changes.

Before you can configure MAC address filtering, you must do one of the following:

- Enable and define an explicit allow list. The DHCP server provides DHCP services only to clients whose MAC addresses are in the allow list. Any client that previously received IP addresses is denied address renewal if its MAC address isn't on the allow list.

- Enable and define an explicit deny list. The DHCP server denies DHCP services only to clients whose MAC addresses are in the deny list. Any client that previously received IP addresses is denied address renewal if its MAC address is on the deny list.

- Enable and define an allow list and a block list. The block list has precedence over the allow list. This means that the DHCP server provides DHCP services only to clients whose MAC addresses are in the allow list, if no corresponding matches are in the deny list. If a MAC address has been denied, the address is always blocked even if the address is on the allow list.

To enable an allow list, deny list, or both, follow these steps:

1. In the DHCP console, press and hold or right-click the IPv4 node, and then tap or click Properties.

2. On the Filters tab, you'll find the current filter configuration details. To use an allow list, select Enable Allow List. To use a deny list, select Enable Deny List.

3. Tap or click OK to save your changes.

NOTE As an alternative, you can press and hold or right-click the Allow or Deny node, under the Filters node, and then select Enable to enable allow or deny lists. If you press and hold or right-click the Allow or Deny node and then select Disable, you disable allow or deny lists.

After you enable filtering, you define your filters by using the MAC address for the client computer or device's network adapter. On a client computer, you can obtain the MAC address by entering the command **ipconfig /all** at the command prompt. The Physical Address entry shows the client's MAC address. You must enter this value exactly for the address filter to work.

A MAC address is defined by eight pairings of two-digit hexadecimal numbers separated by a hyphen, as shown here:

FE-01-56-23-18-94-EB-F2

When you define a filter, you can specify the MAC address with or without the hyphens. This means that you could enter FE-01-56-23-18-94-EB-F2 or FE0156231894EBF2.

You also can use an asterisk (*) as a wildcard for pattern matching. To allow any value to match a specific part of the MAC address, you can insert * where the values usually would be, as shown here:

FE-01-56-23-18-94-*-F2

FE-*-56-23-18-94-*-*

FE-01-56-23-18-*-*-*

FE01*

To configure a MAC address filter, follow these steps:

1. In the DHCP console, double-tap or double-click the IPv4 node, and then double-tap or double-click the Filters node.

2. Press and hold or right-click Allow or Deny as appropriate for the type of filter you are creating, and then tap or click New Filter.

3. Enter the MAC address to filter, and then if you want to you can enter a comment in the Description text box. Tap or click Add. Repeat this step to add other filters.

4. Tap or click Close when you have finished.

Setting a new exclusion range

You can exclude IPv4 or IPv6 addresses from a scope by defining an exclusion range. Scopes can have multiple exclusion ranges. To define an exclusion range for a scope with IPv4 addresses, follow these steps:

1. In the DHCP console, expand the scope with which you want to work, and then press and hold or right-click the Address Pool folder or Exclusions folder. On the shortcut menu, tap or click New Exclusion Range.

2. Enter a start address and an end address in the Start IP Address and End IP Address boxes, and then tap or click Add. The range specified must be a subset of the range set for the current scope and must not be currently in use. Repeat this step to add other exclusion ranges.

3. Tap or click Close when you have finished.

> **TIP** To exclude a single IP address, enter a start address and leave the end address blank.

To define an exclusion range for a scope with IPv6 addresses, follow these steps:

1. In the DHCP console, expand the scope with which you want to work, and then press and hold or right-click the Exclusions folder. On the shortcut menu, tap or click New Exclusion Range.

2. Enter a start address and an end address in the Start IPv6 Address and End IPv6 Address boxes, and then tap or click Add. The range specified must be a subset of the range set for the current scope and must not be currently in use. Repeat this step to add other exclusion ranges.

3. Tap or click Close when you have finished.

If you don't need an exclusion anymore, you can delete it. Select Address Pool or Exclusions as appropriate. In the main pane, press and hold or right-click the exclusion, select Delete, and then tap or click Yes in response to the confirmation message.

Reserving DHCP addresses

DHCP provides several ways to assign permanent addresses to clients. One way is to use the Unlimited setting in the Scope dialog box to assign permanent addresses to all clients that use the scope. Another way is to reserve DHCP addresses on a per-client basis. When you reserve a DHCP address, the DHCP server always assigns the client the same IP address, and you can do so without sacrificing the centralized management features that make DHCP so attractive.

If the client is on the network and has a current IPv4 or IPv6 lease, you can create a reservation by completing the following steps:

1. In the DHCP console, expand the scope with which you want to work, and then select the Address Leases folder.

2. Press and hold or right-click the lease you want to work with. On the shortcut menu, tap or click Add To Reservation.

Otherwise, to manually reserve an IPv4 address for a client, follow these steps:

1. In the DHCP console, expand the scope with which you want to work, and then press and hold or right-click the Reservations folder. On the shortcut menu, tap or click New Reservation.

2. In the Reservation Name text box, enter a short but descriptive name for the reservation. This name is used only for identification purposes.

3. In the IP Address box, enter the IPv4 address you want to reserve for the client.

   NOTE This IP address must be within the valid range of addresses for the currently selected scope.

4. The MAC Address box specifies the MAC address for the client computer's NIC. You can obtain the MAC address by entering the command **ipconfig /all** at the command prompt on the client computer. The Physical Address entry shows the client's MAC address. You must enter this value exactly for the address reservation to work.

5. Enter an optional comment in the Description text box.

6. By default, both DHCP and BOOTP clients are supported. This option is fine, and you need to change it only if you want to exclude a particular type of client.

7. Tap or click Add to create the address reservation. Repeat this step to add other address reservations.

8. Tap or click Close when you have finished.

To manually reserve an IPv6 address for a client, follow these steps:

1. In the DHCP console, expand the scope with which you want to work, and then press and hold or right-click the Reservations folder. On the shortcut menu, tap or click New Reservation.

2. In the Reservation text box, enter a short but descriptive name for the reservation. This information is used only for identification purposes.

3. In the IPv6 Address box, enter the IPv6 address you want to reserve for the client.

> **NOTE** This IP address must be within the valid range of addresses for the currently selected scope.

4. The device unique identifier (DUID) box specifies the MAC address for the client computer's NIC. You can obtain the MAC address by entering the command **ipconfig /all** at the command prompt on the client computer. The Physical Address entry shows the client's MAC address. You must enter this value exactly for the address reservation to work.

5. The identity association identifier (IAID) sets a unique identifier prefix for the client. Typically, this is a nine-digit value.

6. Enter an optional comment in the Description text box.

7. Tap or click Add to create the address reservation. Repeat this step to add other address reservations.

8. Tap or click Close when you have finished.

Releasing addresses and leases

When you work with reserved addresses, you should take note of a couple caveats:

- Reserved addresses aren't automatically reassigned. If the address is already in use, you need to release the address to ensure that the appropriate client can obtain it. You can force a client to release an address by terminating the client's lease or by logging on to the client and entering the command **ipconfig /release** at an elevated command prompt.

- Clients don't automatically switch to the reserved address. If the client is using a different IP address, you need to force the client to release the current lease and request a new one. You can do this by terminating the client's lease or by logging on to the client and entering the command **ipconfig / renew** at an elevated command prompt.

Modifying reservation properties

You can modify the properties of reservations by following these steps:

1. In the DHCP console, expand the scope with which you want to work, and then tap or click the Reservations folder.

2. Press and hold or right-click a reservation, and then tap or click Properties. You can now modify the reservation properties. You can't modify options that are shaded, but you can modify other options. These options are the same options described in the previous section.

Deleting leases and reservations

You can delete active leases and reservations by following these steps:

1. In the DHCP console, expand the scope with which you want to work, and then tap or click the Address Leases folder or Reservations folder, as appropriate.

2. Press and hold or right-click the lease or reservation you want to delete, and then tap or click Delete.

3. Confirm the deletion by tapping or clicking Yes.

4. The lease or reservation is now removed from DHCP; however, the client isn't forced to release the IP address. To force the client to release the IP address, log on to the client that holds the lease or reservation and enter the command **ipconfig /release** at an elevated command prompt.

Backing up and restoring the DHCP database

DHCP servers store DHCP lease and reservation information in database files. By default, these files are stored in the %SystemRoot%\System32\DHCP directory. The key files in this directory are used as follows:

- **Dhcp.mdb**   The primary database file for the DHCP server
- **J50.log**   A transaction log file used to recover incomplete transactions in case of a server malfunction
- **J50.chk**   A checkpoint file used in truncating the transaction log for the DHCP server
- **J50000NN.log**   A reserved log file for the DHCP server
- **Tmp.edb**   A temporary working file for the DHCP server

Backing up the DHCP database

The %SystemRoot%\System32\DHCP\Backup folder contains the backup information for the DHCP configuration and the DHCP database. By default, the DHCP database is backed up every 60 minutes automatically. To manually back up the DHCP database at any time, follow these steps:

1. In the DHCP console, press and hold or right-click the server you want to back up, and then tap or click Backup.

2. In the Browse For Folder dialog box, select the folder that will contain the backup DHCP database, and then tap or click OK.

Registry keys that control the location and timing of DHCP backups, in addition to other DHCP settings, are located under HKEY_LOCAL_MACHINE\SYSTEM \CurrentControlSet\Services\DHCPServer\Parameters.

The following keys control the DHCP database and backup configuration:

- **BackupDatabasePath**   Sets the location of the DHCP database. You should set this option through the DHCP Properties dialog box. Tap or click the Advanced tab, and then set the Database Path as appropriate.

- **DatabaseName**   Sets the name of the primary DHCP database file. The default value is DHCP.mdb.

- **BackupInterval**   Determines how often the DHCP client information database is backed up. The default is 60 minutes.

- **DatabaseCleanupInterval**   Determines how often the DHCP service deletes expired records from the DHCP client information database. The default is four hours.

Restoring the DHCP database from backup

In the case of a server crash and recovery, you might need to restore and then reconcile the DHCP database. To force DHCP to restore the database from backup, follow these steps:

1. If necessary, restore a good copy of the %SystemRoot%\System32\DHCP \Backup directory from the archive. Afterward, start the DHCP console, press and hold or right-click the server you want to restore, and then tap or click Restore.

2. In the Browse For Folder dialog box, select the folder that contains the backup you want to restore, and then tap or click OK.

3. During the restoration of the database, the DHCP Server service is stopped. As a result, DHCP clients are temporarily unable to contact the DHCP server to obtain IP addresses.

Using backup and restore to move the DHCP database to a new server

If you need to rebuild a server providing DHCP services, you might want to move the DHCP services to another server prior to rebuilding the server. To do this, you need to perform several tasks on the source and destination servers. On the destination server, do the following:

1. Install the DHCP Server service on the destination server, and then restart the server.

2. Stop the DHCP Server service in the Services console.

3. Delete the contents of the %SystemRoot%\System32\DHCP folder.

On the source server, do the following:

1. Stop the DHCP Server service in the Services console.

2. After the DHCP Server service is stopped, disable the service so that it can no longer be started.

3. Copy the entire contents of the %SystemRoot%\System32\DHCP folder to the %SystemRoot%\System32\DHCP folder on the destination server.

Now all the necessary files are on the destination server. Start the DHCP Server service on the destination server to complete the migration.

Forcing the DHCP Server service to regenerate the DHCP database

If the DHCP database becomes corrupt and Windows is unable to repair the database when you stop and restart the DHCP Server service, you can attempt to restore the database as described in "Restoring the DHCP database from backup" earlier in this chapter. If this fails or you prefer to start with a fresh copy of the DHCP database, follow these steps:

1. Stop the DHCP Server service in the Services console.

2. Delete the contents of the %SystemRoot%\System32\DHCP folder. If you want to force a complete regeneration of the database and not allow the server to restore from a previous backup, you should also delete the contents of the Backup folder.

   CAUTION Don't delete DHCP files if the DHCPServer registry keys aren't intact. These keys must be available to restore the DHCP database.

3. Restart the DHCP Server service.

4. No active leases or other information for scopes are displayed in the DHCP console. To regain the active leases for each scope, you must reconcile the server scopes as discussed in the next section.

5. To prevent conflicts with previously assigned leases, you should enable address conflict detection for the next few days, as discussed in "Avoiding IP address conflicts" earlier in this chapter.

Reconciling leases and reservations

Reconciling checks the client leases and reservations against the DHCP database on the server. If inconsistencies are found between what is registered in the Windows registry and what is recorded in the DHCP server database, you can select and reconcile any inconsistent entries. After the entries you select are reconciled, DHCP either restores the IP address to the original owner or creates a temporary reservation for the IP address. When the lease time expires, the address is recovered for future use.

You can reconcile scopes individually, or you can reconcile all scopes on a server. To reconcile a scope individually, follow these steps:

1. In the DHCP console, press and hold or right-click the scope with which you want to work, and then tap or click Reconcile.

2. In the Reconcile dialog box, tap or click Verify.

3. Inconsistencies are reported in the status window. Select the displayed addresses, and then tap or click Reconcile to repair inconsistencies.

4. If no inconsistencies are found, tap or click OK.

To reconcile all scopes on a server, follow these steps:

1. In the DHCP console, expand the server entry, press and hold or right-click the IPv4 node, and then tap or click Reconcile All Scopes.

2. In the Reconcile All Scopes dialog box, tap or click Verify.

3. Inconsistencies are reported in the status window. Select the displayed addresses, and then tap or click Reconcile to repair inconsistencies.

4. If no inconsistencies are found, tap or click OK.

CHAPTER 9

Optimizing DNS

This chapter discusses the techniques you use to set up and manage Domain Name System (DNS) on a network. DNS is a name-resolution service that resolves computer names to IP addresses. When you use DNS, a fully qualified host name—omega.microsoft.com, for example—can be resolved to an IP address, which enables computers to find one another. DNS operates over the TCP/IP protocol stack and can be integrated with Windows Internet Name Service (WINS), Dynamic Host Configuration Protocol (DHCP), and Active Directory Domain Services (AD DS). Fully integrating DNS with these Windows networking features enables you to optimize DNS for Windows Server domains.

Understanding DNS

DNS organizes groups of computers into domains. These domains are organized into a hierarchical structure that can be defined on an Internet-wide basis for public networks or on an enterprise-wide basis for private networks (also known as *extranets* and *intranets*, respectively). The various levels within the hierarchy identify individual computers, organizational domains, and top-level domains. For the fully qualified host name omega.microsoft.com, *omega* represents the host name for an individual computer, *microsoft* is the organizational domain, and *com* is the top-level domain.

Top-level domains are at the root of the DNS hierarchy and are also called *root domains*. These domains are organized geographically, by organization type, and by function. Typical corporate domains, such as microsoft.com, are also referred to as *parent domains* because they're the parents of an organizational structure. You can divide parent domains into subdomains you can use for groups or departments within your organization.

Subdomains are often referred to as *child domains*. For example, the fully qualified domain name (FQDN) for a computer within a human resources group could be designated as jacob.hr.microsoft.com. Here, *jacob* is the host name, *hr* is the child domain, and *microsoft.com* is the parent domain.

Integrating Active Directory and DNS

Active Directory domains use DNS to implement their naming structure and hierarchy. Active Directory and DNS are tightly integrated, so much so that you should install DNS on the network before you can install Active Directory Domain Services.

During installation of the first domain controller on an Active Directory network, you have the opportunity to automatically install DNS if a DNS server can't be found on the network. You can also specify whether DNS and Active Directory should be integrated fully. In most cases, you should respond affirmatively to both requests. With full integration, DNS information is stored directly in Active Directory, which enables you to take advantage of Active Directory's capabilities.

Understanding the difference between partial integration and full integration is very important:

- **Partial integration** With partial integration, the domain uses standard file storage. DNS information is stored in text-based files that end with the .dns extension. The default location of these files is %SystemRoot%\System32\Dns. Updates to DNS are handled through a single authoritative DNS server. This server is designated as the primary DNS server for the particular domain or an area within a domain called a *zone*. Clients that use dynamic DNS updates through DHCP must be configured to use the primary DNS server in the zone. If they aren't, their DNS information won't be updated. Likewise, dynamic updates through DHCP can't be made if the primary DNS server is offline.

- **Full integration** With full integration, the domain uses directory-integrated storage. DNS information is stored directly in Active Directory and is available through the container for the *dnsZone* object. Because the information is part of Active Directory, any domain controller can access the data, and you can use a multimaster approach for dynamic updates through DHCP. This enables any domain controller running the DNS Server service to handle dynamic updates. Furthermore, clients that use dynamic DNS updates through DHCP can use any DNS server within the zone. An added benefit of directory integration is the ability to use directory security to control access to DNS information.

If you look at the way DNS information is replicated throughout the network, you will find more advantages to full integration with Active Directory. With partial integration, DNS information is stored and replicated separately from Active Directory. By having two separate structures, you reduce the effectiveness of both DNS and Active Directory and make administration more complex. Because DNS is less efficient than Active Directory at replicating changes, you might also increase network traffic and the amount of time required to replicate DNS changes throughout the network.

In early releases of the DNS Server service for Windows servers, restarting a DNS server could take an hour or more in large organizations with extremely large AD DS–integrated zones. The operation took this much time because the zone data was loaded in the foreground while the server was starting the DNS service. To ensure that DNS servers can be responsive after a restart, the DNS Server service for Windows Server 2008 R2 and later has been enhanced to load zone data from AD DS in the background while the service restarts. This ensures that the DNS server is responsive and can handle requests for data from other zones.

At startup, DNS servers running Windows Server 2008 R2 and later perform the following tasks:

- Enumerate all zones to be loaded.
- Load root hints from files or AD DS storage.
- Load all zones that are stored in files rather than in AD DS.
- Begin responding to queries and Remote Procedure Calls (RPCs).
- Create one or more threads to load the zones that are stored in AD DS.

Because separate threads load zone data, the DNS server is able to respond to queries while zone loading is in progress. If a DNS client performs a query for a host in a zone that has already been loaded, the DNS server responds appropriately. If the query is for a host that has not yet been loaded into memory, the DNS server reads the host's data from AD DS and updates its record list accordingly.

Enabling DNS on the network

To enable DNS on the network, you need to configure DNS clients and servers. When you configure DNS clients, you tell the clients the IP addresses of DNS servers on the network. By using these addresses, clients can communicate with DNS servers anywhere on the network, even if the servers are on different subnets.

NOTE Configuring a DNS client is explained in Chapter 7, "Managing TCP/IP networking." Configuring a DNS server is explained in the next section of this chapter.

The DNS client built into computers running Windows 7 and later, in addition to Windows Server 2008 R2 or later, supports DNS traffic over Internet Protocol version 4 (IPv4) and Internet Protocol version 6 (IPv6). By default, IPv6 automatically configures the site-local address of DNS servers. To add the IPv6 addresses of your DNS servers, use the properties of the Internet Protocol Version 6 (TCP/IPv6) component in Network Connections or the following command:

```
netsh interface IPV6 ADD DNSSERVERS
```

In Windows PowerShell, you can use Get-NetIPInterface to list the available interfaces and then use Set-DNSClientServerAddress to set the IPv6 address on a specified interface.

DNS servers running Windows Server 2008 R2 or later support IPv6 addresses as fully as they support IPv4 addresses. In the DNS Manager console, host addresses are displayed as IPv4 or IPv6 addresses. The Dnscmd command-line tool also accepts addresses in either format. Additionally, DNS servers can now send recursive queries to IPv6-only servers, and the server forwarder list can contain both IPv4 and IPv6 addresses. Finally, DNS servers now support the ip6.arpa domain namespace for reverse lookups.

When the network uses DHCP, you should configure DHCP to work with DNS. DHCP clients can register IPv6 addresses along with or instead of IPv4 addresses. To ensure proper integration of DHCP and DNS, you need to set the DHCP scope options as specified in "Setting scope options" in Chapter 8, "Running DHCP clients and servers." For IPv4, you should set the 006 DNS Servers and 015 DNS Domain Name scope options. For IPv6, you should set the 00023 DNS Recursive Name Server IPV6 Address List and 00024 Domain Search List scope options. Additionally, if computers on the network need to be accessible from other Active Directory domains, you need to create records for them in DNS. DNS records are organized into zones, where a *zone* is an area within a domain.

DNS client computers running Windows 7 or later, in addition to Windows Server 2008 R2 or later, can use Link-Local Multicast Name Resolution (LLMNR) to resolve names on a local network segment when a DNS server is not available. They also periodically search for a domain controller in the domain to which they belong. This functionality helps avoid performance problems that might occur if a network or server failure causes a DNS client to create an association with a distant domain controller located on a slow link rather than a local domain controller. Previously, this association continued until the client was forced to seek a new domain controller, such as when the client computer was disconnected from the network for a long period of time. By periodically renewing its association with a domain controller, a DNS client can reduce the probability that it will be associated with an inappropriate domain controller.

The DNS client service for Windows 8 and later has several interoperability and security enhancements specific to LLMNR and NetBIOS. To improve security for mobile networking, the service

- Does not send outbound LLMNR queries over mobile broadband or VPN interfaces.
- Does not send outbound NetBIOS queries over mobile broadband.

For better compatibility with devices in power-saving mode, the LLMNR query timeout is set to 410 milliseconds (msec) for the first retry and 410 msec for the second retry, making the total timeout value 820 msec. To improve response times for all queries, the DNS client service does the following:

- Issues LLMNR and NetBIOS queries in parallel, and optimizes for IPv4 and IPv6
- Divides interfaces into networks to send parallel DNS queries
- Uses asynchronous DNS cache with an optimized response timing

NOTE You can configure a DNS client computer running Windows 7 or later, in addition to Windows Server 2008 R2 or later, to locate the nearest domain controller instead of searching randomly. This can improve performance in networks containing domains that exist across slow links. However, because of the network traffic this process generates, locating the nearest domain controller can have a negative impact on network performance.

Windows Server 2008 and later support read-only primary zones and the Global-Names zone. To support read-only domain controllers (RODCs), the primary read-only zone is created automatically. When a computer becomes an RODC, it replicates a full read-only copy of all the application directory partitions that DNS uses, including the domain partition, ForestDNSZones, and DomainDNSZones. This ensures that the DNS server running on the RODC has a full read-only copy of any DNS zones. As an administrator of an RODC, you can view the contents of a primary read-only zone. You cannot, however, change the contents of a zone on the RODC. You can change the contents of the zone only on a standard domain controller.

To support all DNS environments and single-label name resolution, you can create a zone named *GlobalNames*. For optimal performance and cross-forest support, you should integrate this zone with AD DS and configure each authoritative DNS server with a local copy. When you use Service Location (SRV) resource records to publish the location of the GlobalNames zone, this zone provides unique, single-label computer names across the forest. Unlike WINS, the GlobalNames zone is intended to provide single-label name resolution for a subset of host names—typically, the CNAME resource records for your corporate servers. The GlobalNames zone is not intended to be used for peer-to-peer name resolution, such as name resolution for workstations. This is what LLMNR is for.

When the GlobalNames zone is configured appropriately, single-label name resolution works as follows:

1. The client's primary DNS suffix is appended to the single-label name that the client is looking up, and the query is submitted to the DNS server.

2. If that computer's full name is not resolved, the client requests resolution by using its DNS suffix search lists, if any.

3. If none of those names can be resolved, the client requests resolution by using the single-label name.

4. If the single-label name appears in the GlobalNames zone, the DNS server hosting the zone resolves the name. Otherwise, the query fails over to WINS.

The GlobalNames zone provides single-label name resolution only when all authoritative DNS servers are running Windows Server 2008 R2 and later. However, other DNS servers that are not authoritative for any zone can be running other operating systems. Dynamic updates in the GlobalNames zone are not supported.

Configuring name resolution on DNS clients

The best way to configure name resolution for DNS clients depends on the configuration of your network. If computers use DHCP, you probably want to configure DNS through settings on the DHCP server. If computers use static IP addresses or you want to configure DNS specifically for an individual system, you should configure DNS manually.

You can configure DNS settings on the DNS tab of the Advanced TCP/IP Settings dialog box. To access this dialog box, follow these steps:

1. Open Network And Sharing Center, and then tap or click Change Adapter Settings.

2. In Network Connections, press and hold or right-click the connection with which you want to work, and then tap or click Properties.

3. Double-tap or double-click Internet Protocol Version 6 (TCP/IPv6) or Internet Protocol Version 4 (TCP/IPv4), depending on the type of IP address you are configuring.

4. If the computer is using DHCP and you want DHCP to specify the DNS server address, select Obtain DNS Server Address Automatically. Otherwise, select Use The Following DNS Server Addresses, and then enter primary and alternate DNS server addresses in the text boxes provided.

5. Tap or click Advanced to display the Advanced TCP/IP Settings dialog box. In this dialog box, tap or click the DNS tab.

You use the options of the DNS tab as follows:

- **DNS Server Addresses, In Order Of Use**   Use this area to specify the IP address of each DNS server that is used for domain name resolution. Tap or click Add if you want to add a server IP address to the list. Tap or click Remove to remove a selected server address from the list. Tap or click Edit to edit the selected entry. You can specify multiple servers for DNS resolution. Their priority is determined by the order. If the first server isn't available to respond to a host name resolution request, the next DNS server in the list is accessed, and so on. To change the position of a server in the list box, select it, and then use the up or down arrow.

- **Append Primary And Connection Specific DNS Suffixes**   Typically, this option is selected by default. Select this option to resolve unqualified computer names in the primary domain. For example, if the computer name Gandolf is used and the parent domain is microsoft.com, the computer name would resolve to gandolf.microsoft.com. If the fully qualified computer name doesn't exist in the parent domain, the query fails. The parent domain used is the one set on the Computer Name tab in the System Properties dialog box. (Tap or click System And Security\System in Control Panel, tap or click Change Settings, and then display the Computer Name tab to check the settings.)

- **Append Parent Suffixes Of The Primary DNS Suffix**   This option is selected by default. Select this option to resolve unqualified computer names by using the parent/child domain hierarchy. If a query fails in the immediate parent domain, the suffix for the parent of the parent domain is used to try to resolve the query. This process continues until the top of the DNS domain hierarchy is reached. For example, if the computer name Gandolf is used in the dev.microsoft.com domain, DNS would attempt to resolve the computer name to gandolf.dev.microsoft.com. If this didn't work, DNS would attempt to resolve the computer name to gandolf.microsoft.com.

- **Append These DNS Suffixes (In Order)** Select this option to set specific DNS suffixes to use rather than resolving through the parent domain. Tap or click Add if you want to add a domain suffix to the list. Tap or click Remove to remove a selected domain suffix from the list. Tap or click Edit to edit the selected entry. You can specify multiple domain suffixes, which are used in order. If the first suffix is not resolved properly, DNS attempts to use the next suffix in the list. If this fails, the next suffix is used, and so on. To change the order of the domain suffixes, select the suffix, and then use the up or down arrow to change its position. This option is especially useful in hybrid namespaces where there are multiple parent domain names.

- **DNS Suffix For This Connection** This option sets a specific DNS suffix for the connection that overrides DNS names already configured for use on this connection. You usually set the DNS domain name on the Computer Name tab of the System Properties dialog box.

- **Register This Connection's Addresses In DNS** Select this option if you want all IP addresses for this connection to be registered in DNS under the computer's fully qualified domain name. This option is selected by default.

  NOTE Dynamic DNS updates are used in conjunction with DHCP to enable a client to update its A (Host Address) record if its IP address changes and to enable the DHCP server to update the PTR (Pointer) record for the client on the DNS server. You can also configure DHCP servers to update both the A and PTR records on the client's behalf. Dynamic DNS updates are supported by DNS servers with BIND 8.2.1 or later in addition to all server versions of Windows.

- **Use This Connection's DNS Suffix In DNS Registration** Select this option if you want all IP addresses for this connection to be registered in DNS under the parent domain.

Installing DNS servers

You can configure any Windows Server 2012 R2 system as a DNS server. Four types of DNS servers are available:

- **Active Directory–integrated primary server** A DNS server that's fully integrated with Active Directory. All DNS data is stored directly in Active Directory.

- **Primary server** The main DNS server for a domain that is partially integrated with Active Directory. This server stores a master copy of DNS records and the domain's configuration files. These files are stored as text files with the .dns extension.

- **Secondary server** A DNS server that provides backup services for the domain. This server stores a copy of DNS records obtained from a primary server and relies on zone transfers for updates. Secondary servers obtain their DNS information from a primary server when they are started, and they maintain this information until the information is refreshed or expired.

- **Forwarding-only server** A server that caches DNS information after lookups and always passes requests to other servers. These servers maintain DNS information until it's refreshed or expired or until the server is restarted. Unlike secondary servers, forwarding-only servers don't request full copies of a zone's database files. This means that when you start a forwarding-only server, its database contains no information.

Before you configure a DNS server, you must install the DNS Server service. Then you can configure the server to provide integrated, primary, secondary, or forwarding-only DNS services.

Installing and configuring the DNS Server service

All domain controllers can act as DNS servers, and you might be prompted to install and configure DNS during installation of the domain controller. If you respond affirmatively to the prompts, DNS is already installed, and the default configuration is set automatically. You don't need to reinstall.

If you're working with a member server instead of a domain controller, or if you haven't installed DNS, follow these steps to install DNS:

1. In Server Manager, tap or click Manage, and then tap or click Add Roles And Features, or select Add Roles And Features in the Quick Start pane to start the Add Roles And Features Wizard. If the wizard displays the Before You Begin page, read the Welcome text, and then tap or click Next.

2. On the Installation Type page, Role-Based Or Feature-Based Installation is selected by default. Tap or click Next.

3. On the Server Selection page, you can choose to install roles and features on running servers or virtual hard disks. Either select a server from the server pool or select a server from the server pool on which to mount a virtual hard disk (VHD). If you are adding roles and features to a VHD, tap or click Browse and then use the Browse For Virtual Hard Disks dialog box to locate the VHD. When you are ready to continue, tap or click Next.

   NOTE Only servers running Windows Server 2012 R2 and that have been added for management in Server Manager are listed.

4. On the Server Roles page, select DNS Server. If additional features are required to install a role, you'll get an additional dialog box. Tap or click Add Features to close the dialog box, and add the required features to the server installation. When you are ready to continue, tap or click Next three times.

5. If the server on which you want to install the DNS Server role doesn't have all the required binary source files, the server gets the files via Windows Update by default or from a location specified in Group Policy.

NOTE You also can specify an alternate path for the required source files. To do this, click the Specify An Alternate Source Path link, enter that alternate path in the box provided, and then tap or click OK. For network shares, enter the UNC path to the share, such as \\CorpServer82\WinServer2012\. For mounted Windows images, enter the Windows Imaging (WIM) path prefixed with WIM: and including the index of the image to use, such as WIM:\\CorpServer82\WinServer2012\install.wim:4.

6. Tap or click Install to begin the installation process. The Installation Progress page tracks the progress of the installation. If you close the wizard, tap or click the Notifications icon in Server Manager, and then tap or click the link provided to reopen the wizard.

7. When Setup finishes installing the DNS Server role, the Installation Progress page will be updated to reflect this. Review the installation details to ensure that the installation was successful.

8. From now on, the DNS Server service should start automatically each time you restart the server. If it doesn't start, you need to start it manually. (See "Starting and stopping a DNS server" later in this chapter.)

9. After you install a DNS server, you use the DNS console to configure and manage DNS. In Server Manager, tap or click Tools, and then tap or click DNS to open the DNS Manager console, shown in Figure 9-1.

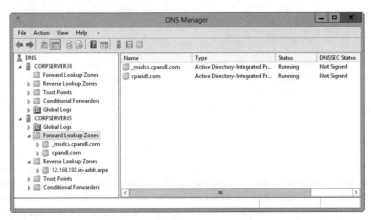

FIGURE 9-1 Use the DNS Manager console to manage DNS servers on the network.

10. If the server you want to configure isn't listed in the tree view, you need to connect to the server. Press and hold or right-click DNS in the tree view, and then tap or click Connect To DNS Server. Now do one of the following:

   ■ If you're trying to connect to a local server, select This Computer, and then tap or click OK.

   ■ If you're trying to connect to a remote server, select The Following Computer, enter the server's name or IP address, and then tap or click OK.

11. An entry for the DNS server should be listed in the tree view pane of the DNS Manager console. Press and hold or right-click the server entry, and then tap or click Configure A DNS Server to start the Configure A DNS Server Wizard. Tap or click Next.

12. On the Select Configuration Action page, shown in Figure 9-2, select Configure Root Hints Only to specify that only the base DNS structures should be created at this time.

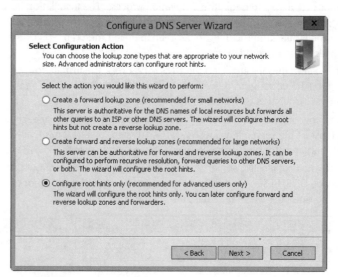

FIGURE 9-2 Configure the root hints only to install the base DNS structures.

13. Tap or click Next. The wizard searches for existing DNS structures and modifies them as necessary.

14. Tap or click Finish to complete the process.

REAL WORLD If the wizard wasn't able to configure the root hints, you might need to configure them manually or copy them from another server. However, a default set of root hints is included with DNS Server, and these root hints should be added automatically. To confirm, press and hold or right-click the server entry in the DNS console, and then select Properties. In the Properties dialog box, the currently configured root hints are shown on the Root Hints tab.

Configuring a primary DNS server

Every domain should have a primary DNS server. You can integrate this server with Active Directory, or it can act as a standard primary server. Primary servers should have forward lookup zones and reverse lookup zones. You use forward lookups to resolve domain names to IP addresses. You need reverse lookups to authenticate DNS requests by resolving IP addresses to domain names or hosts.

After you install the DNS Server service on the server, you can configure a primary server by following these steps:

1. Start the DNS Manager console. If the server you want to configure isn't listed, connect to it as described previously in "Installing and configuring the DNS Server service."

2. An entry for the DNS server should be listed in the tree view pane of the DNS Manager console. Press and hold or right-click the server entry, and then tap or click New Zone to start the New Zone Wizard. Tap or click Next.

3. As Figure 9-3 shows, you can now select the zone type. If you're configuring a primary server integrated with Active Directory (on a domain controller), select Primary Zone and be sure the Store The Zone In Active Directory check box is selected. If you don't want to integrate DNS with Active Directory, select Primary Zone, and then clear the Store The Zone In Active Directory check box. Tap or click Next.

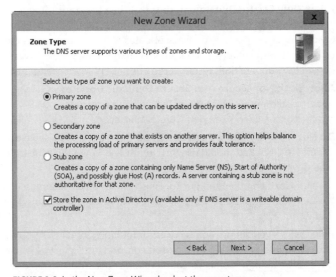

FIGURE 9-3 In the New Zone Wizard, select the zone type.

4. If you're integrating the zone with Active Directory, choose one of the following replication strategies; otherwise, proceed to step 6.

   ■ **To All DNS Servers Running On Domain Controllers In This Forest** Choose this strategy if you want the widest replication strategy. Remember, the Active Directory forest includes all domain trees that share the directory data with the current domain.

   ■ **To All DNS Servers Running On Domain Controllers In This Domain** Choose this strategy if you want to replicate DNS information within the current domain.

   ■ **To All Domain Controllers In This Domain (For Windows 2000 Compatibility)** Choose this strategy if you want to replicate DNS information to all domain controllers within the current domain, as needed for

Windows 2000 compatibility. Although this strategy gives wider replication for DNS information within the domain and supports compatibility with Windows 2000, not every domain controller is a DNS server as well (nor do you need to configure every domain controller as a DNS server).

5. Tap or click Next. Select Forward Lookup Zone, and then tap or click Next.

6. Enter the full DNS name for the zone. The zone name should help determine how the server or zone fits into the DNS domain hierarchy. For example, if you're creating the primary server for the microsoft.com domain, you would enter **microsoft.com** as the zone name. Tap or click Next.

7. If you're configuring a primary zone that isn't integrated with Active Directory, you need to set the zone file name. A default name for the zone's DNS database file should be filled in for you. You can use this name or enter a new file name. Tap or click Next.

8. Specify whether dynamic updates are allowed. You have three options:

   - **Allow Only Secure Dynamic Updates**   When the zone is integrated with Active Directory, you can use access control lists (ACLs) to restrict which clients can perform dynamic updates. With this option selected, only clients with authorized computer accounts and approved ACLs can dynamically update their resource records in DNS when changes occur.

   - **Allow Both Nonsecure And Secure Dynamic Updates**   Choose this option to allow any client to update its resource records in DNS when changes occur. Clients can be secure or nonsecure.

   - **Do Not Allow Dynamic Updates**   Choose this option to disable dynamic updates in DNS. You should use this option only when the zone isn't integrated with Active Directory.

9. Tap or click Next, and then tap or click Finish to complete the process. The new zone is added to the server, and basic DNS records are created automatically.

10. A single DNS server can provide services for multiple domains. If you have multiple parent domains, such as microsoft.com and msn.com, you can repeat this process to configure other forward lookup zones. You also need to configure reverse lookup zones. Follow the steps listed in "Configuring reverse lookups" later in this chapter.

11. You need to create additional records for any computers you want to make accessible to other DNS domains. To do this, follow the steps listed in "Managing DNS records" later in this chapter.

REAL WORLD   Most organizations have private and public areas of their network. The public network areas might be where web and external email servers reside. Your organization's public network areas shouldn't allow unrestricted access. Instead, public network areas should be configured as part of perimeter networks. (Perimeter networks are also known as *DMZs*, demilitarized zones, and *screened subnets*. These are areas protected by your organization's firewall that have restricted external access and no access to the internal network.) Otherwise, public network areas should be in a completely separate and firewall-protected area.

The private network areas are where the organization's internal servers and work stations reside. On the public network areas, your DNS settings are in the public Internet space. Here, you might use a .com, .org, or .net DNS name that you've registered with an Internet registrar and public IP addresses that you've purchased or leased. On the private network areas, your DNS settings are in the private network space. Here, you might use adatum.com as your organization's DNS name and private IP addresses, as discussed in Chapter 7.

Configuring a secondary DNS server

Secondary servers provide backup DNS services on the network. If you're using full Active Directory integration, you don't really need to configure secondaries. Instead, you should configure multiple domain controllers to handle DNS services. Active Directory replication will then handle replicating DNS information to your domain controllers. On the other hand, if you're using partial integration, you might want to configure secondaries to lessen the load on the primary server. On a small or medium-size network, you might be able to use the name servers of your Internet service provider (ISP) as secondaries. In this case, you should contact your ISP to configure secondary DNS services for you. Alternatively, you can put your public DNS records on a dedicated, external DNS service while hosting your private DNS records entirely on your internal DNS servers.

Because secondary servers use forward lookup zones for most types of queries, you might not need reverse lookup zones. But reverse lookup zone files are essential for primary servers, and you must configure them for proper domain name resolution.

If you want to set up your own secondaries for backup services and load balancing, follow these steps:

1. Start the DNS Manager console. If the server you want to configure isn't listed, connect to it as described previously.

2. Press and hold or right-click the server entry, and then tap or click New Zone to start the New Zone Wizard. Tap or click Next.

3. For Zone Type, select Secondary Zone. Tap or click Next.

4. Secondary servers can use both forward and reverse lookup zone files. You create the forward lookup zone first, so select Forward Lookup Zone, and then tap or click Next.

5. Enter the full DNS name for the zone, and then tap or click Next.

6. Tap or click in the Master Servers list, enter the IP address of the primary server for the zone, and then press Enter. The wizard then attempts to validate the server. If an error occurs, be sure the server is connected to the network and that you've entered the correct IP address. Also ensure that you've enabled zone transfers on the primary. If you want to copy zone data from other servers in case the first server isn't available, repeat this step.

7. Tap or click Next, and then tap or click Finish. On a busy or large network, you might need to configure reverse lookup zones on secondaries. If so, follow the steps listed in the next section.

Configuring reverse lookups

Forward lookups are used to resolve domain names to IP addresses. Reverse lookups are used to resolve IP addresses to domain names. Each segment on your network should have a reverse lookup zone. For example, if you have the subnets 192.168.10.0, 192.168.11.0, and 192.168.12.0, you should have three reverse lookup zones.

The standard naming convention for reverse lookup zones is to enter the network ID in reverse order and then use the suffix *in-addr.arpa*. With the previous example, you'd have reverse lookup zones named 10.168.192.in-addr.arpa, 11.168.192. in-addr.arpa, and 12.168.192.in-addr.arpa. Records in the reverse lookup zone must be in sync with the forward lookup zone. If the zones get out of sync, authentication might fail for the domain.

You create reverse lookup zones by following these steps:

1. Start the DNS Manager console. If the server you want to configure isn't listed, connect to it as described previously.

2. Press and hold or right-click the server entry, and then tap or click New Zone to start the New Zone Wizard. Tap or click Next.

3. If you're configuring a primary server integrated with Active Directory (a domain controller), select Primary Zone and be sure that Store The Zone In Active Directory is selected. If you don't want to integrate DNS with Active Directory, select Primary Zone, and then clear the Store The Zone In Active Directory check box. Tap or click Next.

4. If you're configuring a reverse lookup zone for a secondary server, select Secondary Zone, and then tap or click Next.

5. If you're integrating the zone with Active Directory, choose one of the following replication strategies:

   - **To All DNS Servers Running On Domain Controllers In This Forest** Choose this strategy if you want the widest replication strategy. Remember, the Active Directory forest includes all domain trees that share the directory data with the current domain.

   - **To All DNS Servers Running On Domain Controllers In This Domain** Choose this strategy if you want to replicate DNS information within the current domain.

   - **To All Domain Controllers In This Domain (For Windows 2000 Compatibility)** Choose this strategy if you want to replicate DNS information to all domain controllers within the current domain, as needed for Windows 2000 compatibility. Although this strategy gives wider replication for DNS information within the domain, not every domain controller is a DNS server as well (and you don't need to configure every domain controller as a DNS server either).

6. Select Reverse Lookup Zone, and then tap or click Next.

7. Choose whether you want to create a reverse lookup zone for IPv4 or IPv6 addresses, and then tap or click Next. Do one of the following:

   - If you are configuring a reverse lookup zone for IPv4, enter the network ID for the reverse lookup zone. The values you enter set the default name for the reverse lookup zone. Tap or click Next.

   - If you have multiple subnets on the same network, such as 192.168.10 and 192.168.11, you can enter only the network portion for the zone name. For example, you could enter 192.168. In this case, you'd have 168.192.in-addr.arpa as the zone name and allow the DNS Manager console to create the necessary subnet zones when needed.

   - If you are configuring a reverse lookup zone for IPv6, enter the network prefix for the reverse lookup zone. The values you enter are used to automatically generate the related zone names. Depending on the prefix you enter, you can create up to eight zones. Tap or click Next.

8. If you're configuring a primary or secondary server that isn't integrated with Active Directory, you need to set the zone file name. A default name for the zone's DNS database file should be filled in for you. You can use this name or enter a new file name. Tap or click Next.

9. Specify whether dynamic updates are allowed. You have three options:

   - **Allow Only Secure Dynamic Updates**   When the zone is integrated with Active Directory, you can use ACLs to restrict which clients can perform dynamic updates. With this option selected, only clients with authorized computer accounts and approved ACLs can dynamically update their resource records in DNS when changes occur.

   - **Allow Both Nonsecure And Secure Dynamic Updates**   Choose this option to allow any client to update its resource records in DNS when changes occur. Clients can be secure or nonsecure.

   - **Do Not Allow Dynamic Updates**   Choosing this option disables dynamic updates in DNS. You should use this option only when the zone isn't integrated with Active Directory.

10. Tap or click Next, and then tap or click Finish. The new zone is added to the server, and basic DNS records are created automatically.

After you set up the reverse lookup zones, you need to ensure that delegation for the zones is handled properly. Contact your networking team or your ISP to ensure that the zones are registered with the parent domain.

Configuring global names

The GlobalNames zone is a specially named forward lookup zone that should be integrated with AD DS. When all the DNS servers for your zones are running Windows Server 2008 or later releases, deploying a GlobalNames zone creates static, global records with single-label names, without relying on WINS. This enables users to access hosts by using single-label names rather than fully qualified domain names. You should use the GlobalNames zone when name resolution depends on DNS, such as when your organization is no longer using WINS and you are planning to deploy only IPv6. Because dynamic updates cannot be used to register updates in the GlobalNames zone, you should configure single-label name resolution only for your primary servers.

You can deploy a GlobalNames zone by completing the following steps:

1. In the DNS Manager console, select a DNS server that is also a domain controller. If the server you want to configure isn't listed, connect to it as described previously in "Installing and configuring the DNS Server service."

2. Press and hold or right-click the Forward Lookup Zones node, and then tap or click New Zone. In the New Zone Wizard, tap or click Next to accept the defaults to create a primary zone integrated with AD DS. On the Active Directory Zone Replication Scope page, choose to replicate the zone throughout the forest, and then tap or click Next. On the Zone Name page, enter **GlobalNames** as the zone name. Tap or click Next twice, and then tap or click Finish.

3. On every authoritative DNS server in the forest now and in the future, you need to enter the following at an elevated shell prompt:

```
Set-DnsServerGlobalNameZone -ComputerName ServerName -Enable $True
```

ServerName is the name of the DNS server that hosts the GlobalNames zone. To specify the local computer, just omit the –ComputerName parameter, such as

```
Set-DnsServerGlobalNameZone -Enable $True
```

4. For each server that you want users to be able to access by using a single-label name, add an alias (CNAME) record to the GlobalNames zone. In the DNS Manager console, press and hold or right-click the GlobalNames node, select New Alias (CNAME), and then use the dialog box provided to create the new resource record.

NOTE An authoritative DNS server tries to resolve queries in the following order: by using local zone data, by using the GlobalNames zone, by using DNS suffixes, by using WINS. For dynamic updates, an authoritative DNS server checks the GlobalNames zone before checking the local zone data.

TIP If you want DNS clients in another forest to use the GlobalNames zone for resolving names, you need to add an SRV resource record with the service name _globalnames._msdcs to that forest's forestwide DNS partition. The record must specify the FQDN of the DNS server that hosts the GlobalNames zone.

Managing DNS servers

The DNS Manager console is the tool you use to manage local and remote DNS servers. As shown in Figure 9-4, the DNS Manager console's main window is divided into two panes. The left pane makes it possible for you to access DNS servers and their zones. The right pane shows the details for the currently selected item. You can work with the DNS Manager console in three ways:

- Double-tap or double-click an entry in the left pane to expand the list of files for the entry.
- Select an entry in the left pane to display details such as zone status and domain records in the right pane.
- Press and hold or right-click an entry to display a context menu.

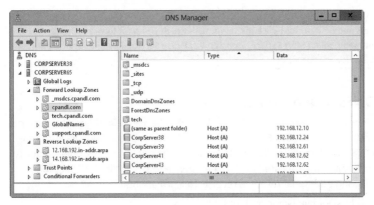

FIGURE 9-4 Manage local and remote DNS servers by using the DNS Manager console.

The Forward Lookup Zones and Reverse Lookup Zones folders provide access to the domains and subnets configured for use on this server. When you select domain or subnet folders in the left pane, you can manage DNS records for the domain or subnet.

Adding and removing servers to manage

You can use the DNS Manager console to manage servers running DNS by following these steps:

1. Press and hold or right-click DNS in the console tree, and then tap or click Connect To DNS Server.

2. If you're trying to connect to the local computer, select This Computer. Otherwise, select The Following Computer, and then enter the IP address or fully qualified host name of the remote computer with which you want to connect.

3. Tap or click OK. Windows Server 2012 R2 attempts to contact the server. If it makes contact, it adds the server to the console.

NOTE If a server is offline or otherwise inaccessible because of security restrictions or problems with the Remote Procedure Call (RPC) service, the connection fails. You can still add the server to the console by tapping or clicking Yes when prompted.

In the DNS Manager console, you can delete a server by selecting its entry and then pressing Delete. When prompted, tap or click Yes to confirm the deletion. Deleting a server only removes it from the server list in the console tree. It doesn't actually delete the server.

Starting and stopping a DNS server

To manage DNS servers, you use the DNS Server service. You can start, stop, pause, resume, and restart the DNS Server service in the Services node of Server Manager or from the command line. You can also manage the DNS Server service in the DNS Manager console. Press and hold or right-click the server you want to manage in the DNS Manager console, point to All Tasks, and then tap or click Start, Stop, Pause, Resume, or Restart as appropriate.

> **NOTE** In Server Manager, under the DNS Server node, expand the DNS node and then press and hold or right-click the server with which you want to work. On the shortcut menu, select Start Service, Stop Service, Pause Service, Resume Service, or Restart Service as appropriate.

Using DNSSEC and Signing Zones

Windows 7 or later versions, in addition to Windows Server 2008 R2 or later, support DNS Security Extensions (DNSSEC). DNSSEC is defined in several Request For Comments (RFCs), including RFCs 4033, 4034, and 4035. These RFCs add origin authority, data integrity, and authenticated denial of existence to DNS. With DNSSEC, there are the following additional resource records to learn about:

- DNSKEY (Domain Name System Key)
- RRSIG (Resource Record Signature)
- NSEC (NextSECure)
- DS (Domain Services)

The DNS client running on these operating systems can send queries that indicate support for DNSSEC, process related records, and determine whether a DNS server has validated records on its behalf. On Windows servers, DNSSEC allows your DNS servers to securely sign zones, to host DNSSEC-signed zones, to process related records, and to perform both validation and authentication. The way a DNS client works with DNSSEC is configured through the Name Resolution Policy Table (NRPT), which stores settings that define the DNS client's behavior. Typically, you manage the NRPT through Group Policy.

When a DNS server hosting a signed zone receives a query, the server returns the digital signatures in addition to the requested records. A resolver or another server configured with a trust anchor for a signed zone or for a parent of a signed zone can obtain the public key of the public/private key pair and validate that the responses are authentic and have not been tampered with.

As part of your predeployment planning, you need to identify the DNS zones to secure with digital signatures. DNS Server for Windows Server 2012 R2 has the following significant enhancements for DNSSEC:

- Support for dynamic updates in Active Directory–integrated zones. Previously, if an Active Directory domain zone was signed, you needed to manually update all SRV records and other resource records. This is no longer required because DNS Server now does this automatically.

- Support for online signing, automated key management, and automated trust anchor distribution. Previously, you needed to configure and manage signings, keys, and trust anchors. This is no longer required because DNS Server now does this automatically.

- Support for validations of records signed with updated DNSSEC standards including NSEC3 and RSA/SHA-2.

With Windows Server 2012 R2, an authoritative DNS server also can act as the Key Master for DNSSEC. The Key Master generates and manages signing keys for both Active Directory-integrated zones protected by DNSSEC and standard (file-backed) zones protected by DNSSEC. When a zone has a designated Key Master, the Key Master is responsible for the entire key signing process from key generation to storage, rollover, retirement, and deletion.

Although key signing and management tasks can only be initiated from the Key Master, other primary DNS servers can continue to use zone signing—they just do so via the Key Master. You must choose a key master when you sign a zone with DNSSEC. You can transfer the key master role to another DNS server that hosts the zone at any time.

Additionally, keep the following in mind:

- For file-backed zones, the primary server and all secondary servers hosting the zone must be a Windows Server 2008 R2 or later DNS server or a DNS-SEC-aware server that is running an operating system other than Windows.

- For Active Directory–integrated zones, every domain controller that is a DNS server in the domain must be running Windows Server 2008 R2 or later if the signed zone is set to replicate to all DNS servers in the domain. Every domain controller that is a DNS server in the forest must be running Windows Server 2008 R2 or later if the signed zone is set to replicate to all DNS servers in the forest.

- For mixed environments, all servers that are authoritative for a DNSSEC-signed zone must be DNSSEC-aware servers. DNSSEC-aware Windows clients that request DNSSEC data and validation must be configured to issue DNS queries to a DNSSEC-aware server. Non-DNSSEC-aware Windows clients can be configured to issue DNS queries to DNSSEC-aware servers. DNSSEC-aware servers can be configured to recursively send queries to a non-DNSSEC-aware DNS server.

Securing DNS zones with digital signatures is a multistep process. As part of that process, you need to designate a *key master*. Any authoritative server that hosts a primary copy of a zone can act as the key master. Next, you need to generate a Key Signing Key and a Zone Signing Key. A Key Signing Key (KSK) that is an authentication key has a private key and a public key associated with it. The private key is used for signing all of the DNSKEY records at the root of the zone. The public key is used as a trust anchor for validating DNS responses. A Zone Signing Key (ZSK) is used for signing zone records.

After you generate keys, you create resource records for authenticated denial of existence by using either the more secure NSEC3 standard or the less secure NSEC standard. Because trust anchors are used to validate DNS responses, you also need to specify how trust anchors are updated and distributed. Typically, you'll want to automatically update and distribute trust anchors. By default, records are signed with SHA-1 and SHA-256 encryption. You can select other encryption algorithms as well.

You don't need to go through the configuration process each time you sign a zone. The signing keys and other signing parameters are available for reuse.

To sign a zone while customizing the signing parameters, follow these steps:

1. In the DNS Manager console, press and hold or right-click the zone you want to secure. On the shortcut menu, select DNSSEC, and then select Sign The Zone. This starts the Zone Signing Wizard. If the wizard displays a welcome page, read the Welcome text, and then tap or click Next.

2. On the Signing Options page, select Customize Zone Signing Parameters, and then tap or click Next.

3. Select a key master for the zone. Any authoritative server that hosts a primary copy of a zone can act as the key master. When you are ready to continue, tap or click Next twice.

4. On the Key Signing Key page, configure a KSK by tapping or clicking Add, accepting or changing the default values for key properties and rollover, and then tapping or clicking OK. When you are ready to continue, tap or click Next twice.

5. On the Zone Signing Key page, configure a ZSK by tapping or clicking Add, accepting or changing the default values for key properties and rollover, and then tapping or clicking OK. When you are ready to continue, tap or click Next five times.

6. After the wizard signs the zone, click Finish.

To sign a zone and use existing signing parameters, follow these steps:

1. In the DNS Manager console, press and hold or right-click the zone you want to secure. On the shortcut menu, select DNSSEC and then select Sign The Zone. This starts the Zone Signing Wizard. If the wizard displays a welcome page, read the Welcome text, and then tap or click Next.

2. On the Signing Options page, select Sign The Zone With Parameters Of An Existing Zone. Enter the name of an existing signed zone, such as **cpandl.com**, and then tap or click Next.

3. On the Key Master page, select a key master for the zone. Any authoritative server that hosts a primary copy of a zone can act as the key master. Tap or click Next twice.

4. After the wizard signs the zone, tap or click Finish.

Creating child domains within zones

By using the DNS Manager console, you can create child domains within a zone. For example, if you create the primary zone microsoft.com, you could create the subdomains hr.microsoft.com and mis.microsoft.com for the zone.

You create child domains by following these steps:

1. In the DNS Manager console, expand the Forward Lookup Zones folder for the server with which you want to work.

2. Press and hold or right-click the parent domain entry, and then tap or click New Domain.

3. Enter the name of the new domain, and then tap or click OK. For hr.microsoft.com, you would enter **hr**. For mis.microsoft.com, you would enter **mis**.

Creating child domains in separate zones

As your organization grows, you might want to organize the DNS namespace into separate zones. At your corporate headquarters, you could have a zone for the parent domain microsoft.com. At branch offices, you could have zones for each office, such as memphis.microsoft.com, newyork.microsoft.com, and la.microsoft.com.

You create child domains in separate zones by following these steps:

1. Install a DNS server in each child domain, and then create the necessary forward and reverse lookup zones for the child domain as described earlier in "Installing DNS Servers."

2. On the authoritative DNS server for the parent domain, you delegate authority to each child domain. Delegating authority enables the child domain to resolve and respond to DNS queries from computers inside and outside the local subnet.

You delegate authority to a child domain by following these steps:

1. In the DNS Manager console, expand the Forward Lookup Zones folder for the server with which you want to work.

2. Press and hold or right-click the parent domain entry, and then tap or click New Delegation to start the New Delegation Wizard. Tap or click Next.

3. As shown in Figure 9-5, enter the name of the delegated domain, such as **service**, and then tap or click Next. The name you enter updates the value in the Fully Qualified Domain Name text box.

FIGURE 9-5 Entering the name of the delegated domain sets the fully qualified domain name (FQDN).

4. Tap or click Add. This displays the New Name Server Record dialog box.

5. In the Server Fully Qualified Domain Name text box, type the fully qualified host name of a DNS server for the child domain, such as **corpserver01.memphis.adatum.com**, and then tap or click Resolve. The server then performs a lookup query and adds the resolved IP address to the IP Address list.

6. Repeat step 5 to specify additional name servers. The order of the entries determines which IP address is used first. Change the order as necessary by using the Up and Down buttons. When you are ready to continue, tap or click OK to close the New Name Server Record dialog box.

7. Tap or click Next, and then tap or click Finish.

Deleting a domain or subnet

Deleting a domain or subnet permanently removes it from the DNS server. To delete a domain or subnet, follow these steps:

1. In the DNS Manager console, press and hold or right-click the domain or subnet entry.

2. On the shortcut menu, tap or click Delete, and then confirm the action by tapping or clicking Yes.

3. If the domain or subnet is integrated with Active Directory, you'll receive a warning prompt. Confirm that you want to delete the domain or subnet from Active Directory by tapping or clicking Yes.

NOTE Deleting a domain or subnet deletes all DNS records in a zone file but doesn't actually delete the zone file on a primary or secondary server that isn't integrated with Active Directory. The actual zone file remains in the %SystemRoot%\System32 \Dns directory. You can delete this file after you have deleted the zones from the DNS Manager console.

Managing DNS records

After you create the necessary zone files, you can add records to the zones. Computers that need to be accessed from Active Directory and DNS domains must have DNS records. Although there are many types of DNS records, most of these record types aren't commonly used. So rather than focus on record types you probably won't use, let's focus on the ones you will use:

- **A (IPv4 address)** Maps a host name to an IPv4 address. When a computer has multiple adapter cards, IPv4 addresses, or both, it should have multiple address records.

- **AAAA (IPv6 address)** Maps a host name to an IPv6 address. When a computer has multiple adapter cards, IPv6 addresses, or both, it should have multiple address records.

- **CNAME (canonical name)** Sets an alias for a host name. For example, by using this record, zeta.microsoft.com can have an alias of www.microsoft.com.

- **MX (mail exchanger)**   Specifies a mail exchange server for the domain, which enables email messages to be delivered to the correct mail servers in the domain.

- **NS (name server)**   Specifies a name server for the domain, which enables DNS lookups within various zones. Each primary and secondary name server should be declared through this record.

- **PTR (pointer)**   Creates a pointer that maps an IP address to a host name for reverse lookups.

- **SOA (start of authority)**   Declares the host that's the most authoritative for the zone and, as such, is the best source of DNS information for the zone. Each zone file must have an SOA record (which is created automatically when you add a zone). Also declares other information about the zone, such as the responsible person, refresh interval, retry interval, and so on.

- **SRV (service location)**   Locates a server providing a specific service. Active Directory uses SRV records to locate domain controllers, global catalog servers, LDAP servers, and Kerberos servers. Most SRV records are created automatically. For example, Active Directory creates an SRV record when you promote a domain controller. LDAP servers can add an SRV record to indicate they are available to hanVdle LDAP requests in a particular zone.

Adding address and pointer records

You use the A and AAAA records to map a host name to an IP address, and the PTR record creates a pointer to the host for reverse lookups. You can create address and pointer records at the same time or separately.

You create a new host entry with address and pointer records by following these steps:

1. In the DNS Manager console, expand the Forward Lookup Zones folder for the server with which you want to work.

2. Press and hold or right-click the domain you want to update, and then tap or click New Host (A Or AAAA). This opens the dialog box shown in Figure 9-6.

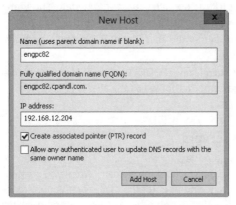

FIGURE 9-6 Create address records and pointer records simultaneously with the New Host dialog box.

3. Enter the single-part computer name, such as **servicespc85**, and then the IP address, such as **192.168.10.58**.

4. Select the Create Associated Pointer (PTR) Record check box.

   NOTE You can create PTR records only if the corresponding reverse lookup zone is available. You can create this file by following the steps listed in "Configuring reverse lookups" earlier in this chapter. The Allow Any Authenticated User option is available only when a DNS server is configured on a domain controller.

5. Tap or click Add Host, and then tap or click OK. Repeat these steps as necessary to add other hosts.

6. Tap or click Done when you have finished.

Adding a PTR record later

If you need to add a PTR record later, you can do so by following these steps:

1. In the DNS Manager console, expand the Reverse Lookup Zones folder for the server with which you want to work.

2. Press and hold or right-click the subnet you want to update, and then tap or click New Pointer (PTR).

3. Type the host IP address, such as **192.168.1.95**, and then enter the host name, such as **servicespc54**. Tap or click OK.

Adding DNS aliases with CNAME

You specify host aliases by using CNAME records. Aliases enable a single host computer to appear to be multiple host computers. For example, the host gamma.microsoft.com can be made to appear as www.microsoft.com and ftp.microsoft.com.

To create a CNAME record, follow these steps:

1. In the DNS Manager console, expand the Forward Lookup Zones folder for the server with which you want to work.

2. Press and hold or right-click the domain you want to update, and then tap or click New Alias (CNAME).

3. In the Alias Name text box, enter the alias. The alias is a single-part host name, such as *www* or *ftp*.

4. In the Fully Qualified Domain Name (FQDN) For Target Host text box, enter the full host name of the computer for which the alias is to be used.

5. Tap or click OK.

Adding mail exchange servers

MX records identify mail exchange servers for the domain. These servers are responsible for processing or forwarding email within the domain. When you create an MX record, you must specify a preference number for the mail server. A preference number is a value from 0 to 65,535 that denotes the mail server's priority within the domain. The mail server with the lowest preference number has the highest priority and is the first to receive mail. If mail delivery fails, the mail server with the next lowest preference number is tried.

You create an MX record by following these steps:

1. In the DNS Manager console, expand the Forward Lookup Zones folder for the server with which you want to work.

2. Press and hold or right-click the domain you want to update, and then tap or click New Mail Exchanger (MX).

3. You can now create a record for the mail server by filling in these text boxes:

   - **Host Or Child Domain**   Using a single-part name, enter the name of the subdomain for which the server specified in this record is responsible. In most cases, you will leave this box blank, which specifies that there is no subdomain and the server is responsible for the domain in which this record is created.

   - **Fully Qualified Domain Name (FQDN)**   Enter the FQDN of the domain to which this mail exchange record should apply, such as **cpandl.com**.

   - **Fully Qualified Domain Name (FQDN) Of Mail Server**   Enter the FQDN of the mail server that should handle mail receipt and delivery, such as **corpmail.cpandl.com**. Email for the previously specified domain is routed to this mail server for delivery.

   - **Mail Server Priority**   Enter a preference number for the host from 0 to 65,535.

   NOTE   Assign preference numbers that leave room for growth. For example, use 10 for your highest priority mail server, 20 for the next, and 30 for the one after that.

   REAL WORLD   You can't enter a multipart name in the Host Or Child Domain text box. If you need to enter a multipart name, you are creating the MX record at the wrong level of the DNS hierarchy. Create or access the additional domain level, and then add an MX record at this level for the subdomain.

4. Tap or click OK.

Adding name servers

NS records specify the name servers for the domain. Each primary and secondary name server should be declared through this record. If you obtain secondary name services from an ISP, be sure to insert the appropriate NS records.

You create an NS record by following these steps:

1. In the DNS Manager console, expand the Forward Lookup Zones folder for the server with which you want to work.

2. Display the DNS records for the domain by selecting the domain folder in the tree view.

3. Press and hold or right-click an existing NS record in the view pane, and then tap or click Properties. This opens the Properties dialog box for the domain with the Name Servers tab selected, as shown in Figure 9-7.

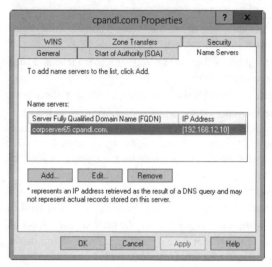

FIGURE 9-7 Configure name servers for the domain through the domain's Properties dialog box.

4. Tap or click Add. This displays the New Name Server Record dialog box.

5. In the Server Fully Qualified Domain Name text box, enter the name of a DNS server for the child domain, such as **corpserver01.cpandl.com** and then tap or click Resolve. The server then performs a lookup query and adds the resolved IP address to the IP Address list.

6. Repeat step 5 to specify additional name servers. The order of the entries determines which IP address is used first. Change the order as necessary by using the Up and Down buttons. When you are ready to continue, tap or click OK to close the New Name Server Record dialog box.

7. Tap or click OK to save your changes.

Viewing and updating DNS records

To view or update DNS records, follow these steps:

1. Double-tap or double-click the zone with which you want to work. Records for the zone should be displayed in the right pane.

2. Double-tap or double-click the DNS record you want to view or update. This opens the record's Properties dialog box. Make the necessary changes, and then tap or click OK.

Updating zone properties and the SOA record

Each zone has separate properties you can configure. These properties set general zone parameters by using the SOA record, change notification, and WINS integration. In the DNS Manager console, you set zone properties by doing one of the following:

- Press and hold or right-click the zone you want to update, and then tap or click Properties.
- Select the zone, and then tap or click Properties on the Action menu.

The Properties dialog boxes for forward and reverse lookup zones are identical except for the WINS and WINS-R tabs. In forward lookup zones, you use the WINS tab to configure lookups for NetBIOS computer names. In reverse lookup zones, you use the WINS-R tab to configure reverse lookups for NetBIOS computer names.

Modifying the SOA record

An SOA record designates the authoritative name server for a zone and sets general zone properties, such as retry and refresh intervals. You can modify this information by following these steps:

1. In the DNS Manager console, press and hold or right-click the zone you want to update, and then tap or click Properties.
2. Tap or click the Start Of Authority (SOA) tab, and then update the text boxes shown in Figure 9-8.

FIGURE 9-8 In the zone's Properties dialog box, set general properties for the zone and update the SOA record.

You use the text boxes on the Start Of Authority (SOA) tab as follows:

- **Serial Number**   A serial number that indicates the version of the DNS database files. The number is updated automatically whenever you make changes to zone files. You can also update the number manually. Secondary servers use this number to determine whether the zone's DNS records have changed. If the primary server's serial number is larger than the secondary server's serial number, the records have changed, and the secondary server can request the DNS records for the zone. You can also configure DNS to notify secondary servers of changes (which might speed up the update process).

- **Primary Server**   The FQDN for the name server followed by a period. The period is used to terminate the name and ensure that the domain information isn't appended to the entry.

- **Responsible Person**   The email address of the person in charge of the domain. The default entry is *hostmaster* followed by a period followed by your domain name, meaning hostmaster@your_domain.com. If you change this entry, substitute a period in place of the @ symbol in the email address and terminate the address with a period.

- **Refresh Interval**   The interval at which a secondary server checks for zone updates. The default value is 15 minutes. You reduce network traffic by increasing this value. However, keep in mind that if the interval is set to 60 minutes, NS record changes might not be propagated to a secondary server for up to an hour.

- **Retry Interval**   The time the secondary server waits after a failure to download the zone database. If the interval is set to 10 minutes and a zone database transfer fails, the secondary server waits 10 minutes before requesting the zone database once more.

- **Expires After**   The period of time for which zone information is valid on the secondary server. If the secondary server can't download data from a primary server within this period, the secondary server lets the data in its cache expire and stops responding to DNS queries. Setting Expires After to seven days enables the data on a secondary server to be valid for seven days.

- **Minimum (Default) TTL**   The minimum time-to-live (TTL) value for cached records on a secondary server. The value can be set in days, hours, minutes, or seconds. When this value is reached, the secondary server causes the associated record to expire and discards it. The next request for the record needs to be sent to the primary server for resolution. Set the minimum TTL to a relatively high value, such as 24 hours, to reduce traffic on the network and increase efficiency. Keep in mind that a higher value slows down the propagation of updates through the Internet.

- **TTL For This Record**   The TTL value for this particular SOA record. The value is set in the format Days : Hours : Minutes : Seconds and generally should be the same as the minimum TTL for all records.

Allowing and restricting zone transfers

Zone transfers send a copy of zone information to other DNS servers. These servers can be in the same domain or in other domains. For security reasons, Windows Server 2012 R2 disables zone transfers. To enable zone transfers for secondaries you've configured internally or with ISPs, you need to permit zone transfers and then specify the types of servers to which zone transfers can be made.

Although you can allow zone transfers with any server, this opens the server to possible security problems. Instead of opening the floodgates, you should restrict access to zone information so that only servers you've identified can request updates from the zone's primary server. This enables you to funnel requests through a select group of secondary servers, such as your ISP's secondary name servers, and to hide the details of your internal network from the outside world.

To allow zone transfers and restrict access to the primary zone database, follow these steps:

1. In the DNS Manager console, press and hold or right-click the domain or subnet you want to update, and then tap or click Properties.

2. Tap or click the Zone Transfers tab, as shown in Figure 9-9.

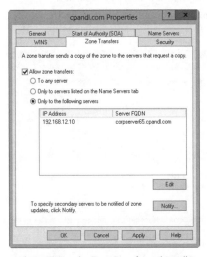

FIGURE 9-9 Use the Zone Transfers tab to allow zone transfers to any server or to designated servers.

3. To restrict transfers to name servers listed on the Name Servers tab, select the Allow Zone Transfers check box, and then choose Only To Servers Listed On The Name Servers Tab.

4. To restrict transfers to designated servers, select the Allow Zone Transfers check box and then choose Only To The Following Servers. Then tap or click Edit as appropriate to display the Allow Zone Transfers dialog box. Tap or click in the IP Address list, enter the IP address of the secondary server for the zone, and then press Enter. Windows then attempts to validate the server. If an error occurs, make sure the server is connected to the network and that you've entered the correct IP address. If you want to copy zone data from other servers in case the first server isn't available, you can add IP addresses for other servers as well. Tap or click OK.

5. Tap or click OK to save your changes.

Notifying secondaries of changes

You set properties for a zone with its SOA record. These properties control how DNS information is propagated on the network. You can also specify that the primary server should notify secondary name servers when changes are made to the zone database. To do this, follow these steps:

1. In the DNS Manager console, press and hold or right-click the domain or subnet you want to update, and then tap or click Properties.

2. On the Zone Transfers tab, tap or click Notify. This displays the Notify dialog box shown in Figure 9-10.

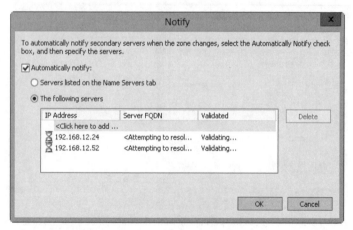

FIGURE 9-10 In the Notify dialog box, notify all secondaries listed on the Name Servers tab of the Properties dialog box or specific servers that you designate.

3. To notify secondary servers listed on the Name Servers tab, select the Automatically Notify check box, and then choose Servers Listed On The Name Servers Tab.

4. If you want to designate specific servers to notify, select the Automatically Notify check box, and then choose The Following Servers. Tap or click in the IP Address list, enter the IP address of the secondary server for the zone, and then press Enter. Windows then attempts to validate the server. If an error occurs, make sure the server is connected to the network and that you entered the correct IP address. If you want to notify other servers, add IP addresses for those servers as well.

5. Tap or click OK twice.

Setting the zone type

When you create zones, they're designated as having a specific zone type and an Active Directory integration mode. You can change the type and integration mode at any time by following these steps:

1. In the DNS Manager console, press and hold or right-click the domain or subnet you want to update, and then tap or click Properties.

2. Under Type on the General tab, tap or click Change. In the Change Zone Type dialog box, select the new type for the zone.

3. To integrate the zone with Active Directory, select the Store The Zone In Active Directory check box.

4. To remove the zone from Active Directory, clear the Store The Zone In Active Directory check box.

5. Tap or click OK twice.

Enabling and disabling dynamic updates

Dynamic updates enable DNS clients to register and maintain their own address and pointer records. This is useful for computers dynamically configured through DHCP. By enabling dynamic updates, you make it easier for dynamically configured computers to locate one another on the network. When a zone is integrated with Active Directory, you have the option of requiring secure updates. With secure updates, you use ACLs to control which computers and users can dynamically update DNS.

You can enable and disable dynamic updates by following these steps:

1. In the DNS Manager console, press and hold or right-click the domain or subnet you want to update, and then tap or click Properties.

2. Use the following options in the Dynamic Updates list on the General tab to enable or disable dynamic updates:

   - **None** Disable dynamic updates.
   - **Nonsecure And Secure** Enable nonsecure and secure dynamic updates.
   - **Secure Only** Enable dynamic updates with Active Directory security. This is available only with Active Directory integration.

3. Tap or click OK.

   NOTE DNS integration settings must also be configured for DHCP. See "Integrating DHCP and DNS" in Chapter 8.

Managing DNS server configuration and security

You use the Server Properties dialog box to manage the general configuration of DNS servers. Through it, you can enable and disable IP addresses for the server and control access to DNS servers outside the organization. You can also configure monitoring, logging, and advanced options.

Enabling and disabling IP addresses for a DNS server

By default, multihomed DNS servers respond to DNS requests on all available network interfaces and the IP addresses they're configured to use.

Through the DNS Manager console, you can specify that the server can answer requests only on specific IP addresses. Generally, you'll want to ensure that a DNS server has at least one IPv4 interface and one IPv6 interface.

To specify which IP addresses are used for answering requests, follow these steps:

1. In the DNS Manager console, press and hold or right-click the server you want to configure, and then tap or click Properties.

2. On the Interfaces tab, select Only The Following IP Addresses. Select an IP address that should respond to DNS requests, or clear an IP address that should not respond to DNS requests. Only the selected IP addresses will be used for DNS. All other IP addresses on the server will be disabled for DNS.

3. Tap or click OK.

Controlling access to DNS servers outside the organization

Restricting access to zone information enables you to specify which internal and external servers can access the primary server. For external servers, this controls which servers can get in from the outside world. You can also control which DNS servers within your organization can access servers outside of your organization. To do this, you need to set up DNS forwarding within the domain.

With DNS forwarding, you configure DNS servers within the domain as one of the following:

- **Nonforwarders**   Servers that must pass DNS queries they can't resolve to designated forwarding servers. These servers essentially act like DNS clients to their forwarding servers.

- **Forwarding-only**   Servers that can only cache responses and pass requests to forwarders. These are also known as *caching-only* DNS servers.

- **Forwarders**   Servers that receive requests from nonforwarders and forwarding-only servers. Forwarders use standard DNS communication methods to resolve queries and to send responses back to other DNS servers.

- **Conditional forwarders**   Servers that forward requests based on the DNS domain. Conditional forwarding is useful if your organization has multiple internal domains.

NOTE You can't configure the root server for a domain for forwarding (except for conditional forwarding used with internal name resolution). You can configure all other servers for forwarding.

Creating nonforwarding and forwarding-only servers

To create a nonforwarding or forwarding-only DNS server, follow these steps:

1. In the DNS Manager console, press and hold or right-click the server you want to configure, and then tap or click Properties.

2. Tap or click the Advanced tab. To configure the server as a nonforwarder, ensure that the Disable Recursion check box is cleared, tap or click OK, and then skip the remaining steps. To configure the server as a forwarding-only server, be sure that the Disable Recursion check box is selected.

3. On the Forwarders tab, tap or click Edit. This displays the Edit Forwarders dialog box.

4. Tap or click in the IP Address list, type the IP address of a forwarder for the network, and then press Enter. Windows then attempts to validate the server. If an error occurs, make sure the server is connected to the network and that you've entered the correct IP address. Repeat this process to specify the IP addresses of other forwarders.

5. Set the Forward Queries Time Out interval. This value controls how long the nonforwarder tries to query the current forwarder if it gets no response. When the Forward Time Out interval passes, the nonforwarder tries the next forwarder on the list. The default is three seconds. Tap or click OK.

Creating forwarding servers

Any DNS server that isn't designated as a nonforwarder or a forwarding-only server will act as a forwarder. Thus, on the network's designated forwarders you should be sure that the Disable Recursion option is not selected and that you haven't configured the server to forward requests to other DNS servers in the domain.

Configuring conditional forwarding

If you have multiple internal domains, you might want to consider configuring conditional forwarding, which enables you to direct requests for specific domains to specific DNS servers for resolution. Conditional forwarding is useful if your organization has multiple internal domains and you need to resolve requests between these domains.

To configure conditional forwarding, follow these steps:

1. In the DNS Manager console, select and then press and hold or right-click the Conditional Forwarders folder for the server with which you want to work. Tap or click New Conditional Forwarder on the shortcut menu.

2. In the New Conditional Forwarder dialog box, enter the name of a domain to which queries should be forwarded, such as **adatum.com**.

3. Tap or click in the IP Address list, type the IP address of an authoritative DNS server in the specified domain, and then press Enter. Repeat this process to specify additional IP addresses.

4. If you're integrating DNS with Active Directory, select the Store This Conditional Forwarder In Active Directory check box, and then choose one of the following replication strategies:

   - **All DNS Servers In This Forest**   Choose this strategy if you want the widest replication strategy. Remember, the Active Directory forest includes all domain trees that share the directory data with the current domain.

   - **All DNS Servers In This Domain**   Choose this strategy if you want to replicate forwarder information within the current domain and child domains of the current domain.

   - **All Domain Controllers In This Domain**   Choose this strategy if you want to replicate forwarder information to all domain controllers within the current domain and child domains of the current domain. Although this strategy gives wider replication for forwarder information within the domain, not every domain controller is a DNS server as well (nor do you need to configure every domain controller as a DNS server).

5. Set the Forward Queries Time Out interval. This value controls how long the server tries to query the forwarder if it gets no response. When the Forward Time Out interval passes, the server tries the next authoritative server on the list. The default is five seconds. Tap or click OK.

6. Repeat this procedure to configure conditional forwarding for other domains.

Enabling and disabling event logging

By default, the DNS service tracks all events for DNS in the DNS Server event log. This log records all applicable DNS events and is accessible through the Event Viewer node in Computer Management. This means that all informational, warning, and error events are recorded. You can change the logging options by following these steps:

1. In the DNS Manager console, press and hold or right-click the server you want to configure, and then tap or click Properties.

2. Use the options on the Event Logging tab to configure DNS logging. To disable logging altogether, choose No Events.

3. Tap or click OK.

Using debug logging to track DNS activity

You typically use the DNS Server event log to track DNS activity on a server. This log records all applicable DNS events and is accessible through the Event Viewer node in Computer Management. If you're trying to troubleshoot DNS problems, it's sometimes useful to configure a temporary debug log to track certain types of DNS events. However, don't forget to clear these events after you finish debugging.

To configure debugging, follow these steps:

1. In the DNS Manager console, press and hold or right-click the server you want to configure, and then tap or click Properties.

2. On the Debug Logging tab, shown in Figure 9-11, select the Log Packets For Debugging check box, and then select the check boxes for the events you want to track temporarily.

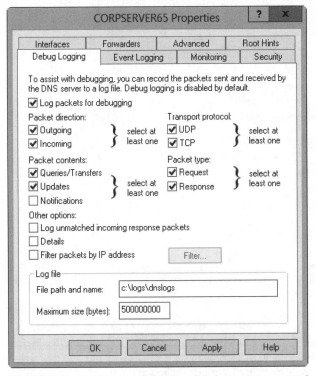

FIGURE 9-11 Use the Debug Logging tab to select the events you want to log.

3. In the File Path And Name text box, enter the name of the log file, such as **dns.logs**. Logs are stored in the %SystemRoot%\System32\Dns directory by default.

4. Tap or click OK. When finished debugging, turn off logging by clearing the Log Packets For Debugging check box.

Monitoring a DNS server

Windows Server 2012 R2 has built-in functionality for monitoring a DNS server. Monitoring is useful to ensure that DNS resolution is configured properly.

You can configure monitoring to occur manually or automatically by following these steps:

1. In the DNS Manager console, press and hold or right-click the server you want to configure, and then tap or click Properties.

2. Tap or click the Monitoring tab, shown in Figure 9-12. You can perform two types of tests. To test DNS resolution on the current server, select the A Simple Query Against This DNS Server check box. To test DNS resolution in the domain, select the A Recursive Query To Other DNS Servers check box.

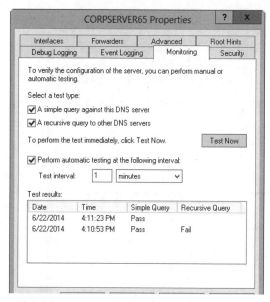

FIGURE 9-12 Configure a DNS server for manual or automatic monitoring on the Monitoring tab.

3. You can perform a manual test by tapping or clicking Test Now. You can schedule the server for automatic monitoring by selecting th e Perform Automatic Testing At The Following Interval check box and then setting a time interval in seconds, minutes, or hours.

4. The Test Results panel shows the results of testing. You'll receive a date and time stamp indicating when the test was performed and a result, such as Pass or Fail. Although a single failure might be the result of a temporary outage, multiple failures typically indicate a DNS resolution problem.

NOTE If all recursive query tests fail, the advanced server option Disable Recursion might be selected. Tap or click the Advanced tab and check the server options.

REAL WORLD If you're actively troubleshooting a DNS problem, you might want to configure testing to occur every 10–15 seconds. This interval will provide a rapid succession of test results. If you're monitoring DNS for problems as part of your daily administrative duties, you'll want a longer time interval, such as two or three hours.

CHAPTER 10

Administering network printers and print services

As an administrator, you need to take two main steps to enable users throughout a network to access print devices connected to Windows Server 2012 R2. First, you need to set up a print server, and then you need to use the print server to share print devices on the network.

This chapter covers the essentials of setting up shared printing and describes how users access printers on the network. You'll also find advice on administering printers and troubleshooting printer problems, which is where we'll begin.

Managing the Print and Document Services role

A provides a central location for sharing printers on a network. When many users require access to the same printers, you should configure print servers in the domain. In earlier releases of the Windows Server operating system, all servers were installed with basic print services. With Windows Server 2012 R2, you must specifically configure a server to be a print server.

Using print devices

Two types of print devices are used on a network:

- **Local print device**   A print device that's physically attached to a user's computer and employed only by the user who's logged on to that computer.

- **Network print device**   A print device that's set up for remote access over the network. This can be a print device attached directly to a print server or a print device attached directly to the network through a network interface card (NIC).

NOTE   The key difference between a local printer and a network printer is that a local printer isn't shared. You can easily make a local printer a network printer. To learn how to do this, see "Starting and stopping printer sharing" later in this chapter.

You install new network printers on print servers or as separate print devices attached to the network. A *print server* is a workstation or server configured to share one or more printers. These printers can be physically attached to the computer or connected to the network. The disadvantage of running a print server with a workstation operating system instead of a server operating system is the limited number of allowed connections. With Windows Server 2012 R2, you don't have to worry about operating system–enforced connection limits.

You can configure any Windows Server 2012 R2 system as a print server. The print server's primary job is to share print devices on the network and to handle print spooling. The main advantages of print servers are that printers have a centrally managed print queue and you don't have to install printer drivers on client systems.

You don't have to use a print server, however. You can connect users directly to a network-attached printer. When you do this, the network printer is handled much like a local printer attached directly to the user's computer. The key differences are that multiple users can connect to the printer and that each user has a different print queue. Each individual print queue is managed separately, which can make administration and problem resolution difficult.

Printing essentials

An understanding of how printing works can go a long way when you're trying to troubleshoot printer problems. When you print documents, many processes, drivers, and devices work together to print the documents. If you use a printer connected to a print server, the key operations are as follows:

- **Printer driver**   When you print a document in an application, your computer uses a printer driver to handle the printing process. If the print device is attached to your computer physically, the printer driver is accessed from a local disk drive. If the print device is located on a remote computer, the printer driver might be downloaded from the remote computer. The availability of printer drivers on the remote computer is configurable by operating system and chip architecture. If the computer can't obtain the latest printer driver, an administrator probably hasn't enabled the driver for the computer's operating system. For more information, see "Managing printer drivers" later in this chapter.

- **Local print spool and print processor**   The application from which you print uses the printer driver to translate the document into a file format that the selected print device can understand. Your computer then passes the document to the local print spooler. The local spooler in turn passes the document to a print processor, which creates the raw print data necessary for printing on the print device.

- **Print router and print spooler on the print server**   The raw data is passed back to the local print spooler. If you're printing to a remote printer, the raw data is then routed to the print spooler on the print server. On Windows Server 2012 R2 systems, the printer router, Winspool.drv, handles the tasks of locating the remote printer, routing print jobs, and downloading printer drivers to the local system if necessary. If any of these tasks fails, the print router is usually the culprit. See "Solving spooling problems" and "Setting printer access permissions" later in this chapter to learn about possible fixes for this problem. If these procedures don't work, you might want to replace or restore Winspool.drv.

  The main reason for downloading printer drivers to clients is to maintain a single location for installing driver updates. This way, instead of having to install a new driver on all the client systems, you install the driver on the print server and enable clients to download the new driver. For more information on working with printer drivers, see "Managing printer drivers" later in this chapter.

- **Printer (print queue)**   The document goes from the print spooler to the printer stack—which in some operating systems is called the *print queue*—for the selected print device. When in the queue, the document is referred to as a *print job*—a task for the print spooler to handle. The length of time the document waits in the printer stack is based on its priority and position within the printer stack. For more information, see "Scheduling and prioritizing print jobs" later in this chapter.

- **Print monitor**   When the document reaches the top of the printer stack, the print monitor sends the document to the print device, where it's actually printed. If the printer is configured to notify users that the document has been printed, you get a confirmation message.

  The specific print monitor used by Windows Server 2012 R2 depends on the print device configuration and type. You might also have monitors from the print device manufacturer. This dynamic-link library (DLL) is required to print to the print device. If it's corrupted or missing, you might need to reinstall it.

- **Print device**   The print device is the physical device that prints documents on paper. Common print device problems and display errors include Insert Paper Into Tray X, Low Toner, Out Of Paper, Out Of Toner or Out Of Ink, Paper Jam, and Printer Offline.

Group Policy can affect your ability to install and manage printers. If you're having problems and believe they're related to Group Policy, you should examine the key policies in the following locations:

- Computer Configuration\Administrative Templates\Printers
- User Configuration\Administrative Templates\Control Panel\Printers
- User Configuration\Administrative Templates\Start Menu And Taskbar

REAL WORLD   Windows Server 2012 R2 is a 64-bit operating system and a print queue running on this operating system cannot function without a native 64-bit printer driver. Because of this, you should verify the availability of required 64-bit print drivers before migrating print queues from servers running 32-bit operating systems to Windows Server 2012 R2. Keep in mind that if your organization has older printers still in use, those printers might have third-party 32-bit drivers and there might not be 64-bit equivalents.

Configuring print servers

You configure a server as a print server by adding the Print and Document Services role and configuring this role to use one or more of the following role services:

- **Print Server**   Configures the server as a print server and installs the Print Management console. You can use the Print Management console to manage multiple printers and print servers, to migrate printers to and from other print servers, and to manage print jobs.

- **Line Printer Daemon (LPD) Service**   Enables UNIX-based computers or other computers using the Line Printer Remote (LPR) service to print to shared printers on the server.

- **Internet Printing**   Creates a website where authorized users can manage print jobs on the server. It also lets users who have Internet Printing Client installed to connect and print to shared printers on the server by using the Internet Printing Protocol (IPP). The default Internet address for Internet Printing is http://*ServerName*/Printers, where *ServerName* is a placeholder for the internal or external server name, such as http://PrintServer15/Printers or http://www.cpandl.com/Printers.

- **Distributed Scan Server**   Establishes the server as a scan server, which is used to run scan processes. Scan processes are rules that define scan settings and control delivery of scanned documents on your network. The Scan Management snap-in is installed when you install this role service. Scan Management enables you to manage Web Services on Devices (WSD)–enabled scanners, scan servers, and scan processes.

You can add the Print and Document Services role to a server by following these steps:

1. In Server Manager, tap or click Manage, and then tap or click Add Roles And Features, or select Add Roles And Features in the Quick Start pane. This starts the Add Roles And Features Wizard. If the wizard displays the Before You Begin page, read the Welcome text, and then select Next.

2. On the Installation Type page, Role-Based Or Feature-Based Installation is selected by default. Select Next.

3. On the Server Selection page, you can choose to install roles and features on running servers or virtual hard disks. Either select a server from the server pool or select a server from the server pool on which to mount a virtual hard disk (VHD). If you are adding roles and features to a VHD, tap or click Browse, and then use the Browse For Virtual Hard Disks dialog box to locate the VHD. When you are ready to continue, select Next.

4. On the Select Roles page, select Print And Document Services. When you are ready to continue, select Next three times.

5. On the Select Role Services page, select one or more role services to install. To allow for interoperability with UNIX, be sure to add LPD Service. Tap or click Next.

6. When you install Internet Printing, you must also install Web Server (IIS) and some related components. You are prompted to automatically add the required role services. Select Add Features to continue.

NOTE If the server on which you want to install the Print And Document Services role doesn't have all the required binary source files, the server gets the files via Windows Update by default or from a location specified in Group Policy. You also can specify an alternate path for the required source files by clicking the Specify An Alternate Source Path link, entering that alternate path in the box provided, and then tapping or clicking OK. For network shares, enter the UNC path to the share, such as \\CorpServer82\WinServer2012\. For mounted Windows images, enter the Windows Imaging (WIM) path prefixed with *WIM:* and including the index of the image to use, such as WIM:\\CorpServer82\WinServer2012\install.wim:4.

7. After you review the installation options and save them as necessary, select Install to begin the installation process. The Installation Progress page tracks the progress of the installation. If you close the wizard, select the Notifications icon in Server Manager, and then select the link provided to reopen the wizard.

8. When Setup finishes installing the Print And Document Services role, the Installation Progress page will be updated to reflect this. Review the installation details to ensure that all phases of the installation were completed successfully.

9. When you install Distributed Scan Server, you'll get a notification that additional configuration is required. Select the link provided to open Scan Management, which you can use to specify scanners to manage. In Scan Management, expand the Scan Management node in the left pane, press and hold or right-click the Managed Scanners node, and then select Manage to open the Add Or Remove Scanners dialog box. Use the Add Or Remove Scanners dialog box to identify the distributed scanners in your organization.

When you install Distributed Scan Server, a security group called Scan Operators is added to the Users container in Active Directory Domain Services (AD DS) for the current logon domain. Any users who need to manage the Distributed Scan service should be added to this group.

REAL WORLD You have several additional options for adding required binaries. At an elevated command prompt, you can enter **DISM /Online /Enable-Feature /FeatureName:PrintServer /All /LimitAccess /Source:E:\Sources\SxS**, where *E:* is a mounted ISO or DVD. At an elevated shell prompt, you can enter **Enable-WindowsOptionalFeature -Online –FeatureName "PrintServer" -All -LimitAccess Source "E:\Sources\SxS"**, where *E:* is a mounted ISO or DVD.

Enabling and disabling file and printer sharing

File and printer sharing settings control access to file shares and printers that are attached to a computer. You can manage a computer's file and printer sharing configuration by following these steps:

1. In File Explorer, select Network in the left pane. On the toolbar in Network Explorer, select Network, and then select Network And Sharing Center.

2. In Network And Sharing Center, select Change Advanced Sharing Settings in the left pane. Select the network profile for the network for which file and printer sharing should be enabled. Typically, this is the Domain profile.

3. Standard file and printer sharing controls network access to shared resources. To configure standard file sharing, do one of the following:

   ▪ Select Turn On File And Printer Sharing to enable file and printer sharing.

   ▪ Select Turn Off File And Printer Sharing to disable file and printer sharing.

Getting started with Print Management

Print Management should be your tool of choice for working with printers and print servers. After you install the Print and Document Services role, Print Management is available on the Tools menu in Server Manager as a stand-alone console. You can also add Print Management as a snap-in to any custom console you create.

By using Print Management, shown in Figure 10-1, you can install, view, and manage the printers and Windows print servers in your organization. Print Management also displays the status of printers and print servers. When you expand a server-level node and select the Printers node, you get a list of printers the server is hosting. If you are accessing the selected print server by using a Remote Desktop connection, you might also find entries for printers being redirected from your logon computer. Redirected printers are listed clearly as such with a (redirected) suffix.

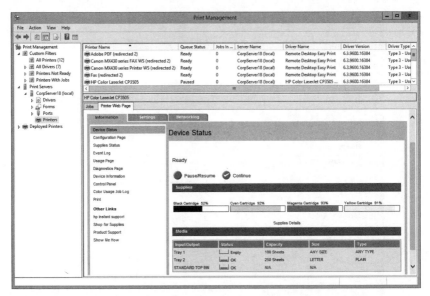

FIGURE 10-1 Use Print Management to work with print servers and printers throughout your organization.

By default, Print Management enables you to manage local print servers. You can manage and monitor other print servers in the organization by adding them to the console. Additionally, to manage a remote print server, you must be a member of the local Administrators group on the print server or a member of the Domain Admins group in the domain of which the print server is a member.

When you select a print server's Printers node, the main pane lists the associated printer queues by printer name, queue status, number of jobs in a queue, and server name. If you press and hold or right-click Printers, and then tap or click Show Extended View, you can turn on Extended view. Extended view makes it easy to track the status of both printers and print jobs by displaying information about the status of a print job, its owner, the number of pages, the size of the job, when it was submitted, its port, and its priority.

In addition, when a printer has a webpage, Extended view displays a Printer Web Page tab that lets you directly access the printer's webpage. This webpage provides details about the printer's status, its physical properties, and its configuration, and it sometimes allows remote administration.

You can add print servers to Print Management by following these steps:

1. In Print Management, press and hold or right-click the Print Servers node in the left pane, and then tap or click Add/Remove Servers.

2. In the Add/Remove Servers dialog box, shown in Figure 10-2, you'll find a list of the print servers you previously added.

FIGURE 10-2 Add print servers to Print Management so that you can manage and monitor them.

Do one of the following, and then tap or click Add To List:

- In the Add Servers list, enter or paste the names of the print servers you want to add. Use commas to separate computer names.
- Tap or click Browse to display the Select Print Server dialog box. Tap or click the print server you want to use, and then tap or click Select Server.

3. Repeat the previous step as necessary, and then tap or click OK.

You can remove print servers from Print Management by following these steps:

1. In Print Management, press and hold or right-click the Print Servers node in the left pane, and then tap or click Add/Remove Servers.

2. In the Add/Remove Servers dialog box, you'll find a list of the print servers that are being monitored. Under Print Servers, select one or more servers, and then tap or click Remove.

Installing printers

The following sections examine techniques you can use to install printers. Windows Server 2012 R2 makes it possible for you to install and manage printers anywhere on the network. To install or configure a new printer on Windows Server 2012 R2, you must be a member of the Administrators, Print Operators, or Server Operators group. To connect to and print documents to the printer, you must have the appropriate access permissions. See "Setting printer access permissions" later in this chapter for details.

Using the autoinstall feature of Print Management

Print Management can automatically detect all network printers located on the same subnet as the computer on which the console is running. After detection, Print Management can automatically install the appropriate printer drivers, set up print queues, and share the printers. To automatically install network printers and configure a print server, follow these steps:

1. Start Print Management by tapping or clicking Tools in Server Manager, and then tapping or clicking Print Management.

2. In Print Management, expand the Print Servers node by double-tapping or double-clicking it.

3. Press and hold or right-click the entry for the local or remote server with which you want to work, and then tap or click Add Printer to start the Network Printer Installation Wizard.

4. On the Print Installation page, select Search The Network For Printers, and then tap or click Next.

5. The wizard searches the local subnet for network printers. If printers are found, you'll get a list of printers by name and IP address (see Figure 10-3). Tap or click a printer to install, tap or click Next, and then continue this procedure to install the automatically detected printer.

   If a printer you want to use is not listed, you should ensure that the printer is powered on and is online and then repeat this procedure. If a printer you want to use is powered on and online but is not listed, see "Installing network-attached print devices" to complete the installation.

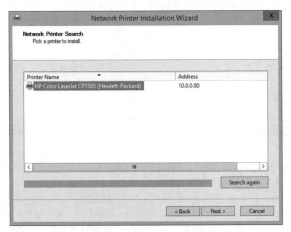

FIGURE 10-3 Printers located by the wizard are listed by name and IP address.

6. The wizard automatically detects the TCP/IP port configuration of the selected printer and then communicates with the printer to obtain the information required to configure the printer. Afterward, the wizard sets the default name and share name of the printer as shown in Figure 10-4. The printer is configured as a shared resource as well.

The printer name is the name you use when you work with the printer in Print Management. The share name is the name users use when they work with the printer.

Optionally, enter information in the Location and Comment text boxes that will help users locate and identify the printer. For example, you might want to specify the printer location as: Room 314 in Building 7.

NOTE The printer name and share name can be up to 256 characters and can include spaces. In a large organization, you'll want the share name to be logical and helpful in locating the printer. For example, you might want to give the name Twelfth Floor NE to the printer that points to a print device in the northeast corner of the twelfth floor.

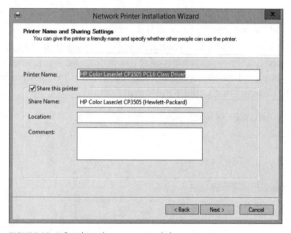

FIGURE 10-4 Set the printer name and share name.

7. The next page lets you review the settings. When you're ready to complete the installation, tap or click Next.

8. When you share a printer, Windows Server automatically makes drivers available so that users can download them when they first connect to the printer. The status page should confirm that printer driver and printer installation were successful. If there was a problem with the installation, note the errors provided. For example, someone might have powered off the printer while you were trying to configure it. If so, you'll need to power the printer back on and repeat this procedure.

9. If you'd like to print a test page on the printer, select the Print Test Page check box, and then tap or click Finish. Otherwise, just tap or click Finish.

10. By default, the printer share is not listed in Active Directory. Listing the printer share in Active Directory enables users to search for and find the printer more easily. If you want the printer share to be listed in Active Directory, select the Printers node in the left pane, press and hold or right-click the printer in the main window, and then select List In Directory.

11. By default, print jobs are sent to the print server where they are rendered and then sent to the printer. You can change this behavior by using Branch Office Direct Printing. With Branch Office Direct Printing, print jobs are rendered on client computers and then sent directly to the printer. If you want to enable direct printing, select the Printers node in the left pane, press and hold or right-click the printer in the main window, and then select Enable Branch Office Direct Printing.

Installing and configuring physically attached print devices

Most physically attached print devices are connected to a computer directly through a USB cable. You can configure physically attached printers as local print devices or as network print devices. The key difference is that a local device is accessible only to users logged on to the computer and a network device is accessible to network users as a shared print device. Remember that the workstation or server you're logged on to becomes the print server for the device you're configuring. If the computer is sleeping or turned off, the printer will not be available.

You can install physically attached print devices locally by logging on to the print server you want to configure; you can install the print devices remotely through Remote Desktop. If you're configuring a local Plug and Play printer and are logged on to the print server, installing a print device is a snap. After the printer is installed, you need to configure it for use.

You can install and configure a print device by following these steps:

1. Power on the printer, and then connect the print device to the server by using the appropriate cable.

2. If Windows Server automatically detects the print device, Windows begins installing the device and the necessary drivers. If the necessary drivers aren't found, you might need to insert the printer's driver disc into the CD/DVD drive.

3. If Windows Server doesn't detect the print device automatically, you need to install the print device manually as described in the next set of instructions.

4. After you install the printer, you can configure the printer. In Print Management, expand the Print Servers node and the node for the server with which you want to work. When you select the Printers node for the server you are configuring, you'll find a list of available printers in the main pane. Press and hold or right-click the printer you want to configure, and then tap or click Manage Sharing. This displays the printer's Properties dialog box with the Sharing tab selected, as shown in Figure 10-5.

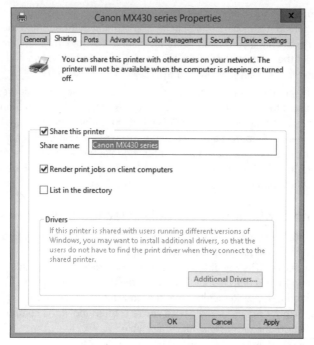

FIGURE 10-5 Configure the printer by using the Properties dialog box.

5. When you select the Share This Printer check box, Windows Server sets the default share name to the name of the printer. You can enter a different name for the printer share in the Share Name text box.

6. By default, the Render Print Jobs On Client Computers check box is selected, which configures the printer for Branch Office Direct Printing. With Branch Office Direct Printing, print jobs are rendered on client computers and then sent directly to the printer. If you want print jobs to be sent to the print server for rendering and then sent to the printer, clear the Render Print Jobs On Client Computers check box.

7. Listing the printer share in Active Directory enables users to search for and find the printer more easily. If you want the printer share to be listed in Active Directory, select the List In The Directory check box.

8. Tap or click OK.

Sometimes Windows Server won't detect your printer. In this case, follow these steps to install the print device:

1. In Print Management, expand the Print Servers node and the node for the server with which you want to work.

2. Press and hold or right-click the server's Printers node, and then tap or click Add Printer to start the Network Printer Installation Wizard.

3. On the Printer Installation page, shown in Figure 10-6, select Add A New Printer Using An Existing Port, and then choose the appropriate LPT, COM, or USB port. You can also print to a file. If you do, Windows Server 2012 R2 prompts users for a file name each time they print. Tap or click Next.

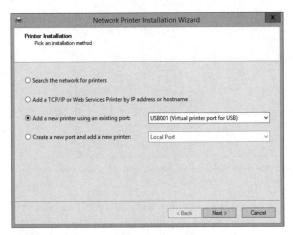

FIGURE 10-6 Choose the existing port to use.

4. On the Printer Driver page, shown in Figure 10-7, choose one of the following options:

- If Windows detected the printer type on the selected port and a compatible driver was found automatically, a printer driver is listed that reflects the printer manufacturer and model and the Use The Printer Driver That The Wizard Selected option is selected by default. To accept this setting, tap or click Next.

- If a compatible driver is not available and you want to choose an existing driver installed on the computer, select the Use An Existing Driver On The Computer option. After you choose the appropriate driver from the selection list, tap or click Next.

- If multiple drivers are available for a printer, such as both PCL and PostScript drivers, and you want to use a driver other than the selected default, select the Use An Existing Driver On The Computer option. After you choose the appropriate driver from the selection list, tap or click Next.

- If a compatible driver is not available and you want to install a new driver, select Install A New Driver, and then tap or click Next. You must now specify the print device manufacturer and model. This enables Windows Server 2012 R2 to assign a printer driver to the print device. After you choose a print device manufacturer, choose a printer model.

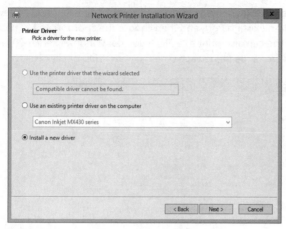

FIGURE 10-7 Select the driver to use for the printer or install a new driver.

REAL WORLD If the device manufacturer and model you're using aren't displayed in the list, tap or click Windows Update. Windows will then connect to the Windows Update website to update the list of printers to show additional models. This automatic driver provisioning process can take several minutes. When the update process is complete, you should then be able to select your printer manufacturer and model. If you can't, download the driver from the manufacturer's website, and then extract the driver files. Tap or click Have Disk. In the Install From Disk dialog box, tap or click Browse. In the Locate File dialog box, locate the .inf driver file for the device, and then tap or click Open.

NOTE If a driver for the specific printer model you're using isn't available, you often can select a generic driver or a driver for a similar print device. Consult the print device documentation for pointers.

5. Assign a name to the printer. This is the name that will be listed in Print Management.

6. Specify whether the printer is available to remote users. To create a printer accessible to remote users, select the Share This Printer option, and then enter a name for the shared resource. In a large organization you'll want the share name to be logical and helpful in locating the printer. For example, you could give the name Twelfth Floor NE to the printer that points to the print device in the northeast corner of the twelfth floor.

7. If you like, you can enter a location description and comment. This information can help users find a printer and determine its capabilities. Tap or click Next.

8. The final page lets you review the settings. When you're ready to complete the installation, tap or click Next.

9. After Windows installs the printer driver and configures the printer, you'll get a status page. Ensure that the driver and printer installation succeeded before continuing. If there were errors, you need to correct any problems and repeat this process. To test the printer, select Print Test Page, and then tap or click Finish.

When the Network Printer Installation Wizard finishes installing the new printer, the Printers folder will have an additional icon with the name set the way you specified. You can change the printer properties and check printer status at any time. For more information, see "Configuring printer properties" later in this chapter.

> **TIP**   If you repeat this process, you can create additional printers for the same print device. All you need to do is change the printer name and share name. Having additional printers for a single print device makes it possible for you to set different properties to serve different needs. For example, you could have a high-priority printer for print jobs that need to be printed immediately and a low-priority printer for print jobs that aren't as urgent.

Installing network-attached print devices

A network-attached print device is attached directly to the network through a network adapter card or a wireless network card. Network-attached printers are configured as network print devices so that they're accessible to network users as shared print devices. Remember that the server on which you configure the print device becomes the print server for the device you're configuring.

Install a network-attached print device by following these steps:

1. In Print Management, expand the Print Servers node and the node for the server with which you want to work.

2. Press and hold or right-click the server's Printers node, and then tap or click Add Printer to start the Network Printer Installation Wizard.

3. On the Printer Installation page, select Add A TCP/IP Or Web Services Printer By IP Address Or Hostname, and then tap or click Next.

4. On the Printer Address page, choose one of the following options in the Type Of Device list:

   - **Autodetect**   Choose this option if you are unsure of the printer device type. Windows Server will try to detect the type of device automatically.

   - **TCP/IP Device**   Choose this option if you are sure the printer is a TCP/IP device.

   - **Web Services Printer**   Choose this option if you are sure the printer is a Web Services for Devices (WSD) capable printer.

   - **Web Services Secure Printer**   Choose this option if you are sure the printer supports WSD Secure Printing.

REAL WORLD With WSD Secure Printing, print servers can create a private secure channel to the print device on the network without the need for additional security technologies such as IPsec. However, users and computers that work with the secure printer must be members of an Active Directory domain. You use the domain settings to manage printer permissions and Active Directory Domain Services acts as the trust arbitrator between the print server and the printer.

5. Enter the host name or IP address for the printer, such as 192.168.1.90. With the Autodetect and TCP/IP Device options, the wizard sets the port name to the same value, but you can also choose to use a different value.

   TIP The port name doesn't matter as long as it's unique on the server. If you're configuring multiple printers on the print server, be sure to record the port-to-printer mapping.

6. The Auto Detect The Printer Driver To Use check box is selected by default. When you tap or click Next, the wizard attempts to contact the printer and automatically configure the print device. If the wizard is unable to detect the print device, be sure that the following are true:
   - You selected the correct type of print device.
   - The print device is turned on and connected to the network.
   - The printer is configured properly.
   - You entered the correct IP address or printer name.

7. If the device type, IP address, or printer name is incorrect, tap or click OK to close the warning dialog box. Next, tap or click Back, and then reenter the required printer information.

8. On the Printer Driver page, choose one of the following options:
   - If Windows detected the printer type on the selected port and a compatible driver was found automatically, a printer driver is listed that reflects the printer manufacturer and model and the Use The Printer Driver That The Wizard Selected option is selected by default. To accept this setting, tap or click Next.
   - If a compatible driver is not available and you want to choose an existing driver installed on the computer, select the Use An Existing Driver option. After you use the selection list to choose the appropriate driver, tap or click Next.
   - If a compatible driver is not available and you want to install a new driver, select Install A New Driver, and then tap or click Next. Specify the print device manufacturer to enable Windows Server to assign a printer driver to the print device. After you choose a print device manufacturer, choose a printer model.

REAL WORLD If the device manufacturer and model you're using aren't displayed in the list, tap or click Windows Update. Windows will then connect to the Windows Update website to update the list of printers to show additional models. This feature is part of the automatic driver provisioning feature. It can take several minutes to retrieve the updated list. You should then be able to select your printer manufacturer and model. If you can't, download the driver from the manufacturer's website, and then extract the driver files. Tap or click Have Disk. In the Install From Disk dialog box, tap or click Browse. In the Locate File dialog box, locate the .inf driver file for the device, and then tap or click Open.

9. Assign a name to the printer. This is the name that will be listed in Print Management.

10. Specify whether the printer is available to remote users. To create a printer accessible to remote users, select the Share Name option, and then enter a name for the shared resource. In a large organization, you should use a share name that is logical and helpful in locating the printer. For example, Twelfth Floor NE would be a good name for the printer that points to the print device in the northeast corner of the twelfth floor.

11. If you like, you can enter a location description and comment. This information can help users find a printer and determine its capabilities. Tap or click Next.

12. The final page lets you review the settings. When you're ready to complete the installation, tap or click Next.

13. After Windows installs the printer driver and configures the printer, you'll get a status page. Ensure that the driver and printer installation succeeded before continuing. If there were errors, you need to correct any problems and repeat this process. To test the printer, select Print Test Page, and then tap or click Finish. To install another printer, select Add Another Printer, and then tap or click Finish.

14. By default, the printer share is not listed in Active Directory. Listing the printer share in Active Directory makes it possible for users to search for and find the printer more easily. If you want the printer share to be listed in Active Directory, select the Printers node in the left pane, press and hold or right-click the printer in the main window, and then select List In Directory.

15. By default, print jobs are sent to the print server where they are rendered and then sent to the printer. You can change this behavior by using Branch Office Direct Printing. With Branch Office Direct Printing, print jobs are rendered on client computers and then sent directly to the printer. If you want to enable direct printing, select the Printers node in the left pane, press and hold or right-click the printer in the main window, and then select Enable Branch Office Direct Printing.

When the Network Printer Installation Wizard finishes installing the new printer, the Printers folder will have an additional icon with the name set the way you specified. You can change the printer properties and check printer status at any time. For more information, see "Configuring printer properties" later in this chapter.

TIP If you repeat this process, you can create additional printers for the same print device. All you need to do is change the printer name and share name. Having additional printers for a single print device makes it possible for you to set different properties to serve different needs. For example, you could have a high-priority printer for print jobs that need to be printed immediately and a low-priority printer for print jobs that aren't as urgent.

Connecting to printers created on the network

After you create a network printer, remote users can connect to it and use it much as they do any other printer. You need to set up a connection on a user-by-user basis or have users do this themselves. To create a connection to the printer on a Windows 7 system, follow these steps:

1. With the user logged on, tap or click Start, and then tap or click Devices And Printers. In Devices And Printers, tap or click Add A Printer to start the Add Printer Wizard.

2. Select Add A Network, Wireless Or Bluetooth Printer. The wizard searches for available devices.

3. If the printer you want is listed in the Select A Printer list, tap or click it, and then tap or click Next.

4. If the printer you want is not listed in the Select A Printer list, tap or click The Printer That I Want Isn't Listed. On the Find A Printer By Name Or TCP/IP Address page, do one of the following:

   - To browse the network for shared printers, choose Find A Printer In The Directory, Based On Location Or Feature, and then tap or click Next. Tap or click the printer to use, and then tap or click Select.

   - To specify the printer to use by its share path, choose Select A Shared Printer By Name. Enter the UNC path to the shared printer, such as **\\PrintServer12\Twelfth Floor NE**, or the Web path to an Internet Printer, such as **http://PrintServer12/Printers/IPrinter52/.printer**.

   - To specify a printer to use by TCP/IP address or host name, select Add A Printer Using A TCP/IP Address Or Hostname, and then tap or click Next. Choose a device type, and then enter the host name or IP address for the printer, such as **192.168.1.90**. If you select the Autodetect or TCP/IP Device options, the wizard will set the port name to the same value, but you can also choose a different value. Tap or click Next.

5. On the Type A Printer Name page, the printer name is set for you. You can accept the default name or enter a new name. Tap or click Next to install the printer, and then tap or click Finish. The user can now print to the network printer by selecting the printer in an application. The Device And Printers folder on the user's computer shows the new network printer as well.

To create a connection to the printer on a Windows 8.1 system, follow these steps:

1. In Devices And Printers, tap or click Add A Printer. The Add Printer Wizard attempts to detect the printer automatically.

   If the wizard finds the printer with which you want to work, tap or click it in the list provided, follow the prompts, and skip the rest of the steps in this procedure.

   If the wizard doesn't find the printer, tap or click The Printer That I Want Isn't Listed, and then complete the rest of this procedure.

2. In the Add Printer Wizard, tap or click Add Bluetooth, Wireless Or Network Discoverable Printer.

3. In the list of available printers, select the printer you want to use, and then tap or click Next.

4. If prompted, install the printer driver on your computer. Complete the additional steps in the wizard, and then tap or click Finish. You can confirm the printer is working by printing a test page.

If you have trouble connecting to the printer, try the following as part of troubleshooting:

- Be sure that a firewall isn't blocking connectivity to the printer. You might need to open a firewall port to enable access between the computer and the printer.

- Be sure the printer is turned on and connected to the same network as the computer. If your network consists of multiple subnets connected together, try to connect the printer to the same network subnet. You can determine the subnet by looking at the computer's IP address.

- Be sure the printer is configured to broadcast its presence on the network. Most network printers automatically do this.

- Be sure the printer has an IP address and proper network settings. If DHCP is configured on the network, DHCP assigns IP addresses automatically as printers connect to the network.

Deploying printer connections

Connecting to printers is fairly easy, but you can make the process even easier by deploying printer connections through Group Policy. You can deploy printer connections to computers or users via the Group Policy objects (GPOs) that Windows applies. Deploy the connections to groups of users when you want users to be able to access the printers from any computer they log on to. Deploy the connections to groups of computers when you want all users of the computers to access the printers. For per-computer connections, Windows adds or removes printer connections when the computer starts. For per-user connections, Windows adds or removes printer connections when the user logs on.

To deploy printer connections to computers, you must follow these steps:

1. In Print Management, expand the Print Servers node and the node for the server with which you want to work.

2. Select the server's Printers node. In the main pane, press and hold or right-click the printer you want to deploy, and then tap or click Deploy With Group Policy. This displays the Deploy With Group Policy dialog box, shown in Figure 10-8.

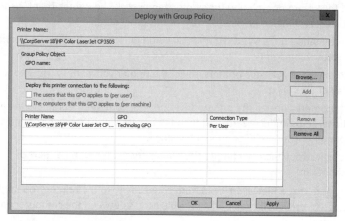

FIGURE 10-8 Select the GPO to use for deploying the printer connection.

3. Tap or click Browse. In the Browse For Group Policy Object dialog box, select the GPO to use, and then tap or click OK.

4. Do one or both of the following:

   ▪ To deploy to the printer connection on a per-user basis, under Deploy This Printer Connection To The Following, select The Users That This GPO Applies To.

   ▪ To deploy to the printer connection on a per-computer basis, under Deploy This Printer Connection To The Following, select The Computers That This GPO Applies To.

5. Tap or click Add to create a print connection entry.

6. Repeat steps 3–5 to deploy the printer connection to other GPOs.

7. Tap or click OK to save the changes to the GPO. In the confirmation dialog box, ensure that all operations were completed successfully. If an error occurred, tap or click Details to get more information about the error. The most common errors involve editing permissions for the GPO with which you are working. If the account you are using doesn't have appropriate permissions, you need to use an account with additional privileges. Tap or click OK.

Configuring point and print restrictions

In Group Policy, the Point And Print Restrictions setting controls security warnings and elevation prompts when users point and print and when drivers for printer connections need to be configured. This setting is found in the Administrative Templates for Computer Configuration under the Printers node.

Table 10-1 summarizes how the Point And Print Restrictions setting is used. Note that prior to Windows 7 and Windows Vista Service Pack 2, Point And Print Restrictions were implemented by using User Configuration policy. If you configure Point And Print Restrictions in User Configuration policy, the settings will be ignored by computers running Windows Vista Service Pack 2, Windows 7, and later versions of Windows.

TABLE 10-1 Point and print restrictions

WHEN THE POLICY SETTING IS	THE POLICY WORKS AS FOLLOWS
Enabled	Clients can point and print to any server. You can configure Clients to show or hide warning and elevation prompts when users point and print and when a driver for an existing printer connection needs to be updated.
Not Configured	Clients can point and print to any server in the forest. Clients also will not show a warning and elevation prompt when users point and print or when a driver for an existing printer connection needs to be updated.
Disabled	Clients can point and print to any server. Clients also will not show a warning and elevation prompt when users point and print or when a driver for an existing printer connection needs to be updated.

By default, Windows allows a user who is not a member of the local Administrators group to install only trustworthy printer drivers, such as those provided by Windows or in digitally signed printer driver packages. When you enable the Point And Print Restrictions setting, you also make it possible for users who are not members of the local Administrators group to install printer connections deployed in Group Policy that include additional or updated printer drivers that are not in the form of digitally signed printer driver packages. If you do not enable this setting, users might need to provide the credentials of a user account that belongs to the local Administrators group.

You can enable and configure the Point And Print Restrictions setting in Group Policy by following these steps:

1. In the Group Policy Management Console, press and hold or right-click the GPO for the site, domain, or organizational unit with which you want to work, and then tap or click Edit. This opens the policy editor for the GPO.

2. In the Group Policy Management Editor, expand the Administrative Templates for Computer Configuration, and then select the Printers node.

3. In the main pane, double-tap or double-click Point And Print Restrictions.

4. In the Point And Print Restrictions dialog box, shown in Figure 10-9, select Enabled.

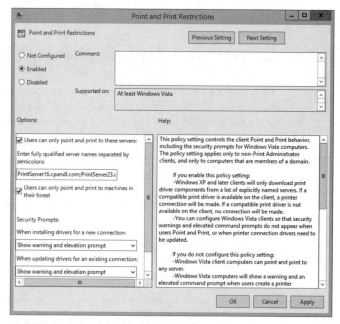

FIGURE 10-9 Configure point and print restrictions.

5. When you enable point and print restrictions, you can configure policy so that users can point and print only to a named list of servers. To enforce this restriction, select the related check box and enter a list of fully qualified server names separated by semicolons. To remove this restriction, clear the related check box.

6. When you enable point and print restrictions, you can configure policy so that users can point and print only to servers in their forest. To enforce this restriction, select the related check box. To remove this restriction, clear the related check box.

7. When you install drivers for a new connection, clients can show or not show a warning or elevation prompt. Use the related selection list to choose the option you want to use.

8. When you update drivers for an existing connection, clients can show or not show a warning or elevation prompt. Use the related selection list to choose the option you want to use.

9. Tap or click OK to apply the configuration.

Moving printers to a new print server

You can use the Printer Migration Wizard to move print queues, printer drivers, printer processors, and printer ports from one print server to another. This is an efficient way to consolidate multiple print servers or replace an older print server.

When you move printers, the server on which the printers are currently located is the source server, and the server to which you want to move the printers is the destination server. With this in mind, you can move printers to a new print server by following these steps:

1. In Print Management, press and hold or right-click the source server, and then tap or click Export Printers To A File. This starts the Printer Migration Wizard.

2. On the initial page, note the printer-related objects that will be exported, and then tap or click Next.

3. On the Select The File Location page, tap or click Browse. In the dialog box provided, select a save location for the printer migration file. After you enter a name for the file, tap or click Save.

4. Printer migration files are saved with the .printerExport extension. Tap or click Next to save the printer settings to this file.

5. After the wizard completes the export process, tap or click Open Event Viewer to review the events generated during the export process. If an error occurred during processing, you can use the event entries to determine what happened and possible actions to take to resolve the problem. When you have finished, exit the Event Viewer.

6. On the Exporting page, tap or click Finish to exit the Printer Migration Wizard.

7. In Print Management, press and hold or right-click the destination server, and then tap or click Import Printers From A File. This launches the Printer Migration Wizard.

8. On the Select The File Location page, tap or click Browse. In the dialog box provided select the printer migration file you created in steps 3 and 4, and then tap or click Open.

9. Tap or click Next. Note the objects that will be imported, and then tap or click Next. On the Select Import Options page, choose one of the following options in the Import Mode list:

- **Keep Existing Printers**   When you choose this option and existing printer queues have the same names as those you are importing, the wizard creates copies to ensure that the original printer queues and the imported printer queues are both available.

- **Overwrite Existing Printers**   When you choose this option and existing printer queues have the same names as those you are importing, the wizard overwrites the existing printer queues with the information from the printer queues you are importing.

10. On the Select Import Options page, choose one of the following options in the List In The Directory list:

- **List Printers That Were Previously Listed**   Choose this option to specify that only printers that were previously listed are listed in Active Directory.

- **List All Printers**   Choose this option to specify that all printers are listed in Active Directory.

- **Don't List Any Printers**   Choose this option to specify that no printers are listed in Active Directory.

11. Tap or click Next to begin the import process. After the wizard completes the import process, tap or click Open Event Viewer to review the events generated during the import process. If an error occurred during processing, you can use the event entries to determine what happened and possible actions to take to resolve the problem. When you have finished, exit the Event Viewer.

12. On the Importing page, tap or click Finish to exit the Printer Migration Wizard.

Monitoring printers and printer queues automatically

Printer filters display only the printers, printer queues, and printer drivers that meet specific criteria. Through automated notification, you can use printer filters to automate monitoring of printers.

In Print Management, you can view existing filters by expanding the Custom Filters node. If you expand the Custom Filters node and then select a filter, the main pane shows all printers or print drivers that match the filter criteria. Print Management includes the following default printer filters:

- **All Printers**   Lists all printers associated with print servers that have been added to the console

- **All Drivers**   Lists all printer drivers associated with print servers that have been added to the console

- **Printers Not Ready**   Lists all printers that are not in a Ready state, such as those with errors

- **Printers With Jobs**   Lists all printers associated with print servers that have active or pending print jobs

You can create a new custom filter by follow these steps:

1. In Print Management, press and hold or right-click the Custom Filters node, and then tap or click Add New Printer Filter to start the New Printer Filter Wizard.

2. On the Printer Filter Name And Description page, enter a filter name and description. If you'd like the number of matching items to be displayed after the filter name, select the Display The Total Number Of Printers check box. Tap or click Next.

3. On the Define A Filter page, define the filter by specifying the text box, condition, and value to match in the first row. If you want to further narrow the possible matches, define additional criteria in the second, third, and subsequent rows. Tap or click Next when you are ready to continue.

   NOTE When you use filters for monitoring and notification, you use the Queue Status text box the most. This text box enables you to receive a notification when a printer has a specific status. You can match the following status values: Attention Required, Busy, Deleting, Door Open, Error, Initializing, IO Active, Manual Feed Required, No Toner Ink, Not Available, Offline, Out of Memory, Out of Paper, Output Bin Full, Page Punt, Paper Jam, Paper Problem, Paused, Printing, Processing, Ready, Toner Ink Low, Waiting, and Warming Up

   TIP When you are matching conditions in a filter, you can match an exact condition that does exist or one that does not exist. For example, if you want to be notified only of conditions that need attention, you can look for Queue Status conditions that are not exactly the following: Deleting, Initializing, IO Active, Printing, Processing, Waiting, Warming Up, and Ready.

4. On the Set Notifications (Optional) page, you can specify whether to send an email message, run a script, or take both actions when the specified criteria are met. Tap or click Finish to complete the configuration.

You can modify an existing custom filter by following these steps:

1. In Print Management, expand the Custom Filters node. Select and then press and hold or right-click the filter with which you want to work. On the shortcut menu, tap or click Properties.

2. In the filter's Properties dialog box, use the options provided to manage the filter settings. This dialog box has the following three tabs:

   - **General**   Shows the name and description of the printer filter. Enter a new name and description as necessary.
   - **Filter Criteria**   Shows the filter criteria. Enter new filter criteria as necessary.
   - **Notification**   Shows the email and script options. Enter new email and script options as necessary.

Solving spooling problems

Windows Server 2012 R2 uses the Print Spooler service to control the spooling of print jobs. If this service isn't running, print jobs can't be spooled. Use the Services console to check the status of the Print Spooler. Follow these steps to check and restart the Print Spooler service:

1. On the Tools menu in Server Manager, tap or click Computer Management.

2. If you want to connect to a remote computer, press and hold or right-click the Computer Management entry in the console tree, and then tap or click Connect To Another Computer. You can now choose the system whose services you want to manage.

3. Expand the Services And Applications node, and then tap or click Services.

4. Select the Print Spooler service. The Status should be Started. If it isn't, press and hold or right-click Print Spooler, and then tap or click Start. The Startup Type should be Automatic. If it isn't, double-tap or double-click Print Spooler and set Startup Type to Automatic.

TIP Spoolers can become corrupted. Symptoms of a corrupted spooler include a frozen printer or one that doesn't send jobs to the print device. Sometimes the print device might print pages of garbled data. In most of these cases, you can resolve the problem by stopping and starting the Print Spooler service. Other spooling problems might be related to permissions. See "Setting printer access permissions" later in this chapter.

Configuring printer properties

The sections that follow explain how to set commonly used printer properties. After you install a network printer, you can set its properties by following these steps:

1. In Print Management, expand the Print Servers node and the node for the server with which you want to work.

2. Select the server's Printers node. In the main pane, press and hold or right-click the printer with which you want to work, and then tap or click Properties. You can now set the printer properties.

Adding comments and location information

To make it easier to determine which printer to use and when, you can add comments and location information for printers. Comments provide general information about the printer, such as the type of print device and who is responsible for it. Location describes the actual site of the print device. After set, applications can display these text boxes. For example, Microsoft Word displays this information in the Comment and Where text boxes when you select Print from the File menu.

You can add comments and location information to a printer by using the text boxes on the General tab of the printer's Properties dialog box. Enter your comments in the Comment text box. Enter the printer location in the Location text box.

Listing printers in Active Directory

Listing printers in Active Directory makes it easier for users to locate and install printers. You can list a printer in Active Directory by doing one of the following:

- Press and hold or right-click the printer's name, and then tap or click List In Directory.

- Open the printer's Properties dialog box, and then tap or click the Sharing tab. Select the List In Directory check box, and then tap or click OK.

Managing printer drivers

In a Windows Server 2012 R2 domain you should configure and update printer drivers only on your print servers. You don't need to update printer drivers on Windows clients. Instead, you configure the network printer to provide the drivers to client systems as necessary.

Updating a printer driver

You can update a printer's driver by following these steps:

1. Open the printer's Properties dialog box, and then tap or click the Advanced tab.

2. In the Driver list, you can select the driver from a list of currently installed drivers. Use the Driver list to select a new driver from a list of known drivers.

3. If the driver you need isn't listed or if you obtained a new driver, tap or click New Driver to start the Add Printer Driver Wizard. Tap or click Next.

4. If the device manufacturer and model you're using aren't displayed in the list, tap or click Windows Update. Windows connects to the Windows Update Web site to update the list of printers to show additional models. This feature is part of the automatic driver provisioning feature. It can take several minutes to retrieve the updated list. You should then be able to select your printer manufacturer and model.

5. If the device manufacturer and model you're using still aren't displayed in the list, choose Have Disk to install the new driver from a file or disc. In the Install From Disk dialog box, enter the folder path to the printer driver file or tap or click Browse to find the printer driver file by using the Locate File dialog box. Tap or click OK.

6. Tap or click Next, and then tap or click Finish.

Configuring drivers for network clients

After you install a printer or change drivers, you might want to select the operating systems that should download the driver from the print server. By enabling clients to download the printer driver, you provide a single location for installing driver updates. This way, instead of having to install a new driver on all the client systems, you install the driver on the print server and enable clients to download the new driver.

You can enable clients to download the new driver by following these steps:

1. Press and hold or right-click the icon of the printer you want to configure, and then tap or click Printer Properties.

2. Tap or click the Sharing tab, and then tap or click Additional Drivers.

3. In the Additional Drivers dialog box, select operating systems that can download the printer driver. As necessary, insert the Windows Server 2012 R2 installation media, printer driver discs, or both for the selected operating systems. The Windows Server 2012 R2 installation media has drivers for most Windows operating systems.

Setting a separator page and changing print device mode

Separator pages have two uses on Windows Server 2012 R2 systems:

- You can use them at the beginning of a print job to make it easier for users to find a document on a busy print device.

- You can use them to change the print device mode, such as whether the print device uses PostScript or Printer Control Language (PCL).

To set a separator page for a print device, follow these steps:

1. On the Advanced tab of the printer's Properties dialog box, tap or click Separator Page.

2. In the Separator Page dialog box, enter the name of the separator file to use. Typically, you'll want to use one of these available separator pages:

   - **Pcl.sep** Switches the print device to PCL mode and prints a separator page before each document

   - **Pscript.sep** Sets the print device to PostScript mode but doesn't print a separator page

   - **Sysprint.sep** Sets the print device to PostScript mode and prints a separator page before each document

   NOTE Sysprintj.sep is an alternate version of Sysprint.sep. If fonts for Japanese are available and you want to use them, you can use Sysprintj.sep.

3. To stop using the separator page, open the Separator Page dialog box and remove the file name.

NOTE When you work with a local server, tap or click the Browse button in the Separator Page dialog box to open the %SystemRoot%\Windows\System32 folder for browsing. In this case, you can browse and select the separator page to use. In contrast, when you work with a remote server, the Browse button is typically not available, so you must enter the exact file name for the separator page.

Changing the printer port

You can change the port used by a print device at any time by using the Properties dialog box for the printer you're configuring. Open the Properties dialog box, and then tap or click the Ports tab. You can now add a port for printing by selecting its check box or remove a port by clearing its check box. To add a new port type, tap or click Add Port. In the Printer Ports dialog box, select the port type, and then tap or click New Port. Enter a valid port name, and then tap or click OK. To remove a port permanently, select it, and then tap or click Delete Port.

Scheduling and prioritizing print jobs

You can use the Properties dialog box for the printer you're configuring to set default settings for print job priority and scheduling. Open the dialog box, and then tap or click the Advanced tab. You can now set the default schedule and priority settings by using the text boxes shown in Figure 10-10. Each of these text boxes is discussed in the sections that follow.

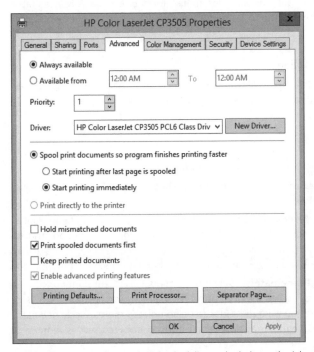

FIGURE 10-10 You configure print job scheduling and priority on the Advanced tab.

Scheduling printer availability

Printers are always available or available only during the hours specified. You set printer availability on the Advanced tab. Select Always Available to make the printer available at all times. Select Available From to set specific hours of operation.

> **TIP** As I mentioned before, you can create additional printers for the same print device. All you need to do is change the printer name and share name. To handle long print jobs that would interfere with the normal use of a printer, you might want to create a new printer for a print device and then set the availability to off-hours for your location. That printer could then be used for long print jobs that you don't want to run during the normal workday. The key to success with this approach is to ensure that the off-hours printer is clearly named as such and that users know how to use the various printers.

Setting printer priority

You can set the default priority for print jobs in the Priority box on the Advanced tab. Print jobs always print in order of priority. Jobs with higher priority print before jobs with lower priority.

Configuring print spooling

For print devices attached to the network, you usually want the printer to spool files rather than print files directly. Print spooling makes it possible to use a printer to manage print jobs.

ENABLING SPOOLING

To enable spooling, use one of the following options:

- **Spool Print Documents So Program Finishes Printing Faster**   Select this option to spool print jobs.
- **Start Printing After Last Page Is Spooled**   Select this option if you want the entire document to be spooled before printing begins. This option ensures that the entire document makes it into the print queue before printing. If for some reason printing is canceled or not completed, the job won't be printed.
- **Start Printing Immediately**   Select this option if you want printing to begin immediately when the print device isn't already in use. This option is preferable when you want print jobs to be completed more quickly or when you want to ensure that the application returns control to users as soon as possible.

OTHER SPOOLING OPTIONS

You can disable spooling by selecting the Print Directly To The Printer option. The following additional check boxes let you configure other spooling options:

- **Hold Mismatched Documents** If you select this option, the spooler holds print jobs that don't match the setup for the print device. Selecting this option is a good idea if you frequently have to change printer form or tray assignments.

- **Print Spooled Documents First** If you select this option, jobs that have completed spooling will print before jobs in the process of spooling, regardless of whether the spooling jobs have higher priority.

- **Keep Printed Documents** Typically, documents are deleted from the queue after they're printed. To keep a copy of documents in the printer, select this option. Use this option if you're printing files that can't easily be re-created. In this way, you can reprint the document without having to re-create it. For details, see "Pausing, resuming, and restarting individual document printing" later in this chapter.

- **Enable Advanced Printing Features** When you enable this option, you can use advanced printing options (if available), such as Page Order and Pages Per Sheet. If you note compatibility problems when using advanced options, you should disable the advanced printing features by clearing this check box.

Starting and stopping printer sharing

You set printer sharing in the Properties dialog box of the printer you're configuring. Press and hold or right-click the icon of the printer you want to configure, and then tap or click Manage Sharing. This opens the printer's Properties dialog box with the Sharing tab selected. You can use this tab to change the name of a network printer and to start sharing or stop sharing a printer. Printer sharing tasks that you can perform include the following:

- **Sharing a local printer (thus making it a network printer)** To share a printer, select Share This Printer, and then specify a name for the shared resource in the Share Name text box. Tap or click OK when you have finished.

- **Changing the shared name of a printer** To change the shared name, just enter a new name in the Share Name text box, and then tap or click OK.

- **Stopping the sharing of a printer** To quit sharing a printer, clear the Share This Printer check box, and then tap or click OK.

Setting printer access permissions

Network printers are shared resources. As such, you can set access permissions for them. You set access permissions in the Properties dialog box of the printer you're configuring. Open the printer's Properties dialog box, and then tap or click the Security tab. Permissions that you can grant or deny for printers are Print, Manage Documents, and Manage This Printer. Table 10-2 summarizes the capabilities of these permissions.

TABLE 10-2 Printer permissions used by Windows Server 2012 R2

PERMISSION	PRINT	MANAGE DOCUMENTS	MANAGE THIS PRINTER
Print documents	X	X	X
Pause, restart, resume, and cancel own documents	X	X	X
Connect to printers	X	X	X
Control settings for print jobs		X	X
Pause, restart, and delete print jobs		X	X
Share printers			X
Change printer properties			X
Change printer permissions			X
Delete printers			X

The default permissions are used for any new network printer you create. These settings are as follows:

- Members of the Administrators, Print Operators, and Server Operators groups have full control over printers by default. This makes it possible for you to administer a printer and its print jobs.

- The creator or owner of the document can manage his or her own document. This enables the person who printed a document to change its settings and to delete it.

- Everyone can print to the printer. This makes the printer accessible to all users on the network.

As with other permission sets, you create the basic permissions for printers by combining special permissions into logical groups. Table 10-3 shows special permissions used to create the basic permissions for printers. By using Advanced permission settings, you can assign these special permissions individually if necessary.

TABLE 10-3 Special permissions for printers

SPECIAL PERMISSIONS	PRINT	MANAGE DOCUMENTS	MANAGE THIS PRINTER
Print	X		X
Manage Documents		X	
Manage This Printer			X
Read Permissions	X	X	X
Change Permissions		X	X
Take Ownership		X	X

Auditing print jobs

Windows Server 2012 R2 lets you audit common printer tasks by following these steps:

1. Open the printer's Properties dialog box, and then tap or click the Security tab. Tap or click Advanced to open the Advanced Security Settings dialog box.

   NOTE Actions aren't audited by default. You must first enable auditing by establishing a group policy to audit the printer.

2. On the Auditing tab, add the names of users or groups you want to audit by using the Add button and remove names of users or groups by using the Remove button.

3. Select the events you want to audit by selecting the check boxes under the Successful and Failed headings, as appropriate.

4. Tap or click OK.

Setting document defaults

Document default settings are used only when you print from applications that are not based on Windows, such as when you print from the command prompt. You can set document defaults by following these steps:

1. Open the printer's Properties dialog box, and then tap or click the General tab.

2. Tap or click Preferences.

3. Use the text boxes on the tabs provided to configure the default settings.

Configuring print server properties

Windows Server 2012 R2 enables you to control global settings for print servers by using the Print Server Properties dialog box. In Print Management, press and hold or right-click the server entry for the print server with which you want to work, and then tap or click Properties. If the print server isn't listed, you can add it in the Add/Remove Servers dialog box. To open the dialog box, press and hold or right-click Print Servers, and then tap or click Add/Remove Servers.

The sections that follow examine some of the print server properties that you can configure.

Locating the Spool folder and enabling printing on NTFS

The Spool folder holds a copy of all documents in the printer spool. By default, this folder is located at %SystemRoot%\System32\Spool\Printers. On the NTFS file system, all users who access the printer must have Modify permission on this directory. If they don't, they won't be able to print documents.

If you're experiencing problems, check the permission on this directory by following these steps:

1. Access the Print Server Properties dialog box.

2. Tap or click the Advanced tab. The location of the Spool folder is shown in the Spool Folder text box. Note this location.

3. Press and hold or right-click the Spool folder in Windows Explorer, and then tap or click Properties.

4. Tap or click the Security tab. Now you can verify that the permissions are set appropriately.

Managing high-volume printing

Printers used in corporate environments can print hundreds or thousands of documents daily. This high volume puts a heavy burden on print servers and can cause printing delays, document corruption, and other problems. To alleviate some of this burden, you should do the following:

- Use network-attached printers rather than directly attached printers. Network-attached printers use fewer system resources (namely CPU time) than do other printers.

- Use Branch Office Direct Printing to render print jobs on client computers, and then send the print jobs directly to a printer. Otherwise, print jobs are sent to the print server where they are rendered, and then sent to the printer.

- Dedicate the print server to handle print services only. If the print server is handling other network duties, it might not be very responsive to print requests and management. To increase responsiveness, you can move other network duties to other servers.

- Move the Spool folder to a drive dedicated to printing. By default, the Spool folder is on the same file system as the operating system. To further improve disk input/output (I/O), use a drive that has a separate controller.

Enabling print job error notification

Print servers can beep to notify users when a remote document fails to print. By default, this feature is turned off because it can be annoying. If you want to activate or remove notification, access the Advanced tab of the Print Server Properties dialog box, and then select or clear the check box labeled Beep On Errors Of Remote Documents.

Managing print jobs on local and remote printers

You manage print jobs and printers by using the print management window. If the printer is configured on your system, you can access the print management window by using one of the following techniques:

- Access the Devices And Printers folder on the print server you want to manage. Double-tap or double-click the icon of the printer with which you want to work. If the printer isn't configured on your system, you can manage the printer remotely by using the Network console. Double-tap or double-click the icon of the print server with which you want to work, and then double-tap or double-click the Devices And Printers folder or the Printers folder.

- In Print Management, double-tap or double-click the Print Servers node, and then double-tap or double-click the entry for the print server itself. Select Printers. Press and hold or right-click the printer with which you want to work, and then tap or click Open Printer Queue.

- In Print Management, press and hold or right-click the Printers node, and then tap or click Show Extended View. With the printer selected in the upper pane, the upper and lower panes in the main window provide functionality similar to that of the print management window.

Viewing printer queues and print jobs

You can now manage print jobs and printers by using the print management window shown in Figure 10-11. The print management window shows information about documents in the printers. This information tells you the following:

- **Document Name**   The document file name, which can include the name of the application that printed it.

- **Status**   The status of the print job, which can include the document's status and the printer's status. Document status entries you'll find include Printing, Spooling, Paused, Deleting, and Restarting. Document status can be preceded by the printer status, such as Printer Off-Line.

- **Owner**   The document's owner.

- **Pages**   The number of pages in the document.

- **Size**   The document size in kilobytes or megabytes.

- **Submitted**   The time and date the print job was submitted.

- **Port**   The port used for printing, such as LPT1, COM3, File, or IP address (if applicable).

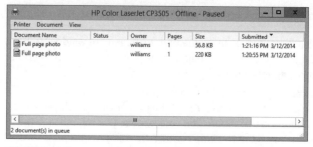

FIGURE 10-11 You manage print jobs and printers by using the print management window.

Pausing the printer and resuming printing

Sometimes you need to pause a printer. You do this by using the print management window and selecting the Pause Printing option from the Printer menu. (A check mark indicates that the option is selected.) When you pause printing, the printer completes the current job and then puts all other jobs on hold.

To resume printing, select the Pause Printing option a second time. This should remove the check mark next to the option.

Emptying the print queue

You can use the print management window to empty the print queue and delete all its contents. To do this, choose Cancel All Documents from the Printer menu. Emptying the print queue is especially useful when a printer has had an issue and users have printed the same documents multiple times.

Pausing, resuming, and restarting individual document printing

You set the status of individual documents by using the Document menu in the print management window. To change the status of a document, press and hold or right-click the document, and then use one of the following options on the shortcut menu to change the status of the print job.

- **Pause** Puts the document on hold and lets other documents print
- **Resume** Tells the printer to resume printing the document from where it left off
- **Restart** Tells the printer to start printing the document again from the beginning

Removing a document and canceling a print job

To remove a document from the printer or cancel a print job, select the document in the print management window. Press and hold or right-click the document, and tap or click Cancel or press the Delete key.

NOTE When you cancel a print job that's currently printing, the print device might continue to print part or all of the document. This occurs because most print devices cache documents in an internal buffer and the print device might continue to print the contents of this cache.

Checking the properties of documents in the printer

Document properties can tell you many things about documents that are in the printer, such as the page source, orientation, and size. You can check the properties of a document in the printer by doing either of the following:

- Press and hold or right-click the document in the print management window, and then tap or click Properties.
- Double-tap or double-click the document name in the print management window.

Setting the priority of individual documents

Scheduling priority determines when documents print. Documents with higher priority print before documents with lower priority. You can set the priority of individual documents in the printer by following these steps:

1. Press and hold or right-click the document in the print management window, and then tap or click Properties.
2. On the General tab, use the Priority slider to change the document's priority. The lowest priority is 1 and the highest is 99.

Scheduling the printing of individual documents

In a busy printing environment, you might need to schedule the printing of documents in the printer. For example, you might want large print jobs of low priority to print at night. To set the printing schedule, follow these steps:

1. Press and hold or right-click the document in the print management window, and then tap or click Properties.
2. On the General tab, select the Only From option, and then specify a time interval. The time interval you set determines when the job can print. For example, you can specify that the job can print only between midnight and 5:00 A.M.

Data backup and recovery

Because data is the heart of the enterprise, protecting it is crucial. And to protect your organization's data, you need to implement a data backup and recovery plan. Backing up files can protect against accidental loss of user data, database corruption, hardware failures, and even natural disasters. Your job as an administrator is to make sure that backups are performed and that backups are stored in a secure location.

Creating a backup and recovery plan

Data backup is an insurance plan. Important files are accidentally deleted all the time. Mission-critical data can become corrupt. Natural disasters can leave your office in ruin. With a solid backup and recovery plan, you can recover from any of these events. Without one, you're left with nothing to fall back on.

Figuring out a backup plan

It takes time to create and implement a backup and recovery plan. You need to figure out what data needs to be backed up, how often the data should be backed up, and more. To help you create a plan, consider the following questions:

- **How important or sensitive is the data on your systems?**   Knowing the importance of data can go a long way toward helping you determine whether you need to back it up, in addition to when and how it should be backed up. For critical data, such as a database, you should have redundant backup sets that cover several backup periods. For sensitive data, you should be sure that backup data is physically secure or encrypted. For less impor-tant data, such as daily user files, you won't need such an elaborate backup plan, but you do need to back up the data regularly and ensure that the data can be recovered easily.

- **What type of information does the data contain?** Data that doesn't seem important to you might be very important to someone else. The type of information the data contains can help you determine whether you need to back up the data, in addition to when and how the data should be backed up.

- **How often does the data change?** The frequency of change can affect your decision on how often certain data should be backed up. For example, data that changes daily should be backed up daily.

- **Can you supplement backups with shadow copies?** *Shadow copies* are point-in-time copies of documents in shared folders. These point-in-time copies make recovering documents easy because you can quickly go back to an older version in case a document is deleted or overwritten accidentally. You should use shadow copies in addition to standard backups, not to replace backup procedures.

- **How quickly do you need to recover the data?** Recovery time is an important factor in a backup plan. For critical systems, you might need to get back online swiftly. To make this possible, you might need to alter your backup plan.

- **Do you have the equipment to perform backups?** You must have backup hardware to perform backups. To perform timely backups, you might need several backup devices and several sets of backup media. Backup hardware includes hard disk drives, tape drives, optical drives, and removable disk drives. In most environments, hard disk drives have become the preferred back up media.

- **Who will be responsible for the backup and recovery plan?** Ideally, someone should be a primary contact for the organization's backup and recovery plan. This person might also be responsible for performing the actual backup and recovery of data.

- **What's the best time to schedule backups?** Scheduling backups when system use is as low as possible will speed up the backup process. However, you can't always schedule backups for off-peak hours, so you need to carefully plan when key system data is backed up.

- **Do you need to store backups off site?** Storing copies of backups off site is essential to recovering your systems in the event of a natural disaster. In your off-site storage location, you should also include copies of the software you might need to install to reestablish operational systems.

REAL WORLD Recovery time objective (RTO) and recovery point objective (RPO) are important factors to consider. RTO represents the time to recover, which might be two hours for one server and four hours for another server. RPO represents your potential data loss, which might be one business day of data with one server or two business days with another server. A high RTO environment is an environment in which you can recover server functionality quickly after an outage. A high RPO environment is an environment in which the data recovered is as up to date as possible.

The frequency of your full server backups will vary according to the speed of your backup system and the amount of data you need to back up. The frequency at which you can create backups controls both the RPO and the RTO available to you. For example, with nightly backups, your RPO will be one business day, meaning that any server outage will likely result in the loss of an entire business day of data. Meanwhile, your RTO, indicating how long it actually takes to recover, will vary according to the amount of data you have to restore, the speed of your backup system, the load and available resources of the server on which you are performing a restore, and what I like to call the X factor—the X factor being any unforeseen issues you might encounter, such as a failure of the backup system itself or a tape in a set, and so forth.

Basic types of backup

There are many techniques for backing up files. The techniques you use depend on the type of data you're backing up, how convenient you want the recovery process to be, and more.

If you view the properties of a file or directory in File Explorer, you'll find an attribute called *archive*. You often use this attribute to determine whether a file or directory should be backed up. If the attribute is on, the file or directory might need to be backed up. You can perform the following basic types of backups:

- **Normal/full backups**   All files that have been selected are backed up, regardless of the *archive* attribute's setting. When a file is backed up, the *archive* attribute is cleared. If the file is later modified, this attribute is set, indicating that the file needs to be backed up.

- **Copy backups**   All files that have been selected are backed up, regardless of the *archive* attribute's setting. Unlike in a normal backup, the *archive* attribute on files isn't modified. This enables you to perform other types of backups on the files at a later date.

- **Differential backups**   Designed to create backup copies of files that have changed since the last normal backup. The presence of the *archive* attribute indicates that the file has been modified, and only files with this attribute set are backed up. However, the *archive* attribute on files isn't modified. This enables you to perform other types of backups on the files at a later date.

- **Incremental backups**   Designed to create backups of files that have changed since the most recent normal or incremental backup. The presence of the *archive* attribute indicates that the file has been modified, and only files with this attribute set are backed up. When a file is backed up, the *archive* attribute is cleared. If the file is later modified, this attribute is set, indicating that the file needs to be backed up.

- **Daily backups**   Designed to back up files by using the modification date on the file itself. If a file has been modified on the same day as the backup, the file will be backed up. This technique doesn't change the *archive* attribute of files.

As part of your backup operations, you'll probably want to perform full backups on a weekly basis and supplement this with daily, differential, or incremental backups. You might also want to create an extended backup set for monthly and quarterly backups that includes additional files that aren't being backed up regularly.

> **TIP** You'll often find that weeks or months go by before anyone notices that a file or data source is missing. This doesn't mean the file isn't important. Although some types of data aren't used often, they're still needed. So don't forget that you might also want to create extra sets of backups for monthly or quarterly periods, or for both periods, to ensure that you can recover historical data.

Differential and incremental backups

The difference between differential and incremental backups is extremely important. To understand the distinction, examine Table 11-1. As you will find, with differential backups you back up all the files that have changed since the last full backup (which means that the size of the differential backup grows over time). With incremental backups, you back up only files that have changed since the most recent full or incremental backup (which means the size of the incremental backup is usually much smaller than a full backup).

TABLE 11-1 Incremental and differential backup techniques

DAY OF WEEK	WEEKLY FULL BACKUP WITH DAILY DIFFERENTIAL BACKUP	WEEKLY FULL BACKUP WITH DAILY INCREMENTAL BACKUP
Sunday	A full backup is performed.	A full backup is performed.
Monday	A differential backup contains all changes since Sunday.	An incremental backup contains changes since Sunday.
Tuesday	A differential backup contains all changes since Sunday.	An incremental backup contains changes since Monday.
Wednesday	A differential backup contains all changes since Sunday.	An incremental backup contains changes since Tuesday.
Thursday	A differential backup contains all changes since Sunday.	An incremental backup contains changes since Wednesday.
Friday	A differential backup contains all changes since Sunday.	An incremental backup contains changes since Thursday.
Saturday	A differential backup contains all changes since Sunday.	An incremental backup contains changes since Friday.

After you determine what data you're going to back up and how often, you can select backup devices and media that support these choices. These options are covered in the next section.

Selecting backup devices and media

Many tools are available for backing up data. Some are fast and expensive, and others are slow but very reliable. The backup solution that's right for your organization depends on many factors, including the following:

- **Capacity**   The amount of data you need to back up on a routine basis. Can the backup hardware support the required load given your time and resource constraints?
- **Reliability**   The reliability of the backup hardware and media. Can you afford to sacrifice reliability to meet budget or time needs?
- **Extensibility**   The extensibility of the backup solution. Will this solution meet your needs as the organization grows?
- **Speed**   The speed with which data can be backed up and recovered. Can you afford to sacrifice speed with server or service downtime to reduce costs?
- **Cost**   The cost of the backup solution. Does it fit your budget?

Common backup solutions

Capacity, reliability, extensibility, speed, and cost are the issues driving your backup plan. If you understand how these issues affect your organization, you'll be on track to select an appropriate backup solution. Some of the most commonly used backup solutions include the following:

- **Tape drives**   Tape drives are the most common backup devices. Tape drives use magnetic tape cartridges to store data. Magnetic tapes are relatively inexpensive but aren't highly reliable. Tapes can break or stretch. They can also lose information over time. The average capacity of tape cartridges ranges from 24 gigabytes (GB) to 160 GB. Compared with other backup solutions, tape drives are slow. Still, the selling point is the low cost.
- **Digital audio tape (DAT) drives**   DAT drives are quickly replacing standard tape drives as the preferred backup devices. Many DAT formats are available. The most commonly used formats are Digital Linear Tape (DLT) and Super DLT (SDLT). With SDLT 320 and 600, tapes have a capacity of either 160 GB or 300 GB uncompressed (320 GB or 600 GB compressed). Large organizations might want to look at Linear Tape Open (LTO) tape technologies. LTO-3, LTO-4, and LTO-5 tapes have uncompressed capacity of 400 GB, 800 GB, and 1500 GB, respectively (and compressed capacity of twice that).
- **Autoloader tape systems**   Autoloader tape systems use a magazine of tapes to create extended backup volumes capable of meeting an enterprise's high-capacity needs. With an autoloader system, tapes within the magazine are automatically changed as necessary during the backup or recovery process. Most autoloader tape systems use DAT tapes formatted for DLT, SDLT, or LTO. Typical DLT drives can record up to 45 GB per hour, and you can improve that speed by purchasing a tape library system with multiple

drives. In this way, you can record on multiple tapes simultaneously. In contrast, most SDLT and LTO drives record over 100 GB per hour, and by using multiple drives in a system you can record hundreds of GB per hour. An example enterprise solution uses 16 LTO drives to achieve data-transfer rates of more than 13.8 terabytes (TB) per hour and can store up to 500 tapes, for a total storage capacity of more than 800 TB.

- **Disk drives** Disk drives provide one of the fastest ways to back up and restore files. With disk drives, you can often accomplish in minutes what takes a tape drive hours. When business needs mandate a speedy recovery, nothing beats a disk drive. The drawback to disk drives is a relatively high cost compared to tapes (though you'd also need to compare the initial hardware investment).

- **Disk-based backup systems** Disk-based backup systems provide complete backup and restore solutions by using large arrays of disks to achieve high performance. High reliability can be achieved when you use redundant array of independent disks (RAID) to build in redundancy and fault tolerance. Typical disk-based backup systems use virtual library technology so that Windows perceives them as autoloader tape library systems, which makes them easier to work with. An example enterprise solution has 128 virtual drives and 16 virtual libraries per node for total storage of up to 7.5 TB per node. When fully scaled, this enterprise solution can store up to 640 TB and transfer up to 17.2 TB per hour.

NOTE Disks and disk-based backup systems can be used between the servers you are backing up and an enterprise autoloader. Servers are backed up to disk first (because this is very fast compared to tape) and later backed up to an enterprise autoloader. Having data on tapes also makes it easier to rotate backup sets to off-site storage. That said, tape backups are increasingly being replaced with disk backups. If you back up to disk arrays, you can move data off site by replicating the data to a secondary array at an alternative data center and that data center can be in your private cloud or a third-party service's cloud.

Before you can use a backup device, you must install it. When you install backup devices other than standard tape and DAT drives, you need to tell the operating system about the controller card and drivers that the backup device uses.

Buying and using backup media

Selecting a backup device is an important step toward implementing a backup and recovery plan. But you also need to purchase the tapes, disks, or both that enable you to implement your plan. The number of tapes or disks you need depends on how much data you have to back up, how often you need to back up the data, and how long you need to keep additional data sets.

The typical way to use backup tapes is to set up a rotation schedule whereby you rotate through two or more sets of tapes. The idea is that you can increase tape longevity by reducing tape usage and, at the same time, reduce the number of tapes you need to ensure that you have historic data on hand when necessary.

One of the most common tape-rotation schedules is the 10-tape rotation. With this rotation schedule, you use 10 tapes divided into two sets of 5 (one for each weekday). The first set of tapes is used one week, and the second set of tapes is used the next week. On Fridays, full backups are scheduled. On Mondays through Thursdays, incremental backups are scheduled. If you add a third set of tapes, you can rotate one of the tape sets to an off-site storage location on a weekly basis.

The 10-tape rotation schedule is designed for the 9-to-5 workers of the world. If you're in a 24 hours a day, seven days a week environment, you'll definitely want extra tapes for Saturday and Sunday. In this case, use a 14-tape rotation with two sets of 7 tapes. On Sundays, schedule full backups. On Mondays through Saturdays, schedule incremental backups.

As disk drives have become more affordable, many organizations have been using disk backup instead of tape backup. With disks, you can use a rotation schedule similar to the one you use with tapes. You will, however, need to modify the way you rotate disks to accommodate the amount of data you are backing up. The key task to remember is to periodically rotate disks to off-site storage.

Selecting a backup utility

Many backup and recovery solutions are available for use with Windows Server 2012 R2. When selecting a backup utility, you need to keep in mind the types of backups you want to perform and the types of data you are backing up. Windows Server 2012 R2 includes the following installable backup and recovery features:

- **Windows Server Backup** A basic and easy-to-use backup and recovery utility. When this feature is installed on a server, you can open the tool by using the Tools menu in Server Manager.

- **Backup Command-Line Tools** A set of backup and recovery commands accessible through the Wbadmin command-line tool. You run and use Wbadmin from an elevated, administrator command prompt. Enter **wbadmin /?** for a full list of supported commands. Windows PowerShell cmdlets for managing backups are also available.

- **Windows Server Backup Module for Windows PowerShell** A set of backup and recovery cmdlets accessible through Windows PowerShell. You run and use these cmdlets from an elevated, administrator Windows PowerShell prompt. Enter **get-help *wb*** for a full list of supported cmdlets.

- **Microsoft Online Backup Service** This service is an add-on that can be downloaded and installed from within Windows Server Backup to schedule backups from a server to Microsoft's Internet cloud-based service. Online backups are possible only for fixed NTFS volumes that don't use BitLocker Drive Encryption. Volumes cannot be shares and must also be configured for read/write access.

- **Repair Your Computer** You can restore a server by using repair options if you cannot access recovery options provided by the server manufacturer.

NOTE Windows Server Backup and the backup command-line tools are available only for management of backups when you add the Windows Server Backup feature to a server. If you add server administration tools to a server, you might be able to open Windows Server Backup. However, you won't be able to use Windows Server Backup to configure and manage backups.

Windows Server Backup is the feature you'll use the most. You can use Windows Server Backup to perform full or copy backups. You cannot use Windows Server Backup to perform differential backups. Windows Server Backup uses the Volume Shadow Copy Service (VSS) to create fast, block-level backups of the operating system, files and folders, and disk volumes. After you create the first full backup, you can configure Windows Server Backup to automatically run full or incremental backups on a recurring basis.

When you use Windows Server Backup, you need separate, dedicated media for storing archives of scheduled backups. You can back up to external and internal disks, DVDs, and shared folders. Although you can recover full volumes from DVD backups, you cannot recover individual files, folders, or application data from DVD backups.

NOTE You cannot back up to tape by using Windows Server Backup. If you want to back up to tape, you need a third-party backup utility.

You can use Windows Server Backup to easily recover individual folders and files. Rather than manually restoring files from multiple backups if the files are stored in incremental backups, you can recover folders and files by choosing the date on which you backed up the version of the item or items you want to restore. Windows Server Backup also works with the Windows Recovery tools, making it easier for you to recover the operating system. You can recover to the same server or to a new server that has no operating system. Because Windows Server Backup uses VSS, you can easily back up data from compliant applications, such as Microsoft SQL Server and Windows SharePoint Services.

Windows Server Backup also includes automatic disk management. You can run backups to multiple disks in rotation simply by adding each disk as a scheduled backup location. After you configure a disk as a scheduled backup location, Windows Server Backup automatically manages the disk storage, ensuring that you no longer need to worry about a disk running out of space. Windows Server Backup reuses the space of older backups when creating newer backups. To help ensure that you can plan for additional storage needs, Windows Server Backup displays the backups that are available and the current disk usage information.

Backing up your data: the essentials

Windows Server 2012 R2 provides Windows Server Backup for creating backups. You use Windows Server Backup to archive files and folders, restore archived files and folders, create snapshots of the system state for backup and restore, and schedule automated backups.

Installing the Windows backup and recovery utilities

The Windows Server backup and recovery tools are available in all editions of Windows Server 2012 R2. However, you cannot install the graphical components of these utilities on core installations of Windows Server 2012 R2. On servers running with a core installation, you need to use the command line, Windows PowerShell, or manage backups via a remote session from another computer.

You can install the Windows backup and recovery tools by following these steps:

1. In Server Manager, select Add Roles And Features on the Manage menu. This starts the Add Roles And Features Wizard. If the wizard displays the Before You Begin page, read the introductory text, and then tap or click Next.

2. On the Installation Type page, Role-Based Or Feature-Based Installation is selected by default. Tap or click Next.

3. On the Server Selection page, you can choose to install roles and features on running servers or virtual hard disks. Either select a server from the server pool or select a server from the server pool on which to mount a virtual hard disk (VHD). If you are adding roles and features to a VHD, tap or click Browse and then use the Browse For Virtual Hard Disks dialog box to locate the VHD. When you are ready to continue, tap or click Next twice.

4. On the Select Features page, select Windows Server Backup. Tap or click Next.

5. Tap or click Install. When the wizard finishes installing the selected features, tap or click Close. From now on, Windows Server Backup and the related command-line tools and the Windows Server Backup module for Windows PowerShell are available for managing backups.

Getting started with Windows Server Backup

You can start Windows Server Backup by selecting the related option on the Tools menu in Server Manager. Alternatively, enter **Wbadmin.msc** in the Everywhere Search box or at a prompt.

When you start Windows Server Backup, you'll get a message about online backup. If you want to use online backups, you need to sign up for the service, register your server, and download the Microsoft Online Backup Service agent. With the Windows Server Backup node selected, you can start this process by clicking the Continue button. Before using the service, I would suggest determining what your costs would be to use the service and to compare those costs to other options.

In Windows Server Backup, shown in Figure 11-1, select the Local Backup node to work with backups. The first time you use Windows Server Backup, you'll get a warning that no backup has been configured for the computer. You clear this warning by creating a backup by using the Backup Once feature, located on the Action menu, or by scheduling backups to run automatically by using the Backup Schedule feature.

FIGURE 11-1 Windows Server Backup provides a user-friendly interface for backup and restore.

To perform backup and recovery operations, you must have certain permissions and user rights. Members of the Administrators and Backup Operators groups have full authority to back up and restore any type of file, regardless of who owns the file and the permissions set on it. File owners and those who have been given control over files can also back up files, but they can do so only for files they own or for which they have Read, Read & Execute, Modify, or Full Control permissions.

NOTE Keep in mind that although local accounts can work only with local systems, domain accounts have domain-wide privileges. Therefore, a member of the local Administrators group can work only with files on the local system, but a member of the Domain Admins group can work with files throughout the domain.

Windows Server Backup provides extensions for working with the following special types of data:

- **System state data** Includes essential system files needed to recover the local system. All computers have system state data, which must be backed up in addition to other files to restore a complete working system.

- **Application data** Includes application data files. You must back up application data if you want to be able to fully recover applications. Windows Server Backup creates block-level backups of application data by using VSS.

Windows Server Backup enables you to perform full, copy, and incremental backups. Although you can schedule a full or incremental backup to be performed one or more times each day, you cannot use this feature to create separate run schedules for performing both full and incremental backups. Further, you cannot select the day or days of the week to run backups. This occurs because each server has a single master schedule that is set to run one or more times daily. If your servers have a single master schedule, you can work around this limitation by configuring Windows Server Backup to perform daily incremental backups and then creating a scheduled task via the Task Scheduler that uses the Wbadmin command-line tool to create a full backup on the day of the week or month you want to use.

When you use Windows Server Backup, the first backup of a server is always a full backup. This is because the full backup process clears the archive bits on files so that Windows Server Backup can track which files are updated subsequently. Whether Windows Server Backup performs full or incremental backups subsequently depends on the default performance settings you configure. You can configure the default performance settings by following these steps:

1. Start Windows Server Backup. In the Actions pane or on the Action menu, tap or click Configure Performance Settings. This displays the Optimize Backup Performance dialog box, shown in Figure 11-2.

2. Do one of the following, and then tap or click OK:

   ■ Choose Normal Backup Performance to perform full backups of all attached drives.

   ■ Choose Faster Backup Performance to perform incremental backups of all attached drives.

   ■ Choose Custom. In the option lists provided, specify whether to perform full or incremental backups for individual attached drives.

FIGURE 11-2 Configure the default backup settings.

3. After you configure the default performance settings, you can start a full or copy backup by tapping or clicking Backup Once on the Action menu or in the Actions pane. You can configure a backup schedule by tapping or clicking Backup Schedule on the Action menu or in the Actions pane.

Getting started with the Backup Command-Line utility

Wbadmin is the command-line counterpart to Windows Server Backup. You use Wbadmin to manage all aspects of backup configuration that you would otherwise manage in Windows Server Backup. This means you can typically use either tool to manage backup and recovery.

After you install the Backup Command-Line Tools feature as discussed earlier in the chapter, you can use Wbadmin to manage backup and recovery. Wbadmin is located in the %SystemRoot%\System32\ directory. This directory is in your command path by default, so you do not need to add it. You can run Wbadmin by following these steps:

1. Open an elevated, administrator command prompt. One way to do this is to enter **cmd** in the Everywhere Search box, press and hold or right-click Command Prompt in the Apps list, and then tap or click Run As Administrator.

2. In the Command Prompt window, enter the necessary command text or run a script that invokes Wbadmin.

REAL WORLD By default with Windows Server 2012 R2, the command prompt and the administrator command prompt are options on the shortcut menu that is displayed when you right-click in the lower left corner or press Windows key + X. The alternative is for the Windows PowerShell prompt and the administrator Windows PowerShell prompt to be displayed on this menu. To configure which options are available, on the desktop, press and hold or right-click the taskbar, and then select Properties. In the Taskbar And Navigation Properties dialog box, on the Navigation tab, select or clear the Replace Command Prompt With Windows PowerShell check box as appropriate.

Wbadmin has a number of associated commands, which are summarized in Table 11-2.

TABLE 11-2 Wbadmin management commands

COMMAND	DESCRIPTION
DELETE SYSTEMSTATEBACKUP	Deletes the system state backup or backups from a specified location.
DISABLE BACKUP	Disables scheduled daily backups so that they no longer run.
DELETE BACKUP	Deletes one or more backups.
ENABLE BACKUP	Enables or modifies a scheduled daily backup.
GET DISKS	Lists the disks that are currently online for the local computer. Disks are listed by manufacturer name, type, disk number, GUID, total space, used space, and associated volumes.
GET ITEMS	Lists items contained in a specified backup.

COMMAND	DESCRIPTION
GET STATUS	Reports the status of the currently running backup or recovery job.
GET VIRTUAL MACHINES	Lists the currently configured virtual machines.
GET VERSIONS	Lists details about the available backups stored in a specific location, including the backup time and backup destination.
START BACKUP	Starts a one-time backup by using the specified parameters. If no parameters are passed and scheduled backups are enabled, the backup uses the settings for scheduled backups.
START RECOVERY	Initiates a recovery of volumes, applications, or files by using the specified parameters.
START SYSTEMSTATEBACKUP	Starts a system state backup by using the options specified.
START SYSTEMSTATERECOVERY	Starts a system state recovery by using the specified parameters.
STOP JOB	Stops the currently running backup or recovery job. Stopped jobs cannot be restarted from where they were stopped.

When you are working with Wbadmin, you can get help on available commands:

- To view a list of management commands, enter **wbadmin /?** at the command prompt.

- To view the syntax for a specific management command, enter **wbadmin** *Command* **/?**, where *Command* is the name of the management command you want to examine, such as **wbadmin stop job /?**.

When you work with Wbadmin, you'll find that just about every command accepts parameters and specific parameter values that qualify what you want to work with. To understand more clearly how this works, consider the following syntax example:

```
wbadmin get versions [-backupTarget:{VolumeName | NetworkSharePath}]
  [-machine:BackupMachineName]
```

The brackets tell you that *–backupTarget* and *–machine* are optional. Thus, you could enter the following to get information on recoverable backups on the local computer:

```
wbadmin get versions
```

You could enter the following to get information on recoverable backups stored on the F drive:

```
wbadmin get versions -backupTarget:f:
```

Or you could enter the following to get information on recoverable backups stored on the F drive on Server96:

```
wbadmin get versions -backupTarget:f: -machine:server96
```

Many Wbadmin commands use the –backupTarget and –machine parameters. The backup target is the storage location with which you want to work and can be expressed as a local volume name, such as F:, or as a network share path, such as \\FileServer32\backups\Server85. The –machine parameter identifies the computer you want to work with for backup or recovery operations.

Working with Wbadmin commands

You use Wbadmin commands to manage the backup configuration of your servers. These commands work with a specific set of parameters. The following sections provide an overview of the available commands and their most commonly used syntaxes.

Using general-purpose commands

The following general-purpose commands are provided for getting information about backups and the system with which you are working:

- **GET DISKS**   Lists the disks that are currently online for the local computer. Disks are listed by manufacturer name, type, disk number, GUID, total space, used space, and associated volumes.

  ```
  wbadmin get disks
  ```

- **GET ITEMS**   Lists items contained in a specified backup.

  ```
  wbadmin get items  -version:VersionIdentifier
    [-backupTarget:{VolumeName | NetworkSharepath}]
    [-machine:BackupMachineName]
  ```

- **GET STATUS**   Reports the status of the currently running backup or recovery job.

  ```
  wbadmin get status
  ```

- **GET VERSIONS**   Lists details about the available backups stored in a specific location, including the backup time and backup destination.

  ```
  wbadmin get versions [-backupTarget:{VolumeName | NetworkSharepath}]
    [-machine:BackupMachineName]
  ```

Using backup management commands

You can manage backups and their configurations by using the following commands and command-line syntaxes:

- **DELETE SYSTEMSTATEBACKUP**   Deletes the system state backup or backups from a specified location.

  ```
  wbadmin delete systemstateBackup [-backupTarget:{VolumeName}]
      [-machine:BackupMachineName]
      [-keepVersions:NumberOfBackupsToKeep | -version:VersionIdentifier |
      -deleteOldest]
      [-quiet]
  ```

- **DISABLE BACKUP**   Disables scheduled daily backups so that they no longer run.

  ```
  wbadmin disable backup [-quiet]
  ```

- **ENABLE BACKUP**   Enables or modifies a scheduled daily backup.

  ```
  wbadmin enable backup [-addTarget:{BackupTargetDisk}]
      [-removeTarget:{BackupTargetDisk}]
      [-schedule:TimeToRunBackup]
      [-include:VolumesToInclude]
      [-allCritical]
      [-quiet]
  ```

- **START BACKUP**   Starts a one-time backup by using the specified parameters. If no parameters are passed and scheduled backups are enabled, the backup uses the settings for scheduled backups.

  ```
  wbadmin start backup [-backupTarget:{TargetVolume |
  TargetNetworkShare}]
      [-include:VolumesToInclude]
      [-allCritical]
      [-noVerify]
      [-user:username]
      [-password:password]
      [-inheritAcl:InheritAcl]
      [-vssFull]
      [-quiet]
  ```

- **STOP JOB**   Stops the currently running backup or recovery job. Stopped jobs cannot be restarted from where they were stopped.

  ```
  wbadmin stop job [-quiet]
  ```

Using recovery management commands

You can recover your computers and data by using the following commands and command-line syntaxes:

- **START RECOVERY** Initiates a recovery of volumes, applications, or files by using the specified parameters:

```
wbadmin start recovery -version:VersionIdentifier
-items:VolumesToRecover | AppsToRecover | FilesOrFoldersToRecover
-itemType:{volume | app | file}
[-backupTarget:{VolumeHostingBackup | NetworkShareHostingBackup}]
[-machine:BackupMachineName]
[-recoveryTarget:TargetVolumeForRecovery | TargetPathForRecovery]
[-recursive]
[-overwrite:{Overwrite | CreateCopy | skip}]
[-notRestoreAcl]
[-skipBadClusterCheck]
[-noRollForward]
[-quiet]
```

- **START SYSTEMSTATEBACKUP** Starts a system state backup by using the options specified:

```
wbadmin start systemstateBackup -backupTarget:{VolumeName}
[-quiet]
```

- **START SYSTEMSTATERECOVERY** Starts a system state recovery by using the specified parameters:

```
wbadmin start systemstateRecovery -version:VersionIdentifier
-showSummary
[-backupTarget:{VolumeName | NetworkSharePath}]
[-machine:BackupMachineName]
[-recoveryTarget:TargetPathForRecovery]
[-authSysvol]
[-quiet]
```

Performing server backups

As part of your planning for each server you intend to back up, you should consider which volumes you want to back up and whether backups will include system-state recovery data, application data, or both. Although you can manually back up to shared volumes and DVD media, you need a separate, dedicated hard disk for running scheduled backups. After you configure a disk for scheduled backups, the backup utilities automatically manage the disk usage and automatically reuse the space of older backups when creating new backups. After you schedule backups, you need to check periodically to ensure that backups are being performed as expected and that the backup schedule meets current needs.

When you create or schedule backups, you need to specify the volumes you want to include, and this affects the ways you can recover your servers and your data. You have the following options:

- **Full server (all volumes with application data)**   Back up all volumes with application data if you want to be able to fully recover a server, along with its system state and application data. Because you are backing up all files, the system state, and application data, you should be able to fully restore your server by using only the Windows backup tools.

- **Full server (all volumes without application data)**   Back up all volumes without application data if you want to be able to restore a server and its applications separately. With this technique, you back up the server by using the Windows backup tools but exclude locations where applications and application data are stored. Then you back up applications and related data by using third-party tools or tools built into the applications. You can fully recover a server by using the Windows backup utilities, and then use a third-party utility to restore backups of applications and application data.

- **Critical volumes/bare metal recovery**   Back up only critical volumes if you want to be able to recover only the operating system.

- **Noncritical volumes**   Back up only individual volumes if you want to be able to recover only files, applications, or data from those volumes.

As part of the backup process, you also need to specify a storage location for backups. Keep the following in mind when you choose storage locations:

- When you use an internal hard disk for storing backups, you are limited in how you can recover your system. You can recover the data from a volume, but you cannot rebuild the entire disk structure.

- When you use an external hard disk for storing backups, the disk will be dedicated for storing your backups and will not be visible in File Explorer. Choosing this option will format the selected disk or disks, removing any existing data.

- When you use a remote shared folder for storing backups, your backup will be overwritten each time you create a new backup. Do not choose this option if you want to store multiple backups for each server.

- When you use removable media or DVDs for storing backups, you can recover only entire volumes, not applications or individual files. The media you use must be at least 1 GB in size.

The sections that follow discuss techniques for performing backups. The procedures you use to back up servers with Windows Server Backup and Wbadmin are similar.

Configuring scheduled backups

With Windows Server Backup, you can schedule automated backups for a server by following these steps:

1. In Windows Server Backup, tap or click Backup Schedule on the Action menu or in the Actions pane to start the Backup Schedule Wizard. Tap or click Next.

2. On the Select Backup Configuration page, note the backup size listed under the Full Server option, as shown in Figure 11-3. This is the storage space required to back up the server data, applications, and the system state. To back up all volumes on the server, select the Full Server option, and then tap or click Next. To back up selected volumes on the server, select the Custom option, and then tap or click Next.

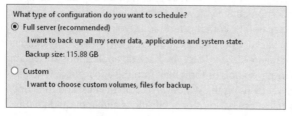

FIGURE 11-3 Note the backup size before you continue.

NOTE Volumes that contain operating system files or applications are included in the backup by default and cannot be excluded. Unfortunately, this means that on a server on which you installed Windows Server 2012 R2 on the D drive, you must also back up the entire C drive because the C drive in this case includes the boot manager and other boot files.

3. If you select Custom, the Select Items For Backup page is displayed. Tap or click Add Items. As shown in Figure 11-4, you can select the check boxes for the volumes you want to back up and clear the check boxes for the volumes you want to exclude. Select the Bare Metal Recovery option if you want to be able to fully recover the operating system. Select the System State option if you want to back up the system state. If the server is a Hyper-V host, you'll have a Hyper-V option and can expand the Hyper-V node to select individual virtual servers to back up by using their saved state and the host component. Tap or click OK, and then tap or click Next.

TIP After you select items, you might want to tap or click Advanced Settings before continuing. You can then use the options on the Exclusions tab to identify locations and file types that should not be backed up. You also can then use the options on the VSS Settings tab to specify whether you want to create a full backup or a copy backup. Keep in mind that when you select anything less than a full volume for backup, the backup is performed file by file rather than as an image.

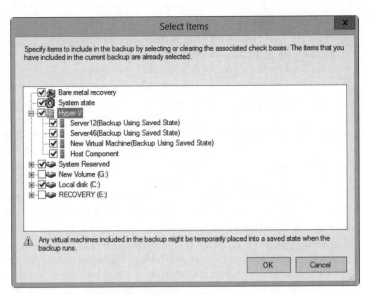

FIGURE 11-4 Select the items to include in the backup.

4. On the Specify Backup Time page, shown in Figure 11-5, you can specify how often and when you want to run backups. To perform backups daily at a specific time, choose Once A Day, and then select the time to start running the daily backup. To perform backups multiple times each day, choose More Than Once A Day. Next, tap or click a start time under Available Time, and then tap or click Add to move the time under Scheduled Time. Repeat this process for each start time you want to add. Tap or click Next when you are ready to continue.

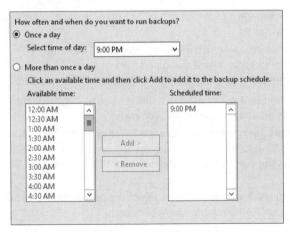

FIGURE 11-5 Select the time to start running the backup.

5. On the Specify Destination Type page, you have these options:

- **Back Up To A Hard Disk That Is Dedicated For Backups** Enables you to specify a dedicated hard disk for backups. Although you can use multiple disks for backups, any disk you select will be formatted, and then dedicated only to backups. This option is recommended because you'll get the best performance. If you select this option, tap or click Next, select the disk or disks to use, and then tap or click Next again.

- **Back Up To A Volume** Enables you to write backups to individual volumes on a hard disk. Because any volume you select is not dedicated to backups, it can be used for other purposes. However, the performance of any of the selected volumes is reduced while backups are being written. If you select this option, tap or click Next, use the Add and Remove options to select the volumes to use, and then tap or click Next again.

- **Back Up To A Shared Network Folder** Enables you to specify a shared network folder for backups. With this option, you can have only one backup at a time because each new backup overwrites the previous backup. If you select this option, tap or click Next. When prompted, tap or click OK. Enter the UNC path to the network share, such as \\FileServer25\Backups\Exchange. If you want the backup to be accessible to everyone who has access to the shared folder, select Inherit under Access Control. If you want to restrict access to the shared folder to the current user and members of the Administrators and Backup Operators groups, select Do Not Inherit under Access Control. Tap or click Next. When prompted to provide access credentials, enter the user name and password for an account authorized to access and write to the shared folder.

6. On the Confirmation page, review the details, and then tap or click Finish. The wizard formats the disk. The formatting process might take several minutes or considerably longer depending on the size of the disk.

7. On the Summary page, tap or click Close. Your backups are now scheduled for the selected server.

With Wbadmin, you can schedule backups by using the ENABLE BACKUP command. ENABLE BACKUP accepts the following parameters:

- **–addTarget** Sets the storage location for backups according to the GUID of the disk you want to use. The GUID of a disk is listed as the disk identifier in the output of the Wbadmin GET DISKS command.

- **–removeTarget** Sets the storage location to remove from the backup schedule according to the GUID of the disk you want to use. The GUID of a disk is listed as the disk identifier in the output of the Wbadmin GET DISKS command.

- **–include** Sets a comma-delimited list of volume drive letters, volume mount points, and GUID volume names to back up.

- **–allCritical** Includes all operating system volumes in the backup automatically.

- **–quiet** Specifies that you want to run the command with no prompts to the user.

To understand how ENABLE BACKUP is used, consider the following examples:

Schedule a backup for C and D at 9:00 P.M. daily

```
wbadmin enable backup -addTarget:{06d88776-0000-0000-0000-000000000000}
 -schedule:18:00 -include:c:,d:
```

Schedule a backup for all operating system volumes at 6:00 A.M. and 9:00 P.M. daily

```
wbadmin enable backup -addTarget:{06d88776-0000-0000-0000-000000000000}
 -schedule:06:00,18:00 -allCritical
```

Modifying or stopping scheduled backups

After you've configured scheduled backups on a server, you can modify or stop the scheduled backups by following these steps:

1. Start Windows Server Backup. Tap or click Backup Schedule on the Action menu or in the Actions pane to start the Backup Schedule Wizard. Tap or click Next.

2. On the Modify Scheduled Backup Settings page, tap or click Modify Backup if you want to add or remove backup items, times, or targets, and then follow steps 3–7 in the section "Configuring scheduled backups" earlier in the chapter. If you want to stop the scheduled backups from running, tap or click Stop Backup, tap or click Next, and then tap or click Finish. When prompted to confirm, tap or click Yes, and then tap or click Close.

NOTE Stopping backups releases backup disks for ordinary use. Backup archives are not deleted from the backup disks and remain available for use in recovery.

With Wbadmin, you can modify scheduled backups by using the ENABLE BACKUP command. For targets, you must use the –addTarget and –removeTarget parameters to modify the target disks. For the run schedule and included volumes, you just set the new values you want to use. Consider the following examples:

Adding a new target to scheduled backups

```
wbadmin enable backup -addTarget:{41cd2567-0000-0000-0000-000000000000}
```

Removing a target from scheduled backups

```
wbadmin enable backup -removeTarget:{06d88776-0000-0000-0000-000000000000}
```

Modifying the run schedule and included volumes

```
wbadmin enable backup -schedule:03:00 -include:c:,d:,e:
```

Creating and scheduling backups with Wbadmin

One way to create manual backups is to use the Wbadmin START BACKUP command. START BACKUP accepts the following parameters:

- **–backupTarget** Sets the storage location for the backup as either a drive letter or UNC path to a shared folder on a remote server.

- **–include** Sets a comma-delimited list of volume drive letters, volume mount points, and GUID volume names to back up.

- **–allCritical** Includes all operating system volumes in the backup automatically.

- **–inheritAcl** Specifies that you want the backup folder at the remote shared folder to inherit the security permissions of the shared folder. If you do not specify this parameter, the backup folder is accessible only to the user you specify in the –user parameter, administrators, and backup operators.

- **–noVerify** Specifies that you do not want to verify backups written to removable media. If you do not specify this parameter, backups written to removable media are verified.

- **–password** Sets the password to use when connecting to the remote shared folder.

- **–quiet** Specifies that you want to run the command with no prompts to the user.

- **–user** Sets the user name to use when connecting to the remote shared folder.

- **–vssFull** Specifies that you want to perform a full backup by using VSS, which ensures that all server and application data is backed up. Do not use this parameter if you are using a third-party backup utility to back up application data.

To understand how START BACKUP is used, consider the following examples:

Performing a full backup of the server

```
wbadmin start backup -backupTarget:f: -vssfull
```

Backing up C and D to F

```
wbadmin start backup -backupTarget:f: -include:c:,d:
```

Backing up all critical volumes

```
wbadmin start backup -backupTarget:f: -allCritical
```

Backing up C and D to a remote shared folder

```
wbadmin start backup -backupTarget:\\fileserver27\backups -include:c:,d:
-user:williams
```

If you want to create a schedule to run backups at different times on different days, you can use Task Scheduler to create the necessary tasks to run this command on the schedule you set. You can use Task Scheduler and Wbadmin to schedule tasks to run backups by following these steps:

1. In Computer Management, tap or click Task Scheduler. You are connected to the local computer by default. As necessary, connect to the computer that you want to access.

2. Press and hold or right-click the Task Scheduler node, and then tap or click Create Task. This opens the Create Task dialog box.

3. On the General tab, enter the name of the task, and then set security options for running the task.

   - If the task should run under a user other than the current user, tap or click Change User Or Group. In the Select User Or Group dialog box, select the user or group under which the task should run, and then provide the appropriate credentials when prompted later.

   - Set other run options as necessary. By default, tasks run only when a user is logged on. If you want to run the task regardless of whether a user is logged on, select Run Whether User Is Logged On Or Not. You can also elect to run with highest privileges and configure the task for earlier releases of Windows.

4. On the Triggers tab, tap or click New. In the New Trigger dialog box, select On A Schedule in the Begin The Task list. Use the options provided to set the run schedule, and then tap or click OK.

5. On the Actions tab, tap or click New. In the New Action dialog box, select Start A Program in the Action list.

6. In the Program/Script text box, enter **%windir%\System32\wbadmin.exe**.

7. In Add Arguments, enter the START BACKUP command you want to use along with its parameters, such as the following:

   ```
   start backup -backupTarget:f: -include:c:,d:,e:\mountpoint,
   \\?\volume{be345a23-32b2-432d-43d2-7867ff3e3432}\
   ```

8. Tap or click OK to close the New Action dialog box.

9. On the Conditions tab, specify any limiting conditions for starting or stopping the task.

10. On the Settings tab, choose any additional optional settings for the task.

11. Tap or click OK to create the task.

Running manual backups

You can use Windows Server Backup to back up servers manually by following these steps:

1. Start Windows Server Backup. Tap or click Backup Once on the Action menu or in the Actions pane to start the Backup Once Wizard.

2. If you want to back up the server by using the same options you use for the Backup Schedule Wizard, select Scheduled Backup Options, tap or click Next, and then tap or click Backup to perform the backup. Skip the remaining steps.

3. If you want to back up the server by using different options, select Different Options, and then tap or click Next.

4. On the Select Backup Configuration page, note the backup size listed under the Full Server option. This is the storage space required to back up the server data, applications, and the system state. To back up all volumes on the server, select the Full Server option, and then tap or click Next. To back up selected volumes on the server, tap or click Custom, and then tap or click Next.

5. If you select Custom, the Select Items For Backup page is displayed. Tap or click Add Items. Select the check boxes for the volumes you want to back up, and clear the check boxes for the volumes you want to exclude. Select the Bare Metal Recovery option if you want to be able to fully recover the operating system. Tap or click OK, and then tap or click Next.

   TIP After you select items, you might want to tap or click Advanced Settings before continuing. You can then use the options on the Exclusions tab to identify locations and file types that should not be backed up. You also can then use the options on the VSS Settings tab to specify whether you want to create a full backup or a copy backup.

6. On the Specify Destination Type page, do one of the following:
   - If you want to back up to local drives, select Local Drives, and then tap or click Next. On the Backup Destination page, select the internal or external disk or DVD drive to use as the backup target. When stored on a DVD, backups are compressed and you can recover only full volumes. As a result, the size of the backup on a DVD might be smaller than the volume on the server. Tap or click Next.
   - If you want to back up to a remote shared folder, select Remote Shared Folder, and then tap or click Next. On the Specify Remote Folder page, enter the UNC path to the remote folder, such as \\FileServer43\Backups. If you want the backup to be accessible to everyone who has access to the shared folder, select Inherit under Access Control. If you want to restrict access to the shared folder to the current user, administrators, and backup operators, select Do Not Inherit under Access Control. Tap or click Next. When prompted to provide access credentials, enter the user name and password for an account authorized to access and write to the shared folder.

7. Tap or click Next, and then tap or click Backup. The Backup Progress dialog box shows you the progress of the backup process. If you tap or click Close, the backup will continue to run in the background.

Recovering your server from hardware or startup failure

Windows Server 2012 R2 includes an extensive diagnostics and resolution architecture. These features can help you recover from many types of hardware, memory, and performance issues and either resolve them automatically or help users through the process of resolving them.

Windows Server 2012 R2 includes more reliable and better-performing device drivers to prevent many common causes of hangs and crashes. Improved I/O cancellation for device drivers ensures that the operating system can recover gracefully from blocking calls and that there are fewer blocking disk I/O operations.

To reduce downtime and restarts required for application installations and updates, Windows Server 2012 R2 can use the update process to mark in-use files for update, and then automatically replace the files the next time the application is started. In some cases, Windows Server 2012 R2 can save the application's data, close the application, update the in-use files, and then restart the application. To improve overall system performance and responsiveness, Windows Server 2012 R2 uses memory efficiently, provides ordered execution for groups of threads, and provides several process-scheduling mechanisms. By optimizing memory and process usage, Windows Server 2012 R2 ensures that background processes have less performance impact on system performance.

Windows Server 2012 R2 provides improved guidance on the causes of unresponsive conditions. By including additional error-reporting details in the event logs, Windows Server 2012 R2 makes it easier to identify and resolve issues. To automatically recover from service failures, Windows Server 2012 R2 uses service recovery policies more extensively than its predecessors. When recovering a failed service, Windows Server 2012 R2 automatically handles both service and nonservice dependencies. Any necessary dependent services and system components are started prior to starting the failed service.

In earlier versions of Windows, an application crash or hang is marked as not responding, and it is up to the user to exit and then restart the application. Windows Server 2012 R2 attempts to resolve the issue of unresponsive applications by using Restart Manager. Restart Manager can shut down and restart unresponsive applications automatically. Thanks to Restart Manager, you might not have to intervene to try to resolve issues with frozen applications.

Failed installation and nonresponsive conditions of applications and drivers are also tracked through Action Center, and the built-in diagnostics display a warning message. By tapping or clicking the Action Center icon in the system tray, you can view recent messages. If you tap or click a message, Windows Server 2012 R2 opens the Message Details page in Action Center, which might provide a solution for the problem.

You also can view a list of current problems at any time by following these steps:

1. In Control Panel, under the System And Security heading, tap or click Review Your Computer's Status.

2. In Action Center, a list of known problems is displayed. For some issues, you'll be able to select a related View Message Details button to display a Message Details page. If a solution is available, tap or click the link provided to download the solution or visit a related website to get more information.

While you are working with Action Center, you can have Windows Server check for solutions to problems by tapping or clicking the Check For Solutions link on the Maintenance panel.

Windows Server 2012 R2 attempts to resolve issues related to running out of virtual memory by providing Resource Exhaustion Detection And Recovery. This feature monitors the systemwide virtual memory commit limit and alerts you if the computer is running low on virtual memory. To help you to correct this issue, it also identifies the processes consuming the largest amount of memory, enabling you to close any or all of these high resource–consuming applications directly from the Close Programs To Prevent Information Loss dialog box. The resource exhaustion alert is also logged in the system event log.

In early versions of Windows, corrupted system files are one of the most common causes of startup failure. Windows Server 2012 R2 includes built-in diagnostics to automatically detect corrupted system files during startup and guide you through automated or manual recovery. To resolve startup problems, Windows Server 2012 R2 uses the Startup Repair tool (StR), which is installed automatically and started when a system fails to boot. Once started, StR attempts to determine the cause of the startup failure by analyzing startup logs and error reports. Then StR attempts to fix the problem automatically. If StR is unable to resolve the problem, it restores the system to the last known working state and then provides diagnostic information and support options for further troubleshooting.

Hardware problems addressed by built-in diagnostics include error detection and disk failure detection. If a device is having problems, hardware diagnostics can detect error conditions and either repair the problem automatically or guide the user through a recovery process. With disk drives, hardware diagnostics can use fault reports provided by disk drives to detect potential failures and alert you before they happen. Hardware diagnostics can also help guide you through the backup process after alerting you that a disk might be failing.

Performance problems addressed by built-in diagnostics include slow application startup, slow boot, slow standby/resume, and slow shutdown. If a computer is experiencing degraded performance, performance diagnostics can detect the problem and provide possible solutions for resolving the problem. For advanced performance issues, you can track related performance and reliability data in the Performance Diagnostics console, which includes a performance monitor and a reliability monitor.

Memory problems addressed by built-in diagnostics include both memory leaks and failing memory. A memory leak occurs if an application or a system component doesn't completely free areas of physical memory after it is done with them. If you suspect that a computer has a memory problem that is not being automatically detected, you can run Windows Memory Diagnostics manually during startup by selecting the related option. If the Windows Memory Diagnostics option is not provided during startup, you can run the program by following these steps:

1. Start Windows Memory Diagnostics. One way to do this is to enter **mdsched.exe** in the App Search box, and then press Enter.

2. Choose whether to restart the computer now and run the tool immediately or schedule the tool to check for problems at the next restart.

3. Windows Memory Diagnostics runs automatically after the computer restarts, by using the standard test mix and performing two test passes by default.

You can change the run options by using the F1 key. Three different levels of memory testing can be performed, including Basic, Standard, and Extended. Use a basic test to quickly check the memory. Use the standard test to perform a standard test of the memory. Use the extended test when you want to perform more extensive testing. Set the number of test passes by using the Pass Count option.

To detect system crashes possibly caused by failing memory, memory diagnostics work with the Microsoft Online Crash Analysis tool. If a computer crashes because of failing memory, and memory diagnostics detect this, you are prompted to schedule a memory test the next time the computer is restarted.

Recovering from a failed start

If Windows Server 2012 R2 fails to start, the server typically will go into recovery mode during the next startup. After preparing automated recovery and attempting to diagnose the server, you'll see an Automatic Repair screen. From this screen, you can select Restart to shut down and start the computer again or Advanced Options to display additional options that might help you repair the server.

If you elect to restart the computer, Windows will do a full restart, which can sometimes resolve the problem. If you choose Advanced Options, you'll have the following options:

- **Continue** Exits the repair menu, and continues to load the operating system
- **Use Another Operating System** Exits the repair menu, and enables you to select the operating system to load (if multiple operating system are installed)
- **Troubleshoot** Displays the Advanced Options menu
- **Turn Off Your PC** Exits the repair menu, and shuts down the server

If you select, Troubleshoot, the Advanced Options screen has the following options:

- **System Image Recovery** Enables you to recover the server by using a system image file. The image file can come from a remote computer.
- **Command Prompt** Enables you to access a command prompt and work with the commands and tools available in the recovery environment.
- **Startup Settings** Enables you to change the startup behavior and start the server in safe mode. Here, you click Restart to restart the computer in safe mode so that you can disable driver signature enforcement, early-launch anti-malware protection, and automatically restart on system failure. You can also enable low-resolution video mode, debugging mode, boot logging, and safe mode.

Starting a server in safe mode

Many startup problems occur because something on the system has changed; for example, a device might have been incorrectly installed. The system configuration or registry might have been updated improperly, causing a conflict. Often you can resolve startup issues by using safe mode to recover or troubleshoot system problems. When you have finished using safe mode, be sure to restart the server by using a normal startup. You will then be able to use the server as you usually would.

In safe mode, Windows Server 2012 R2 loads only basic files, services, and drivers. The drivers loaded include those for the mouse, monitor, keyboard, mass storage, and base video. The monitor driver sets the basic settings and modes for the server's monitor; the base video driver sets the basic options for the server's graphics card. No networking services or drivers are started unless you choose the Safe Mode With Networking option. Because safe mode loads a limited set of configuration information, it can help you troubleshoot problems.

You can start a server in safe mode by following these steps:

1. If the computer won't start as usual, the Recovery screen is displayed during startup. On the Recovery screen, tap or click Troubleshoot.

2. On the Advanced Options screen, tap or click Startup Settings. Next, on the Windows Startup Settings screen, tap or click Restart.

3. Use the arrow keys to select the safe mode you want to use, and then press Enter. The safe mode option you use depends on the type of problem you're experiencing. The key options are as follows:

   - **Repair Your Computer**   Loads the Startup Repair tool. Choose this option to restart the server and go back to the Recovery screen.

   - **Safe Mode**   Loads only basic files, services, and drivers during the initialization sequence. The drivers loaded include the mouse, monitor, keyboard, mass storage, and base video. No networking services or drivers are started.

   - **Safe Mode With Networking**   Loads basic files, services, and drivers, in addition to services and drivers needed to start networking.

   - **Safe Mode With Command Prompt**   Loads basic files, services, and drivers, and then starts a command prompt instead of the Windows graphical interface. No networking services or drivers are started.

   TIP   In Safe Mode With Command Prompt, you can start the Explorer shell from the command-line interface by pressing Ctrl+Shift+Esc and entering **explorer.exe** in the New Process window on the File menu of Task Manager.

   - **Enable Boot Logging**   Enables you to create a record of all startup events in a boot log.

   - **Enable Low-Resolution Video**   Enables you to start the system in low-resolution 640 × 480 display mode, which is useful if the system display is set to a mode that can't be used with the current monitor or the system has a bad driver.

   - **Last Known Good Configuration**   Starts the computer in safe mode by using registry information that Windows saved at the last shutdown, including the HKEY_CURRENT_CONFIG (HKCC) hive. This registry hive stores information about the hardware configuration with which you previously and successfully started the computer.

- **Debugging Mode**   Starts the system in debugging mode, which is useful only for troubleshooting operating system bugs.

- **Directory Services Restore Mode**   Starts the system in safe mode, and enables you to restore the directory service. This option is available on Windows Server 2008 R2 and later domain controllers.

- **Disable Automatic Restart On System Failure**   Prevents Windows Server from automatically restarting after an operating system crash.

- **Disable Driver Signature Enforcement**   Starts the computer in safe mode without enforcing digital signature policy settings for drivers. If a driver with an invalid or missing digital signature is causing startup failure, this option resolves the problem temporarily so that you can start the computer and resolve the problem by getting a new driver or changing the driver signature enforcement settings.

- **Disable Early Launch Anti-Malware Driver**   Starts the computer in safe mode without running the boot driver for the computer's anti-malware software. If the boot driver for the computer's anti-malware software is preventing startup, you need to check the software developer's website for an update to resolve the boot problem or configure the software without boot protection.

- **Start Windows Normally**   Starts the computer with its regular settings.

4. If a problem doesn't reappear when you start in safe mode, you can eliminate the default settings and basic device drivers as possible causes. If a newly added device or updated driver is causing problems, you can use safe mode to remove the device or reverse the update.

Backing up and restoring the system state

In Windows Server 2012 R2, there are approximately 50,000 system state files, which use approximately 4 GB of disk space in the default installation of an x64-based computer. The fastest and easiest way to back up and restore a server's system state is to use Wbadmin. With Wbadmin, you can use the START SYSTEMSTATEBACKUP command to create a backup of the system state for a computer, and the START SYSTEMSTATERECOVERY command to restore a computer's system state.

> **TIP**   When you select a system state restore on a domain controller, you have to be in the Directory Services Restore mode. To learn how to restore Active Directory, see the next section.

To back up a server's system state, enter the following at an elevated command prompt:

```
wbadmin start systemstatebackup -backupTarget:VolumeName
```

Here *VolumeName* is the storage location for the backup, such as F:.

To restore a server's system state, enter the following at an elevated command prompt:

```
wbadmin start systemstaterecovery -backupTarget:VolumeName
```

Here *VolumeName* is the storage location that contains the backup you want to recover, such as F:. Additionally, you can do the following:

- Use the –recoveryTarget parameter to restore to an alternate location.
- Use the –machine parameter to specify the name of the computer to recover if the original backup location contains backups for multiple computers.
- Use the –authSysvol parameter to perform an authoritative restore of the SYSVOL.

You can also recover the system state by using a backup that includes the system state or by performing a recovery.

Restoring Active Directory

When restoring system state data to a domain controller, you must choose whether you want to perform an authoritative or nonauthoritative restore. The default is nonauthoritative. In this mode, Active Directory and other replicated data are restored from backup and any changes are replicated from another domain controller. Thus, you can safely restore a failed domain controller without overwriting the latest Active Directory information. On the other hand, if you're trying to restore Active Directory throughout the network by using archived data, you must use an authoritative restore. With an authoritative restore, the restored data is restored on the current domain controller and then replicated to other domain controllers.

> **CAUTION** An authoritative restore overwrites all Active Directory data throughout the domain. Before you perform an authoritative restore, you must be certain that the archive data is the correct data to propagate throughout the domain and that the current data on other domain controllers is inaccurate, outdated, or otherwise corrupted.

To restore Active Directory on a domain controller and enable the restored data to be replicated throughout the network, follow these steps:

1. Make sure the domain controller server is shut down.
2. Restart the domain controller server, and enter safe mode.
3. Select Directory Services Restore Mode.
4. When the system starts, use the Backup utility to restore the system state data and other essential files.
5. After restoring the data but before restarting the server, use the Ntdsutil.exe tool to mark objects as authoritative. Be sure to check the Active Directory data thoroughly.
6. Restart the server. When the system finishes startup, the Active Directory data should begin to replicate throughout the domain.

Restoring the operating system and the full system

As discussed previously, Windows Server 2012 R2 includes startup repair features that can recover a server in case of corrupted or missing system files. The startup repair process can also recover from some types of boot failures involving the boot manager. If these processes fail and the boot manager is the reason you cannot start the server, you can use the Windows Server 2012 R2 installation disc or system recovery options to restore the boot manager and enable startup.

System recovery options are available only with full server installations and not with Server Core installations. With Server Core installations, you need to use the installation disc to initiate recovery.

System recovery options include the following tools:

- **System Image Recovery** Enables you to recover a server's operating system or perform a full system recovery. With an operating system or full system recovery, make sure your backup data is available and that you can log on with an account that has the appropriate permissions. With a full system recovery, keep in mind that data that was not included in the original backup will be deleted when you recover the system, including any in-use volumes that were not included in the backup.

- **Windows Memory Diagnostics Tools** Enables you to diagnose a problem with the server's physical memory. Three different levels of memory testing can be performed: basic, standard, and exhaustive.

You can also access a command prompt. This command prompt gives you access to the command-line tools available during installation in addition to these other programs:

- **Startup Repair Wizard (X:\Sources\Recovery\StartRep.exe)** Typically, this tool is started automatically on boot failure if Windows detects an issue with the boot sector, boot manager, or Boot Configuration Data (BCD) store.

- **Startup Recovery Options (X:\Sources\Recovery\Recenv.exe)** Enables you to start the Startup Recovery Options Wizard. If you previously entered the wrong recovery settings, you can provide different options.

As an administrator, you can perform command-line troubleshooting by following these steps:

1. If the computer won't start as usual, the Recovery screen is displayed during startup. On the Recovery screen, tap or click Troubleshoot.

2. On the Advanced Options screen, tap or click Command Prompt.

3. When prompted to choose an account, tap or click the Administrator account. Next, enter the password for the Administrator account, and tap or click Continue.

4. Use the command prompt to perform troubleshooting. For example, you could run the Startup Repair Wizard by entering **x:\sources\recovery \startrep.exe**.

You can recover a server's operating system or perform a full system recovery by using a backup image you created earlier with Windows Server Backup. With an operating system recovery, you recover all critical volumes but do not recover non-system volumes. If you recover your full system, Windows Server Backup reformats and repartitions all disks that were attached to the server. Therefore, you should use this method only when you want to recover the server data onto separate hardware or when all other attempts to recover the server on the existing hardware have failed.

NOTE When you recover the operating system or the full system, make sure that your backup data is available and that you can log on with an account that has the appropriate permissions. With a full system recovery, keep in mind that existing data that was not included in the original backup will be deleted when you recover the system. This includes any volumes that are currently used by the server but were not included in the backup.

You can recover the operating system by using a backup image by following these steps:

1. If the computer won't start as usual, the Recovery screen is displayed during startup. On the Recovery screen, tap or click Troubleshoot.

2. On the Advanced Options screen, tap or click System Image Recovery.

3. When prompted to choose an account, tap or click the Administrator account. Next, enter the password for the Administrator account, and tap or click Continue. This starts the Re-Image Your Computer Wizard.

4. On the Select A System Image Backup page, tap or click Use The Latest Available System Image (Recommended), and then tap or click Next. Or tap or click Select A System Image, and then tap or click Next.

5. If you select an image to restore, do one of the following on the Select The Location Of The Backup page:

   ■ Tap or click the location that contains the system image you want to use, and then tap or click Next. Afterward, tap or click the system image you want to use, and then tap or click Next.

   ■ To browse for a system image on the network, tap or click Advanced, and then tap or click Search For A System Image On The Network. When you are prompted to confirm that you want to connect to the network, tap or click Yes. In the Network Folder text box, specify the location of the server and shared folder in which the system image is stored, such as **\\FileServer22\Backups**, and then tap or click OK.

   ■ To install a driver for a backup device that doesn't show up in the location list, tap or click Advanced, and then tap or click Install A Driver. Insert the installation media for the device, and then tap or click OK. After Windows installs the device driver, the backup device should be listed in the location list.

6. On the Choose Additional Restore Options page, do the following optional tasks, and then tap or click Next:

   ■ Select the Format And Repartition Disks check box to delete existing partitions and reformat the destination disks to be the same as the backup.

   ■ Select Only Restore System Drives to restore only the drives from the backup that are required to run Windows: the boot, system, and recovery volumes. If the server has data drives, they will not be restored.

   ■ Tap or click Install Drivers to install device drivers for the hardware to which you are recovering.

- Tap or click Advanced to specify whether the computer is restarted and the disks are checked for errors immediately after the recovery operation is completed.

7. On the Confirmation page, review the details for the restoration, and then tap or click Finish. The wizard then restores the operating system or the full server as appropriate for the options you selected.

Restoring applications, nonsystem volumes, and files and folders

Windows Server 2012 R2 provides separate processes for system state and full server recovery and the recovery of individual volumes and files and folders. You can use the Recovery Wizard in Windows Server Backup to recover nonsystem volumes and files and folders from a backup. Before you begin, you should be sure that the computer you are recovering files to is running Windows Server 2012 R2. If you want to recover individual files and folders, you should be sure that at least one backup exists on an internal or external disk or in a remote shared folder. You cannot recover files and folders from backups saved to DVDs or removable media.

With this in mind, you can recover nonsystem volumes, files and folders, or application data by following these steps:

1. Start Windows Server Backup. In the Actions pane or on the Action menu, tap or click Recover to start the Recovery Wizard.

2. On the Getting Started page, specify whether you will recover data from the local computer or from another location, and then tap or click Next.

3. If you are recovering data from another location, specify whether the backup you want to restore is on a local drive or in a remote shared folder, tap or click Next, and then specify location-specific settings. When you are recovering from a local drive, on the Select Backup Location page, select the location of the backup from the drop-down list. When you are recovering from a remote shared folder, on the Specify Remote Folder page, enter the path to the folder that contains the backup. In the remote folder, the backup should be stored at *BackupServer*\WindowsImageBackup*ComputerName*.

4. If you are recovering from another location, on the Select Server page, select which server's data you would like to recover. Tap or click Next.

5. On the Select Backup Date page, select the date and time of the backup you want to restore by using the calendar and the time list. Backups are available for dates shown in bold. Tap or click Next.

6. On the Select Recovery Type page, do one of the following:
   - To restore individual files and folders, tap or click Files And Folders, and then tap or click Next. On the Select Items To Recover page, under Available Items, tap or click the plus sign (+) to expand the list until the folder you want is visible. Tap or click a folder to display the contents of the folder in the adjacent pane, tap or click each item you want to restore, and then tap or click Next.

- To restore noncritical, nonoperating system volumes, tap or click Volumes, and then tap or click Next. On the Select Volumes page, you'll find a list of source and destination volumes. Select the check boxes associated with the source volumes you want to recover, and then select the location to which you want to recover the volumes by using the Destination Volume lists. Tap or click Next. If prompted to confirm the recovery operation, tap or click Yes. Skip steps 7 and 8.

- To restore application data, tap or click Applications, and then tap or click Next. On the Select Application page, under Applications, tap or click the application you want to recover. If the backup you are using is the most recent, you might encounter a check box labeled Do Not Perform A Roll-Forward Recovery Of The Application Databases. Select this check box if you want to prevent Windows Server Backup from rolling forward the application database that is currently on your server. Tap or click Next. Because any data on the destination volume will be lost when you per-form the recovery, make sure that the destination volume is empty or does not contain information you will need later.

7. Next, you can specify whether you want to restore data to its original loca-tion (nonsystem files only) or an alternate location. For an alternate location, enter the path to the restore location or tap or click Browse to select it. With applications, you can copy application data to an alternate location. You cannot, however, recover applications to a different location or computer.

8. For file and folder recovery, choose a recovery technique to apply when files and folders already exist in the recovery location. You can create copies so that you have both versions of the file or folder, overwrite existing files with recovered files, or skip duplicate files and folders to preserve existing files. You also can restore the original security permissions to files and folders being recovered.

9. On the Confirmation page, review the details, and then tap or click Recover to restore the specified items.

Managing encryption recovery policy

If you're an administrator for an organization that uses the Encrypting File System (EFS), your disaster-recovery planning must include additional procedures and prep-arations. You need to consider how to handle issues related to personal encryption certificates, EFS recovery agents, and EFS recovery policy. These issues are discussed in the sections that follow.

Understanding encryption certificates and recovery policy

File encryption is supported on a per-folder or per-file basis. Any file placed in a folder marked for encryption is automatically encrypted. Files in encrypted format can be read only by the person who encrypted the file. Before other users can read an encrypted file, the user must decrypt the file.

Every file that's encrypted has a unique encryption key. This means that encrypted files can be copied, moved, and renamed just like any other file—and in most cases these actions don't affect the encryption of the data. The user who encrypted the file always has access to the file if the user's private key is available in the user's profile on the computer or the user has credential roaming with Digital Identification Management Service (DIMS). For this user, the encryption and decryption process is handled automatically and is transparent.

EFS is the process that handles encryption and decryption. The default setup for EFS makes it possible for users to encrypt files without needing special permission. Files are encrypted by using a public/private key that EFS generates automatically on a per-user basis. By default, Windows uses the Advanced Encryption Standard (AES) algorithm for encrypting files with EFS. Internet Information Services 7 and later can use an AES provider for encrypting passwords by default.

Encryption certificates are stored as part of the data in user profiles. If a user works with multiple computers and wants to use encryption, an administrator needs to configure a roaming profile for that user. A roaming profile ensures that the user's profile data and public-key certificates are accessible from other computers. Without this, users won't be able to access their encrypted files on another computer.

TIP An alternative to a roaming profile is to copy the user's encryption certificate to the computers the user uses. You can do this by using the certificate backup and restore process discussed in "Backing up and restoring encrypted data and certificates" later in this chapter. Just back up the certificate on the user's original computer, and then restore the certificate on each of the other computers the user logs on to.

EFS has a built-in, data-recovery system to guard against data loss. This recovery system ensures that encrypted data can be recovered if a user's public-key certificate is lost or deleted. The most common scenario in which this occurs is when a user leaves the company and the associated user account is deleted. Although a manager might have been able to log on to the user's account, check files, and save important files to other folders, encrypted files will be accessible afterward only if the encryption is removed by the manager acting as the user who encrypted the files or, if while logged on as the user, the manager moves the files to a FAT or FAT32 volume (where encryption isn't supported).

To access encrypted files after the user account has been deleted, you need to use a recovery agent. Recovery agents have access to the file encryption key that's necessary to unlock data in encrypted files. However, to protect sensitive data, recovery agents don't have access to a user's private key or any private key information.

Recovery agents are designated automatically, and the necessary recovery certificates are generated automatically as well to ensure that encrypted files can always be recovered.

EFS recovery agents are configured at two levels:

- **Domain** The recovery agent for a domain is configured automatically when the first Windows Server 2012 R2 domain controller is installed. By default, the recovery agent is the domain administrator. Through Group Policy, domain administrators can designate additional recovery agents. Domain administrators can also delegate recovery agent privileges to designated security administrators.

- **Local computer** When a computer is part of a workgroup or in a stand-alone configuration, the recovery agent is the administrator of the local computer by default. You can designate additional recovery agents. Further, if you want local recovery agents in a domain environment rather than domain-level recovery agents, you must delete the recovery policy from the Group Policy for the domain.

You can delete recovery policies if you don't want them to be available. However, deleting recovery policies is not recommended because there can be severe unintentional consequences.

Configuring the EFS recovery policy

Recovery policies are configured automatically for domain controllers and workstations. By default, domain administrators are the designated recovery agents for domains, and the local administrator is the designated recovery agent for a stand-alone workstation.

Through Group Policy, you can view, assign, and delete recovery agents by following these steps:

1. Access the Group Policy console for the local computer, site, domain, or organizational unit with which you want to work. For details on working with Group Policy, see Chapter 6, "Managing users and computers with Group Policy."

2. Expand Computer Configuration, Windows Settings, Security Settings, and Public Key Policies, and then tap or click Encrypting File System to access the configured Recovery Agents in Group Policy.

3. The pane at the right lists the recovery certificates currently assigned. Recovery certificates are listed according to who they are issued to, who issued them, their expiration date and purpose, and more.

4. To designate an additional recovery agent, press and hold or right-click Encrypting File System, and then tap or click Add Data Recovery Agent. This starts the Add Recovery Agent Wizard, which you can use to select a previously generated certificate that has been assigned to a user and mark it as a designated recovery certificate. Tap or click Next. On the Select Recovery Agents page, tap or click Browse Directory, and in the Find Users, Contacts, And Groups dialog box, select the user you want to work with. Tap or click OK, and then tap or click Next. Tap or click Finish to add the recovery agent.

5. To delete a recovery agent, select the recovery agent's certificate in the right pane, and then press Delete. When prompted to confirm the action, tap or

click Yes to permanently and irrevocably delete the certificate. If the recovery policy is empty (meaning it has no other designated recovery agents), EFS is turned off so that users can no longer encrypt files.

NOTE Before you can designate additional recovery agents, you should set up a root certificate authority (CA) in the domain. Afterward, you must use the Certificates snap-in to generate a personal certificate that uses the EFS Recovery Agent template. The root CA must then approve the certificate request so that the certificate can be used. You can also use Cipher.exe to generate the EFS recovery agent key and certificate.

Backing up and restoring encrypted data and certificates

You can back up and restore encrypted data like you can any other data. The key thing to remember is that you must use backup software that understands EFS, such as the built-in backup and restore tools. You must be careful when using this type of software, however.

The backup or restore process doesn't necessarily back up or restore the certificate needed to work with the encrypted data. The user's profile data contains that certificate. If the user's account exists and the profile still contains the necessary certificate, the user can still work with the encrypted data.

If the user's account exists and you previously backed up the user's profile and then restored the profile to recover a deleted certificate, the user can still work with the encrypted data. Otherwise, there's no way to work with the data, and you need to have a designated recovery agent access the files, and then remove the encryption.

Being able to back up and restore certificates is an important part of any disaster-recovery* plan. The next sections examine the techniques you can use to perform these tasks.

Backing up encryption certificates

You use the Certificates snap-in to back up and restore personal certificates. Personal certificates are saved with the Personal Information Exchange (.pfx) format.

To back up personal certificates, follow these steps:

1. Log on as the user to the computer where the personal certificate you want to work with is stored. Tap or click Start, enter **mmc** in the Search box, and then press Enter. This opens the Microsoft Management Console (MMC).

2. In the MMC, select File, and then select Add/Remove Snap-In. This opens the Add Or Remove Snap-Ins dialog box.

3. In the Available Snap-Ins list, select Certificates, and then tap or click Add. Select My User Account, and then tap or click Finish. This adds the Certificates snap-in to the Selected Snap-Ins list. The focus for the snap-in is set to the currently logged-on user account.

4. Tap or click OK to close the Add Or Remove Snap-Ins dialog box.

5. Expand Certificates—Current User, expand Personal, and then select Certificates. Press and hold or right-click the certificate you want to save, tap or click All Tasks, and then tap or click Export. This starts the Certificate Export Wizard. Tap or click Next.

6. Select Yes, Export The Private Key. Tap or click Next twice.

7. On the security page, use the options provided to specify security principals that should have access to the certificate. The default security principal is the Administrator account. Afterward, enter and confirm a password for opening the certificate. Tap or click Next.

8. Tap or click Browse. Use the dialog box provided to specify a file location for the certificate file, and then tap or click Save. Be sure that this location is secure, because you don't want to compromise system security. The file is saved with the .pfx extension.

9. Tap or click Next, and then tap or click Finish. If the export process is successful, you'll get a message box confirming this. Tap or click OK to close the message box.

Restoring encryption certificates

When you have a backup of a certificate, you can restore the certificate to any computer on the network—not just the original computer. The backup and restore process is, in fact, how you move certificates from one computer to another.

Follow these steps to restore a personal certificate:

1. Copy the Personal Information Exchange (.pfx) file onto removable media, such as a flash drive or a floppy disk, and then log on as the user to the computer where you want to use the personal certificate.

   NOTE Log on to the target computer as the user whose certificate you're restoring. If you don't do this, the user won't be able to work with his encrypted data.

2. Access the Certificates snap-in for My User Account as described previously.

3. Expand Certificates—Current User, and then press and hold or right-click Personal. Tap or click All Tasks, and then tap or click Import. This starts the Certificate Import Wizard.

4. Tap or click Next, and then insert the removable media.

5. Tap or click Browse. In the Open dialog box, locate the personal certificate on the removable media. Be sure to select Personal Information Exchange as the file type. After you locate the file, select it, and then tap or click Open.

6. Tap or click Next. Enter the password for the personal certificate, and then tap or click Next again.

7. The certificate should be placed in the Personal store by default. Accept the default by tapping or clicking Next. Tap or click Finish. If the import process is successful, you'll get a message box confirming this. Tap or click OK.

Index

Numbers & Symbols

64-bit print drivers, 300
512b drives, 5
512e drives, 5
$ symbol, 101, 103

A

A records
  described, 282
  updating, 267
AAAA records, 282
access-based enumeration, 92
access controls, claims-based, 132–134
access permissions. *See* NTFS permissions
account policies
  changing template settings, 160
  described, 157
Action Center
  changing run time for automatic
    maintenance, 75
  network diagnostics and, 207
  storage spaces and, 66
  viewing known problems and
    solutions, 359
Active Directory
  access tracking, 135
  auditing policies, 135
  authorizing DHCP servers in, 228
  central access policies, 133
  DNS and, 262, 263, 270–272
  dynamic updates and, 278, 291
  integrated primary server, 267
  integration modes, 291
  listing printer shares in, 307, 308, 313
  listing printers in, 320, 323
  objects, auditing, 139
  publishing shares in, 94
  restoring, 364
  SRV records and, 283
  storing data and objects, 101
Active Directory Certificate Services, 196
Active Directory Domain Services, security
  policies and, 175
Active Directory Users And Computers
  assigning logon scripts, 189
  object auditing, 135, 139

active partition or volume, 19
adaptive query timeout, 207
Add-DhcpServerInDC cmdlet, 228
address conflict detection, 236
address records, 282–284
Address Resolution Protocol (ARP) test, 218
ADMIN$ share, 100
administrative installation, 191
administrative shares, 100
administrator access, object ownership
  and, 122
administrator command prompt, shortcuts
  to, 346
Advanced Encryption Standard (AES)
  algorithm, 369
Advanced Format hard drives, 5
Advanced Sharing Settings, 83
Advanced TCP/IP Settings, 266
advertising software, 191
alias (CNAME) records, 276
allocating space
  storage pools and, 57, 58, 61
  to virtual disks, 62
allocation unit size, 27, 29, 43
allow lists, MAC address filtering and, 253
allowing special permissions, 131
analyzing disks, 78–80
AppData (Roaming) folder, redirecting, 181
applications, recovering, 367, 368
Apply Policy To Removable Media policy, 143
applying security policies, 177, 178
archive attribute, 337
assigning drive letters and paths, 67
asynchronous DNS cache, 264
attaching VHDs, 24
Audit Account Logon Events option, 135
Audit Account Management option, 135
Audit Directory Service Access option,
  135, 139
Audit Logon Events option, 136
Audit Object Access option, 116, 136, 138
Audit Policy Change option, 136
Audit Privilege Use option, 136
Audit Process Tracking option, 136
Audit System Events option, 136
auditing
  Active Directory objects, 139, 140
  DHCP servers, 229

F

Failed Redundancy volume status
    described, 40
    mirrored sets and, 50
Failed volume status, 40
failover, DHCP, 218
failover scopes, 223, 249–252
failures, recovering from
    failed start, 361
    hardware or startup, 358–361
FAT file system, 10
FAT32 file system, 10
fault tolerance
    disk mirroring and, 47
    disk striping with parity and, 49
    failover scopes and, 250
    incomplete volumes, 40
    RAID and, 44, 45
Favorites folder, redirecting, 181
FAX$ share, 100
file and printer sharing, enabling and
    disabling, 302
File And Storage Services
    configuring role, 4, 5
    configuring share permissions, 98
    creating a sync share, 117
    creating shared folders, 91–93
    NFS sharing, 108
    role services, 2
    shared folders, modifying settings
        for, 94
    viewing NTFS permissions, 124
    Work Folders, 117
File Explorer
    accessing Work Folders, 120
    claims-based permissions and, 133
    connecting to special shares, 101
    disconnecting network drives, 114
    mapping network drives, 113
    NFS sharing and, 107
    restoring a shadow copy, 110
    shadow copies and, 109
    sharing local folders, 88
    showing hidden items, 83
    viewing NTFS permissions, 124
file paths, security settings for, 166
file screening, 11
File Server Resource Manager
    creating disk quotas, 155, 156
    creating disk quota templates, 154
    modifying disk quota templates, 153
    role services, 11
File Server role service, 3
File Server VSS Agent Service role service, 3

file servers
    described, 1
    role services for, 2
File Services And Storage role, 54
file sharing. *See* standard file sharing; public
    folder sharing; shared folders
file systems
    described, 1, 10, 11
    local vs. remote, 1
    policies for, 157, 164–167
    specifying type, 27, 29, 43
files
    auditing, 136–138
    compressing, 30
    decrypting, 36
    encrypting, 32–34
    expanding compressed, 31
    permissions, list of, 125
    recovering, 367, 368
    setting basic permissions, 127–129
    setting special permissions, 129–132
filesystem log buffer, time stamp update
    records and, 65
filtering
    by MAC address, 253
    printers, 320, 321
firewalls, security policies and, 175
FireWire (IEEE 1394)
    data transfer and, 14
    Unreadable drive status and, 17
firmware interfaces, 8
folder redirection
    based on group membership, 184–186
    described, 181
    removing, 186
    to a single location, 182
folders
    auditing, 136–138
    permissions, list of, 125
    permissions, setting basic, 127–129
    permissions, setting special, 129
    recovering, 292
forcing files to close, 106
Foreign drive status, 17
formatting partitions, 28, 29
formatting volumes, 43
Formatting volume status, 40
forward lookup zones
    global names, 275, 276
    primary DNS servers and, 272
    purpose, 274
    secondary DNS servers and, 273
    updating properties, 287
forwarder servers, 292, 293
forwarding-only servers, 268, 292, 293

About the author

WILLIAM STANEK (*www.williamstanek.com*) is the award-winning author and series editor of the bestselling Pocket Consultant series. William is one of the world's leading technology experts and has more than 20 years of hands-on experience with advanced programming and development. Over the years, his practical advice has helped millions of programmers, developers, and network engineers all over the world. Dubbed "A Face Behind the Future" in 1998 by *The Olympian*, William has been helping to shape the future of the written word for more than two decades. William's 150th book was published in 2013, and more than 7.5 million people have read his many works. William's current books include *Exchange Server 2013: Configuration & Clients*, *Windows Server 2012 R2 Pocket Consultant: Essentials & Configuration*, and *Windows Server 2012 Inside Out*.

William has been involved in the commercial Internet community since 1991. His core business and technology experience comes from more than 11 years of military service. He has substantial experience in developing server technology, encryption, and Internet solutions. He has written many technical white papers and training courses on a wide variety of topics. He frequently serves as a subject matter expert and consultant.

William has an MS with distinction in information systems and a BS in computer science, magna cum laude. He is proud to have served in the Persian Gulf War as a combat crew member on an electronic warfare aircraft. He flew on numerous combat missions into Iraq and was awarded nine medals for his wartime service, including one of the United States of America's highest-flying honors, the Air Force Distinguished Flying Cross. Currently, he resides in the Pacific Northwest with his wife and children.

William recently rediscovered his love of the great outdoors. When he's not writing, he can be found hiking, biking, backpacking, traveling, or trekking in search of adventure with his family!

Find William on Twitter at WilliamStanek and on Facebook at *www.facebook.com/William.Stanek.Author*. Please visit *www.Pocket-Consultant.com* to find links to stay in touch with William.

Now that you've read the book...

Tell us what you think!

Was it useful?
Did it teach you what you wanted to learn?
Was there room for improvement?

Let us know at http://aka.ms/tellpress

Your feedback goes directly to the staff at Microsoft Press,
and we read every one of your responses. Thanks in advance!